Mrs H. E. Gaines

A GUIDE TO THE

# Religions of America

THE FAMOUS LOOK MAGAZINE SERIES
ON RELIGION—PLUS FACTS, FIGURES,
TABLES, CHARTS, ARTICLES, AND COM-
PREHENSIVE REFERENCE MATERIAL
ON CHURCHES AND RELIGIOUS GROUPS
IN THE UNITED STATES; EDITED BY

## LEO ROSTEN

SIMON AND SCHUSTER 1955

PUBLISHED BY SIMON AND SCHUSTER, INC.
ROCKEFELLER CENTER, 630 FIFTH AVENUE
NEW YORK 20, N. Y.

SEVENTH PRINTING
LIBRARY OF CONGRESS CATALOG CARD NUMBER: 55-7133
DEWEY DECIMAL CLASSIFICATION NUMBER: 200
MANUFACTURED IN THE UNITED STATES OF AMERICA
PRINTED BY THE MURRAY PRINTING COMPANY
BOUND BY F. M. CHARLTON COMPANY, NEW YORK

*To Madeline*

# Contents

PART TWO    FACTS AND FIGURES
ON RELIGION IN THE UNITED STATES

## Doctrines and Beliefs

## Church Membership

xii  *Contents*

# Editor's Note

It is surprising how little we really know about the faith of our neighbors, or the prayers and practices of the churches we pass every day. This is all the more curious if we consider how widespread has been the revival of religious interest in our nation, and how intense the effort, over the past twenty years, to heighten understanding among our churches and broaden cooperation between our creeds.

In June of 1952, *Look* Magazine began to publish a series of articles on the major religious groups in the United States. Each article was framed in question-and-answer form. Each question was as clear, direct, and candid as possible—designed to elicit as simple, clear, and direct an answer as could be given. Each article, that is, tried to answer the kind of questions which an ordinary man might ask of a religious body to which he did not belong, or of which he knew not much. For each article a writer was sought who could describe the tenets of his faith with the utmost clarity and vigor, who could initiate a very large audience (over 20,000,000 readers) into the canons and structure of his creed.

The series won quite extraordinary response from churchmen and laymen and organizations throughout the land. Sigma Delta Chi, the Laymen's Movement for a Christian World, the National Religious Publicity Council, the University of Illinois—these, among others, honored *Look* Magazine with awards for the judgment, authority, and taste with which the articles were presented to the American public.

This book contains the complete series of articles on religion published in *Look* from 1952–1955 (many are substantially expanded from their original length)—plus a sizable appendix of facts, figures, charts, and rather striking information specially collected and collated for this volume.

LEO ROSTEN

# PART ONE

# RELIGIOUS BELIEFS

# What Is a Baptist?

## by WILLIAM B. LIPPHARD

MR. LIPPHARD writes from a background of more than forty years of professional association with the American Baptist Convention, which consists of more than 6,500 churches. Views of some members of the American Baptist Convention differ on certain points (for example, the doctrine of the Virgin Birth) from those held by some members of the Southern Baptist Convention. It should be emphasized that neither the American Baptist Convention nor the Southern Baptist Convention has ever adopted an "official" statement of doctrine and faith; accordingly, minor differences among Baptists, on specific points of creed or practice, may be regarded as individual, not official, variations.

William B. Lipphard, president of the Associated Church Press from 1947 to 1949, was for twenty years editor of the Baptist publication, *Missions* magazine. He has long been associated with the American Baptist Convention and served as a delegate to Baptist World Congresses in Sweden, Germany, Canada, and Denmark.

Mr. Lipphard was born in Evansville, Indiana, in 1886. He was edu-
cated at Yale, from which he received a B.A. and an M.A. degree, and Colgate-Rochester Divinity School, where he won his B.D. His honorary degrees include a D.D. from Franklin College, and a Litt.D. from Ottawa University, Kansas. He has traveled widely in Europe, to which he has made over twenty separate trips, the Far East, and South America.

From 1940 to 1943, Mr. Lipphard was secretary of the World Relief Committee of the American Baptist Convention. He was a member of the Joint Commission on Missionary Education of the National Council of the Churches of Christ, is a member of the American Friends of the World Council of Churches, the Foreign Policy Association, and is a former vice-president of the American Baptist Historical Society.

In 1951, Mr. Lipphard received an award from the Associated Church Press for his eminence in editorial writing. He is the author of four books: *The Ministry of Healing, The Second Century, Communing with Communism,* and *Out of the Storm in China.*

## What is a Baptist?

A Baptist is a faithful follower of Jesus Christ, who sincerely endeavors to establish His way of life among mankind, is a staunch believer in the historic Baptist principle of religious liberty, has been baptized by

*1*

immersion, and is a member of a parish church which is identified by the name Baptist.

Baptists believe that religion is a personal relationship between the human soul and God. In this realm, nothing may intrude—no ecclesiastical system, no governmental regulation, no ordinance, no sacrament, no preacher, no priest. The saving grace of Christ and the infinite mercy of God are available to every individual, without the mediation of any priest or minister or church or system. Baptists believe in the "priesthood of all believers."

**What are the basic tenets of the Baptist creed?**

Baptists have no single, official creed. Periodically, efforts have been made by extreme conservatives to secure the adoption of a statement which would become a test for service or fellowship. Each time, such a proposal has been defeated. The nearest statement to a formal creed is the so-called "Grand Rapids Affirmation," adopted on May 23, 1946, by the Northern Baptist Convention (later the American Baptist Convention), which declares:

> "RESOLVED: That we reaffirm our faith in the New Testament as a divinely inspired record and therefore a trustworthy, authoritative and all-sufficient rule of our faith and practice. We rededicate ourselves to Jesus Christ as Lord and Savior and we call all our churches to the common task of sharing the whole gospel with the whole world."

Despite their wide differences of theological interpretation, Baptists *are* united in one fellowship and committed to a common purpose. They are motivated by a transcending loyalty to Jesus Christ, as Lord and Savior. For Baptists, Christ stands at the door of every human heart and knocks, waiting to be invited in to take possession of that person's life, to make him a living reincarnation of Christ Himself. As the Apostle Paul expressed it: ". . . I live; yet not I, but Christ liveth in me." To that concept of the reincarnation of Christ, every Baptist gives wholehearted assent.

**What are the distinctive characteristics of the Baptist faith?**

The answer can best be expressed in two words: religious liberty. Throughout their history, Baptists have contended for full, complete, unrestricted religious freedom. And the freedom they demand for themselves they just as zealously demand for those of all other religions—Catholic, Moslem, Hindu, Jewish, or pagan—as well as those of no religion.

Baptists claim that an atheist has just as much right to cherish his views, and to persuade others to accept his views, as any advocate of any religion—provided only that nobody in the profession of his convictions interferes with the right of all others to do likewise.

Baptists believe that religious error can never be suppressed or eradicated by legislation, force, or persecution—whether by state or church. The Baptist contention is not for mere "tolerance" but for absolute liberty. Tolerance means concession and expediency; liberty means inalienable right. The English philosopher John Locke said: "The Baptists were the first propounders of absolute liberty, just and true liberty, equal and impartial liberty."

### Why do Baptists prefer to be called a denomination instead of a church?

Because most Baptists do not admit that they constitute a "church" —but are organized into local "churches." The local parish church is the sovereign, all-powerful ecclesiastical unit. The term "Baptist Church" is used for convenience; "denomination" is preferred by most Baptists.

Baptists have no hierarchy, no centralized control of religious activity, no headquarters' "oversight" of churches or liturgies, practices or regulations. The local parish church is a law unto itself. Its relations with other churches, its compliance with recommendations from national church headquarters, its acceptance of any resolutions formulated at a convention—all these are entirely voluntary, without the slightest degree of compulsion.

### Do Baptists accept the literal interpretation of the Bible?

Yes and no. All Baptists believe in the inspiration of the Bible, but only the extreme fundamentalists accept it literally or regard it as infallible in every detail. All Baptists accept the Bible as infallible in religious teachings and as a trustworthy record of the progressive revelation of God, climaxed by the supreme revelation of Himself in Jesus Christ. Progressive and liberal Baptists regard some sections of the Bible as written in the thought patterns of Biblical times—allegorical, figurative, legendary, yet conveying eternal religious truths. No official dogma prescribes how an individual Baptist shall interpret the Bible.

**Why do Baptists baptize only by immersion?**

For two reasons: (1) Immersion was the mode of baptism in the New Testament; John the Baptist immersed his converts in the Jordan River; Christ Himself was so immersed. (2) Baptists regard baptism as a public confession of Christian faith and a symbol of the burial and resurrection of Christ, as stated by Paul in his Epistle to the Colossians. Hence, Baptists look upon immersion as realistic symbolism, through which the life of sin is buried in baptism and the new life of faith emerges.

Immersion is limited to adults and to such children as have reached an age where they can understand the meaning of baptism. "Baptize" is a transliteration of the Greek word *baptizein* (meaning "to immerse"), not a translation. To say that Baptists baptize by immersion is redundant, since baptism originally was immersion.

**Why don't Baptists baptize infants?**

Since baptism is a voluntary public profession of Christian faith, only persons old enough to understand its significance and its symbolism should be accepted for baptism. Moreover, Baptists give their children the right to decide for themselves whether or not they wish to be baptized as a public profession of Christian faith. Such a decision makes religion and the ceremony of baptism more meaningful.

**Do Baptists accept the doctrine of the Virgin Birth of Christ?**

A great majority undoubtedly do. A substantial minority do not. For the majority, the doctrine of the Virgin Birth is essential to faith in the deity of Christ. The minority need no such support, since they find no reference to the Virgin Birth in the writings of Paul or in the gospels of Mark and John.

Since Baptists have no authoritarian creed to control their faith and practice, each local parish church has the right to decide whether or not to make acceptance of the doctrine of the Virgin Birth a condition of church membership.

Baptists pay no special homage to Mary but respect her as the noblest of women. They have never accepted the doctrine of *her* immaculate conception or the doctrine, recently announced by **Pope Pius XII**, of the Assumption of Mary.

## Do Baptists accept the doctrine of the Trinity?

Yes. This is a basic doctrine of Christianity. The trinitarian formula, "in the name of the Father, and of the Son, and of the Holy Ghost," is used at every baptism. The sublime mystery of the Trinity, of the eternal and infinite essence of God manifested in three persons, the Baptist leaves to the theologians to interpret. He simply accepts it.

## What is the Baptist position on sin and salvation?

A Baptist affirms the competency of the individual, under God, in matters of religion. Every true believer in Christ as personal Savior is saved—without the intervention of preacher or church. Each individual must give evidence of his personal redemption by faith, good works, and the Christian way of life. The confession of sin is a personal matter between the individual and God. Hence no priestly mediation or resort to the confessional is needed.

With most Protestants, Baptists believe that man sins against the holiness and righteousness of God, that he willfully disobeys God's commands, allows his selfishness to motivate his life, and is therefore in need of salvation. A good Baptist definition of sin explains it as "lack of conformity to the moral law or God, either in act, disposition or state." Man cannot save himself. He needs and finds in Jesus Christ a divine redeemer who unites in Himself both the human nature and the divine. By His death on the Cross, man was reconciled to God and God to man. Through faith in this reconciling ministry of Christ, man is saved from his sins.

## Do Baptists believe in heaven and hell?

A categorical answer, applicable to all Baptists, is impossible. Most Baptists believe in some form of life beyond the grave. They cannot conceive of the total annihilation of spiritual values; nor can they imagine the continued existence of spiritual values without the continuing existence of personalities to express them. As to the precise nature of life hereafter, Baptists cherish a vast range of ideas, from some nebulous, indefinable existence to some definite place, like a city of golden streets or a region of everlasting torment as envisaged by the extreme literalists. Some Baptists find it difficult to reconcile the fact of an all-merciful God with endless punishment for sins committed within the short span of a lifetime on earth. Still others, with·sublime confidence and trust, simply accept the assurance of Christ: "Where I am, there ye may be also."

### Do Baptists have sacraments?

No. What are known as sacraments are regarded by Baptists as simple dignified ordinances with no supernatural significance and no sacramental values. The Lord's Supper, or Communion Service, is usually observed on the first Sunday of the month. It is a reminder of the death of Christ and is observed in obedience to His command the night before He was crucified. Whatever grace a Baptist derives from participating in the Lord's Supper depends on his own awareness of what the Supper signifies as a memorial service. No supernatural grace is bequeathed to him by the officiating clergyman or by his partaking of the bread and of the cup. Whatever blessing he receives comes through some new rededication to a life of righteousness and service to his fellow men.

### Do Baptists approve of divorce?

No, except for adultery. But there is no regulation among Baptist churches regarding divorce. Annual conventions of Baptists have often condemned the rising divorce rate in the United States. Each Baptist clergyman depends on his conscience in deciding whether or not to officiate at the marriage of divorced persons. No church law prescribes what he must do.

### Do Baptists sanction birth control?

No parish Baptist church and no ecclesiastical convention of Baptists has ever by resolution expressed approval or disapproval of birth control or planned parenthood. Even if it had, such resolution would not be binding on any Baptist. Most Baptists would resent and repudiate any such resolution as an unwarranted intrusion into the private life of husband and wife.

### How do Baptists propagate their faith?

The historic Baptist view holds that *every* church member, and every professing Christian, is an evangelist. By word, deed, and character, he is committed to proclaim his Christian faith and to seek to win others to its acceptance. Throughout their history, Baptists have engaged in very active missionary effort, at home and abroad. Foreign missions have been successful on every continent.

## How many Baptists are there in the world? In the United States?

There are approximately 22,000,000 Baptists in the world. An accurate tabulation is impossible because religious statistics cannot be compiled in countries behind the Iron Curtain. It is estimated that there are 3,000,000 Baptists in Soviet Russia. *The World Almanac* for 1953 records 17,500,734 Baptists in the United States, divided among the four larger national groups and eighteen smaller bodies, all of whom identify themselves as Baptists. Since Baptists do not baptize infants or children until they have reached the age when they understand the meaning of baptism, the figures for church membership do not include children. About one third of the Protestants in the United States are Baptists.

## How did the Baptist movement begin?

Most Baptists like to trace their ancestry directly back to John the Baptist. But there is no historical evidence of any definite, organized body of Baptists before the year 1611 when groups in England began to maintain that only believers in Christ, not infants, could be baptized and that baptism had to be by immersion.

Baptist *principles,* however, go back to the teachings and practices of the churches in the New Testament, before they became organized and controlled under the hierarchical system known as Roman Catholicism. Prof. Hans von Schubert of Heidelberg acknowledged that "in the ancient church, it was not the general custom to baptize children; preparation for baptism and the baptismal ceremony were designed for grown persons."

During the early centuries and through the Middle Ages, small groups of Christians sought to maintain the purity and simplicity of the early churches. Later groups emerged who became known as Anabaptists, because they insisted on rebaptism. They regarded their original baptism as infants as not in accord with the New Testament and therefore invalid.

Among them was Balthazar Hubmeier, who died at the stake on March 10, 1528, and his wife, who was drowned in the Danube a few days later, because of their unswerving fidelity to three basic Baptist principles: (1) the supremacy of the Scriptures, rather than the Church, in matters of faith and doctrine; (2) religious liberty; and (3) the baptism of believers rather than infants.

Anabaptist groups flourished for nearly four centuries, mostly in

Switzerland, Germany, and the Netherlands. They were the ecclesiastical ancestors of the Baptists of today. Since 1611 in England, and since 1639 in the United States, when Roger Williams founded the first Baptist church in Providence, Rhode Island, the denomination has grown in the number of its local parish churches, its adherents, its prestige, and its influence.

# What Is a Catholic?

## by JOHN COGLEY

JOHN COGLEY is executive editor of *The Commonweal,* the distinguished weekly journal edited by Catholic laymen. He was founding editor of the Catholic student magazine, *Today,* and is a member of the Commission on Religious Organizations of the National Conference of Christians and Jews. During World War II, he served as a radio operator and military counselor in the Air Force.

Mr. Cogley was born in Chicago in 1916, studied at Loyola University and the University of Chicago, and pursued graduate studies in philosophy and theology at the University of Fribourg (Switzerland).

He is the editor of *Catholicism in America,* a collection of seventeen articles which first appeared in *The Commonweal.*

This article was submitted to the proper authorities in the New York Archdiocese, who declared that it presents a correct understanding of Catholic doctrinal and moral teachings. The author alone is responsible for non-doctrinal opinions.

**Do Catholics believe theirs is the only true religion?**

Yes. The fact that there are many religions, all holding different—often contradictory—doctrines about God and man strikes the Catholic as tragic. The idea that they are all equally true (those that hold Christ was divine and those that hold He was merely human, for instance) seems absurdly illogical.

Catholics believe that Christ, the Son of God, founded the Church and promised to remain with it, "even unto the consummation of the world." But when they say theirs is the only true religion, Catholics do not mean that they alone are the children of God or that only Catholics are righteous and God-fearing. Many non-Catholics are saints; some Catholics are scoundrels. Nor do Catholics believe that only Catholics go to heaven. Pope Pius IX wrote: "It is to be held as of faith that none can be saved outside the Apostolic Roman Church . . . but, nevertheless, it is equally certain that those who are ignorant of the true religion, if that ignorance is invincible, will not be held guilty in the eyes of the Lord." Catholics believe that in the sight of God, all who love Him and sincerely desire to do His will are related

9

in some way to the Church which His Son founded and so can be saved.

## What are the chief differences between the Catholic and Jewish faiths? The Catholic and Protestant?

The Catholic Church claims four distinctive marks: it is *one* (in doctrine, authority, and worship), *holy* (perfect observance of its teachings leads inevitably to sanctity), *catholic* (it is unchanging in its essential teachings and preaches the same gospel and administers the same sacraments to men of all times in all places), and *apostolic* (it traces its ancestry back to the Apostles and, like them, carries the message of Christ to all, regardless of race, nationality, station, or class).

Judaism: Pope Pius XI at the time of the Hitler persecutions wrote: "Spiritually, we are Semites." In the Mass, reference is made to "our father Abraham." The Catholic recognizes the unique religious role of the Jewish people before Christ. He shares their belief in God the Father, in the brotherhood of man, and in the moral teachings handed down by the patriarchs and prophets. Christianity, as he sees it, is the fulfillment of Judaism. "I came not to destroy the law but to fulfill it," Christ said.

The big difference is that Catholics believe that Jesus Christ was the promised Messiah, true God and true Man. They believe that mankind was redeemed by Christ's atonement, though individual men must still work out their own personal salvation by faith and good works. Catholics accept the New Testament with its "new law" of charity—by which is meant the love of God for His own sake and of all men (even of enemies) because they too are children of God. The Catholic believes that with the coming of Christ, all races and nations became "chosen people."

Protestantism embraces a variety of doctrines. Some Protestants are closer to Catholic belief than others. Two of the chief differences seem to be these:

*The Bible:* Protestants believe in private interpretation. Catholics believe that the Church is the divinely appointed custodian of the Bible and has the final word on what is meant in any specific passage. The Church guards orthodoxy (including interpretation of the Scriptures) and passes down essential Christian tradition from one generation to another.

*Universal Priesthood:* Most Protestants affirm the "priesthood of all believers," in opposition to the Catholic idea of a specially ordained priesthood. Catholics, too, believe that by virtue of the sacraments laymen share in the priesthood of Christ. But the "priesthood of the laity" is subordinated to that of the clergy, who alone have received the sacrament of Holy Orders.

The Catholic Mass is not the same as a Protestant Communion Service—not only in ceremony but in what each congregation believes is taking place. Protestantism provides for a greater variety of opinion on such matters as divorce and birth control, which the Catholic feels have been settled once and for all either by the natural law or by revelation. The average Protestant thinks of "the Church" as a broad spiritual unity; the Catholic using the same words has a precise institution—the Roman Catholic Church—in mind.

**May Catholic priests take part in interreligious services?**

No. The public worship of Catholics, and the priest's exercise of his spiritual office, are subject to the authority of the Church. Since the Church's authority is not recognized by the other participants at an interfaith service, Catholics at such services—be they priests or laity —are placed in an untenable position. They are implicitly called upon to deny their own Church's claims and sometimes, by the wording of prayers and hymns, to assent explicitly to beliefs they do not hold.

**Do Catholics believe the Pope can do no wrong? Must Catholics accept everything the Pope says?**

Catholics do not believe the Pope can do no wrong. Nor does the Pope. He confesses regularly to a simple priest, like the humblest peasant in the Church. Catholics admit freely that there were Popes who were wicked men (I first learned of them in parochial schools), though their number and the enormity of their sins have often been exaggerated.

Catholics do believe that the Pope, be he saint or sinner, is preserved by God from leading the Church into doctrinal error. These are the conditions of a papal pronouncement which Catholics consider infallible: (1) It must come under the heading of faith or morals; (2) the Pope must be speaking as head of the Church with the intention of obliging its members to assent to his definition.

Everything that the Church teaches as infallible doctrine, a Catholic must accept. On questions that have not been defined as articles of faith (the miracles at Fatima, for instance), he is under no such obligation.

## What do Catholics believe about the Virgin Mary? Does the recent doctrine of the Assumption mean that Mary is now in an actual place?

Catholics believe that from the moment of her conception in *her* mother's womb, the Mother of Christ was preserved free from original sin. This is what is known as the Immaculate Conception, often confused with the Virgin Birth—which, of course, refers to the birth of Christ. Mary remained a virgin throughout her life. Soon after her death, her body was reunited with her soul in heaven. Because of her stainless life and vast dignity as the Mother of the God-Man, Catholics believe Mary is the greatest of the saints. Catholics pray *to* God *through* Mary because they believe that she is a powerful intercessor and that when Christ on Calvary said, "Behold thy mother!" she became the mother of mankind.

The Assumption (the belief that Mary's body was preserved from corruption and taken to heaven and reunited to her soul) is not a new belief. Fifteen hundred years ago, the feast was celebrated. What took place during 1950 was this: Pope Pius XII solemnly declared that the ancient belief was now a formal doctrine, to which all Catholics must give assent. The Pope made this solemn declaration in answer to a widespread popular request by clergy and laity.

The word "heaven" is used to mean both a place and a state of being. Of the state, Catholics believe that it consists essentially in seeing God "face to face" (1 Cor. 13, 12). Of the place, we have no knowledge beyond the fact that it *exists*. "Eye hath not seen, ear hath not heard, nor hath it entered into the heart of man what God hath prepared for those who love Him" (1 Cor. 2, 9).

## Do Catholics believe that unbaptized babies cannot go to heaven because of "original sin"?

Yes. It is Catholic belief that no one by nature has a "right" to heaven. Man does not have a claim on the *supernatural* happiness which he enjoys in seeing God "face to face." It is a free gift of God. The loss of supernatural life—generally called the fall from grace—was incurred by Adam at the time of his rebellion against God. Because Adam was head of the human race, all mankind was involved in the historic sin of disobedience by which the first man rejected the gifts God had given him above and beyond the needs of human nature.

Since the redemption by Christ ("the new Adam"), it has been possible for men to regain the life of grace. Baptism restores supernatural life. Without that life, man simply does not have the capacity to enjoy heaven. In the case of adults, the Church teaches, the life of grace may be gained by an act of perfect contrition or pure love of God ("baptism of desire"). Infants are incapable of such an act of the will.

Unbaptized babies (in limbo) do not suffer in any way, even from a sense of loss. St. Thomas Aquinas taught that they, too, have knowledge of God—but according to a "natural" capacity. Their happiness is greater than any known by man on earth, however limited in comparison with that of the saints in heaven.

### How do Catholics look on the Devil?

Catholics believe that Satan (the leader of the fallen angels) and his cohorts are pure spirits with an intelligence of a very high order and a will which is now obstinately bent on evil. The Devil and the other fallen angels can tempt and torment men, though all temptations are not directly attributable to them. Many religious thinkers have said that the Devil's greatest triumph lies in convincing the world that he doesn't exist.

Hell, to Catholics, means two things: a place and a state of punishment. The Devil is not confined to hell as a place, and will not be until the last day; but he exists "in hell"—as a state of eternal punishment.

### Why do Catholics worship "graven images"?

They don't. Like any religion, Catholicism uses symbols to heighten the meaning of spiritual truths. The Council of Trent summed up the Catholic position on images four hundred years ago: "The images of Christ and the Virgin Mother of God, and of the other saints, are to be had and to be kept, especially in the churches, and due honor and veneration are to be given to them; *not that any divinity or virtue is believed to be in them, on account of which they are to be worshiped, or that anything is to be asked of them, or that trust is to be put in images,* as was done of old by the Gentiles, who placed their hopes in idols; but because *the honor which is shown them is referred to the prototypes which these images represent.*" [My italics.]

### Why do Catholics sprinkle holy water on buildings, farm implements, etc.?

Water is an ancient symbol of spiritual purification. Holy water in the

Church is an adaptation of an old Jewish custom. Catholics do not believe that the water has any power in itself. When it is sprinkled, with appropriate prayers, on buildings, farm implements and the like, the ceremony signifies that the Church is humbly calling upon God to drive away the forces of Satan and accept for His own glory the uses to which the thing blessed will be put. Man is a unity of body and spirit, and the Church has never hesitated to recognize this by using material objects to signify spiritual realities.

**What is purgatory?**

Like "heaven" or "hell," the word "purgatory" refers to a place and a state. Catholics believe that purgatory exists to *purge* those souls who are not yet pure enough for heaven but have not died in a state of serious (mortal) sin. Such near-saints must undergo the pain of intense longing for God until they have paid the debt of temporal punishment due them because of their sins on earth. In a word, purgatory exists to make saints who will be ready for the purity of God's presence. If one does not succeed in becoming a saint on earth but yet escapes eternal hell, he is purified in purgatory.

**What is the real meaning of the Mass?**

The Mass is the central act of worship in the Catholic Church. It is the true sacrifice of the Body and Blood of Christ, made present on the altar by the words of consecration (over the bread, "This is my body"; over the wine, "This is . . . my blood . . ."). "In this divine sacrifice," the Council of Trent declared, "the same Christ is present and immolated in a bloodless manner who once for all offered himself in a bloody manner on the altar of the cross; . . . only the manner of offering is different."

Mass must be celebrated by a priest or bishop, with whom the congregation joins in offering to God "a re-presentation and a renewal of the offering made on Calvary."

Catholics believe that after the priest pronounces the words of consecration in the Mass, the whole substance of the bread becomes the Body of Christ, the whole substance of the wine becomes the Blood of Christ. They believe that Christ is truly and substantially present in the Eucharist, body and soul, humanity and divinity.

Mass is said in various tongues—in the West, mainly in Latin. The priest performs an act of social worship; he does not preach or teach in Latin. Catholics use missals (which contain translations) and know, in most cases, what the standard Mass prayers mean.

**Do Catholics regard the human body and the act of love as shameful?**

The Church puts great stress on modesty—but precisely because it disapproves so strongly of any cheapening of sex, which it regards as a sacred trust. How could a Church that teaches the Son of God became flesh and blood regard the human body as shameful? Far from looking upon the act of love as unclean, the Church teaches that it is the means by which men share in the work of the Creator.

**Is it true that Catholics consider all non-Catholic children illegitimate?**

No. It is Church law that the wedding of a Catholic must be performed in the presence of a priest and two witnesses. In the case of non-Catholics, the Church recognizes the sacredness and binding nature of all ceremonies which mark "the conjugal union of man and woman, contracted between two qualified persons, which obliges them to live together throughout life."

**Does the Church forbid intermarriage?**

Yes. But while never approving of mixed marriages, the Church for a serious reason will lift the ban provided (a) the non-Catholic party agrees in writing not to interfere with the religion of the Catholic; (b) both parties agree to have all children baptized and brought up as Catholics; and (c) there is moral certainty that the promises will be kept.

**Is a Catholic permitted to get a divorce?**

Catholics believe that marriage, by its nature, must be a contract "till death do us part." The Church does not recognize any absolute divorce between a couple who are validly married, where one or the other would be free to marry again. For good reasons (infidelity, cruelty), the Church may approve separation from bed and board. In such cases, a Catholic may be permitted to get a civil divorce in order to satisfy some legal requirement. He may not, however, remarry during the lifetime of the other party. In cases where the Church has decreed nullity—where, according to Church law, there was no marriage in the first place—a civil annulment or divorce may sometimes be necessary.

**In a case where doctors agree that a mother may die during childbirth, must Catholic doctors save the child rather than the mother?**

No. The Catholic doctor is bound to make every effort to save both. Both mother and child have an inherent right to life. *Neither may be killed so the other can live.* This is the answer the Church has to give either to a grief-stricken young husband who needs the help of his wife in raising a family, or to a royal figure who feels a greater need for a son and heir than for his queen. Directly to take the life of an innocent is never permitted—even as a means to a good end.

The question, incidentally, is largely academic. Statistics show that maternity deaths in the nation's Catholic hospitals are as low as any.

**Why don't priests and nuns marry?**

For hundreds of years, the Western Church has required that its clergy remain unmarried. This is a disciplinary matter which could (but undoubtedly won't) be changed overnight. The rule leaves priests wholly free from the responsibilities of family life for pastoral and missionary work. It is wholeheartedly accepted by the clergy and is popular with the Catholic laity.

Nuns and monks take a vow of chastity—not because they despise marriage and human love but in order to dedicate themselves wholly to the service of God in a religious order. Nuns (and those monks who have not received priestly orders) may marry with the Church's blessing any time they are dispensed from their vows by the proper authority. But as long as they choose to remain in the cloister, nuns and monks are obliged to observe the life of poverty, chastity, and obedience to which they have freely dedicated themselves.

Such self-chosen celibacy is quite in keeping with the teaching of Saint Paul on the superiority (in the spiritual order) of virginity.

Incidentally, thousands of Catholic priests *are* married. They are members of the Eastern rites, in union with Rome. Among these Catholics, it is customary to ordain married men, though second marriages are forbidden.

**Why does the Catholic Church oppose birth control? Why does the Church oppose the dissemination of birth control information among non-Catholics (as in Massachusetts voting)?**

The Catholic position on birth control is based on the belief that (a) artificial contraception is against the law of God, and (b) because it is immoral, it cannot be employed as a means, even to a good end.

Strictly speaking, it is artificial birth *prevention* (by means of contraceptive devices, chemicals, etc.) which the Church condemns as intrinsically evil. The proper end of the sex act is procreation. The physical expression of love is surely good but is subordinated to the ultimate reason for sexual relations. The pleasure connected with sex, like the satisfaction that goes with eating, is good, too, as long as it is taken for what it is—a means to an end.

Basing its objections on the natural law, the Church says that deliberately to frustrate the proper end of the sex act is contrary to right reason, is conduct unbecoming to rational beings and, for this reason, is immoral.

Birth prevention is regarded by Catholics as being evil in itself— circumstances cannot change it into something morally good or indifferent. The natural law binds all men, Catholics and non-Catholics alike. Therefore, whenever there is a question of relaxing legislation on contraception (often put on the books, as in Massachusetts, not by Catholic but by Protestant legislators), Catholics will vote in accordance with their consciences. Can one really expect an American to vote for a practice which he believes is against the law of God?

"Natural" birth control—the so-called rhythm theory—is permitted (as the Pope recently stated) in cases where undue medical or economic hardship makes family limitation imperative. His Holiness, along with condemning artificial birth control, urged that the nations make greater efforts to support the present population of the world by opening underpopulated areas to immigration, by increasing food production, by sharing technical advances with the have-not nations, and by developing more natural resources.

**What actually happens in confession? Can a Catholic gain absolution for a sin, repeat the same sin, and receive absolution repeatedly?**

Confessions are usually heard in the boxlike "confessionals" found in every Catholic church. It is dark inside. Sometimes you can see the priest dimly, but often a white cloth is tacked to the grille separating priest and penitent. Before you enter the confessional, you prepare yourself by examining your conscience.

Inside, you kneel and whisper to the priest on the other side of the grille. You tell him how long it has been since your last confession. Then, as completely as you can, you name your sins, giving their number and such details as are necessary to supply a clear idea of what you did that was wrong.

When you finish, the priest usually says a few words of spiritual counsel and encouragement. Then he gives you your "penance." This is a certain number of prayers or prayerful acts that you must perform to signify your genuine sorrow and your resolution to do better. You say the Act of Contrition, a formal prayer which expresses love for God, sorrow for sin, and "purpose of amendment." As you recite this prayer, you can hear the priest's words of absolution. The priest sends you out with a "God bless you" and usually asks you to pray for him, a sinner like yourself.

The Bible says that even the just man falls seven times a day, and it is true that Catholics, like other people, find themselves repeating the same old sins. But no one sins *because* he goes to confession regularly. If one does not intend to make a sincere effort to break sinful habits, there is no point in going to confession. A "bad confession" (where sins are withheld or where genuine sorrow or the "purpose of amendment" are not present) is considered invalid and sacrilegious.

**What is the attitude of the Church toward drinking and gambling?**

Neither is considered evil in itself, though both may become sinful by excess or abuse. The Church approves total abstinence in the same way that it puts its approval upon voluntary celibacy. Both sex and alcoholic drinks are the creation of God; they may be forsworn but must not be condemned as intrinsically evil.

Gambling is regarded as an innocent pastime unless one or all of the following conditions are present: (a) the subject matter of the bet is sinful; (b) one party is *forced* to play; (c) one party is certain of the outcome; (d) one party is left in ignorance of the real terms of the gamble; (e) cheating and fraud are present; (f) the money staked is needed to pay debts or for the support of oneself or family; (g) the gambling game is forbidden by legitimate public authority.

**Why do Catholics have their own schools? Do they seek financial support from public funds (including taxes paid by non-Catholics) for parochial schools?**

American Catholics have made great sacrifices to build their own school system because they believe there is no ignorance as tragic as religious ignorance and that imparting a religious attitude related to life and learning is a seven-day-a-week, not a Sunday-morning, task.

Millions are spent on their parochial schools by Catholics. If they were closed down, many Americans would soon feel the difference in school taxes. Besides supporting their own schools, Catholics pay their full share of public-school taxes, as cheerfully as taxes are ever paid, because they believe that free public education should be available to all Americans who want it for their children.

Catholics have not sought support for their schools from public funds. When there was a question of providing such "auxiliary aids" as bus rides and school lunches from Federal funds, Catholics asked that their children—not their schools!—share in the benefits. Parochial schools actually mean lower taxes for everybody—because Catholics do not use the schools they pay for. If there is a tax issue in the parochial-school question, this is it.

### Why does the Church forbid Catholics to read or see certain books, plays, and movies?

What a Catholic believes by faith, he believes absolutely. He is ready to take the Church's word on what constitutes a danger to this faith.

Catholics regard their Church as a moral teacher. When books, plays, movies, etc., are forbidden, it is because it is the Church's judgment that, for the ordinary person, such books, plays, etc., may provide either a temptation to sin, a false religious understanding, or a challenge to faith which he is not equipped to handle. Many of the works on the index of forbidden books are theological studies written in good faith by devout Catholics; the Church has proscribed them because they contain some theological error.

In the case of clearly obscene books, there is the added obligation not to encourage immorality. Where pornography is not the issue, a Catholic may ask for permission (from a representative of the local bishop) to read a forbidden book or see a proscribed play. If it is felt he is sufficiently well instructed to meet the challenge to his faith, and there is good reason for his request, the permission is readily granted.

### Do Catholics believe in religious tolerance?

American Catholics believe in and practice religious tolerance, as their Protestant and Jewish neighbors amply testify. There are bigots in the Church, as in every group, but this is a psychological failing of individuals, not something that derives from Catholic belief.

In certain Catholic countries (as in a few Protestant countries), religious tolerance is not wholeheartedly accepted as a political idea. On the other hand, the Catholic can point to a country like Eire, where not long ago a Protestant was elected President. Even in the United States, it is doubtful whether a Catholic, or a Jew, could reach the White House.

Often by "religious tolerance" is understood something more properly called "religious indifferentism"—the idea that "one religion is as good (or as bad) as another." This is a proposition which Catholics cannot accept. It should not be imposed on American citizens as a test of patriotism—especially in the name of tolerance!

If by tolerance is meant living in peace with one's neighbor, making no attempts to interfere with his religious practices and recognizing his civil right to pick his own church (or no church), then the record of American Catholics is second to none.

On this score, Catholics have probably been more sinned against than sinning, what with the Know-Nothing movement, the Ku Klux Klan, the Al Smith campaign.

**The Catholic Church is an authoritarian institution. Does this contradict democratic principle?**

The Church is a religious, not a political, society. Democracy is a system of government in which each man is free to serve God—that is, to acknowledge the authority of God—according to his own conscience. How can one "contradict democratic principle" by following the religious dictates of his conscience?

# What Is a Christian Scientist?

## by GEORGE CHANNING

GEORGE CHANNING is known internationally as a Christian Science lecturer, teacher, and practitioner. He has served as First Reader in the Mother Church, Boston, and was a trustee of the Christian Science Publishing Society, which publishes the *Christian Science Monitor* and the religious periodicals of Christian Science. He has been editor of the *Christian Science Journal,* the *Christian Science Sentinel,* and the *Herald of Christian Science.* From 1950 to 1953, he was manager of the Committees on Publication.

Mr. Channing was born in Providence, Rhode Island, in 1888. He is a graduate of Brown University and studied law at Yale and Boston Universities. He has had a broad career in journalism, beginning on the Providence *Journal.* He was city editor of the Seattle *Star* and worked for the Detroit *Free Press* and *Journal.*

During the First World War, Mr. Channing was a first lieutenant and served in France. In 1953, he received the "Brown Bear Award" from Brown University for distinguished activities as an alumnus.

The views expressed by Mr. Channing in this article were officially approved by the Mother Church, The First Church of Christ, Scientist, Boston, Massachusetts.

**What is a Christian Scientist?**

A Christian Scientist is one who accepts and practices Christian Science as his religion. Christian Science has been defined by its discoverer and founder, Mary Baker Eddy: "As the law of God, the law of good, interpreting and demonstrating the divine Principle and rule of universal harmony."

**Why do you consider it Christian?**

Because it is based wholly on the teachings of Christ Jesus which make clear the spiritual meaning of the Holy Scriptures. It requires its adherents to be active in obeying all the commandments of Jesus, including healing the sick.

**Why do you consider it scientific?**

Because it is exact in premise and conclusion and is completely demonstrable.

**What is the basic premise of Christian Science?**

That God is divine Mind, the conceiver of man and the universe, and Mind is all that exists. Mind expresses itself and its expression is man.

Spirit is eternal and real; matter is an unreal illusion subject to decay and dissolution.

Evil has to do with matter—therefore evil is unreal, an illusion.

Spirit and its expression, man, are indestructible. Death is an illusion of mortal sense, which may continue to appear until destroyed by spiritual sense, either on this or the other side of the grave. The individual continues to live even though unseen by persons on our plane of existence.

**What is the relation of man to God?**

Man and the universe are made in the image and likeness of the divine Mind, God, which conceives them. Mind is synonymous with Spirit, Soul, Life, Truth, Love, Principle (which means cause or origin).

Man, the idea and image of God, is immortal, perfect, wholly good, untouched and untainted by evil because man expresses God.

**What is health to the Christian Scientist?**

Health is a spiritual reality; therefore health is eternal. Disease and illness are aspects of falsehood—delusions of the human mind which can be destroyed by the prayer of spiritual understanding. The divinely mental can and does replace the materially mental.

**Who was Mary Baker Eddy?**

Mary Baker Eddy (1821–1910) was the discoverer and founder of Christian Science. She is regarded by Christian Scientists as the revelator of truth to this age. She brought the Comforter that Jesus foretold. This Comforter is the Science of Christianity and is available, through Mrs. Eddy's achievement, to all who desire to utilize God's power and God's law as Jesus did.

Each person, of any religion, can find what is satisfying to him as the spiritual meaning in the Bible. But Christian Scientists feel that Mrs. Eddy's book, *Science and Health with Key to the Scriptures,* offers the *complete* spiritual meaning of the Bible. They believe that this full meaning would not have been available to them without Mrs. Eddy's discovery.

### Do Christian Scientists consider themselves Protestants?

Yes. Christian Science is a truly Protestant religion, although it embodies several distinguishing characteristics:

Christian Science holds that good is infinite, that sin, death, and disease are unreal, and that evil is a delusion.

Christian Science maintains that healing is a *religious* function.

Christian Science has no ordained clergy or personal pastors. Though Christian Scientists know the pure consecration of Christian martyrs, martyrdom has no place in Christian Science. The Christian Scientist does not die for his religion; he lives in it.

There is no personal preacher in a Christian Science service. The Bible in the King James version and *Science and Health with Key to the Scriptures,* by Mrs. Eddy, are the only "pastors" of the denomination. Texts are read aloud from these books by a first and second reader.

Prayer, to the Christian Scientist, is scientific and achieves healing; Christians who understand such prayer are equipped to fulfill the promise of the Master Christian: "In my name shall they cast out devils; they shall speak with new tongues; they shall take up serpents; and if they drink any deadly thing it shall not hurt them; *they shall lay hands on the sick, and they shall recover"* (Mark 16:17–18).

Christian Scientists do not practice baptism in the material form; to Christian Scientists, baptism means purification from all material sense.

Salvation, to Christian Scientists, consists of being saved from the illusions and delusions of mortal sense—which means the sense of being capable of becoming sick and dying.

Protestantism, it should be remembered, began as a protest against certain organizations or forms of worship. Christian Science also protests—against mortal sense.

### What do Christian Scientists believe about Jesus?

Christian Science accepts the divinity of Christ, but does not deify Jesus—which means that to Christian Scientists, Christ Jesus was not God, but was the Son of God. The true mission of Christ Jesus was to redeem mankind from the beliefs of mortality by showing that man in his real nature is spiritual. Man is not God, but bears witness to God's presence.

The healings of Christ Jesus are regarded by Christian Scientists not as miracles, but as the result of the application of natural spiritual law.

Christian Science completely accepts the Virgin Birth.

By the Trinity, Christian Scientists mean the unity of Father, Son and Holy Spirit—but do not accept the Trinity as three persons in one. Life, Truth, and Love are "the triune Principle called God" (*Science and Health*).

**What role does prayer play in Christian Science?**

An all-important role. To the Christian Scientist, living is basically praying. "Men ought always to pray" (Luke 18:1). The understanding of God is reached through praying. The true Christian Scientist applies his thought in an effort to attain perfect praying. Real devotion and experience are needed to pray the perfect prayer.

A Christian Scientist may not always pray perfectly. The efficacy of his prayer reflects the degree of his own spiritual understanding. If he has attained high spiritual understanding, and if he applies his understanding honestly and with devotion, results may follow which seem miraculous to others.

Healing is accomplished by spiritual understanding. Christian Science distinguishes faith from understanding: Faith means acceptance before proof. Through faith, degrees of evidence appear which serve to *lift* faith into spiritual understanding.

**What is a Christian Science practitioner?**

A practitioner is one who prays for those who ask his prayers in their behalf.

To be registered as a public practitioner, one must be approved by the Mother Church, the First Church of Christ, Scientist in Boston, Massachusetts. To be a practitioner requires systematic instruction, either self-acquired or under authorized teachers, and satisfactory evidence of successful healing work. Candidates must demonstrate a capacity to apply spiritual understanding to the destruction of human ills and discords.

**Can a practitioner treat a patient hundreds of miles away?**

Yes. False beliefs are destroyed by spiritual truth, through prayer, regardless of the geographical location of the person who entertains such false beliefs. Jesus healed the Centurion's servant (Matthew 8:5–13) and the daughter of the Greek woman (Mark 7:25–30) while not physically present with them.

## Do Christian Scientists deny that some diseases are caused by germs, microbes, and viruses?

The Christian Scientist knows that life is divine in origin and that health is a *spiritual* reality. Theories about germs and microbes come from beliefs which hold that life is material and that disease is real. The Christian Scientist knows by experience that his belief is demonstrable despite theories of disease involving germs, microbes, and viruses.

## How can Christian Science maintain its attitude to disease in view of modern medical knowledge?

The Christian Scientist's attitude to disease is supported by reason and by actual demonstration. Christ Jesus demonstrated, as did his followers, what healing and health really mean. Christian Scientists maintain their faith by spiritual intuition and by the proofs they are able to accumulate in their own experience.

Let us remember that the conclusions of material medicine are constantly changing. Recently, the "wonder drugs" (penicillin, aureomycin) were acclaimed almost as panaceas; yet later, their efficacy had to be qualified. Strict warnings had to be issued against too much trust in them. There are countless instances of this kind.

Christian Scientists hold that sickness, sin, and death are aspects of falsehood; and falsehood can be destroyed by exposing it to spiritual truth. Christian Scientists feel they have incontestable evidence that in this way their religion destroys, effectively and permanently, the hatreds, doubts, lusts, and other discords of the human mind and body.

The objective of Christian Science is not *primarily* to heal physical disease—but to regenerate human thought through spiritual understanding. Healing is the effect of attaining this regeneration in some degree. The achievements of medical research do not present any problem to the Christian Scientist, for the results of such research in no way affect the substance and permanency of spiritual truth.

## Do Christian Scientists go to hospitals?

The teaching and faith of Christian Science basically reject medical treatment. To the extent that a man or woman relies on material methods of healing, he or she is not relying fully on Christian Science.

**Do Christian Scientists refuse medical attention when their own children are sick?**

Christian Scientists love their children as deeply as other parents. When their children are ill, they want them to have the most effective and reliable help. They employ the method of Christian Science— prayer, or spiritual understanding—fearlessly and with complete confidence, because they have reason to know that Christian Science is efficacious. (No one is forced to rely on Christian Science against what he may regard as his own good judgment.)

Christian Scientists in many schools and colleges ask for and receive exemption from regulations requiring medical means—*yet their health is as good as that of the rest of the student body, and is often better.* The Christian Scientist knows that he takes good care of his children in one particular way: he prays earnestly for himself and his children every day. He prays not only for their health, but for their spiritual progress.

**Do Christian Scientists call in a doctor at childbirth?**

Yes. The Christian Scientist makes sure that someone who possesses the necessary skills is present at childbirth. The Christian Scientist does not presume to do what he is neither trained nor licensed to do.

**Have not Christian Scientists died because they refused medical attention, or relied entirely on faith and prayer, or called in a doctor too late?**

One might as readily ask, without intending to give offense, "Have not many persons died because they refused the spiritual method of Christian Science, and relied entirely on material aid?"

No statistics prove that the healing methods of material medicine are superior to those of Christian Science. We do know that thousands of men and women who were pronounced "incurable," and who spent years in invalidism and suffering, turned to Christian Science and were healed. Such persons are numerous among the members of the Christian Science Church.

Efforts to understand and apply any rule may appear more successful in some instances than in others. The failure to bring certain facts to light does not alter the verity of the facts themselves. The laws of mathematics, for instance, may fail to reveal a correct answer when improperly applied; indeed, many sciences fail to reveal certain answers even when properly applied.

One does not judge the medical profession by the cases it loses, nor by the overcrowded hospitals and graveyards. May not Christian Science ask that it be judged by its potentialities for good and its achievement in canceling the sense of disease, in erasing sin (and the penalties for sin) from the experience of innumerable persons?

**Do Christian Scientists refuse medical attention in the case of fractures or accidents?**

There are innumerable instances of bone fractures which have been set and healed perfectly under Christian Science treatment—without medical or surgical aid. Results depend upon honest effort, correct understanding, and constancy in Christian Science practice.

A Christian Scientist does not surrender his status as a free man or woman under God. He works out his own salvation by following the course which wisdom dictates to him. If the Christian Scientist has not reached the degree of spiritual understanding which is needed for healing by spiritual means and resorts to some other means, he obviously cannot be said to be employing fully the method of Christian Science. He does not undergo condemnation for this; nor does he assume any burden of guilt. He is always free to improve his spiritual understanding and employ it exclusively, thus restoring his status as a Christian Scientist.

**If God is infinite and good, how does evil exist?**

Evil is hypnotic. It has no more reality than a dream—yet to the dreamer it *appears* real. The nothingness of evil—and of that which sees, feels, or believes in evil—is proved through spiritual awakening.

**Does Christian Science believe in sin?**

Man is really sinless and free. Sin is the belief in the real existence of a mind or minds other than the divine Mind, God. Mortal mind, which believes in decaying and dying, is the sinner. St. Paul called it the "carnal" mind. If a person accepts the carnal mind, *its* sins will appear to be his sins, and its suffering his suffering.

Christian Scientists rid themselves of sin by breaking the false notion that the carnal mind is real, or one's own. Penalty for sin lasts only as long as such false belief lasts. The Christian Scientist tries to live so that the divine Mind is revealed as his mind.

Christian Scientists hold that sin is unreal. But this does not mean that one can sin with impunity. The sinner does not know that sin is unreal; if he did, this would destroy his capacity for sinning.

**Do Christian Scientists believe in heaven or hell?**

Yes—but not in a geographical sense. As Mrs. Eddy said: "The sinner makes his own hell by doing evil, and the saint his own heaven by doing right."

**Why don't Christian Scientists use the word "death"
or the word "died"?**

They do use both words. The words appear in Christian Science periodicals where the context requires them. But the term "passed on" is considered more exact by Christian Scientists, who accept literally the fact that individual life is indestructible. We believe that what is called "death" is not termination, but only an incident in the dream of mortality, an experience of mortal mind, not the divine Mind.

**Does Christian Science maintain that death itself can be eliminated?**

Yes. The Christian Scientist believes that material decay and destruction can be stopped by the full realization of divine truth. Through progressive improvement of one's spiritual understanding which alleviates the circumstances of death, the ultimate elimination of death itself can be achieved. In this way, true immortality can be realized.

**Do Christian Scientists hold funeral services?**

It is perfectly proper for the family to engage a Christian Scientist to read passages from the Bible and from the Christian Science textbook. These passages are intended to remind the hearers that Life, God, and man (who is the individual expression of Life) are eternal. It is also proper to have no reading at all.

**What is the attitude of Christian Science toward birth control?**

There is a whole chapter on marriage in Mrs. Eddy's book, in which this statement occurs (*Science and Health*, p. 56:7–8): "Marriage is the legal and moral provision for generation among human kind." Mrs. Eddy explains that marriage will continue subject to moral regulations needed to secure increasing virtue until mankind attains the spiritual understanding which discerns the perfect spiritual creation, untainted by matter. In accordance with this teaching, married couples are free to follow their own judgment as to having children and as to the number they will have.

**Do Christian Scientists oppose vaccination?**

Christian Scientists do not oppose vaccination for those who want it and believe in it. They do oppose compulsory vaccination for Christian Scientists—as a trespass upon their religious convictions.

Mrs. Eddy specifically instructed Christian Scientists to obey the law, but to seek legal exemption from those laws which violate their religious rights or the rights of conscience. To exempt Christian Scientists from vaccination does no harm to others—especially if vaccination is as effective as it is claimed to be for those who believe in it.

Incidentally, Christian Scientists and their children obey all quarantine regulations because they don't want their neighbors to become fearful of their safety because Christian Scientists refrain from material methods.

**Why do Christian Science students request exemptions from certain examinations—in bacteriology, for instance?**

The only instruction to which Christian Scientists object is that which tends to set up the method of material medicine as the *only* healing method or system. Christian Scientists object to picturing the processes of disease in ways which visualize the terror which begets disease. They also object to compulsory medical regulations because, in effect, such regulations constitute indoctrination which may undermine the religious teaching of the home.

**Would Christian Scientists abolish sanitation and public health measures?**

No. Christian Scientists advocate sanitation because they love cleanliness—inner and outer. They respect the right of the community to take such measures as the community considers essential—so long as these measures do not impose compulsory medication on those who practice their own spiritual method of healing.

Incidentally, Christian Scientists feel that reliance on spiritual means alone, to safeguard public health, is wise *only in proportion to the spiritual understanding of health among the people in the area involved.*

**What is the attitude of Christian Science toward psychiatry and psychoanalysis?**

There is no similarity between medical psychiatry and Christian Science. Christian Science is religion. It treats all ills by prayer. As Mrs. Eddy said: "To heal . . . is to base your practice on immortal Mind, the divine Principle of man's being; and this requires a preparation of the heart and an answer of the lips from the Lord."

Psychiatrists and psychoanalysts investigate the *human* mind; Christian Science is based on the understanding of the divine Mind. Our faith is devoted to the destruction of the false notions of the human mind by exposing them to the spiritual idea of truth. The divine Mind is the only permanent and real remedy for any ill.

**What is the attitude of Christian Science toward other religions?**

The Christian Scientist does not feel superior to the adherents of any denomination. Every man is free to demonstrate the efficacy of his own faith; each is entitled to encouragement in his pursuit of spiritual objectives. Mrs. Eddy said: "A genuine Christian Scientist loves Protestant and Catholic, D.D. and M.D.—loves all who love God, good; and he loves his enemies."

# What Is a Congregationalist?

## by DOUGLAS HORTON

SINCE THIS article was written, the Congregational Christian Churches of America (1,250,000 members) and the Evangelical and Reform Church (760,850 members) have voted to merge into a new body—to be known as the United Church of Christ. The union will be effected in 1957 with the calling of a Convening General Synod of the United Church of Christ.

Douglas Horton is Dean of the Divinity School, Harvard University. For 17 years he was minister of the General Council of Congregational Christian Churches. He was a member of the Central Committee of the World Council of Churches, is a trustee of Princeton University and a trustee of Union Theological Seminary, and chairman of the board of the American University at Cairo.

Mr. Horton was born in Brooklyn, New York, in 1891. He finished his undergraduate studies at Princeton University and proceeded to graduate work in Edinburgh, Oxford, and Ger-

many. He has taught theology at the Newton Theological Institution, the Union Theological Seminary, and the Chicago Theological Seminary. During the First World War, he served as chaplain in the United States Navy. He has received honorary degrees from the Chicago Theological Seminary, Lawrence College, Marietta College, and Carleton College.

Mr. Horton was ordained to the ministry of the Congregational Church in 1915, and has served as minister in Middletown, Connecticut, Brookline, Massachusetts, and Chicago. He is on the editorial board of the *Congregational Quarterly* and was the editor of *The Basic Formula for Church Union*. He has written five books: *Out Into Life, A Legend of the Grail, Taking a City, The Art of Living Today,* and *Congregationalism, A Study in Church Polity*; and he translated, from the German, the work of the distinguished theologian, Karl Barth, *The Word of God and the Word of Man*.

### What is a Congregationalist?

He is a member of a Congregational Christian Church, which in turn is a member of the fellowship of Congregational Churches which encircles the earth.

**What is the Congregational Christian creed?**

If a creed be defined as an attempt to define one's faith in the living God, Congregationalists have been among the greatest creed-makers of history—for each particular congregation is accustomed to write its own creed. A few churches use the Apostles' Creed. Other churches have given up the use of this creed, chiefly because one or two of its phrases are believed to be untrue. Congregationalists remain Puritans, with a passionate regard for truth. They do not adopt a creed unless persuaded that it is all true. The Catholic faith which they hold is fundamentally a belief not in any creed but in the living person of Jesus Christ.

**Is a Congregationalist a Catholic?**

Yes, though not in the sense that he recognizes the sovereignty of the Pope. He is a Catholic in the sense that he holds what he regards as the Catholic faith, that universal faith which is common to all Christians and which binds together the "Holy Catholic Church." He holds the Roman to be *one* of the true branches of the Church.

**Does he believe in the Apostolic Succession?**

Yes. He does not believe that this succession is chiefly visible in the line of Popes, nor in the Anglican or other episcopal lines, nor in the lines of elders or other office-bearers of the Church. Rather, he sees the entire Church of Christ as the succession from the Apostles. He believes that the humblest church member, as well as the most distinguished of prelates, can carry the riches of the Church's belief to succeeding generations.

**What sacraments do Congregational Christians observe?**

Two: Baptism and the Lord's Supper. Baptism is the rite by which the Church takes a child (or adult) to itself. The mode is usually that of "sprinkling," though other forms may be used if desired. The Holy Communion is the ritual meal at which Christ is the host and through which the Church's faith is confirmed and increased. In some Congregational Christian churches the people receive the communion at the altar rail; in most, the elements of Communion are brought by the deacons to the people in the pews.

**Do Congregational Christians believe in the Virgin Birth?**

Probably the majority do not. Undoubtedly many do. It is regarded as a subject for historical research. The fact of Christ, and not the manner in which he was born, is held to be of dominant importance. It is, indeed, the reference to the Virgin Birth in the Apostles' Creed which unfits the latter for use in many churches.

**Do Congregational Christians believe in the Holy Trinity?**

Fully. They believe in God the Father, Creator and Sustainer of the universe, infinite in wisdom, goodness, and love. They believe that God was in Christ reconciling the world to Himself. They believe in the Holy Spirit to such an extent that they are extremely sensitive to the dangers which lie in unchangeable laws and ceremonies which prevent new responses to the Spirit's call.

**What is the Congregational Christian view of sin and salvation?**

The view of most Christians. Sin is opposition or indifference to the will of God. God, however, as Jesus revealed Him, is willing to forgive. When, therefore, a person repents in faith, God accepts him— and when God has accepted a person, he need have no fear of any future in this world or the next. He is "saved."

**Do Congregational Christians believe in heaven and hell?**

Certainly not as *places* of torment and of bliss. They do believe that physical death is not the end of life, that the justice of God cannot finally be escaped, and that it will be heaven to be with God and hell to be without Him.

**What is the Congregational attitude toward the Bible?**

The Bible is regarded as revealing God in a way which will never be superseded. Once one knows that God is love, as Christ shows Him to be, all subsequent knowledge is simply an elaboration of this fundamental truth—and it is this knowledge that God imparts to men through the pages of Scripture.

Congregationalists apply methods of science wholeheartedly to the study of the Bible. As a result they feel they know what God is saying in the Bible better than their fathers who lived in a pre-scientific age.

## Do Congregationalists favor birth control?

On this matter they have made no official statement. They believe that marriage is a holy estate, whether or not it results in the birth of children. In general, however, they do believe that the use by man of the brains which God has given him to invent means of preventing conception is not contrary to God's will.

## What is the Congregational attitude toward divorce?

Though the Congregational Christian Churches have never made a joint official pronouncement on divorce, it is safe to say that they regard the current divorce habits of the American people as a scandal. They are endeavoring to meet this disorder by giving youth better training in the Christian understanding of marriage. They do not oppose legal divorce after a couple have entered into the tragedy of spiritual divorce.

## How and why did the Congregational movement start?

The Congregationalists were one of several groups within the Church of England during the controversial days of the early seventeenth century. They desired that the bishops should have less, and the people more, power over the churches. New England offered them an opportunity to stay nominally within the English Church (for they did not wish to separate) and yet be free from what they regarded as the persecution of the bishops. The tie with the Church of England was broken when, with the coming of Charles II, strict conformity to the Book of Common Prayer was demanded.

## What type of worship is used in the Congregational Christian Churches?

It usually is a moderately formal order of prayers (silent and spoken), hymns, Scripture reading, and preaching designed to express adoration of God, confession of sin, thanksgiving, and commitment to God's will.

## What distinguishes the Congregationalist from other Protestants?

His emphasis upon the place of the *congregation* in the life of the Church. It is in congregations that the Church is visible in its succession from age to age. It is in the congregation that the sacrament is celebrated and the preaching of the Word is heard. The congregation is the point at which God is most likely to reveal his will to a worshiping people. In a congregation all hearts are brought close to each other in brotherhood by being brought close to Christ.

## What is the place of women in Congregationalism?

Here the Congregational view differs from many others. So far as ecclesiastical status is concerned, no distinction is made between men and women. In a situation in which an ordained woman can give better service than an ordained man, the Congregational Churches give ordination to a woman of the proper spiritual qualifications. Only about four per cent of the Congregational Christian ministers are women and of these less than a third are pastors of churches.

## How are Congregational Christian Churches governed?

Ideally, by the mind of Christ through the people who constitute the congregation. When any problem arises, the people seek—through prayer, study, and mutual consultation—to understand His mind concerning it. Though their spiritual shortcomings and ignorance too often stand in their way, these obstacles do not excuse them from seeking the will of Christ and following it.

As in most American denominations, there are county and state associations of churches and a national association—the General Council; but these have no power over the internal life of any of the congregations. This is the reason the Congregational Churches are sometimes known as Free Churches. The freedom of the congregation is inviolable, because the congregation is better able to consult the mind of Christ about itself than is any outside group. No minister beloved by his people can be removed by external pressure. No church can be disbanded except by the wish of its people. The relation between Christ and "two or three gathered together" in His name is sacred.

## What discipline is used by the Congregational Christian Churches?

The chief discipline is brotherly persuasion. Theoretically, public censure is possible and, in extreme cases, the withdrawal of fellowship from an offender. The latter procedure has been invoked only when the well-being of the Church itself seemed at stake. Since the Church's interest is in redemption, a Congregational Christian Church recoils from any discipline which tends to separate an offender from its ministries.

**What attitude does the Congregationalist take toward the Jew?**

That of a brother. Congregational ministers and Jewish rabbis in many cities exchange pulpits regularly, and there are happy friendships between them. Both have a strongly ethical emphasis in their religious teaching; both stand for the establishment of justice and human brotherhood. The Congregationalist considers that fraternity with non-Christians expresses his Christian belief.

**What is the Congregational attitude to the condition of society?**

Like other Christian groups, they are committed to helping humanity. They were leaders in the abolition of slavery. They set up and supported hundreds of schools for Negroes south of the Mason-Dixon line, when they were most needed. The Congregational is the oldest foreign missionary society founded in North America—of the sort that have been called "the greatest international peace agencies on earth."

The Council for Social Action of the Congregational Christian Churches educates the people of the churches to the social needs of the day.

Congregationalists as children of the Reformation believe that the Church stands under the constant judgment of God and must be willing to reform *itself,* if need be, in every age.

**In the Congregational view, for what purpose does the Church exist?**

Congregationalists hold that the mission of the Church of Christ is to proclaim the Gospel to all mankind, to exalt the worship of the one true God, and to labor for the progress of knowledge, the promotion of justice, the reign of peace, and the realization of human brotherhood. An official statement of 1913 reads: "Depending, as did our fathers, upon the continued guidance of the Holy Spirit to lead us into all truth, we work and pray for the transformation of the world into the Kingdom of God; and we look with faith for the triumph of righteousness and the life everlasting."

**What is the Congregational attitude toward education?**

Congregationalists have always believed in an educated ministry and an educated laity. Harvard College was founded by the Congregational fathers "to advance learning and to perpetuate it to posterity." Yale had like beginnings. Congregationalists have set up other institutions of learning across the entire country. The Congregational freedom from imposed forms compels them to do their own thinking in the light of the Gospel—and that makes education indispensable.

## Do Congregationalists believe in cooperation among the denominations?

Unreservedly. They are sometimes called the interdenominational denomination. No other ecclesiastical group has participated in a greater number of unions with other groups. They will cooperate with any Christian communion which will cooperate with them. In any community they oppose religious isolationism and denominational exclusiveness.

The Congregational Churches accept members from other Christian communions without re-confirming them, and clergy from other communions without re-ordaining them.

## How many Congregational Christians are there in the United States? In the world?

According to the latest census (1953), there are 1,283,754 members gathered in 5,573 churches in the United States. There are over two million Congregationalists in the world.

## What role have the Congregationalists played in America?

The Pilgrim Fathers who landed on Plymouth Rock were the first Congregationalists to reach the New World. Shortly thereafter, other shiploads of Congregationalists poured into the Puritan colony of Massachusetts Bay. They gave to New England its early character. They were pious, hardy, and loved learning.

The historian Bancroft calls the Mayflower Compact, which was composed and signed by the Congregational Fathers, "the birth of popular constitutional liberty" in this country. Being itself a pure democracy under God, and summoning all its members to individual responsibility and labor, Congregationalism today conserves, as historically it helped create, American democracy.

# Who Are the Disciples of Christ?

## by JAMES E. CRAIG

WHILE ALL members of this communion use the name "Disciples of Christ," "Church of Christ," and "Christian Church" interchangeably, the term "Disciples of Christ" is more commonly used by those churches which cooperate through the International Convention.

James E. Craig, life Elder and trustee of the Park Avenue Christian Church, New York City, has had a distinguished career in journalism. He was chief editorial writer for the New York *Sun,* editor of its editorial page, and managing editor of *The Protestant World.*

Mr. Craig was born in Norborne, Missouri, in 1881. He was baptized into the Disciples of Christ by his father, a Disciples minister. Mr. Craig studied at the University of Missouri. As reporter, feature writer, and editor, Mr. Craig worked on the Kansas City *Journal, Star,* and *Post,* and the St. Louis *Post-Dispatch.* He was city editor of the St. Louis *Globe-Democrat* and the New York *Evening Mail,* and was managing editor of the Brownsville, Texas, *Herald.* Mr. Craig has written an authoritative history of the Freemasons, and won the *Masonic Outlook* prize essay contest in 1925.

## Who are the Disciples of Christ?

The Disciples of Christ constitute the largest purely indigenous American religious group, with around 1,800,000 adult communicants and some 8,000 autonomous congregations. In point of origin, the beliefs of the Disciples are as American as the Declaration of Independence. In point of individual liberty of conscience, they are as American as the Bill of Rights.

Some will say that the Disciples of Christ are a great evangelical, Protestant denomination. Others will say that they are not a denomination at all, but the pure New Testament Church of Christ. Still others will prefer to describe the Disciples as a brotherhood, or a communion. Perhaps the most favored word among Disciples is movement—a movement back to the New Testament, and forward to ultimate unity under God of all who call themselves Christians.

### What are the basic tenets of their creed?

The Disciples have no creed but Christ and no doctrines save those which are found in the New Testament or are reasonably to be inferred therefrom. The Disciples are God-centered, Christ-centered, Bible-centered, with no creed save one—the answer of the Apostle Peter to a question from Jesus himself: "Thou art the Christ, the Son of the Living God." Open confession of this faith, public acceptance of the Nazarene as Lord and Savior, and baptism by immersion are all that may be demanded of a candidate for admission into the fellowship. The Disciples are inclined to regard formal creeds and historical sects as so many milestones on the long highway of an evolving theology. As for themselves, they put aside ancient speculations and dogmas, and content themselves with Peter's simple exclamation that Jesus was the Messiah promised in the Scriptures.

The Disciples believe in the priesthood of all believers—that is, that the individual believer can reach the Throne of Grace without any human intermediary. According to the authorizations they find in the New Testament, the Disciples have evangelists, pastors, elders, and deacons. But they look upon these officers as useful instruments sanctioned by the Apostles. They never doubt the right of any man to go directly to God, by prayer, for guidance in all problems arising in the forum of conscience. They place absolute trust in the everlasting oversight of Divine mercy and good will. They nevertheless recommend pastoral consultation and guidance.

### What do the Disciples believe about the Bible?

The Disciples share the common Protestant belief that the Bible (except for the Apocryphal Books) is the inspired Word of God, written by different persons at different times under the inspiration of the Holy Spirit. They use the Old Testament for meditation and instruction, a schoolmaster bringing the faithful to Christ.

Many Disciples believe, however, that the Old Testament represents *two* dispensations—one for the patriarchal age before Moses, the other for the age from Moses to the resurrection of Jesus. These Disciples accept the New Testament as a third and purely Christian dispensation, for the guidance of Christian churches and peoples.

In common with other Christian bodies, the Disciples have their fundamentalists and their liberals. The literalists, or fundamentalists, accept every word of the Authorized Version of the Bible as a final and infallible word of God. The liberals believe that newer translations of the original tongues, and the studies of inspired scholars, have thrown new light upon many passages of the Scriptures. There is nothing to prevent literalists and liberals from sitting down together around the Table of the Lord's Supper, each responsible for his own belief and each serving God according to the dictates of his own conscience.

**Do Disciples believe in the Holy Trinity?**

The Disciples have had little trouble in discarding most of the dogmas which sprang up between the first century and the nineteenth. Hence, speculation about the Holy Trinity and the nature of a triune God has bothered them little or not at all. They baptize into the name of the Father, Son and Holy Spirit, as Christ commanded. They believe that the Holy Spirit is the Comforter promised in the New Testament, but they do not worry over its constitution or the nature of its operations. They accept its guidance as constantly enlarging the horizons of Christian thought. They are not concerned about such matters as original sin or predestination.

**Do the Disciples baptize?**

They baptize only those who are adult enough to know what they are doing when they stand up to confess Christ. They baptize by immersion, believing it to have been the New Testament way—an act of obedience and surrender, a symbol of the death, burial, and resurrection of the Lord Jesus.

**Do the Disciples believe in the Virgin Birth?**

It is probable that about 99 per cent of them do. It is possible that others have doubts on the subject. But there is no ecclesiastical or denominational authority that can declare one belief to be orthodox and reject the other as heretical.

**What do the Disciples believe about sin and salvation?**

No answer covering all the congregations is possible. The Disciples as a rule reject the doctrine of original sin; but most of them believe that we are all sinful creatures unless and until redeemed by the saving sacrifice of the Lord Jesus.

Early in the history of the movement, the conception gained ground that a reasonable God would not leave His creatures without a rational plan of salvation which any person could understand and follow. Walter Scott was perhaps the first notable exponent of this idea. He suggested a five-fold plan: faith, repentance, baptism, newness of life, gift of the Holy Spirit. By faith he meant a sincere belief in the power and goodness of God, accompanied by complete surrender to His holy will. By repentance he meant not merely sorrow for past misdeeds, but perfect contrition, coupled with resolution not to sin again. By baptism he meant obedience to a command of the Savior and emulation of the example of the Apostles. By newness of life he meant such conduct thereafter as would be void of further offense to God and scandal to the Church. By the gift of the Holy Spirit he meant the coming of the indwelling Comforter promised in the Gospels.

It was Walter Scott's belief that when a sinner honestly fulfilled these requirements he had no need to look for some mystical and emotional inner manifestation of saving grace. If you do what God has told you to do, he argued, you may be sure that God will reward you accordingly. Although the accent and terminology may have shifted, the essentials of this plan are still widely accepted among the Disciples.

**Do the Disciples believe in heaven and hell?**

Here again it is difficult to give an answer that will prove satisfactory to all members of this great fellowship. Practically all of them believe in the immortality of the soul and in a blissful reunion hereafter for all the faithful who have died in the Lord. Many doubtless believe in a literal paradise and a literal hell. Many others are content to leave the details of future rewards and punishments in the hands of Divine Mercy, without troubling themselves over theories elaborated in medieval theology. Disciple faith in general is a matter of deep personal conviction, rooted in serene confidence that the Kingdom of God will prove invincible in this world and in the life to come.

**How did the Disciples begin?**

The Disciples began by the confluence of two main currents of religious thought: one, the Christian Church, developed in Kentucky and Ohio under the leadership of Barton W. Stone; the other, that of a body which came to call itself Disciples of Christ, developed in western Pennsylvania and western Virginia under the leadership of Thomas

Campbell, his son, Alexander Campbell, and Walter Scott, a kinsman of the great novelist.

All these men, who came to be known as the Big Four, were of Presbyterian antecedents; all were well educated according to the scholarship of their time, which laid emphasis upon proficiency in Greek, Latin, and Hebrew.

These scholars and religious statesmen cast their lot among pioneers and in pioneering conditions. In the early years of the nineteenth century, a great westward migration was in full swing. Men and women of various church allegiances found church homes among denominations with which they were familiar. Many others were unchurched wanderers, tossed about by every wind of doctrine. Out of this emergency a great opportunity and a great vision came into flower.

The opportunity was that of bringing all these drifters into a single Christian fold. The vision was that of an ultimately united and militant Protestant Church. Here and there earnest men had begun asking themselves whether some way could not be found to break down the sectarian barriers which separated Christians into different corrals of creed. From many proposed answers one began to prevail: that a divided church could lay aside its divisive creeds and start afresh, building once more upon the foundations of the primitive churches as laid down in the New Testament.

This revolutionary idea cannot be ascribed to any one person. As early as 1803, Barton W. Stone and his supporters gave voice to it in Kentucky. In 1809, Thomas Campbell gave it cohesive literary expression in his Declaration and Address, long looked upon as the cornerstone of the edifice about to be built. Walter Scott and such powerful and popular preachers as "Raccoon John" Smith (Baptist) of Tennessee imparted to it an evangelistic fervor. Alexander Campbell, a skillful debater, gave it forensic and theological expression up to the time of his death in 1866.

In their enthusiasm for the cause, Calvinists and Arminians did not hesitate to lay many of their traditional beliefs upon the altar of a conviction that Christ died not for a chosen few, but for all; that the New Testament provided a plan of salvation which any adult of reasonable intelligence could understand and adopt.

Simple as the program may sound, the practical business of putting it into effect encountered enormous difficulties. It was easy enough to say there should be no creed but Christ, and to adopt the ordinance of baptism (by immersion) and weekly observance of the Lord's Supper.

After declaring the New Testament to be the guide for Christian faith and practice, it seemed logically possible to ask for strict fidelity to the essentials of faith while allowing complete liberty of opinion regarding the nonessentials. Here, of course, came the rub: how do you decide what the essentials are and who is to make the decision? The distinction has troubled individual Disciples to this very day. Such difficulties are inevitable in a religious system which magnifies individual responsibility and reduces ecclesiastical authority to a minimum.

## Are the "Disciples of Christ," "Christian Church," "Churches of Christ" all the same?

In 1832 the Disciples of the East and the Christians of the West came together in a single union. From that day on, the term "Christian Church" has been more commonly used in the Midwest and South; the term "Disciples of Christ" has been favored in the East. In the International Convention and in many congregations the words are used interchangeably. One of the oldest congregations, on Park Avenue in New York City, calls itself the Park Avenue Christian Church, with "Disciples of Christ" in parentheses.

Two other groups called themselves Christian Churches. One was James O'Kelly's group, which first called itself Republican Methodists and then changed its name to Christian. Another was the fine New England group which has since united with the Congregationalists as the Congregational-Christian Church.

Not long after the Civil War one group of members of the original movement proclaimed independence of the main body and since has gone its separate way. It insists, among other things, that there is no warrant in the New Testament for instrumental music or for missionary societies and the like. This extremely conservative body usually speaks of its congregations as Churches of Christ. (That name is also used by some of the churches cooperating through the International Convention, as well as by individual congregations of other denominations.) This group maintains headquarters in Nashville, Tennessee. Some other conservative congregations are not identified with the International Convention for reasons having to do with New Testament interpretation.

## Do the Disciples of Christ proselytize?

They invite but do not proselytize. No Sunday morning service closes without an offering of fellowship to any adult who cares to take his stand by the Cross of the Risen Lord.

### Do the Disciples have an ordained ministry?

Except in a few remote sections where ordained ministers are not available, practically all of the cooperating churches do have ordained pastors. In an emergency an elder or other layman may fill the pulpit. Elders usually, but not always, conduct the Communion Service.

In the early days, distrust of clericalism was so great that ministers were called "Elder," not "Reverend," and the wearing of gowns or cassocks in the pulpit was looked upon as smacking of "prelacy." (Both these prejudices have now largely passed away.) No important distinction was made between clergy and laity. Indeed, any elder elected by the congregation could perform any ministerial duty—except that of saying marriage ceremonies, a function usually regulated by the state.

As time wore on, certain weaknesses in this system became obvious. Congregations began to demand ordained pastors. Today there are between thirty-four and thirty-eight Disciple colleges, universities, and Biblical Training schools which are trying to fill that demand.

### What are the Disciples' views on divorce?

There is no central church authority on this subject.

In practice, ministers and congregations of the Disciples of Christ differ in their attitudes to divorce. Some believe that the questions propounded to Jesus by the Pharisees on this subject were "trick" questions concerned with then-current Jewish law, and that what Jesus answered must be viewed in that light. Some ministers and congregations take the Master's answer as binding to this day, and therefore oppose any remarriage of divorced persons. Others are willing to consent to the remarriage of any innocent party to a divorce obtained on the ground of adultery. Still others, perhaps a majority, believe that divorce has become a legal function of the state, and do not hesitate to remarry any person to whom the civil government has accorded the right of remarriage.

### What are the Disciples' views on birth control?

The old Disciple rule is that where the Scriptures speak, we speak; where they are silent, we are silent.

There can be no doubt, however, that a majority of Disciple ministers believe that birth control is justifiable under certain circumstances. The one sure test of this attitude rests in the fact that no Disciple minister can be muzzled, either by the Brotherhood at large or by his own congregation. By the terms of his ordination, each considers himself empowered, as were the Prophets of old, to denounce whatever he considers amiss in the life of his people—and silence seems to give at least a modified consent. In general, Disciples are content to leave matters such as birth control to the individual consciences of husband and wife.

**How do the Disciples differ from other Protestants?**

Disciples have no catechism and no prescribed rituals of worship.

Disciples do not accept the doctrine of Apostolic Succession. Hence they have no archbishops or bishops or hierarchy of ecclesiastical authority. Disciples interpret the words "bishop" and "elder" as synonyms for one office—a *lay* office, elected by the members of the congregation and in no sense authorized or regulated from above.

Disciples believe that a confession of faith in Jesus as the Christ requires no added metaphysical doctrine.

They regard conversion as a voluntary, rational act which does not require special personal revelation. In receiving a new member, they take the applicant's simple statement of faith at face value. They employ no formula of interrogation or board of inquiry.

Disciples believe that a Christian's right to Holy Communion is entirely a matter for his own conscience. They admit to the Lord's Supper any baptized person, without regard to his sectarian affiliations.

Perhaps the most notable difference between Disciples and other Protestant groups is the emphasis of Disciples upon individual liberty of opinion, upon the right of each man to interpret the Scriptures in his own way.

Disciples base their whole case and their whole appeal on a simple outline of faith and a democratic system of church government. They have no sense of rivalry between the denominations. They hold that as long as a member accepts the simple faith, and the idea of democratic government in the church, he may believe what his mind dictates about many of the tenets of other Christian bodies.

Disciples observe with joy that the differences among Protestants are receiving less and less attention today, while the many things they have in common receive more and more. To Disciples, the rising trend towards a mutual ground of faith marks a steady advance toward ultimate church unity. And in this field the Disciples have made their influence most heavily felt. They have been in the forefront of almost every important Protestant cooperative and ecumenical movement. Thirty-nine Disciples were active in establishing the old Federal Council of Churches; two hundred are enrolled in the National Council of Churches of Christ in America; fourteen Disciple leaders serve the World Council of Churches.

**What is the church service like?**

With minor variations, Sunday morning service in Disciple churches follows pretty much the same pattern. With or without processions and with or without organ, the worship begins with the singing of hymns. This is followed by responsive readings, recitation of the Lord's Prayer, reading of the Scriptures, pastoral prayer, an anthem or two, the sermon, an invitation to fellowship, gathering of tithes and offerings, Communion Service, benediction, and final hymn or recessional. Sometimes Communion precedes the sermon. On occasion, the sermon may be omitted, but never Communion. (In the sanctuary of the Park Avenue Christian Church in New York City is preserved a little table at which Alexander Campbell and Walter Scott presided over the Lord's Supper. Incidentally, it is a tradition of this congregation that it has not omitted Communion Service on a single Sunday in 144 years.) Many Disciples attribute their large gain in membership to the weekly practice of extending the right hand of fellowship to all who may desire to unite with a congregation.

**How are the Disciples governed?**

The average Disciple church is administered by a pastor, an Official Board of elders and deacons, and perhaps representatives of the Christian Women's Fellowship. Women are taking an increasingly greater part in every branch of Disciple activity—from the pulpit, the prayer meeting, and missionary society to the pew.

Elders look after the spiritual welfare of members; deacons manage incidental business. All matters of fundamental importance must ultimately be decided by the congregation as a whole.

Trials for heresy are almost unknown, although "withdrawals" of fellowship for immoral or scandalous, unchristian conduct are subjects of congregational action. Disciples believe that only the Lord himself can expel any person from the Church Universal.

**Do the Disciples believe theirs the only true religion?**

Certainly not. They believe theirs to be most nearly in accord with the practices of the early Christian churches. They also believe that their greatest mission in life is to bring Christians of all faiths into one Church of Christ. Their ancient retort to an ancient gibe about their name was to say: "We are not the only Christians, but are Christians only."

**What is the International Convention?**

The International Convention of Disciples of Christ is a voluntary and cooperative fellowship of local churches in the United States and Canada, their various missionary, benevolent, and administrative agencies. It is a "reporting convention" rather than a legislative body. It receives reports from sixteen major boards and, in turn, submits these to the local congregations.

Though the cooperating churches send representatives, any Disciple may attend and vote.

The International Convention presents recommendations on every subject affecting the movement. These are advisory only, but because of the great prestige of the Convention and its officials most of the recommendations are accepted by the local congregations. What has been said about the International Convention is similarly true with respect to autonomous conventions in cities, districts, and states.

# What Is an Episcopalian?

## by W. NORMAN PITTENGER

W. NORMAN PITTENGER, professor of Christian Apologetics at General Theological Seminary in New York, is vice-chairman of the Commission on Christ and the Church, appointed under the World Council of Churches. He was born in Bogota, New Jersey, in 1905, and was graduated from General Theological Seminary and the Berkeley Divinity School in New Haven, Connecticut. He became an Episcopal Deacon in 1936, and was ordained into the priesthood in 1937.

Mr. Pittenger has served as examining chaplain in the Diocese of New Jersey, vice-chairman of the Church Congress, and president of the American Theological Society. He is American editor for *Theology,* an English monthly journal, has been contributing editor to the *Journal of the Philosophy of Religion,* and serves on the editorial board of the *Anglican Theological Review* and *Religion in Life.*

Mr. Pittenger has written sixteen books. He is co-author of *The Faith of the Church,* the authoritative and quasi-official statement of the Episcopal creed. Two more volumes from Mr. Pittenger's pen are being published this year: *Theology and Reality* and *Christian Affirmations.*

## What is an Episcopalian?

An Episcopalian is a member of the Protestant Episcopal Church, which is one branch of the Anglican Communion—a religious group spread throughout the world and numbering some forty million Christians. There are "Episcopal Churches" in all parts of the globe. The Church of England is the mother of them all. Many of our churches are self-governing, like the Japanese church (called the Holy Catholic Church in Japan) or the Canadian. They all use the Book of Common Prayer; they all are in communion with the Archbishop of Canterbury; they all recognize bishops as their chief pastors.

"Episcopalian" is derived from the Greek *episkopos,* which means "bishop." It describes the type of "order" or ministry which the Church maintains—that is, the bishop is looked upon as the symbol of the Church's unity and the chief pastor of the flock.

**Is the Episcopalian Church Catholic or Protestant?**

In a profound sense, it is both. It is sometimes called "the bridge church." The Episcopal Church preserves the ancient Catholic sacraments and professes the ancient Catholic creeds; this was the intention of its reformers in the sixteenth century. On the other hand, it is a "reformed" church, for during that century, the authority of the Bishop of Rome (the Pope) was rejected and many modifications were made in worship and doctrine. But in no sense did the early reformers in England intend to deny "Catholic truth." The official title of the Church in America, "the Protestant Episcopal Church," was adopted when the word "Protestant" meant "non-Roman" or "non-papal."

**What is the Episcopal attitude toward Roman Catholicism?**

The Episcopal Church has no official position in regard to present-day Roman Catholicism. It believes that the Anglican Communion possesses all the essential marks of historical Catholicism—the apostolic faith, sacraments, and ministry. But most Episcopalians would seriously question Roman Catholic centralization of power in the Bishop of Rome, and would regard with disfavor what they conceive to be the Roman Church's suppression of freedom in many intellectual areas and elsewhere.

**Did Henry VIII found the Episcopal Church?**

No. Under Henry, the freedom of the English Church from the authority of the Bishop of Rome was achieved; but that was the end of a long period of protest and agitation against what were conceived to be the Pope's unwarranted usurpations of authority. Henry's desire for a divorce provided the occasion but was not the *cause* of the independence of the Church of England. It is unfortunate that in many textbooks the mistake of identifying occasion and cause has led to the propagation of what is in fact an untruth.

**What are the basic beliefs of Episcopalians?**

They are affirmed in the Apostles' Creed and the Nicene Creed. The Apostles' Creed is the ancient baptismal statement of faith. As used in Episcopalian services, it runs: "I believe in God the Father Almighty, Maker of heaven and earth:

"And in Jesus Christ his only Son our Lord: Who was conceived

by the Holy Ghost, Born of the Virgin Mary: Suffered under Pontius
Pilate, Was crucified, dead, and buried: He descended into hell; The
third day he rose again from the dead: He ascended into heaven,
And sitteth on the right hand of God the Father Almighty: From
thence he shall come to judge the quick and the dead.

"I believe in the Holy Ghost: The holy Catholic Church; The
Communion of Saints: The Forgiveness of Sins: The Resurrection of
the body: And the Life everlasting. Amen."

The Nicene Creed, used at the service of Holy Communion, is an
expanded statement of the Christian faith, essentially the same as the
Apostles' Creed.

Both creeds state the main points of Christian belief in a pictorial
and dramatic form. Some of the phrases are clearly "symbolic" (as,
"sitteth on the right hand of God the Father," which of course could
not be *literally* true); some parts are historical in intention (as "born,"
"crucified," "dead," "buried," "rose again"); and some parts are
philosophical, often phrased in the pictorial language which the early
Church acquired from its Jewish background.

### What do Episcopalians believe about Jesus Christ?

They believe that He is "truly God and truly man, united in one person" for the salvation of mankind. There are different ways of understanding and teaching this doctrine, but it is central and unchangeable
for all Episcopalians.

### What is the Episcopal view of the Virgin Birth?

The creeds and the liturgy of the Episcopal Church assert the traditional belief that Jesus was born of Mary without human father.
There is no disagreement within the Church on the *theological* meaning of the Virgin Birth. There has been, and still is, disagreement
about the Virgin Birth in its biological detail. Most Episcopalians
probably accept it as literally true; some regard it as symbolic in
character. The Episcopal Church is able to contain both types of
thinking within it, since all Episcopalians accept the Incarnation—
the true deity and humanity of Jesus—as the central truth about
Christ.

### What about the Trinity?

The Trinity is the Christian teaching about God. In the light of man's
experience of God's working in the world, Christians have been

driven to assert that God *is* as He *reveals* Himself. He is Creative Reality (God the Father); He is Expressive Act (God the Son); He is Responsive Power (God the Holy Spirit). Yet He is *one* God. This is "theology." What matters most, in the Book of Common Prayer, about the Trinity is that we worship God and experience Him in a "trinitarian" fashion.

**What does the Episcopal Church believe about the Lord's Supper?**

Holy Communion, sometimes called the Lord's Supper or Holy Eucharist (from an ancient Christian word for the service), is the chief service of worship in the Episcopal Church, although it does not always occupy the chief place in the Sunday schedule. The teaching of the Church about this sacrament is expressed in these words: "The Sacrament of the Lord's Supper was ordained for the continual remembrance of the sacrifice of the death of Christ, and of the benefits which we receive thereby"; and the Offices of Instruction (Prayer Book, page 293), from which these words are quoted, goes on to say that "the . . . thing signified" in the sacrament "is the Body and Blood of Christ, which are spiritually taken and received by the faithful."

**Do Episcopalians practice private confession?**

They may, since provision is made in the Prayer Book for private confession of sins to a priest, with the declaration of absolution by him. However, this is not enforced, as in the Roman Catholic Church; it is entirely optional. Many Episcopalians avail themselves of the privilege, some frequently, some occasionally. Many do not desire to use this "means of grace" and find satisfaction in the *general* confessions and absolutions which are provided in the regular services of the Church.

**How do Episcopalians regard the Bible?**

The Holy Scriptures are, for Episcopalians, the great source and testing ground of Christian doctrine. Nothing may be taught "as necessary to eternal salvation" excepting what can be "proved" (the Elizabethan word for "tested") by Holy Scripture.

But the Episcopal Church does not hold to the literal inerrancy of Scripture. The Bible is considered sacred for its general inspiration, as the record of God's revelation.

The Episcopal Church maintains a balance between gospel and tradition, on the one hand, and the use of reason on the other. Freedom of investigation, restatements of the Christian faith, and incorporation of scientific truths are possible *without* creating violent fundamentalist-modernist controversies. The Episcopal Church has accepted the theory of evolution as an account of man's origin, as well as other new scientific discoveries, without disturbing its central beliefs. In both freedom of inquiry and biblical criticism, the Episcopal Church's position has sometimes been called a "liberal" or even a "modernist" Catholicism.

## What is the Book of Common Prayer?

At the time of the English reforms, the old service books of the Church were translated into English. Some of the services were combined and edited; many were shortened and simplified. The result was the Book of Common Prayer, completed in 1549. All later Prayer Books, including that used in America today, are re-editings of the 1549 book, whose beautiful, stately language, simplicity, and dignity are unparalleled. The regular services, like the Holy Communion or Holy Eucharist, Morning and Evening Prayer, the Litany, are all taken from the Prayer Book. Episcopalians believe that a prescribed form of service, with parts assigned to clergy and people, is the most fitting way to adore God. Frequent revisions are made to meet the needs of succeeding ages; but the principle of ordered worship remains at the heart of Anglicanism.

The worship of the Episcopal Church is not rigid. Many variations are found in the Prayer Book; the special prayers ("collects") and the different readings from the Bible give considerable variety for each Sunday and holy day.

## Do Episcopalians believe in heaven and hell?

The teachings of the Episcopal Church about death, judgment, heaven, and hell are stated plainly in the Book of Common Prayer. Death marks the end of this period of man's life. He is judged in terms of his real character, by a God "unto whom all hearts are open, all desires known, and from whom no secrets are hid." Heaven is a state in which the vision of God is enjoyed in a "life of perfect service" of God. Hell is alienation from God, and therefore the loss of that goal to which man's whole existence is directed.

Episcopalians do not believe in a *physical* heaven or hell; these are "states of being." The departed in whom there is some possibility of goodness are prepared for the full enjoyment of God by such cleansing and purifying as they may require—in a way, this resembles the idea of "purgatory." But Episcopalians do not use the term in their official teaching because they feel that it is often associated with crude ideas of payment of penalty and the like.

By the "resurrection," the Episcopal Church means not the raising of the physical body we now possess but the re-creation by God of the total personality of man with a "spiritual body"—that is, with an instrument of self-expression appropriate to a heavenly life.

### What then is meant by salvation?

Modern Episcopalians tend to understand by this term "health or wholeness of life." Salvation means that one is given the wholeness which is God's will for man, and is delivered from arrogance and selfishness. Salvation has to do not only with the "hereafter" but also with man's present earthly existence. In man, sinner because he is ridiculously proud and self-centered, there is no real "health"; by fellowship with God in Christ, he is brought into the sphere of healthy and whole life.

### Does the Episcopal Church have a priesthood?

It does. There are three "orders of ministry" included in "Holy Orders": bishops, priests, deacons. The Offices of Instruction state that the bishop's office is "to be a chief pastor in the Church; to confer Holy Orders; and to administer confirmation." A priest's office is "to minister to the people committed to his care; to preach the Word of God; to baptize; to celebrate the Holy Communion; and to pronounce absolution and blessing in God's name." The deacon assists the priest in divine service and other ministrations; he is a minister in the real sense of the word, but without such "higher" privileges as priest and bishop.

The priest is the "ministerial representative" for Christ in his church; he also represents the priesthood of the laity, which is shared by all who are baptized. An Episcopal minister is never called a "preacher," since that is only one aspect of his office; he is also celebrant of the Holy Communion—absolver, teacher, shepherd of his flock.

The ministers of the Episcopal Church may marry or not marry as they see fit, "as they shall judge the same to serve better to godliness."

### Are there monks and nuns in the Episcopal Church?

Yes. There are many orders of Episcopal monks and nuns, both in the United States and elsewhere. Some are purely "contemplative"— that is, engaged in prayer; others are "mixed"—that is, engaged both in prayer and in teaching, writing, preaching. These men and women take the vows of poverty, chastity, and obedience. They do not marry. They live in communities established for the purpose of sharing a common life of work and prayer.

### What is meant by "high," "low," and "broad" Church?

These words are used to describe parishes, but they are misleading. A "high" parish is one which emphasizes sacramental worship, the supreme value of the "Catholic tradition," and a rather elaborate service of worship. A "low" parish is one in which the services are simpler and a stronger emphasis is placed on the gospel and on personal religion. In a "broad" parish, which may be either "high" or "low," the importance of a rational understanding of the Christian tradition is stressed, with a concern for "liberal values." But all these emphases meet in the proclamation of the gospel, sacramental worship, and the reasonable presentation of Christianity. Episcopalians appeal to Scriptures, tradition, and personal experience, as well as reason, for vindication of the truth of the Christian faith. Differences in emphasis are welcomed in the Episcopal Church, as long as the central affirmations are maintained.

### Does the Episcopal Church permit divorce?

In America, the "canons" (or church law) do not recognize divorce, but do provide a number of grounds for annulment—the ecclesiastical declaration that no marriage has in fact existed because of some factor that made such impossible. A bishop may permit a divorced person to remarry if certain conditions are met. He may also admit to Holy Communion persons who have been divorced and remarried—if they can prove that they are in good faith, are struggling to live a Christian life, and have demonstrated their stability and repentance.

### What is the Episcopalian attitude toward birth control?

The Anglican Communion has spoken, through its conference of bishops at Lambeth, on birth control, saying that when practiced without selfish motives, it is permissible. There has been much discussion of the "moral theology" of contraception, but no more clearly defined position has yet been taken.

## What is the Church attitude toward drinking and gambling?

The Episcopal Church has been nonpuritanical in most respects; it believes that God intends men to enjoy life—if they can do so without such excesses as will harm them and spoil their potentialities as children of God. The Episcopal Church's primary concern has been with abuses. It has not taken an official stand on gambling and drinking, although there have been some quasi-official condemnations of the gambling evil and the perils to character which it involves. As to drinking—like card-playing, dancing, and the like, the Episcopal Church has on the whole been "liberal" in attitude, feeling that the evils come when the activities are abused.

## Do Episcopalians believe that theirs is the only true faith?

No. We hold that all who are baptized (whether by Episcopalian or other baptism, provided it is with water and in the name of the Holy Trinity) are members of the Church of Christ. Christ is the "head" of His Church (called in the New Testament "The Body of Christ") and those who belong to Him by baptism are His "members." Confirmation by the bishop is necessary to communicant status, but it is not believed to be "joining the Church." It is a sacramental rite by which, Episcopalians believe, the Holy Spirit is given to a Christian reaching communicant status.

Even those who are not actually baptized, but by intention would be baptized if they were able, are believed to be "saved." The Church is Christ's instrument for fulfilling His purpose in the world and the means by which His continuing presence is made available. Of that one Church, Episcopalians believe they are a part; they have never claimed they are the *only* part.

## How is the Episcopal Church governed?

In different countries the Anglican Communion has different kinds of government. In the United States, there are parishes, with elected laymen to represent the congregation; dioceses, with the "convention" under which the bishop and his clergy carry on the Church's work; and a general convention which meets every three years and represents the entire American Church. The Church is democratic: delegates to the general convention and laymen to diocesan conventions are elected. At the general convention, the House of Deputies, composed of laymen and priests, and the House of Bishops, in which all bishops may sit, must concur in legislative measures. Neither bishops nor parish clergy have any autocratic rights; all must cooperate with the laity.

### What is the Lambeth Conference?

Every ten years, more than three hundred Bishops of the Anglican Communion meet at Lambeth in London, under the presidency of the Archbishop of Canterbury. This assembly has no legal power; its decisions have moral authority only. The meetings are the great symbol of the unity of the whole communion. The presidency of the Archbishop of Canterbury indicates that all the churches in the worldwide Anglican fellowship are at one in their common loyalty and in their communion with the see of Canterbury.

### How many Episcopalians are there in the United States?

Over 2,715,825 Americans have been baptized in the Episcopalian faith. In addition, a quarter-million or so persons look to the Church for ministrations but are not formal members. The Episcopal Church has 6,958 clergy in the United States, in 7,954 parishes and missions.

### Does the Episcopal Church own schools and colleges?

Yes, it either owns or controls such colleges as Hobart, Kenyon, University of the South, Trinity, and such schools as Groton, St. Mark's, St. Paul's, and others. The Church has eleven seminaries, plus one diocesan seminary where the clergy are trained.

### Does the Episcopal Church believe in missionary work?

Yes, it has been active in this field. Apart from any work done by other branches of the Anglican Communion, the Episcopal Church has missionaries in Asia, South America, Africa, and in many parts of the United States, as well as in Alaska. This activity is under the National Council of the Church, whose Director of Overseas Activities is in charge of foreign missions and whose Director of the Home Department is in charge of domestic missions.

### What role has the Episcopal Church played in American history?

The first service of the Anglican Communion in the New World was held at Jamestown, Virginia, in 1607. For many years, the Episcopalians in the colonies were under the Bishop of London; with the War of Independence, they became self-governing.

A majority of the founders of this nation were Episcopalians— including George Washington, Alexander Hamilton, James Madison, James Monroe, John Marshall, and John Jay. From that time to the present, the Church has played a significant part in our national life. Despite its close fellowship with the Church of England, it has been thoroughly American and its members are loyal citizens of this land.

# Who Are Jehovah's Witnesses?

## by MILTON G. HENSCHEL

MILTON G. HENSCHEL is a director of the Watch Tower Bible and Tract Society, the governing body of Jehovah's Witnesses. A third-generation Witness, he was born in Pomona, New Jersey, in 1920, and began house-to-house preaching at the age of eight. By the time he was fourteen, he was devoting himself entirely to the work of the ministry.

Mr. Henschel is an ordained minister of Jehovah's Witnesses and has traveled to eighty countries in his official duties as executive aide to the president of the Watch Tower Bible and Tract Society.

**What is the basic creed professed by Jehovah's Witnesses?**

The Witnesses have no creed. They follow the Bible all the way, not halfway. They feel the Bible is entirely consistent—both the Hebrew and Greek Scriptures—and practical for our day.

**Where did the name come from?**

The name Jehovah's Witnesses is found in the Bible in Isaiah 43:12: "Ye are my witnesses, saith Jehovah, and I am God." A history of Jehovah's Witnesses and their service to God takes us back 6,000 years. Abel and other men of faith before Christ are called "witnesses" in Hebrews 11 and 12:1. Christ is "the faithful and true witness" in Revelation 3:14. He designated others to continue the testimony, saying, "Ye shall be witnesses unto me . . . unto the uttermost part of the earth"—Acts 1:8.

Jehovah's Witnesses today are merely the last of a long line of servants of God. They are not an incorporated body. They use the non-profit Watch Tower Bible and Tract Society, which was incorporated in Pennsylvania by Charles Taze Russell and associated Christians in 1884, as the governing body.

## What are the teachings of Jehovah's Witnesses?

That Jehovah is the only true God. His supremacy has been challenged by Satan, who caused the rebellion in Eden and who puts the integrity of all men to the test. God's primary purpose is the vindication of this supremacy. In carrying out this purpose, God sent Jesus to earth to provide the ransom sacrifice and to lay the foundation for God's new system of things.

Jehovah will not tolerate wickedness on earth forever. The beginning of the end for Satan came when Christ took power in heaven as King. This happened in 1914. Christ's first act was casting Satan out of heaven, and this was followed by great troubles on earth. This will be climaxed in God's battle, Armageddon: the complete destruction of the Devil and his system of things, his world. This is the vindication of Jehovah's name and the beginning of the 1,000-year reign of Christ. Then all that breathe will praise Jehovah.

Christ is now in his second presence. He will always remain invisible to humans, but his presence is proved by world events since 1914, which fulfill all the predictions of Matthew 24.

Now the Christian's duty is to keep integrity to Jehovah, to announce the King's reign, and to help neighbors find the way to godly service and everlasting life.

## Do Jehovah's Witnesses believe in the Virgin Birth?

Jesus was born miraculously, a virgin birth in fulfillment of the prophecy of Isaiah 7:14. He died a ransom to relieve man from sin inherited from the first parents in the Garden of Eden. As 1 Corinthians 15 shows, Christ died a human body but was resurrected as a mighty spirit creature.

## Do Witnesses believe in the Holy Trinity?

Jehovah's Witnesses believe that Jehovah God and Christ Jesus are two distinct persons and are not combined with a so-called "Holy Ghost" in one godhead called a trinity.

## Do Witnesses salute the flag?

Saluting a flag, of any nation, is regarded by Jehovah's Witnesses as unchristian image worship. Any national flag is a symbol of sovereign power, regarded by people as sacred.

Jehovah's Witnesses cannot conscientiously participate in an act that ascribes salvation to the national emblem and to the nation for which it stands, for, in the Ten Commandments, it says: "Thou shalt not make unto thee any graven image, or any likeness of any thing that is in heaven above, or that is in the earth beneath, or that is in the water under the earth:. thou shalt not bow down thyself to them, nor serve them." Jehovah's Witnesses do not wish to incur the wrath of God by acts of worship contrary to his commands. They do not oppose anyone's desire or right to salute the flag. Each must decide for himself what he will do. That is true freedom of worship. The Supreme Court of the United States has so declared in a case involving Jehovah's Witnesses: Its decision was that there is no requirement of the conscientious to salute the flag of the United States.

**Do the Witnesses deny government authority?**

No. Without governments, anarchy and chaos would reign. Earthly governments have the right to make laws to regulate morals, protect persons and property, and maintain public order. Jehovah's Witnesses obey all such laws, *if* they are in accord with God's laws. When there is direct conflict between God's law and that of a government, they obey the supreme law of God as set forth in the Bible.

**Why do the Witnesses claim service exemption?**

Because they have conscientious objections, based on the commandments of God, against taking part in the *world's* wars. Wars between nations today are not the same as Israel's wars in ancient times. Israel was Jehovah's theocratic nation, and the Israelites were fighters in God's wars. No political nation today can properly claim that status.

Though not pacifists, Jehovah's Witnesses fight only when God commands them to do so. Since the days of ancient Israel, God has not commanded men to fight in wars between nations. That is why Christians of the first century refused to serve in the imperial armies of Rome. Besides, ministers of religion are exempted from military service by law in many countries. Because the vocation of each Jehovah's Witness is the ministry, all Witnesses claim exemption under such laws.

They do not oppose the desire of any person to serve in the armed forces of any nation. Nor do they oppose the efforts of any nation to raise an army by conscripting its manpower. They merely keep their own neutrality, refusing to break their allegiance to their God and

Savior. Their position is that of neutral ambassadors for Christ the King.

Having a good conscience toward God does not make a person a weakling or a coward. Fear of death does not cause the Witnesses to take this position; in some lands, they are executed by firing squads because of it. It takes more courage to stand up for unpopular principles than it does to go along with the majority.

**What do the Witnesses believe about hell?**

Hell is the grave; it is *not* a place of fiery, eternal torment. Hell is a place of rest, in hope of resurrection, not a place of torture from which one can never escape. Peter said Jesus was in hell after his death. Death and hell will both be destroyed at the end of the thousand-year rule of Christ. Purgatory is not mentioned once in the Bible. It is an invention of men. There is no "intermediate" state of the dead. Such ideas are found in the ancient pagan religions, not in the Bible.

**What do Witnesses believe about heaven?**

Heaven is the habitation of spirit creatures; it is the place of God's throne. The reward of spiritual life with Christ Jesus in heaven for men on earth is limited to those who inherit the Kingdom of God. In Revelation 7:4, the number of these is given as exactly 144,000.

**What will become of the billions of people who have lived on the earth?**

After mentioning the 144,000 who will go to heaven, Revelation 7 tells of "a great multitude, which no man could number, of all nations," standing before the throne. These are destined to live forever on the earth.

The apostle Peter said: "We, according to his promise, look for new heavens and a new earth." This means the removal of the wicked and oppressive system under Satan and the ushering in of the righteous rule of Christ.

Then the earth will be made a paradise. "There shall be no more death, neither sorrow, nor crying, neither shall there be any more pain"—Revelation 21:4. Jehovah will provide all things needed by the human family, and animals now ferocious will be at peace with man—Isaiah 65. There will be no more national boundaries, no political divisions and no war—Micah 4. It is to such a world that those in the graves will be resurrected.

**Do the Witnesses believe in baptism?**

Yes. Baptism is a symbol of dedication to the will of Jehovah. We consider baptism to be complete submersion, not just sprinkling. The baptism that started with Jesus is not meant for cleansing from sin, because Jesus was no sinner—Hebrews 7. Matthew 28 shows that the baptized ones must first be taught. This, with Jesus' baptism at the age of thirty, shows that baptism is not for infants but for persons of responsible age who have the ability to learn.

**Can any Witness be an ordained minister?**

Yes, for true ordination comes from God. Jehovah, through Christ, ordains his witnesses to serve as ministers—John 15:16. Jesus chose fishermen, tax collectors, and other untrained men, as well as the learned Paul. Similar men may become ordained ministers today. Jehovah's Witnesses are, indeed, a society or body of ministers.

The public ceremony of water immersion identifies one as a minister of God. It marks him as a person who has dedicated his entire life to the service of Jehovah; it implies acceptance of the obligations which the ministry imposes. Jesus set the example by his baptism in the River Jordan, after which he devoted his life to the ministry. We believe that titles like "Reverend" and "Father" are not properly applied to ministers but belong to God alone—Matthew 23:9. Clerical garb is never used.

**Are boys and girls allowed to preach?**

Yes. Youths are not only permitted to preach, but they are invited to do so—just as the boys Samuel, Jeremiah, and Timothy did. Jesus was only twelve when he was about his "Father's business," discussing the Scriptures.

**Are ministers and workers paid?**

Ministers at our national headquarters in Brooklyn, New York, and in the field are voluntary workers. All officers of the Watch Tower Bible and Tract Society and others at headquarters receive $14 allowance per month for personal needs. They are given free room and board. As a means of support, most of the Witnesses do secular work.

**How are Jehovah's Witnesses governed?**

The governing body consists of seven ministers serving as a board of directors. They are elected by the 402 members of the Watch Tower Bible and Tract Society, who reside in 29 countries. The board chooses one director as president. The present president is N. H. Knorr of Brooklyn.

**What is the attitude toward divorce?**

Divorces may be obtained only on the ground of marital unfaithfulness. Adultery is a violation of God's law. If a Witness obtains a divorce on other grounds and remarries, he must be expelled from the congregation.

**What is the attitude toward birth control?**

The purpose of marriage is the rearing of children. Jehovah's Witnesses regard birth control as an entirely personal matter.

**Why do they refuse blood transfusions?**

Leviticus 17:10 says: "Whatsoever man . . . eateth any manner of blood; I will . . . cut him off from among his people." And Acts 15:20: "Abstain from . . . things strangled, and from blood." This is explicit.

Jehovah's Witnesses see no difference between being fed blood through the mouth or nose or intravenously. In emergencies, blood substitutes may be used. The Witnesses would risk "temporary" death rather than accept a blood transfusion and incur God's disapproval.

We do not condemn medical practice; there are many physicians and dentists among Jehovah's Witnesses.

Some defend transfusions because they save lives, and refer to Jesus as the greatest example of giving a blood transfusion. This is shallow reasoning: Christ Jesus' blood was not drained off and preserved. What little of his blood was literally shed, fell to the ground. None of his blood was used to put into the veins of someone else.

**Why do Witnesses enter people's homes to try to convert them?**

Jehovah's Witnesses preach at the homes of the people because Christ Jesus did and they are to take him as their example and follow in his footsteps. Paul said that he taught "publicly and from house to house."

We believe we have the most urgent message of all time and should follow the example in the Bible and take it to people's homes.

### Why do Witnesses distribute literature on street corners?

Many people cannot be reached at their residences. Jehovah's Witnesses believe they must preach to people around the world before this generation passes away, and they use all possible ways of doing it. Preaching in the streets is one way. The apostle Paul preached in the market places. Jesus taught on the streets of the people. Hence this method has its foundation in the Bible.

### Why are Witnesses persecuted?

The Bible says, "All that will live godly in Christ Jesus shall suffer persecution"—2 Timothy 3:12. Jehovah's Witnesses believe their work is of God. They know their real persecutor is the Devil. They have been arrested, beaten, and jailed in many countries, including all Communist countries, where they are banned.

### Do Jehovah's Witnesses believe theirs is the only true faith?

Certainly. If they thought someone else had the true faith, they would preach that. There is only "one faith," said Paul.

Jehovah's Witnesses do not believe that there is more than one way to gain salvation, or that the majority of people will meet the strict requirements of true faith. Jesus showed that only a minority would be right: "Narrow is the way which leadeth unto life, and few there be that find it."

# What Is a Jew?

## by RABBI MORRIS N. KERTZER

MORRIS N. KERTZER, an ordained rabbi, is director of interreligious activities for the American Jewish Committee and a former president of the National Association of Jewish Chaplains in the Armed Forces. He received the Bronze Star Medal for "meritorious achievement" in World War II, and was the only Jewish chaplain on the Anzio beachhead. He has lectured throughout the United States on religious education and interfaith cooperation.

Mr. Kertzer was born in 1910 in the "bush country" of northern Ontario, Canada, where his father was a pioneer. A graduate of the University of Toronto, he was ordained at the Jewish Theological Seminary and pursued graduate studies at three American universities: Columbia, Illinois, and Michigan. He spent seven years as associate professor in the School of Religion at the University of Iowa, and has traveled widely in Europe, Asia, and Africa.

He is the author of three books: *With an "H" on My Dog Tag*, based on his experiences as a chaplain during World War II; *A Faith to Live by*, a booklet designed for men in the Army; and *What Is a Jew?*, an authoritative exposition of Judaism which expanded the following article after it appeared in *Look* Magazine.

### What is a Jew?

It is difficult to find a single definition. A Jew is one who accepts the faith of Judaism. That is the *religious* definition. A Jew is one who, without formal religious affiliation, regards the teachings of Judaism—its ethics, its folkways, its literature—as his own. That is the *cultural* definition of a Jew. A Jew is one who considers himself a Jew or is so regarded by his community. That is the *"practical"* definition of a Jew. Prof. Mordecai Kaplan calls Judaism "a civilization." Jews share a common history, common prayer, a vast literature and, above all, a common moral and spiritual purpose. Judaism is really a way of life.

### What are the principal tenets of Judaism?

Judaism holds that man can most genuinely worship God by imitating those qualities that are godly: As God is merciful, so must we be compassionate; as God is just, so must we deal justly with our neighbor; as God is slow to anger, so must we be tolerant.

Some 1,800 years ago, one of our sages taught: "He who is beloved of his fellow men is beloved of God." To worship God is to love the works of His hands.

The Jewish prayer book speaks of three basic principles of faith:

1. *The love of learning.* As long ago as the first century, Jews had a system of compulsory education. The education of the poor and the fatherless was a responsibility of the Jewish community, as well as of the family. And the ancient rabbis knew something about the psychology of learning. On the first day of school, youngsters were fed honey cakes shaped in the letters of the alphabet so that they would associate learning with sweetness.

2. *The worship of God.* From their earliest childhood, Jews are taught that He is to be worshiped out of love, not out of fear.

3. *Good deeds*—deeds that stem from the heart. There is no Hebrew word for "charity" because, to the devout Jew, there is no such thing as "charity." According to the ancient rabbis: "We are *required* to feed the poor of the gentiles as well as our Jewish brethren. . . ." No one is exempt from obligations to his fellow men. The Talmud informs us that "even one whom the community supports must give to the poor." It is interesting to note that, in Jewish tradition, kindness to animals is the purest form of goodness because it is done without any hope of reward.

### Do Jews believe in heaven and hell?

Jews believe in the immortality of the soul—an immortality whose nature is known only to God—but they no longer accept the literal idea of heaven and hell. There was a time when heaven and hell were accepted in Jewish theology but, even then, rarely as physical entities. A soul tormented with remorse for misdeeds was "in hell"; a soul delighting in a life well lived was "in heaven." The twelfth-century philosopher Maimonides opposed the idea of rewards and punishments for behavior; the reward for virtuous living, he said, is simply the good life itself. (Maimonides makes this point in his *later* writings. He gives a more literal interpretation of the hereafter in his "Thirteen Principles," written at the age of twenty. Thus, Judaism can be said to have two concepts of the hereafter—one sophisticated and philosophical, the other relatively simple.)

### Do Jews believe that Judaism is the only true religion?

Jews do not presume to judge the honest worshiper of any faith. Our prayer book tells us:

"The righteous of *all* nations are worthy of immortality." We Jews know that there are many mountain tops—and all of them reach for the stars.

### Do Christianity and Judaism agree on anything? On what points do they differ?

Christians and Jews share the same rich heritage of the Old Testament, with its timeless truths and its unchanging values. They share their belief in the fatherhood of one God—all-knowing, all-powerful, ever-merciful, the God of Abraham, Isaac, and Jacob. They share their faith in the sanctity of the Ten Commandments, the wisdom of the prophets, and the brotherhood of man. Central to both faiths is the firm belief in the spirit of man; in the pursuit of peace and the hatred of war; in the democratic ideal as a guide to the political and social order; and, above all, in the imperishable nature of man's soul. These are the points of agreement—the broad common ground of Judaism and Christianity that makes up the Judeo-Christian heritage.

The chief areas of disagreement between the two religions are these: Jews do not accept the divinity of Jesus as the "only begotten Son" of God. Jews recognize Jesus as a child of God in the sense that we are all God's children. The ancient rabbis taught us that God's greatest gift is the knowledge that we are made in His image. Jews also cannot accept the principle of incarnation—God becoming flesh. It is a cardinal tenet of our faith that God is purely spiritual; He admits of no human attributes. Nor can Judaism accept the principle of vicarious atonement—the idea of salvation *through* Christ. It is our belief that every man is responsible for his own salvation. We believe that no one can serve as an intermediary between man and God, even in a symbolic sense. We approach God—each man after his own fashion—without a mediator.

Judaism does not accept the doctrine of original sin. We do not interpret the story of Adam and Eve as reflecting man's fall from grace. Nor do we consider our bodies and their appetites as sinful. We look upon them as natural functions of life itself, for God created them.

## Do Jews try to convert Gentiles?

No. Modern Judaism is not a proselytizing creed. There has been no active missionary effort in Jewish religious life for many centuries. Jews have always welcomed converts who embraced Judaism out of true conviction. Our tradition makes no distinction between Jews born in or out of the faith. Conversion to Judaism is not uncommon today. I have participated in the conversion of a number of Protestants and Catholics to the Jewish faith.

## Does Judaism oppose intermarriage?

Practically all religions are opposed to marriage outside their faith. Religious Jews oppose intermarriage for the same reasons. When husband and wife disagree on an issue as basic as their religious creed, the prospect for a lasting and harmonious relationship may be harmed.

## Are Jews forbidden to read the New Testament?

No. Jews cannot conceive of being "forbidden" to read anything. There has certainly never been a ban against reading the New Testament or any other Christian writings. I have even seen pious Jews poring over the contents of missionary literature; and many Jewish scholars know the Gospels as intimately as the Old Testament which is the basis of our creed.

## Are there various creeds and sects among Jews?

American Judaism contains three religious groupings: the Orthodox, the Conservative, and the Reform (sometimes called the Liberal).

The *Orthodox* Jew regards his faith as the main stream of a tradition that has been unaltered for the past three thousand years. He accepts the Bible as the revealed Will of God. He does not change with each new "wind of doctrine"; he says that his way of life yields neither to expediency nor to comfort. Orthodox Jews observe the Sabbath strictly (no work, no travel, no writing, no business dealings, no carrying of money). They observe every detail of the dietary laws. They maintain separate pews for women in the synagogue. They use only Hebrew in prayer and ceremonial services.

*Reform* Judaism differs sharply from Orthodoxy on the matter of Revelation. A Reform Jew accepts as binding only the *moral* laws of the Bible and those ceremonies that "elevate and sanctify our lives." He does not follow customs he believes "not adapted to the views and habits of modern civilization." Reform Jews feel that faith must be rational and capable of withstanding the careful scrutiny of reason and science. The worship of Reform Judaism departs from traditional forms. There is complete equality of the sexes in the temple. Prayer is largely in English (or the vernacular). There is greater flexibility in the choice of prayers. Instrumental music is permitted in the temple. The prayer shawl (*tallith*) is not worn by the male worshipers.

*Conservative* Jews follow the pattern of traditional Judaism, by and large, but regard Judaism as an evolving and ever-growing religion. They feel that change should be the result of natural growth and in consonance with the spirit of Jewish law. They regard Reform Judaism as too sharp a break with the past. The Conservative Jew follows the dietary laws, with only minor relaxations. He observes the Sabbath, high holidays, and festivals in traditional ways. But he has borrowed many of the forms of Reform Judaism—such as the late-Friday-evening service and the use of English in prayers.

**Exactly what is a rabbi and what does he do?**

Literally, rabbi means "teacher." The authority of a rabbi is based not on his position but upon his learning. He has no special privileges. He is in no sense an intermediary between man and God. In Orthodox Jewish practice, the rabbi *rarely* leads in the services: it is the cantor who conducts worship. And any well-informed layman may rise to the pulpit to lead the congregation in prayer. There is no religious hierarchy in the Jewish faith. The influence of an individual rabbi is determined solely by his ability to keep the respect of laymen and colleagues as an interpreter of Jewish law. The modern rabbi, like the minister, is responsible for religious education, for worship in the synagogue, for ceremonials surrounding birth, confirmation, marriage, and death, and for pastoral guidance.

**Is it true that in Judaism the home is more important than the synagogue?**

Yes. Many times in history, Jews have been forbidden to worship publicly: synagogues and temples have been closed by law. Yet Jewish religious life has continued intact. The center of Judaism resides in the family and the home. Jews regard the home as a fitting place of worship—just as they regard marriage as a three-way partnership between husband, wife, and God. Our religion is essentially a family religion. The mother, lighting the Sabbath candles; the father, blessing his children at the table; the many happy rituals that surround holidays; the scroll (*mezuzah*) on the doorpost which signifies that God is in the home—each of these is an integral part of Jewish life.

The Catholic weekly *America* recently said that "the disproportionately small number of Jewish children requiring public care is a tribute to Jewish family life." Juvenile delinquency is rare among Jews and alcoholism almost unheard of. Though divorce is permitted by the laws of the Talmud, the divorce rate is far below the community average. (Divorce is permitted when love and harmony have ceased to exist between a man and a woman, and their marriage has become empty and meaningless.)

**Do all Jews wear hats when they pray?**

No. *Orthodox* Jews wear a hat or skullcap at all times—not only during prayer. *Conservative* Jews cover the head only during acts of worship. *Reform* Jews generally pray without hats. In ancient times, Jews covered their heads during worship by lifting their prayer shawls over their heads in order to cover their eyes. This removed all distraction from prayer and made it possible to attain the greatest concentration during worship. The hat or skullcap is the symbolic descendant of the prayer-shawl covering.

**What are the "kosher" laws?**

The Old Testament (Leviticus) sets down certain definite dietary restrictions: 1—It is forbidden to eat the meat of certain animals (such as the pig and horse) and certain sea foods (shrimp, lobster, crab, oyster). 2—Meats must be slaughtered according to ritual and must meet specific health standards. 3—Meat products and dairy products may not be eaten together. (The Bible says that meat must not be boiled in milk. This was a pre-Biblical, pagan custom.)

Maimonides, a distinguished physician as well as a philosopher, said that "kosher" food restrictions were health measures—particularly in the case of pork, which deteriorates rapidly in warm climates. He also saw important moral values in applying restraint to eating habits—for if we practice discrimination in satisfying our appetite, we may be more self-controlled with the other temptations of life. Many of the laws concerning kosher food deal with the *method* of slaughtering the animal: it must be done without pain to the beast, with the greatest possible speed, and by a God-fearing man. Incidentally, Jews are forbidden to hunt.

Jews who follow the dietary laws do not feel a sense of deprivation. They regard kosher practices as a symbol of their heritage, a daily lesson in self-discipline, and a constant reminder that human beings must feel pity for all living things. How many Jews obey the dietary laws today? No one can answer authoritatively. A safe guess is that less than 20 per cent of the Jews in America conform strictly to the laws governing kosher food.

## What is the Talmud?

The Talmud consists of sixty-three books of legal, ethical, and historical writings of the ancient rabbis. It was edited five centuries after the birth of Jesus. It is a compendium of law and lore. It is the legal code which forms the basis of Jewish religious law and it is the textbook used in the training of rabbis. Interlaced with the legal discussions of the scholars are thousands of wonderful parables, biographical sketches, historical notes, humorous anecdotes and epigrams—a storehouse of wisdom which is as real today as it was many centuries ago. Many of the moral maxims of the Talmud have become household phrases: "Give every man the benefit of the doubt." "An ignorant man cannot be a pious one." "Don't look at the flask but at what it contains." "Words without deeds are like a tree without roots—a puff of wind, and it collapses." "Why are we born into the world with clenched fists and leave it with outstretched fingers? . . . To remind us that we take nothing with us."

## What is the Torah?

The word "Torah" is used in two ways. Broadly, "Torah" means a way of life. It is synonymous with learning, wisdom, love of God. Without this, life has neither meaning nor value. More narrowly, the Torah is the beautiful, handprinted scroll of the Five Books of Moses (the Bible from Genesis to Deuteronomy) which is housed in the Ark of the synagogue. A portion of the Torah is read aloud every Sabbath during worship. The worshiper stands when the Torah is taken out of the Ark. A pious Jew kisses the Torah by placing his prayer shawl on the parchment (so his fingers will not touch the scroll), then lifting the fringes of the shawl to his lips. The Torah is the most sacred *object* in Jewish worship. Throughout history, men have bled and died to save the revered scroll from desecration.

## What is Yom Kippur?

Yom Kippur means "Day of Atonement," the last of the Ten Days of Penitence. It is marked by twenty-four hours of prayer and fasting, during which the worshiper (and the congregation collectively) recounts the catalogue of human transgressions—pride, greed, jealousy, vanity, lust, and so on. Throughout this day runs the prayer: "Father, *we* have sinned before Thee." Judaism stresses that prayer is not the sole avenue to God's grace. Equally important in God's eyes are deeds of love and compassion. A story is told of Rabbi Israel Salanter, who failed to appear for worship one Yom Kippur eve. His congregation was frantic, for it was inconceivable that their beloved rabbi would be absent on this holiest night. After a long search, they found him in the barn of a Christian neighbor. On his way to the synagogue, the rabbi had found his neighbor's calf, lost and tangled in the brush. He had freed the calf tenderly and brought it back to its stall. The rabbi's prayer was his act of mercy.

**What is Rosh Hashanah?**

Rosh Hashanah means New Year. It ushers in the Ten Days of Penitence, during which mankind "passes in judgment before the heavenly throne." It is the season when Jews also sit in judgment on themselves —by comparing their aspirations to their conduct during the year which has just ended. The Rosh Hashanah of 1955 will mark the Jewish year 5716. Among the Rosh Hashanah prayers is one which asks the Lord to hasten the day when "all men shall come to serve Thee"—when mankind will be joined in universal brotherhood under the Fatherhood of God.

**Is an American Jew's first loyalty to Israel or America?**

The only loyalty of an American Jew is to the United States of America—without any ifs, ands, or buts. To the Jew, the state of Israel is the ancestral home of his forefathers, the birthplace of his faith and his Bible. It is the haven for over a million Jews—after the agonies and nightmares and murders of the past twenty years. Surely, it is not surprising that Israel has great and special meaning for Jews all over the world. Nor is it surprising that the courage and the pioneering of the people of Israel have won the respect of men of every religious faith. But spiritual bonds and emotional ties are quite different from political loyalty. Many Americans retain strong attachments to the land of their fathers. But their political loyalty—whether they be Irish or German or Italian; Catholic, Protestant, or Jew—is and will always be to America alone.

# What Is a Lutheran?

## by G. ELSON RUFF

G. ELSON RUFF has been editor of *The Lutheran* for ten years, is editor-in-chief of the United Lutheran Publication House, and president of the Associated Church Press, an organization consisting of 125 Protestant church periodicals. His syndicated feature column, "Church in the News," has several times received the Associated Church Press Award as the most distinguished reporting on religious news in an American denominational paper.

Mr. Ruff was born in Dunkirk, New York, in 1904. He studied at the University of Pennsylvania, from which he received an A.M. degree, Thiel College, which later awarded him an honorary Litt. D., and the Philadelphia Lutheran Theological Seminary. He was ordained to the ministry of the Evangelical Lutheran Church in 1926 and served for fourteen years as a Lutheran pastor in Pennsylvania. His thoughtful and scholarly book, *The Dilemma of Church and State,* was published early in 1954.

## How did Lutheranism originate?

On October 31, 1517, there was only one Protestant—Martin Luther.* A few years later, there were millions. The violent explosion known as the Reformation split the church of the sixteenth century into a number of segments, of which the Lutheran Church is one.

Luther had been a Roman Catholic priest who loved the Church and had no intention of separating from it. But he ventured to protest in 1517 against the Church's sales of certificates, called indulgences, which were said to reduce the time a soul must stay in purgatory. Luther had learned from Scripture that full forgiveness of sin is promised through faith in the merciful God revealed in Christ. This central idea led Luther to criticize many Roman Catholic teachings and practices. Soon the break was beyond repair.

* "Protestant," as a term describing the followers of Luther, was not actually used until 1529, when it was applied to the princes at the Diet of Spires, who protested against the edict decreed by the majority. Of course, there were many before Luther who protested against abuses in the church in the Middle Ages; but Lutherans were the first to be called "Protestants."

## What are the basic tenets of the Lutheran creed?

Lutherans don't claim any doctrines different from the common Christian faith described in the New Testament and first summarized in the Apostles' Creed. We are created by God, but we employ the freedom given us by God to disobey our Creator. The result is continual tragedy in human life. But God does not abandon us in our tragedy. He shares it with us.

In Christ, He reveals Himself as the Savior God, suffering punishment and death so we may share with Him in the resurrection from death. Through faith in Christ, a new life begins in us. It is nourished by God's gifts through His Word and sacraments. The Word is recorded in the Bible, but the Word itself is a living, active thing through which the Holy Spirit stirs us to growth in understanding and obedience to God's will.

## What distinguishes Lutherans from other Protestant groups?

You don't hear Lutherans say, "It doesn't matter what you believe just so you live right." Lutherans think that a way of living is a by-product of a way of believing. Since Lutheranism developed from Luther's intense experience of salvation through faith, it has been marked by concern for faith as the essential part of religion. So Lutherans, more than most of the other Protestants, emphasize doctrine. They insist on unusually thorough education of their pastors and require young people to engage in a long period of study of the Lutheran Catechism before being admitted to full church membership.

Lutherans do not stress prohibitions or blue laws. They think of the Christian life as a grateful response to a loving Father rather than as obedience to a stern monarch. Such life should achieve a high ethical level without emphasis on rules and regulations. In this, Lutheranism is sharply different from some other forms of Protestantism.

Since Luther had been an ardent Roman Catholic before his excommunication, he was less drastic than some later reformers in abandoning Catholic forms of worship. These are retained among Lutherans in a simplified form, and in the language of the people instead of in Latin. Lutherans observe the festivals and seasons of the historic church year. In their churches, they have the altar, cross, candles, vestments, and other equipment of worship which most other Protestants discarded as "too Catholic." Lutherans believe that these forms of liturgy are not required, but are valuable because of their beauty and because, through them, we share in the experiences of the family of Christian worshipers of all the ages. Lutheran music is world-famous, especially the compositions of Johann Sebastian Bach.

### Do Lutherans worship Martin Luther?

Luther had faults. He was of a violent temperament and sometimes scalded his opponents with intemperate abuse. When driven into a corner, in the turbulent events of his career, he made several unfortunate compromises which nobody defends today. Luther asked his followers not to call themselves "Lutherans." The name was given to them by their opponents as a mark of contempt. They called themselves "Evangelicals"—believers in the gospel. Yet Lutherans deeply respect Martin Luther as one of the greatest teachers and liberators of the church. His ideas still stimulate fresh thinking. Every year, Lutheran scholars write many books exploring his thoughts. But nobody worships him.

### Do Lutherans worship any saints?

Every Christian is a saint. In the Apostles' Creed, the church is called "the communion of saints." A saint is not a perfect person but one who, by God's grace, is progressing toward holiness. Every Christian is also a sinner until the day he dies, even such great Christians as Peter and Paul. Lutherans worship God alone. They do not pray to the Virgin Mary or to anyone but God.

### What is the Lutheran concept of sin?

Sin is the word describing the situation of all people as disobedient to God. Sin is not specific wrongdoing (this is the *result* of sin), but the basic condition of our personality. It is our nature to try to make ourselves the center of our lives. Sin means trying to pretend that we are God. It is refusal to accept the restriction on our freedom which is the inescapable consequence of the fact that we are created beings and that the only reason for our existence is doing the will of our Creator. This is portrayed in the old story of Adam and Eve in the garden, who were not satisfied to accept the one limitation placed on them—that they must not eat the fruit of a certain tree.

### How do Lutherans believe mortals are saved?

We can no more escape by our own efforts from our condition as sinners than we could swim to shore if we fell off a ship in mid-Atlantic. Our only hope is to be rescued. Salvation is a gift from God. The only thing we can do about it is to want it. Even this desire comes from God.

In other words, when we recognize our fatal human weakness, and are thoroughly dissatisfied with it, we are prepared to let God come to us with His gift of faith. This was Luther's situation during his long "dark night of the soul," when, as a monk, he was trying to do all the things that were supposed to result in salvation. He discovered, when he got through trying to save himself, that the merciful and loving God was waiting to save him through faith in Christ. If people could be saved by obeying laws or fulfilling ritual requirements, they would be saving themselves. Lutherans believe that only God can save us.

### How do Lutheran sacraments differ from Roman Catholic sacraments?

Luther came to the conviction that the complete sacrifice for man's sin had already been made in our Lord's crucifixion. So the Roman teaching of the Mass as a sacrifice no longer had meaning for Luther. The Lord's Supper, in Lutheran teaching, is an encounter of the believer with the living Lord, Who is truly present in the Holy Communion to forgive sins and renew the spiritual life of believers. But no physical change takes place in the bread and wine of the Communion.

This teaching was perhaps the most radical part of the Reformation. It attacked the whole Roman Catholic idea of the church as a treasury of merit stored up through saying masses, and of the priesthood as divinely ordained to celebrate the sacrifice of the Mass. In the "priesthood of all believers," of which Luther often spoke, each Christian directly encounters God and receives His saving grace.

Lutherans believe that, in baptism, a person is born into the Kingdom of God and becomes an heir of salvation. It is the beginning of the life of faith in which each day our human nature "is to be drowned and destroyed by daily sorrow and repentance, together with all sins and evil lusts, that the new man should daily come forth and rise, that *shall live* in the presence of God in righteousness and purity forever." (*The Small Catechism,* by Martin Luther.)

The remaining five of the seven sacraments of the Roman Catholic Church were discarded by Luther, and by all Protestants since his day, as not true sacraments because they were not established by Christ. Confirmation, marriage, and ordination of the clergy are rites of the church to which no unique promise of divine grace is attached. Penance is not necessary because God promises complete forgiveness to all who ask for it in faith. There is no guilt "left over" which penance can erase or for which one must make amends in purgatory. Anointing of the sick with oil, with prayers for their recovery, is good Christian therapy, but not a Scriptural requirement.

### Do Lutherans believe in the Holy Trinity?

They do, along with orthodox Christians of all ages. God the Father is our Creator. God the Son is our Redeemer. God the Holy Ghost is the Sanctifier and Nourisher of our souls. Yet there is one God in three personalities. It is not possible to make any essential Christian teaching—such as how God could be a man, how the dead can live eternally, how one God can be three personalities—conform to mathematical formulae or submit to scientific proof. Such things are beyond the range of human reasoning and are matters of faith.

### Are there any special rituals in Lutheran worship?

There is no requirement that Lutheran congregations should all worship in the same way. There is wide variation between the ritual of a cathedral of the Church of Sweden, for instance, and of a small country parish in Saskatchewan. The service of confirmation of youth (usually at age fourteen) on Palm Sunday or Pentecost is a rite which has a distinctive form in Lutheran churches. Also preceding each celebration of the Lord's Supper, there is a service of public confession which is characteristically Lutheran. Private confession is practiced by Lutherans in some places but is not required. In the Lord's Supper, the communicants kneel at the altar rail and receive both bread and wine.

### Do Lutherans believe in heaven and hell?

The goal of the Christian life is the perfect existence which will finally be ours when we can be completely obedient to our Creator. Lutherans do not believe this Kingdom of God will come through gradual improvement of human nature. Fulfillment of God's purposes lies beyond the limits of our present life. Those who live and die in faith in Christ will live with Him eternally, freed from the limitations of time and space. Predictions about this eternal life must necessarily be in some sort of picture language, for it is beyond the range of finite minds. Naïve descriptions of heaven and hell, which were common in old times, are obviously inadequate. But victory over death is the certain destiny of God's people.

## What is the attitude of the Lutheran Church to the Pope? To the Roman Catholic Church? To Roman Catholics?

We are more moderate in speaking of the Pope than Luther was. For one thing, the Papacy has been drastically reformed since Luther's time. However, Lutherans absolutely reject any teaching that God has delegated supreme authority over the souls of His people to any man.

There is only one church, we believe, but it is not any visible institution, such as the Roman Catholic Church or the Lutheran Church. It consists of all the congregations of believers in which "the Gospel is rightly taught and the Sacraments rightly administered." (*Augsburg Confession,* Article 7.)

As for our personal attitude toward Roman Catholics, we should love them as Christian brothers, however much we disagree in our understanding of the gospel. The Pope and bishops of the Roman Catholic Church often make profound statements of Christian truth and peace. Lutherans know that among Roman Catholics are many of the finest Christians on earth.

## What is the Lutheran position on divorce?

God intends marriage to be lifelong. He established the family as the training school in which His children may learn to love and serve one another. But human sinfulness crops up in the marriage relation just as everywhere else. Some marriages become so badly eroded by infidelity and selfishness that to declare them no longer existing is less evil than to try to keep them going. Following the New Testament, Lutherans agree that adultery and desertion may be grounds for divorce. Christians should not legislate general principles to apply to all cases. Every case must be considered individually.

There is a good bit of agitation within Lutheran churches now for a restudy of the problem of divorce. The main emphasis ought to be positive, on education of people in the Christian principle of lifelong fidelity rather than on means of dissolving the marriage relation.

## Do Lutherans believe in birth control?

There have not been many statements by Lutheran organizations on this question, but there is no general objection to the well-known fact that countless Lutherans practice birth control. A recent statement of the Commission on Social Relations of the American Lutheran Conference included these words: "The means which a married pair uses to determine the number and the spacing of the births of their children are a matter for them to decide with their own consciences, on the basis of competent medical authority and in the sense of accountability to God. No moral merit or demerit can be attached to any of the medically approved methods for controlling the number or spacing of children. Whether the means used are those labeled 'natural' or 'artificial' is of far less importance than the spirit in which these means are used. Continence in the marriage relationship, when its sole purpose is the selfish avoidance of pregnancy, is equally as wrong as is the use of contraception toward this same selfish goal. An overabundant production of children without regard to the responsibilities involved may be as sinful and selfish as is the complete avoidance of parenthood."

On this and other ethical questions, the Lutheran Church has little tendency to legislate. The church is not a law-making society but an agency through which the Holy Spirit shapes and directs Christian lives in their growth toward holiness.

### How is the Lutheran Church governed?

There is no pattern which prevails in all countries, because Lutherans believe that church government is a practical concern without doctrinal significance. Lutheran churches of Europe have bishops, but none of the Lutheran churches in America follow this example. Church conventions, which elect presidents and other officials, are the main instruments of authority in the American churches.

The foundation of this authority is in the congregations themselves, because in them the free people of God exercise their right to hear the gospel and receive the sacraments. They cannot be held in obedience to an earthly hierarchy. Each Lutheran congregation owns its church building or other property and is self-governing in all of its local affairs. Men are called to the office of the ministry by God through the congregations, and if they cease to perform the functions of their office they cease to be ministers.

### Does the Lutheran Church permit its pastors to marry?

Luther taught that enforced celibacy of the priesthood was a mistake. Eight years after the beginning of the Reformation, he himself married a nun who had left her convent as a result of Luther's teaching. (The date is important because enemies of Luther often assert that "he left the church to get married.")

## Is Lutheranism international?

Lutheranism includes almost the entire population of Denmark, Finland, Iceland, Norway, and Sweden, a majority of the Germans, Latvians, Estonians, and minorities in most other European countries. Mission work has resulted in Lutheran churches in South America, Africa, Asia, Australia. Lutherans constitute almost half of the Protestants of the world. It is impossible to give the total accurately. Of five million Lutherans in Russia in 1918, who knows how many there are now? The same is true in all Iron Curtain countries. Perhaps 70 million would be a reasonable guess at the present world total.

Lutheran membership in the United States at the end of 1953 was 6,666,181. An additional four or five million persons give "Lutheran" as their church preference when they fill out questionnaires.

## Do Lutherans believe in separation of church and state?

In America, they emphatically do. Luther taught that church and state are both ordained by God and that each has separate, clear-cut functions. Church-state separation is a logical application of the Lutheran principle of resistance to attempts of human authorities to rule men's souls.

In the Scandinavian countries and Finland, the Lutheran Church is the state church, under nominal control of Parliament (as is the Anglican Church in England). There has usually been some connection between the Lutheran Church and the government in other European countries, due to the historical development of the churches. Yet, in Norway under the wartime Quisling government, the Lutheran Church rebelled against the authority of the state. All bishops and most pastors refused to obey its orders. In Germany also, some pastors were strong leaders in the opposition to Hitler. They quoted Luther who wrote, "If your worldly master is wrong, and you know for certain he is wrong, then fear God more than man and do not serve him." At present, Lutheran churchmen in the Russian zone of Germany are struggling against Communist tyranny.

Lutherans in the United States have been unanimous in opposing the appointment of an ambassador to the Vatican because they believe it is contrary to a basic American principle to send a diplomatic representative to the headquarters of a church.

**Do Lutherans believe theirs is the only true religion?**

Yes, but they don't believe they are the only ones who have it. There are true Christian believers in a vast majority of the churches, perhaps in all. Lutherans are among the leaders in interchurch assemblies, such as the World Council of Churches, because they are eager for better understanding and cooperation among Christians everywhere.

# What Is a Methodist?

## by RALPH W. SOCKMAN

RALPH W. SOCKMAN was named one of the six leading clergymen in the United States in a poll conducted by the *Christian Century* Magazine. He was president of the Federation of Churches from 1927 to 1929, and has been chairman of the World Peace Commission of the Methodist Church since 1928. He has been minister of Christ Church in New York City (formerly Madison Avenue Methodist Episcopal Church) since 1917. His Sunday morning "National Radio Pulpit" has been broadcast over the radio for twenty-six years. He also writes a nationally syndicated column entitled "Lift for Living."

Mr. Sockman was born in Mount Vernon, Ohio, in 1889. He studied at Ohio Wesleyan University and received an M.A. degree from Columbia University. He was graduated from Union Theological Seminary in 1916, and the following year received his Ph.D. at Columbia University.

Mr. Sockman was president of the Church Peace Union in 1947 and is the director of the Hall of Fame. He has taught at Yale University and Union Theological Seminary, was a member of the Harvard University Board of Preachers, and serves as the chaplain of New York University. He has received fourteen honorary degrees.

Mr. Sockman is the author of fifteen books, the latest of which is the best-seller *How to Believe.* Among his better-known works are *Men of the Mysteries, Morals of Tomorrow, Recoveries in Religion, Date with Destiny, How to Live,* and *The Higher Happiness.*

## What is a Methodist?

The Methodist Church is "a unique blend of New Testament Christianity, the Protestant Reformation and the influence of John Wesley." Wesley himself was fond of saying: "A Methodist is one who has the love of God shed abroad in his heart by the Holy Ghost given unto him, one who loves the Lord his God with all his heart, with all his soul, with all his mind, and with all his strength."

Methodism began in England as a movement within the existing Protestant Church, and not as a new sect.

## How do Methodists regard the Bible?

They regard it as the "Holy Scriptures." Methodists look upon the

Bible as a library of inspired books containing the progressive revelation of God. They recognize the various types of literature in the Bible —law, poetry, prophecy, allegory, gospels, epistles.

Realizing that the Scriptures have been translated from their original tongues, the Methodists make allowance for differences of interpretation. They believe in the "open Bible" and encourage the individual to read it for himself, leaving him free to make his own interpretation under the guidance of the Holy Spirit.

Methodists believe that "the Holy Scriptures contain all things necessary to salvation; so that whatsoever is not read therein, nor may be proved thereby, is not to be required of any man, that it should be believed as an article of faith, or be thought necessary to salvation." [From the Methodist Articles of Religion.]

### How did the Methodist Church begin?

The Methodist Church was born in the Church of England through the work of John Wesley. Educated at Oxford and ordained to the Anglican priesthood, the young Wesley sought in vain for religious satisfaction by the strict observance of religious rules and the ordinances of the church. The turning point in his life came at a prayer meeting in London on May 24, 1738. There he learned what Saint Paul had discovered—that it is not by rules and our own efforts at self-perfection that man may enter upon life and peace, but only by faith in God's mercy.

When Wesley went forth to preach his new, heart-warming experience, the people who had been unreached by the church flocked to hear him. Multitudes came asking Wesley to teach and direct them. He gathered these people into societies "in order to pray together, to receive the word of exhortation, and to watch over one another in love, that they might help each other to work out their own salvation."

He appointed leaders, assigned them to various fields of labor, and supervised their work. The movement spread rapidly over England, then to Ireland and America. Wesley's intention was not to form a new sect but only to organize societies within the Church of England. The preachers were not ordained, and the members were supposed to receive the sacraments in the Anglican church. But the Bishop of London, to whose diocese Wesley belonged, would not ordain ministers to serve the Methodist societies. Nor would he consecrate their meeting places. If Wesley's work was to expand, he had to take the irregular steps of ordination and consecration.

Furthermore, Wesley was confronted with the care of his followers in America, where the Anglican clergy had nearly all returned to England as Tories during the War of the Revolution. The 15,000 American Methodists at the close of the Revolutionary War clamored for clerical leadership. Wesley responded to their demand by asking the Bishop of London to ordain some ministers for America. Failing in his request, Wesley himself ordained two men to "preside over the flock in America."

Under their leadership, the Methodist Episcopal Church in America was organized at Baltimore on December 24, 1784.

**Where did the name Methodist come from?**

It arose from the methodical habits of the "Holy Club" which John and Charles Wesley founded at Oxford University. The members arranged a daily schedule of duties, setting hours for visiting the sick and those in prison, conducting schools among the poor, and observing the religious offices of the church. They prayed aloud three times each day and stopped for silent prayer every hour.

These strict rules of conduct aroused the ridicule of the student body. "Methodists" was almost the mildest epithet hurled at the Holy Club. The name clung to the followers of Wesley because he continued to stress rules of conduct and religious observance.

**What is the Methodist attitude toward the Trinity?**

Methodists do not pretend to understand fully the meaning of the Trinity. Who does? Even Saint Augustine, after writing the classic exposition of the doctrine of the Trinity, confessed that it still remained a mystery. If God could be fully explained, he would cease to be God.

The doctrine of the Trinity is the expression of the three aspects in *our experience* of God. We conceive of God as the Creator, the First Cause of all things—as God the Father. We think of God revealed historically in the personality of Christ—as God the Son. We feel him as a pervading, continuing presence and power in our lives—as God the Holy Spirit.

The doctrine of the Trinity is also our formula for understanding the personality of God. God is Love, but whom did He love before He created man and the universe? Love must have an object. The object of God's love in the pre-Creation period was Christ the Son, co-eternal with the Father. And the divine activity linking God the

Father with the object of his love, God the Son, was and eternally is God the Holy Spirit.

## How do Methodists regard the Virgin Birth?

The original Methodist Articles of Religion declare that Christ the Son "took man's nature in the womb of the blessed Virgin." The great majority of Methodists continue to hold this belief. Some would distinguish the biological aspects of the Virgin Birth from its theological implications. Some believe that the deity of Christ does not rest on the uniqueness of his physical birth but on the inexplicable quality and power of his life and work.

Hence, some Methodists do not feel it necessary to believe that Jesus Christ was born without a human father in order to assert that he is the Only Begotten Son of the Heavenly Father. The Methodist Church does not disown this latter group as long as they believe in the Deity of Christ.

## Do Methodists pray to saints?

No. They believe God is directly accessible to each of his children. Since God is Love, no intermediary is needed to intercede for his children. Methodists, like other Protestants, believe in the "individual priesthood of all believers."

## Do Methodists believe in heaven and hell?

Methodists believe in divine judgment after death. Goodness will be rewarded and evil punished.

The concepts of heaven and hell vary widely, according to the educational and religious background of the believers. Some have very concrete ideas of golden streets in heaven and fiery furnaces in hell. But the majority of Methodists are emancipated from the prescientific view of a physical heaven "up there" and a physical hell "down there." They trust the promise of Christ: "I go to prepare a place for you." Heaven is the realm of mind and spirit where the redeemed keep company with God and His Risen Son, Jesus Christ. Hell is the state where such fellowship is absent.

## Do Methodists believe in purgatory?

No. Methodists find no scriptural warrant for the Roman Catholic belief in purgatory. They do not presume to peer behind the veil of death or departmentalize the processes of divine judgment. Many

Methodists believe that God's punishments are redemptive rather than punitive. They trust the justice and love of God to care for the departed.

**What sacraments do Methodists recognize?**

Methodists hold only two sacraments as ordained of God: baptism and the Lord's Supper. Baptism is not only a sign of profession but also of regeneration, or a new birth. The Supper of the Lord is the sacrament of our redemption by Christ's death and a sign of the love which Christians ought to have among themselves.

Methodists maintain the general Protestant position of only two sacraments because, according to the Gospel record, only two had the direct touch of Jesus. This does not mean that the Methodists have a weakened conception of other rites, such as marriage and confirmation. These are held in high reverence, but Methodists still limit the word "sacrament" to the two ordinances which Christ Himself performed.

**Do Methodists baptize infants?**

Yes. We believe "all men are heirs of life eternal and subjects of the saving grace of the Holy Spirit." Christ himself said, "Suffer the little children to come unto me, and forbid them not, for of such is the Kingdom of God."

While an infant is not aware of the meaning of the sacrament, the parents are—and are thereby committed to the Christian nurture of the child. The church assumes responsibility for her baptized children and awaits the time when they will be mature enough to appreciate and assume for themselves the vows made at baptism.

**Do Methodists accept Roman Catholic baptism as valid?**

Yes. Methodists believe that the sacrament of baptism is a sign of God's grace and man's regeneration. Methodists and Roman Catholics believe in the same God.

**Do Methodists believe in the "real presence" of Christ in the sacrament of the Lord's Supper?**

Yes, but not in the sense that Roman Catholics regard the "real presence." In the Mass, Roman Catholics are taught that the bread becomes the Body of Christ and the wine becomes the Blood of Christ, so that Christ is present in body and soul.

Methodists accept Christ's own words that "God is a spirit: and they that worship him must worship him in spirit and in truth." Hence, they believe that the body of Christ is given, taken, and eaten in the sacrament only in "a heavenly and spiritual manner." And faith is the means whereby the body of Christ is received and eaten in the Lord's Supper.

## Do Methodist ministers hear confessions?

Methodist churches have no "confessionals" as do Roman Catholic churches. Methodist ministers perform a great deal of counseling. Persons often come to confess their sins as well as their troubles. But the pastor does not presume to give "penance" or to pronounce words of absolution. Methodists believe that each individual can go directly to God, trusting the New Testament promise: "If we confess our sins, He is faithful and just to forgive us our sins. . . ."

## What do Methodists mean by salvation?

Salvation means not only security in heaven after death, but a present experience of God's grace and power. When men truly and earnestly repent of their sins, God forgives the guilt of past transgressions. Also, he imparts the power which fortifies men against future sins.

God calls men to that holiness of life which, as Wesley insisted, is "social holiness," the love and service of their fellow men. Man cannot attain this holiness merely by obeying laws and doing good works. Man's salvation comes by faith and through the grace of God. God sent Christ to reveal his love to men. When men behold how Christ died for them, their hearts are moved and their lives are transformed. They confess Christ as their Savior. He is the power of God unto salvation.

## Do Methodists have to accept a creed?

They are not required to sign any formal creed. Those joining the church are asked to answer affirmatively two questions:

"Do you confess Jesus Christ as your Savior and Lord and pledge your allegiance to His Kingdom?"

"Do you receive and profess the Christian faith as contained in the New Testament of Our Lord, Jesus Christ?"

Wesley, the founder, once declared: "I believe the merciful God regards the lives and tempers of men more than their ideas." One of his basic principles was, "Think and let think." With its emphasis on life rather than creed. Methodism has been relatively free from heresy trials.

## Are Methodists stricter than others in matters of personal conduct, especially as to amusements?

Methodists today are about as broad and liberal in their codes of behavior as are other leading Protestants. Methodists traditionally have fought against intemperance, gambling, and licentious indulgence. John Wesley formulated a list of general rules for the members of his societies because he believed they needed concrete standards as well as ideals.

For many years, the church had a provision forbidding diversions such as card playing and dancing. This provision was changed nearly thirty years ago to read, "not taking such diversions as cannot be used in the name of the Lord Jesus."

## What is the Methodist position on birth control?

The General Conference of the Methodist Church has never made an official pronouncement on birth control. The statements of individual leaders suggest that prevailing Methodist opinion approves the use of contraceptives by lawfully married couples when in the interest of the mothers' health and the children's welfare. The justifying motive must be unselfish. The children we bring into the world have a right to a wholesome home life. Toward that end, the spacing of children, the health of parents, and adequate economic support are factors to be considered. The discipline recommends courses of instruction for young married couples on "life adjustments and personality problems."

## What is the Methodist position on divorce?

Methodists deplore the prevalence of divorce and seek to preserve the marriage bond by every means humanly possible. However, they recognize that situations do arise where the sanctity of individual personality requires the severance of the marital relationship. They hold that those who have been wronged have the right to a second chance.

No Methodist minister should solemnize the marriage of a divorced person whose wife or husband is living and unmarried; but this rule shall not apply (1) to the innocent person, when it is clearly established by competent testimony that the true cause for divorce was adultery or other vicious conditions which, through cruelty or physical peril, invalidated the marriage vow; nor (2) to the divorced persons seeking to be reunited in marriage.

**What distinguishes Methodists from other Protestant denominations?**

It is difficult to say, because modern practices and the growing spirit of church unity tend to draw the leading Protestant denominations ever closer together. The Methodist Church retains, in general, the theology of the Anglican Church from which it sprang. Some Methodist parishes preserve much of the Protestant Episcopal liturgy. On the other hand, in some Methodist churches, the services of worship are very informal. Within the 40,000 American Methodist churches, there is probably as wide variation in types of thought and worship as there is between Methodists, Presbyterians, Congregationalists, and others.

Of course, Methodists do have some differences from the other branches of the Protestant Church. For instance, the Protestant Episcopal Church believes that divine grace is imparted through apostolic succession. Methodists do not hold to this doctrine. Hence, a Methodist minister cannot administer the sacraments in an Episcopal church. And the confirmation of members in the Methodist Church is an office not limited to bishops, as in the Protestant Episcopal Church, but can be given by all ordained ministers.

Also, the Methodist Church differs from the Baptist and some others in the matter of baptism. Not only do Methodists believe in infant baptism, which the Baptists do not, but also they baptize usually by sprinkling rather than by immersion. Other differences might be cited if space permitted consideration of the various denominations.

The two most marked Methodist emphases are the inner experience of religion and the social applications of conscience. John Wesley stressed "the witness of the spirit," "an inward impression on the soul whereby the spirit of God immediately and directly witnesses to my spirit that I am a child of God . . . that all my sins are blotted out and I am reconciled to God." Holding this emphasis, Methodism has made much of conversion, revivals, and testimonies of religious experience.

The Methodist social conscience has kept the church in the forefront of reform movements, such as the improvement of labor conditions, the inculcation of temperance, and the abolition of war. In the number of missions, hospitals, and colleges, Methodism leads in Protestantism.

The Methodist Church also emphasizes the democratic principle in its organization and government. Laymen are increasingly given leadership in the church councils.

## How is the Methodist Church governed?

Since British Methodism differs in its organization from that of the American church, we shall speak only of the United States and the main body of Methodists here.

Having been organized at about the time the United States Constitution was adopted, the Methodist Church parallels rather uniquely the pattern of American government. The executive branch consists of a Council of Bishops, whose members are elected by jurisdictional conferences composed of ministers and laymen. Each bishop presides over an area, of which there are now thirty-seven in the United States (and eighteen in mission fields abroad). The bishops appoint the ministers of individual parishes.

The legislative power of the Methodist Church is vested in a General Conference, which meets every four years and is composed of both clergy and laymen—in equal numbers. The delegates to the General Conference are democratically elected by annual conferences and on a proportional basis.

The supreme judicial power of the church rests in a Judicial Council, whose members and qualifications are determined by the General Conference of the church.

## How many Methodists are there?

The latest figures give 9,180,428 members of the Methodist Church in the United States. In addition, there are 845,793 preparatory members.

There are also three main Negro Methodist bodies: the African Methodist Episcopal Church (1,166,300 members); the African Methodist Episcopal Zion Church (728,150); and the Colored Methodist Episcopal Church (392,000).

Methodists throughout the world number approximately 14,500,000 in actual membership and claim a total constituency of 25,000,000 as adherents.

# What Is a "Mormon"?

## by RICHARD L. EVANS

RICHARD L. EVANS is a member of the Council of Twelve, Church of Jesus Christ of Latter-day Saints, and since 1930 has been active in the famed radio programs originating from Station KSL in Salt Lake City. He is the narrator on the Sunday "Tabernacle Choir and Organ" broadcasts.

Mr. Evans was born in Salt Lake City in 1906. He received his B.A. and M.A. degrees at the University of Utah, following which he traveled and did editorial work in Europe. He is editor of *Improvement Era*, a Mormon publication, is a member of the Board of Regents of the University of Utah, serves on the board of trustees of Brigham Young University, and is director of Temple Square, Salt Lake City. In 1938, he was appointed a member of the First Council of the Seventy, Church of Jesus Christ of Latter-day Saints.

For some years Mr. Evans wrote a weekly newspaper column which was syndicated throughout the United States. He has written five books: *Unto the Hills, This Day—And Always, And the Spoken Word, At this Same Hour,* and *Tonic for Our Times.*

This article presents the doctrines and practices of the Church of Christ of Latter-day Saints, Salt Lake City, Utah, the largest "Mormon" body in the world (1,246,362 members in 1953). The position of other Latter-day bodies should be noted:

The Reorganized Church of Jesus Christ of Latter-day Saints, with headquarters in Independence, Missouri (152,850 members), claims to be the legal successor of the church founded by Joseph Smith; it refers to an Ohio court decision (1880) to substantiate this claim. In 1860, Joseph Smith, the son of the founder, became president of the Reorganized Church, which denied the leadership of Brigham Young and has always condemned polygamy.

The Church of Christ, Temple Lot, with headquarters in Independence, Missouri (2,275 members), and several groups with membership under 2,000 (Cutlerites, Bickertonites, Strangites) hold different views on questions concerning succession to the presidency of the Church, the use of temples, and certain matters of organization and procedure.

## What is a "Mormon"?

Strictly speaking, there is no such thing as a "Mormon," and there is no "Mormon" Church. "Mormon" is merely a nickname for a member of the Church of Jesus Christ of Latter-day Saints.

### Are "Mormons" Christians?

Unequivocally yes—both as to the name of the Church and in unqualified acceptance and worship of Jesus the Christ.

### Are "Mormons" Protestants?

No. Joseph Smith (see below) never belonged to any other church. He claimed no authority by succession from any other church or sect. He inferred no authority from the Bible. He and his associates testified that they received their authority by direct divine bestowal.

### When and how was the Church of Jesus Christ of Latter-day Saints founded?

The Latter-day Saint believes that the Gospel of Jesus Christ was proclaimed in the heavens before the world was; that it was on earth anciently, and known to Adam and others; but that mankind has repeatedly departed from it (as in the days of Noah); and that it has had to be "restored" in various "dispensations" (as through Abraham, Moses, and others). He believes that the last such "restoration" occurred in the early nineteenth century, beginning "the dispensation of the fullness of times" (Ephesians 1:10).

In 1820, near Palmyra, in western New York, in a period of religious unrest and "revival," Joseph Smith (then in his fifteenth year) related how (prompted by an impression from reading James 1:5) he retired one morning to a grove near the family farm to petition the Lord in prayer. What he saw and experienced is recorded in a widely published pamphlet (*Joseph Smith's Own Story*), including the appearance of "two Personages, whose brightness and glory defy all description . . . One of them spake unto me . . . and said, pointing to the other—'This is my Beloved Son. Hear Him!'" (See also Matthew 3:17 and 17:5.) The declarations that followed indicated the need for a "restoration" of the Gospel of Jesus Christ (which some among the religious "reformers" had long recognized).

As a legal entity, the "restored Church" was organized at Fayette, Seneca County, New York, April 6, 1830. Membership quickly increased, and so did opposition. The main body first moved to Ohio, then to Missouri, then to Illinois. After Joseph Smith was martyred by an armed mob at Carthage, Illinois, in 1844, the Latter-day Saints moved westward under the leadership of the senior member of the Twelve Apostles, Brigham Young, into the valley of the Great Salt Lake (1847), into "a land that nobody wanted."

In each move they made, they left behind them homes and prosperous farms and other possessions—including Nauvoo (population 20,000), which they had built from a swampland on the Mississippi and which was then (1846) the largest city in Illinois.

In the two following decades, some 80,000 "Mormon" pioneers traversed the thousand miles of plains and Rocky Mountains, from the Missouri River to the Great Basin. Some rode in wagons; some pushed all their possessions in handcarts; some walked—and more than 6,000 died along the way.

It was no passing persuasion that enabled them to do what they did or that induced them, time after time, to leave what they left.

**How do the "Mormons" look upon Joseph Smith?**

They look upon him as one who was commissioned of God to effect a "restoration" of the Gospel of Jesus Christ and to open a new Gospel "dispensation." They look upon him as a prophet of God, in the same literal sense as they look upon other prophets of the Old and New Testaments (and they so accept Joseph Smith's successors; from Brigham Young and including the present president of the Church, David O. McKay).

Joseph Smith was born in Sharon, Vermont, in 1805. His progenitors were early New England settlers, the first arriving in 1638. His forebears fought with the Colonial forces.

**Do "Mormons" believe in the Holy Trinity?**

Yes. The Latter-day Saint accepts the Godhead as three literal, distinct personalities: God the Father; His Son, Jesus the Christ (who is one with the Father in purpose and in thought, but separate from Him in physical fact); and the Holy Ghost, a Personage of spirit (Acts 7:55, etc.). Here, the "Mormon" points to literal scriptural language. He believes in a loving, understanding Father who made His children "in His own image" (Genesis 1:27), and Jesus His Son is said to be in "the express image of his person" (Hebrews 1:3).

**What do the "Mormons" believe about Jesus Christ?**

They believe Him to be the Son of God, "the only begotten of the Father" in the flesh. They believe in His atoning sacrifice and literal resurrection. They accept Him as the Savior and Redeemer of mankind. They look to Him as the "one mediator between God and men" (I Timothy 2:5), and pray to the Father in His name. They believe that He will come again and reign on earth (Acts 1:9–11).

### Do "Mormons" believe in the Virgin Birth?

Yes. The Latter-day Saint accepts the miraculous conception of Jesus the Christ.

### What do "Mormons" believe about the Bible?

The Bible is basic to "Mormon" belief. The King James version is officially used, and is believed "to be the word of God as far as it is translated correctly" (8th Article of Faith).

### What is the Book of Mormon?

The Book of Mormon is not the "Mormon Bible," as is sometimes supposed. It is one of the complementary works that the "Mormon" accepts as scripture. The "Mormon" does not believe that the revelations of God were confined to ancient Israel. He does not believe that a loving Father would restrict his communication to one part of His family, to one time of history, or to one land. He believes "all that God has revealed, all that He does now reveal, and . . . that He will yet reveal many great and important things pertaining to the Kingdom of God" (9th Article of Faith).

The Book of Mormon is part of a record, both sacred and secular, of prophets and peoples who (with supplementary groups) were among the ancestors of the American "Indians." It covers principally the peoples of the period from about 600 B.C. to 421 A.D. These peoples were of Asiatic origin, of the House of Israel, and left Jerusalem during the reign of King Zedekiah, eventually to cross the sea to the Western world, where they built great cities and civilizations. Ultimately, they all but destroyed themselves in warring with one another.

They brought with them certain records of the Old Testament. In addition, their historians, statesmen, and prophets kept records of important events of their own civilization, some of which were engraved on gold plates. It was from such plates "preserved by the gift and power of God" that Joseph Smith translated the Book of Mormon (first published in 1830).

The book takes its title from a man whose name was Mormon, who was one of the later prophets of the thousand-year period, and who was not greatly different from the prophets of Old and New Testament times, except that he lived in the Western Hemisphere among some of the Savior's "other sheep" (John 10:16). The Book of Mormon witnesses that Jesus the Christ visited the inhabitants of this hemisphere after His ascension.

### What does the "Mormon" believe about man's immortality?

Energy, matter, and "intelligence" exist eternally and are indestructible. And man himself has existed from the premortal past and will continue, with his individual identity, into the endless eternal future.

At an appointed time, after the change called death, man will emerge as a resurrected being with a deathless union of spirit and body, literally following the promise and pattern set by the Savior.

### Who will be "saved"?

The Latter-day Saint believes in universal "salvation"—"For as in Adam all die, even so in Christ shall all be made alive. *But every man in his own order* . . ." (I Corinthians 15:22–23.)

The Savior referred to "many mansions" (John 14:2). Paul speaks of the man "caught up to the third heaven" (II Corinthians 12:2), and further observed (I Corinthians 15:40, 41, 42) that there are different "degrees of glory." While "salvation" is universal, "exaltation" (with the highest eternal opportunities) must be earned by obedience to laws, ordinances, and commandments of the Kingdom.

### Do "Mormons" believe in heaven and hell?

The "heaven" the "Mormon" looks to and lives for is a real place of eternal progress, with endless association with loved ones, with families and friends. For those who are willfully indifferent to their opportunities on earth, the knowledge that they have fallen short of their highest possible happiness will be part of the punishment of the "hell" of hereafter.

### Why do the "Mormons" emphasize education?

This can best be answered by quoting three significant sentences:

"The glory of God is intelligence, or . . . light and truth" (Doctrine and Covenants 93:36).

"It is impossible for a man to be saved in ignorance" (*ibid.* 131:6).

"Whatever principle of intelligence we attain unto in this life, it will rise with us in the resurrection" (*ibid.* 130:18).

Brigham Young said: "Our religion is simply the truth. It is all said in this one expression—it embraces all truth, wherever found in all the works of God and man . . ."

Since the Latter-day Saint believes that the "intelligence" each man attains will remain forever with him, his search for knowledge, for truth, for light is not only a permissible privilege but also an inescapable obligation.

## Do "Mormons" practice polygamy?

No. For any Church member, the penalty for plural marriage today is excommunication.

Polygamy or plural marriage was at one time practiced by a part of the "Mormon" people. Federal laws prohibiting this practice were passed, but were questioned by the Church as an unconstitutional infringement of religious liberty. In 1890, after the constitutionality of these laws had been reaffirmed by the Supreme Court of the United States, Wilford Woodruff, then president of the Church, issued a manifesto which, upon acceptance by the Church, proscribed the further practice of polygamy.

Polygamy was practiced at certain periods in Biblical times, righteously and with divine sanction. And those who entered into polygamy in the nineteenth century did so with a conviction that it was also for them so sanctioned. They honored their wives and families.

The practice of polygamy was revoked by the same authority by which it had been sanctioned.

## What is the "Mormon" concept of marriage?

The "Mormon" believes that there can be no heaven for him without his family, and if he fully conforms to the teachings of his Church, he enters into a marriage covenant that lasts not only until "death do us part" but continues "for time and eternity." "Neither is the man without the woman, neither the woman without the man, in the Lord" (I Corinthians 11:11).

Such marriages are performed in "Mormon" temples. Marriages performed outside of temples, by civil ceremony alone, are not believed to be binding beyond death unless they are later solemnized for "eternity."

Marriages with non-"Mormons" are contrary to counsel, and are not solemnized in the temples.

## Do "Mormons" permit divorce?

Divorce is deplored and discouraged. "Temple divorces" (as distinguished from civil divorces) may be granted only by the president of the Church, for serious cause, including infidelity.

## Do "Mormons" believe in baptism? Confirmation? Holy Communion?

As to baptism—yes—by immersion, and by those having authority—according to the pattern set by the Savior, who was baptized by John *in the River Jordan*. The "Mormon" believes that the symbolism of being "buried with Him in baptism" (Colossians 2:12) is not found in any other form but by immersion.

The Latter-day Saint does not believe in baptizing infants, but only those who have become "accountable" for their actions, at the age of eight years and over. He believes "that men will be punished for their own sins, and not for Adam's transgression" (2nd Article of Faith). Infants are innocent and will not be held accountable here or in heaven for the actions or errors of others, "for of such is the Kingdom of God" (Mark 10:14).

A simple confirmation immediately follows baptism, "by the laying on of hands for the gift of the Holy Ghost."

As to Communion: The sacrament of the Lord's Supper is administered in a simple manner. Bread and water are blessed and partaken of by all the congregation "in remembrance" of the Savior, and as a witness that "they are willing to keep His commandments."

## What are "Mormon" temples used for?

All men are welcome to worship in "Mormon" chapels and meeting places throughout the world. But "Mormon" temples (of which there are eight in use) are not places of public worship. Temples are used for solemnizing marriages, and for other sacred ordinances.

God (who is a God of law and order) has set certain requirements for citizenship in the highest "Kingdom" of the hereafter. But obviously all men have not known the laws and commandments and requirements of the "Kingdom." Yet the "Mormon" believes that a just God will give to all those who have ever lived an adequate opportunity to hear and accept the gospel and its required earthly ordinances. In the words of Peter: "For this cause was the gospel preached also to them that are dead . . ." (I Peter 4:6.) Thus these essential ordinances—including baptism—are "vicariously" performed in the temples for those who have died without adequate opportunity to receive them for themselves. Ancient knowledge of this principle and practice is suggested by Paul: ". . . if the dead rise not at all? Why are they then baptized for the dead?" (I Corinthians 15:29.)

The principle of doing for others what they cannot do for themselves is not new. The Savior performed a "vicarious" service for all of us (I Peter 3:18).

**What is the "Mormon" attitude on birth control?**

The Church has always advocated the rearing of large families, and birth control, as commonly understood, is contrary to its teachings.

**Do the "Mormons" have "ministers"?**

Among the Latter-day Saints, there is no "professional" clergy. The Church offers opportunity for participation and responsibility for everyone. Any worthy man may be called to be a bishop or to fill any other priesthood office for an unspecified time, and without financial compensation. For his livelihood, he would usually continue his lay profession or occupation.

A boy or girl of eight or ten may occupy a pulpit for a short talk. Boys beginning at the age of twelve are ordained to an office in the priesthood. There are organizations within the Church that provide for study, for service, and for the cultural and recreational activities of every man, woman, and child of all ages. All are expected to participate and to perform some service.

The "Mormon" is proud of his "practical" religion which takes into account the "wholeness" of man and teaches that "men are that they might have joy" (Book of Mormon, II Nephi 2:25), and touches upon the needs and activities of every day, as well as the hereafter.

**Do "Mormons" believe there is conflict between science and religion?**

To the Latter-day Saint, truth is an eternal whole, and if there are seeming discrepancies between science and religion, it is simply because men do not know enough. And where there is doubt and controversy, the "Mormon" feels that he can afford to wait for final answers—for truth and intelligence and life are everlasting.

**How many "Mormons" are there?**

The Church of Jesus Christ of Latter-day Saints (with headquarters in Salt Lake City, Utah) numbers 1,246,362 (1953) with some 3,300 congregations throughout the world. There are also some schismatic groups with historical and doctrinal differences. The Reorganized

Church of Jesus Christ of Latter-day Saints, Independence, Missouri, numbers 152,850 (1953).

### Do the "Mormons" proselyte other people?

Yes. Missionaries have gone out since the 1830's in an earnest endeavor to carry the message of the "Restoration" "to every nation, and kindred, and tongue, and people" (Revelation 14:6).

This work is done principally by young men about twenty years of age (supplemented by young women and older people also), taken from all walks of life. During their missionary service, they are ordained ministers. They pay their own expenses (assisted by families or friends) and give usually two or more years of their time.

### How is the Church governed?

The 6th Article of Faith affirms that the offices and organization of the Church of Jesus Christ should follow the plan and pattern set by the Savior: "We believe in the same organization that existed in the Primitive Church, viz., apostles, prophets, pastors, teachers, evangelists, etc.," including high priests, seventies, elders, bishops, priests, and deacons, as named in the New Testament.

The Church has a strong central organization, with a First Presidency of three presiding high priests ("after the order of Melchisedec" —Hebrews 5:10), followed in order by the Council of the Twelve Apostles (with assistants); a patriarch; the First Council of the Seventy; also a Presiding Bishopric who preside over the Aaronic Priesthood.

Geographically, the Church is divided into "stakes" and "wards" (somewhat resembling the diocese and parishes), and "missions."

### How is the Church financed?

Principally by tithing—the scriptural tenth (Malachi 3:8–11).

Work, thrift, and industry are taught as the best cure for want. Acceptance of government "dole" or any "unearned" public aid is discouraged. Through the voluntary spare-time labors of men of many occupations and professions, a church welfare program provides means to rehabilitate those in need, and to see that no one goes without the necessities of life.

### What is the "Mormon" attitude on liquor and tobacco?

A code of health and conduct given in 1833 and known as the "Word of Wisdom" disapproves the use of tobacco, alcoholic beverages, and "hot drinks" (specifically tea and coffee). The spirit of the "Word of Wisdom" requires abstinence from all injurious substances and suggests that man should enjoy all the wholesome things of the earth "with prudence and thanksgiving" (Doctrine and Covenants, 89).

### What is the "Mormon" philosophy of freedom?

When Joseph Smith was asked how he governed his people, he replied: ". . . teach them correct principles, and let them govern themselves."

The "Mormon" loves freedom as he loves life. He believes that there is no principle more basic to the Gospel of Jesus Christ than the God-given free agency of every man. He believes that a war in heaven was fought for freedom; that the right of choice is essential to the soul's salvation; and that anyone who seeks to enslave men in any sense is essentially in league with Satan himself.

Further, as to freedom, he cites these Articles of Faith:

"We claim the privilege of worshiping almighty God according to the dictates of our own conscience, and allow all men the same privilege, let them worship how, where, or what they may.

"We believe in being honest, true, chaste, benevolent, virtuous, and in doing good to all men. . . . If there is anything virtuous, lovely or of good report or praiseworthy, we seek after these things."

With these convictions, the "Mormon" stands willing to leave all things and all men in the hands of a just Judge and loving Father.

# What Is a Presbyterian?

## by JOHN SUTHERLAND BONNELL

JOHN S. BONNELL has been minister of the Fifth Avenue Presbyterian Church, New York, for almost twenty years. He has taught at Princeton Theological Seminary, and lectured at Union Theological Seminary in Richmond, Virginia, and Queen's University at Kingston, Ontario, Canada.

Mr. Bonnell was born on Prince Edward Island, Canada, in 1893. He studied at Dalhousie University in Halifax (Nova Scotia), where he received his B.A. degree. He received his D.D. from Pine Hill Divinity Hall in Halifax. He was ordained in 1922 and served as pastor of St. Andrew's Church, New Brunswick, Canada, and Westminster Church in Winnipeg. He has received an honorary LL.D. from Washington and Jefferson College and a D.D. from Lafayette College.

During World War I, Mr. Bonnell served as a sergeant in the Fifth Canadian Siege Battery; he was wounded twice. He has traveled extensively in Europe and made a study of religious freedom in ten European countries— two of them behind the Iron Curtain.

In 1941, he was special delegate to the General Assembly of the Church of Scotland—from the Presbyterian Church in the U.S.A., and the Federal Council of Churches.

Mr. Bonnell has had extraordinarily wide experience in pastoral counseling. He served as an attendant nurse in a hospital for three years, during which he received special training under a psychiatrist. During more than thirty years of his ministry, he has held 7,600 interviews with people who have sought guidance and help.

Mr. Bonnell broadcasts on a national radio network each Sunday from November through April. He has contributed to many magazines and is the author of six books: *Fifth Avenue Sermons, Pastoral Psychiatry, Britons under Fire, Psychology for Pastor and People, What Are You Living For?* and *The Practice and Power of Prayer.*

This article has been considerably expanded by Mr. Bonnell from the article which originally appeared in *Look* Magazine.

### What is a Presbyterian?

A Presbyterian is a Protestant who belongs to a particular form of church government. The word Presbyterian refers not to a special system of doctrine or worship, but to a representative form of church government. In Greek, *presbyteros* means "elder." The Presbyterian Church is governed by elders: teaching elders, who are ordained ministers or pastors, and ruling elders elected from the ranks of the Church.

In each congregation these elders, with a minister at their head as Moderator, form the Session with supreme authority in all spiritual matters in the local church. There are two additional boards in each congregation: the deacons have responsibility for distributing charity and in some congregations other duties have been allocated to them, and the trustees hold the property for the congregation and are entrusted with its upkeep. They are also charged with responsibility for the finances of the church. In some Presbyterian churches the responsibilities of the Board of Trustees are performed by the Board of Deacons.

**What is the basis of the Presbyterian creed?**

In 1643 the Parliament of England appointed 151 laymen, clergymen, and church scholars to draw up a system of Reformation doctrine and government. They labored for six years, holding 1,163 sessions, and produced among other important theological works the Westminster Confession of Faith, which is recognized as the creed of English-speaking Presbyterians. Most Presbyterians accept also the creeds of the early undivided Christian Church—the Nicene and the Apostles' Creeds.

**What do Presbyterians believe about the Bible?**

Presbyterians believe the Scriptures of the Old and New Testaments to be the Word of God and "the only infallible rule of faith and practice," and that they are the source of those truths by which men live. They believe in the "inspiration" of the Scriptures: that God spoke through men whose minds and hearts He had touched. They therefore emphasize inspired men, not inspired words.

Most Presbyterians have rejected the view of inspiration, held by pre-Christian pagan writers, that the personalities of inspired men were "possessed" or entranced by a spirit so that they became "pens of God" or wrote down what Deity had dictated. Rather they believe that God employed the personalities of chosen men in making His Divine revelation. Presbyterians do not equate tradition with the Bible. Tradition plays a decidedly inferior role in Presbyterian thinking.

**Do Presbyterians believe in heaven and hell?**

Yes. The Bible and human experience teach that we are living in a moral universe where sin carries its own appropriate penalty and righteousness its own reward, including the vision of God. The New Testament emphasizes the dread nature of the punishment which sin inevitably incurs, the severest of which is separation from God.

It is understandable that men should think of the spiritual world in material terms: heaven as streets of gold and gates of pearl. Similarly, hell has been pictured in such material imagery as fire and brimstone. While these are symbols, it must not be forgotten that they represent a spiritual reality.

All thoughtful Christians will, however, reject as immoral and unchristian the teaching once proclaimed that the bliss of the redeemed will be heightened by watching the sufferings of the damned.

Heaven and hell are not only places; they are also states of mind and character. They have their commencement in the here and now. An utterly selfish, godless man could find no happiness in the Christian heaven because he carries hell in his heart.

**What sacraments are observed?**

Only two: Holy Communion (the Lord's Supper) and baptism. With the vast majority of Protestants, Presbyterians believe that Jesus instituted only these two sacraments.

**Do Presbyterians believe that Christ is physically present in the sacrament of Holy Communion?**

No. Presbyterians believe that Christ is *spiritually* present in the Lord's Supper. Presbyterians do not believe that Christ is offered up in the sacrament to the Father, or that any real sacrifice is made. The sacrament is a *commemoration* of the sacrifice of Christ once offered for all men.

The Westminster Confession of Faith expresses the doctrine in this way: "Worthy receivers outwardly partaking of the visible elements of this sacrament do then inwardly by faith, really and indeed, yet not carnally and corporally, but spiritually receive and feed upon Christ crucified, and all the benefits of His death, the body and blood of Christ . . . really but spiritually present to the faith of believers. . . ."

**Do Presbyterians believe that baptism is necessary to salvation?**

No. They accept this rite, ordinarily performed by sprinkling water on the person, as a holy sign or seal of the Covenant of Grace—an outward symbol of inward regeneration. While baptism is urgently recommended in the Presbyterian Church, and while its omission is regarded as a grave fault, it is not held to be necessary for salvation. The Confession of Faith declares: "Grace and salvation are not so inseparably annexed unto it that no person can be regenerated or saved without it."

## Do Presbyterians baptize children?

Yes—to signify that they, too, are received as members of the Church and are in union with Christ. When these children have reached the age of discretion, they will assume the obligation taken on their behalf by their parents. Presbyterians do not believe that children, dying without baptism, are excluded from the bliss of heaven or the vision of God.

## Do Presbyterians believe that Jesus Christ is the Son of God?

Yes. This belief is central in Presbyterian doctrine, which teaches that Jesus Christ, the Eternal Son of God, for us and for our salvation became man. Therefore, He is true God and true man: at once the Revealer of God and the Savior of men.

## Do Presbyterians believe in the Trinity?

Yes. The Trinity is frequently invoked in worship, at every baptism, and in the benediction at the close of each service. When God is spoken of as three Persons—Father, Son and Holy Spirit—Presbyterians do not think of Him as three individuals. That is tritheism. One God reveals Himself in three manifestations.

The word "Persons" used of the Godhead is employed in the same sense as "persona." It signifies a character or a representation. Various analogies have been employed by theologians to explain this doctrine but most Presbyterians accept it by faith.

## Do Presbyterians accept the Virgin Birth?

Yes. A majority of Presbyterians, among whom this author is included, undoubtedly believe that the entrance of Jesus into our world was by a miraculous birth as related by St. Matthew and St. Luke. This doctrine is set forth in the Apostles' Creed, the Westminster Confession of Faith, and in the Doctrinal Statement of the Basis of Union of Presbyterian Churches. All Presbyterians believe in the Incarnation—that God was made flesh and came to man in Jesus Christ.

Some find a symbolic rather than a physical meaning in the accounts of the birth of Jesus. They base their views on the contention that the physical details of His birth were not taught by Paul or Jesus Himself.

Presbyterians honor and revere Mary as the Mother of our Lord. But they reject the traditions which have grown up through the centuries concerning her. These have resulted in such dogmas as the Immaculate Conception and the Assumption which, Presbyterians hold, have no foundation in the Scriptures.

### Do Presbyterians employ the confessional?

Not in the same sense as Roman Catholics or High Church Episcopalians. Believing in "the priesthood of all believers," Presbyterians make their confession directly to God—without a human intermediary.

The great increase of spiritual counseling has taught Presbyterians that confession is sometimes more searching and thoroughgoing when it is made to God in the presence of a pastor. Such confession is voluntary, never compulsory; and the confession is made to God, not the pastor.

### What do Presbyterians believe about salvation?

They believe that salvation is not earned by good works but is the gift of God. Good works are the *fruits* of salvation, evidence that we are growing in grace and in the knowledge of Christ.

Presbyterians believe that salvation is found only through a complete commitment and surrender to God as He is revealed in Christ. God pardons our sins and accepts us, not for any merit of our own, but because of our faith in the perfect obedience of Christ and His sacrificial death. Forgiveness, grace, and salvation are obtained through a direct personal relationship to God—without the mediation of ministers or priests. Presbyterians accept the New Testament witness: "For there is one God, and one mediator between God and men, the man Christ Jesus."

### Do Presbyterians believe in the Resurrection?

Yes. With a few exceptions, Presbyterians do not interpret the phrase in the Apostles' Creed, "the resurrection of the body," as meaning the *physical* body. St. Paul writes: "Flesh and blood cannot inherit the kingdom of God; neither doth corruption inherit corruption." They understand "the resurrection of the body" as a reference to the *spiritual* body, which is a medium of growth and self-expression appropriate to a spiritual world.

Presbyterians believe in the Resurrection of Jesus Christ. Our Lord's sinless body did not see corruption. It was transformed into a spiritual body. St. John in his Gospel suggests that the resurrected body of Jesus for evidential purposes retained certain physical properties.

According to the New Testament and especially St. Paul, man's body, unlike that of Jesus', will experience corruption. But the body of believers will be transformed into a spiritual body which will be the body of the resurrection. Paul writes: "It is sown a natural body, it is raised a spiritual body. There is a natural body, and there is a spiritual body" (I Corinthians 15:44).

## Do Presbyterians employ symbolism in worship?

Yes. There was a time when Presbyterian churches were largely devoid of religious symbols and noted for their austere appearance. This was due to the desire of Scottish reformers to avoid everything that might suggest the veneration of religious objects and relics. Such practices were regarded as idolatrous.

The descendants of these reformers, however, came to see that a legitimate use may be made of symbolism in worship and that holiness and beauty are not contradictory, that there is indeed a "beauty of holiness." This change of emphasis brought a return to Gothic architecture, the construction of chancels, the use of organs and choirs, and the employment of candelabra and the cross.

When a cross is used as a religious symbol in Presbyterian churches, it is the cross of the Resurrection—the empty cross—symbolizing the risen, victorious Christ. The crucifix is never employed.

## Can Presbyterians alter their Confession of Faith?

Yes. Presbyterians, believing the promise that God's Holy Spirit will lead us constantly into larger truth, have never adopted a slavish attitude toward the Westminster Confession of Faith. While ministers, ruling elders, and deacons at their ordination are required to "sincerely receive and adopt the Confession of Faith as containing the system of doctrine taught in the Holy Scriptures," the Presbyterian Church, both in Scotland and America, has constantly maintained its right to say in what sense the declarations of this Confession are to be understood.

The Presbyterian Church of the United States, the United Presbyterian Church of North America, and the Presbyterian Church in the United States of America have all from time to time amended the Confession of Faith or adopted Declaratory Statements as "permissible and legitimate interpretations" of the doctrines set forth in this Confession.

**Do Presbyterians believe in predestination?**

Presbyterians believe that God alone determines man's salvation. Salvation is not a human achievement. The wording of the Westminster Confession leads some to believe that predestination deprived man of all freedom of choice—that his fate was "sealed" at birth. But the Declaratory Statement adopted by the Presbyterian Church in the United States in 1903 states: "Men are fully responsible for their treatment of God's gracious offer (of salvation) and . . . no man is hindered from accepting it and . . . no man is condemned except on the ground of his sin."

**Do Presbyterians permit divorced persons to remarry?**

Yes, but with important safeguards. No Presbyterian minister may remarry persons who have been divorced less than twelve months. Divorce is permitted to the innocent party on Scriptural grounds (adultery) and such innocent party may remarry. It is also permitted in case of "such willful desertion as can in no way be remedied by the Church or civil magistrate." In other circumstances if the Presbyterian minister is in doubt as to what ought to be done to avoid injustice, he can consult his Presbytery's Committee on Divorce.

Presbyterian churches are seeking to curb this widespread evil by a more careful examination of persons presenting themselves for marriage and by organizing groups of young people in "Preparation for Marriage" classes.

**Does the Presbyterian Church forbid birth control?**

The Presbyterian Church does not legislate for its people on personal moral issues. Nothing in the Church's teaching, however, can be construed as forbidding an intelligent, conservative, and unselfish employment of birth control. The commandment of God to our first parents, "Be fruitful and multiply," was given at a time when the world was underpopulated. Presbyterians do not believe this precept is relevant today when overpopulation in many areas produces hunger and famine.

### Who was the founder of Presbyterianism?

John Calvin, who broke with the Church of Rome at the age of
twenty-four, did more than any other man to set forth the principles
upon which modern Presbyterianism is built. But it is questionable
whether the term "founder" is appropriate. Calvin summoned Christians to return to a form of government which was prevalent in the first
century A.D. John Knox, during his exile from Britain, lived in Geneva
where he studied Calvin's teaching. Knox was the most powerful
single force in establishing Presbyterianism in Scotland, where it is
the dominant creed.

### Do Presbyterians believe that theirs is the only form of church government authorized by the New Testament?

No. While they find ample evidence in the Gospels and the Epistles
of their type of government, Presbyterians believe that church polity
varied from place to place and time to time.

Presbyterians, in agreement with many able New Testament scholars, believe that no Christian church today can claim exclusive
possession of a system of church government authorized by Christ.

After the second century A.D., the bishop came to be the chief
official of the Church, supplanting the authority of the elders. This
new development gave rise to an autocratic form of church government which in the Middle Ages became corrupt, making inevitable the
Protestant Reformation.

### What is the Presbyterian attitude toward education?

From the time of John Calvin, the denomination has always stressed
the importance of education for the laity as well as the ministry.

In Scotland, from John Knox to this day, the public schoolhouse
has stood beside the kirk. On the mantelpiece of many a crofter's tiny
home in the highlands of Scotland, where Presbyterianism is deeply
rooted, may be seen the pictures of a son or daughter in academic
robes. The fact that the Presbyterian Church has always put the Bible
into the hands of its people, printed in their mother tongue, has been
a powerful incentive to public education and has raised the standard
of literacy in Scotland.

### How is the Presbyterian Church governed?

The Presbyterian system of church government is itself a representative democracy. The people govern the Church through elected representatives. The layman has a prominent role in the Presbyterian Church. All property is vested in laymen—not in ministers or bishops. In the larger courts of the Church, the vote of every minister is balanced by the vote of a layman. Laymen are eligible for the highest office (moderator) in each court.

**What are the courts of the Presbyterian Church?**

There are four: the Session, with which we have already dealt; the Presbytery; the Synod; the General Assembly. Each has its own function. The Presbytery, made up of ministers and elders, has oversight of all congregations within its prescribed area. The Synod is composed of ministers and representative elders from congregations within a specified number of Presbyteries. The General Assembly is the court of final appeal. It is representative of the whole Church and is attended by delegates—ministers and elders—from all the Presbyteries. An equal number of elders and ministers are appointed as delegates to the three highest courts of Presbyterianism.

**How many Presbyterians are there throughout the world?**

Only an approximate answer can be given to this question. There is general agreement, however, that Presbyterians—in the broadest sense —number more than twenty million, constituting one of the largest and most influential Protestant groups in the world. We know that Presbyterian churches are found even behind the Iron Curtain. There are, for instance, more than two million Presbyterians in communist Hungary, six hundred thousand in Rumania, and between one-third and one-half million in Czechoslovakia. In the United States there are over four million communicant members of Presbyterian churches. The Presbyterian form of church government is strong in the Netherlands, and by far the greater part of the population of Scotland is affiliated with the Presbyterian Church.

**What role did Presbyterians play in the establishment of American democracy?**

So great was the participation of Presbyterians in the Revolutionary War that it was described in the British House of Commons as this "Presbyterian rebellion." An historian writing in the *Encyclopaedia Britannica* says: "The Presbyterians exerted a great influence in the construction of the Constitution of the United States, and the government of the Church was assimilated in no slight degree to the civil government of the country."

Presbyterians are proud of the fact that the Rev. John Witherspoon was the only clergyman who signed the Declaration of Independence. At least thirteen other signers of this historic document can be identified as Presbyterians.

Having suffered greatly from persecution in the Old World, Presbyterians had an immense fear of political and religious oppression in the New. The words of John Knox to Mary, Queens of Scots, the Roman Catholic sovereign of Scotland, were frequently quoted during the war in America: "If princes exceed their bounds, Madam, they may be resisted and even deposed."

# What Is a Protestant?

## by HENRY P. VAN DUSEN

HENRY P. VAN DUSEN, president of the faculty of Union Theological Seminary and Auburn Theological Seminary, is one of the most distinguished churchmen in America. He was president of the American Association of Theological Schools from 1942 to 1944, and is president of the Union Settlement Association, vice-president of the Foreign Missions Board of the Presbyterian Church in the U.S.A., chairman of the Study Committee of the World Council of Churches, and was for eight years chairman of the Inter-Seminary Movement. He is a member of the board of trustees of the Rockefeller Foundation, the General Education Board, Yenching University (China), Princeton University, and has been a trustee of Smith College, Vassar College, and the Millbrook School.

Mr. Van Dusen was born in Philadelphia in 1897. He is a graduate of Princeton University, the Union Theological Seminary, and Edinburgh University (Scotland), from which he received his Ph.D. He has taught religion at Union Theological Seminary for over twenty-eight years. He has received honorary degrees from Yale, Heidelberg, Edinburgh, Amherst, Oberlin, and New York University.

Mr. Van Dusen served on the World Council of Churches for fifteen years and has been a delegate to many national and international conferences on religion. He served as chairman of the Study Program of the First Assembly of the World Council of Churches in Amsterdam in 1948. He has been active in the Young Men's Christian Association for thirty years and is a member of the Board of Governors of the Council for Clinical Training of Theological Students.

He is on the editorial board of the *Presbyterian Tribune, The Ecumenical Review,* and *Christianity and Crisis.* He has written fourteen books, edited six others, and contributed to twelve more. Among his better-known works are: *In Quest of Life's Meaning, God in These Times, Reality and Religion,* and *God in Education.*

### What is Protestantism?

Protestantism is the branch of Christianity which sprang up in the sixteenth century in the attempt to recover original, authentic Christian faith and life by purging the Church of the West in that day of its worst perversions, abuses, and excesses.

*111*

## What are Protestants "protesting" against?

They are not protesting *against* anything.

The word "Protestant" comes from the Latin, and means "to profess," "to bear witness," "to declare openly," "to proclaim." Its primary meaning is positive and affirmative. Only secondarily does it mean to "protest" against wrong beliefs, false claims, and unworthy practices.

Much the same misunderstanding attaches to the word "Confession," the name which early Protestants gave to their creedal statements. It does not mean "admit" or "acknowledge" guilt; it means "a solemn declaration or affirmation of religious belief."

Thus, a Protestant is one who affirms or proclaims his faith.

## Are there any beliefs held by all Protestants?

Yes. All Protestants agree in affirming:

Faith in Jesus Christ as Lord and Savior;
The Bible as the primary source of what is true and right;
The loving concern of God for every human being;
Direct and constant fellowship between God and each believer;
God's forgiveness in response to each person's penitence and faith;
The Church as the community of followers of Christ;
The responsibility of every Christian for his faith and life (the "priesthood of all believers");
The duty to discover and do God's will in his daily work (the "divine significance of every 'calling' ");
The obligation to seek to advance the Kingdom of God in the world;
Eternal life with God in the "communion of saints."

## What are the differences between Protestantism and Roman Catholicism?

There are many. Most of them focus in two areas—the authority claimed by the Roman Catholic hierarchy and the dominant trends within the Roman Catholic Church.

The Church of Rome claims that it is the only true Christian Church and that all others, Eastern Orthodox as well as Protestant, are schismatics or heretics or both. Neither Protestants nor Orthodox can accept that claim.

No less serious as an obstacle to Protestant-Roman Catholic collaboration are the dominant trends within Romanism, especially the increasing reliance upon miracles and the elaboration of the cult of the Virgin Mary.

### Does the name "Protestant" cover all non-Roman Catholic Christians?

No. There are *three* main branches of Christianity: Roman Catholicism, Protestantism, and Eastern Orthodoxy. Eastern Orthodoxy includes some twenty independent ("autocephalous," each-with-its-own-head) Churches, each of which draws its members mostly from one nation (the Churches of Greece, Russia, Serbia, Rumania, Bulgaria, etc.). They are all closely related through a common tradition and liturgy.

The first major division within Christendom came not between Roman Catholicism and Protestantism, but between the Eastern and Western Catholic Churches in the eleventh century. The separation of Protestants from Western Catholicism came five centuries later.

In the earlier Christian centuries, a number of groups separated from the main body of Christendom (the Coptic, Syrian, Armenian, and others) and have continued as independent Christian bodies to this day.

### Are Protestants "free" to believe "anything"?

Each individual Christian, as a person endowed by God with freedom, must of course believe what he honestly thinks to be true. But every Church, whether Roman Catholic or Eastern Orthodox or Protestant, has its own standard of belief which its members are expected to affirm.

### What is the final authority for Protestants—the Bible, the Church, conscience?

Each Protestant is responsible to God for his own belief and life.

In seeking to discover and do God's will, he turns to the Bible as the principal source of both light and strength, and finds help in the church as the community of the faithful followers of Christ.

### What do Protestants mean by salvation?

Salvation is trust in Jesus Christ to free the Christian from error and sin, to assure him of God's forgiveness of his past mistakes and misdeeds, and thus to restore him to full and free fellowship with God within the community of the Church.

**What do Protestants believe about heaven and hell?**

Protestants believe that eternal life in fellowship with God is "heaven," and that permanent separation from God is "hell."

It is doubtful whether many educated Protestants today believe in "heaven" and "hell" as literal physical places; rather, they indicate the spiritual state of the soul, especially in relation to God, after death.

**Do Protestants believe in original sin?**

Most Protestants recognize that there is a powerful bent toward will-fulness and wrongdoing in every person. Some hold that this tendency is an inheritance from the ancestry of the race. Others are reluctant to call it "original sin" because of what they consider mistaken associations with the term.

**How do Protestants regard the Holy Trinity?**

All Protestants affirm that God makes Himself known in three ways: as the "Father Almighty, Maker of heaven and earth"; as Jesus Christ, His Son; and as the Holy Spirit, "the Lord and Giver of Life," the "Comforter."

**How do Protestants regard the Bible?**

Protestants revere the Bible as the inspired record of God's disclosure of Himself to man and the major guide for the Christian's faith and life.

**How do Protestants view divorce?**

All Protestants recognize divorce as a lamentable failure of marriage —as God has intended it and as those joined in marriage have pledged themselves to maintain it. Beyond that, Protestants differ as to when and under what circumstances divorce is justified.

**How do Protestants view birth control?**

Virtually all Protestants believe that sexual union is a divine provision, not only for the propagation of children but also for the deepening and sanctifying of the spiritual union of husband and wife. An increasing number of Protestants favor an intelligent and consecrated use of means to assure the number and spacing of children which will best further the divine intention for the family ("planned parenthood").

**Why are so many Protestants being converted to Roman Catholicism?**

They aren't. The most recent nation-wide survey indicates that in the last ten years, *about four times as many former Catholics have become Protestants as ex-Protestants have become Roman Catholics.*

The minister of one of the largest parishes in the East reports that about *one-fifth* of nearly 5,000 persons accepted into the membership of his church, during his twenty-five-year pastorate, have been from Catholic backgrounds. In a metropolitan diocese of the Protestant Episcopal Church, out of a total of 1,891 persons received into membership in 1952, 132 or 7 per cent were of previous Roman Catholic affiliation. In a relatively small Protestant church in a suburban area on the West Coast, among 200 new members added in the past two years, 75 were former Roman Catholics.

**What do Protestants believe about the "separation of church and state"?**

All Protestants accept the fundamental American principle, embedded in our Constitution, that no particular religion or church should be "established" or given preferred privileges.

Beyond that, there is wide divergence of view among Protestants as to the most desirable relation between church and state today. Some favor the erection of an absolute "wall of separation." Others hold that the authentic American tradition recognizes that we are a religious people, that all religious groups should be equally respected as important bulwarks of national life, and that the state should continue, as in the past, to support religion—for example, by granting tax exemption to churches and church contributions, and by providing chaplains for Congress, the Armed Forces, and other government institutions.

**What do Protestants mean by "religious tolerance"?**

"Religious tolerance" recognizes the right and duty of every citizen to worship God, or to refrain from such worship, as his conscience dictates.

**Is Protestantism as strong a shield against communism as Catholicism is?**

The best answer lies in the facts. They are impressive facts.

The countries in which communism or its twin tyranny, fascism, are the gravest threat today are, almost without exception, countries in which Protestantism has *not* been the preponderant form of Christianity—Russia and her satellites, Italy, France, Spain, Portugal, and many Latin American nations.

Even more striking is this fact: there is not a single instance where a country in which Protestantism has been the formative influence—Scandinavia, Holland, Switzerland, Great Britain, the United States —has fallen victim to communism or is seriously threatened by communism.

### Why are there so many different Protestant churches?

For three reasons:

(1) Protestantism sprang up at the Reformation, not as a single movement, but as a number of independent attempts to reform the Church of that day. There were then, and are today, four main types of Protestantism: first, Lutheran; second, Calvinist or "Reformed"; third, Anglican or Episcopalian; and a fourth type, variously called "independent" or "radical" or "free church" Protestantism. All branches of this fourth type stress each person's direct approach to God, the church as an intimate fellowship of believers, the responsibility of the laity, and the church's independence of the state. Among the Communions of this type are the Baptists, Congregationalists, Disciples of Christ, Evangelicals, Friends, Methodists, and many other groups. This type of Protestantism has become the predominant form in the United States and is rapidly becoming so throughout the world.

(2) The large number of different Protestant Communions in the United States is the result of the fact that immigrants from many European countries brought their own traditions with them and reproduced here the churches of their homelands. A good illustration was the division within American Lutheranism into German, Slovak, Norwegian, Danish, Swedish, and Finnish Lutheran churches.

(3) In almost every instance, the birth of a new Protestant Communion was due to a discovery or rediscovery of some genuine and valuable Christian insight or experience which had been neglected or lost.

The major branches of Protestantism, therefore, represent not so much opposed or competing interpretations of Christianity, as complementary emphases upon different Christian truths. The number of Protestant denominations is less an evidence of the pettiness of Protestants than it is a testimony to the greatness and manifoldness of God's disclosure of Himself to men.

**Why don't Protestants begin to get together?**

They have and are doing so more and more every day.

Sir Ernest Barker of Cambridge University wrote several years ago, "Our century has its sad features. But there is one feature in its history which is not sad. That is the gathering tide of Christian union." That "tide" began to flow a century and a half ago. It has been running with steadily accelerating pace straight through the present century. It is flowing more powerfully at this moment than at any previous time in Christian history.

**What progress is being made in church union?**

In thousands of American communities, competing local congregations have been united. Where formerly two or five separate Protestant churches struggled to maintain a precarious existence, today there is a single vigorous Church of Christ.

More significant, and much more difficult, have been the unions of great national church bodies—that is, entire denominations. In the past century, about a hundred "church unions" have taken place between different denominations in various areas of the world. Some have reunited branches of a single Communion, such as the unification of the three major branches of American Methodism to form the Methodist Church. Many have united churches of different denominational families. In 1925, the Presbyterian, Methodist, and Congregational Churches in Canada joined to form the United Church of Canada.

The most far-reaching church unions have occurred in the Orient. In South India, the Anglican, Congregational, Methodist, and Presbyterian-Reformed groups united in 1947 to constitute the Church of South India. In Japan, the Church of Christ embraces more than a score of previously separate bodies, and now includes about 75 per cent of all Protestants in Japan. In different parts of the world, Baptists, Congregationalists, Christians, Episcopalians, Methodists, Presbyterians—all the major Protestant denominations except the Lutherans—have participated in mergers.

**What is the "Ecumenical Movement"?**

"Ecumenical" means "embracing the whole world."

The Ecumenical Movement includes every aspect of the effort for larger Christian fellowship and cooperation throughout the world. It has a double objective: to extend Christianity to the farthest limits of the earth, and to unite the many Christian Churches in fellowship and cooperative action.

*Christian missions* and *Christian unity* are the two closely interrelated phases of Ecumenical Christianity.

**What is the World Council of Churches?**

It is "a fellowship of Churches which accept our Lord Jesus Christ as God and Savior." Projected in 1938, it maintained a difficult yet vigorous existence as a body "in process of formation" all through the strains of World War II. The World Council of Churches increased its membership and expanded its activities year by year, holding its member-churches on both sides of every battlefront in constant communication and living communion. It was the only international institution unbroken by the conflict. It was formally instituted at Amsterdam in 1948. It held its Second Assembly in Evanston, Illinois, in August, 1954.

The World Council is *not* an exclusively Protestant organization. Its membership is drawn from Eastern Orthodoxy as well as Protestantism. At present, it includes 163 member churches (denominations) in 48 countries on every continent. These include almost all the major Protestant Communions (exceptions: Southern Baptists and Missouri Synod Lutherans in the United States) and a number of representatives of Eastern Orthodoxy. In total memberships, the World Council accounts for about a third of all the Christians in the world.

**Are Roman Catholics and Protestants drawing closer together?**

No. It is greatly to be regretted that present tendencies are in the opposite direction. This trend is regretted not only by Protestants but by many liberal-minded Catholic theologians, priests, and laymen. This does not mean, however, that there cannot be cordial understanding and cooperation between individual Catholic bishops, priests, and laymen and their Protestant neighbors. Such collaboration exists and, in many places, is increasing.

**What is the attitude of the Roman Catholic Church toward movements for Christian unity?**

In the early years of the Christian unity development, the Vatican maintained benevolent interest. The Pope was invited to participate. In explaining the necessity for his negative reply, he expressed sympathetic good wishes. At the early Christian unity conferences, numbers of Roman Catholics were welcomed as observers; local Catholic bishops entertained the delegates and authorized prayers for the outcome of the conferences.

But as the Ecumenical Movement has grown in extent and strength, the attitude of the Vatican has appeared to cool and stiffen. At the First Assembly of the World Council of Churches at Amsterdam in 1948, visitors' seats were reserved for Catholics, and a considerable number of individual Catholics applied; but a short time before the Assembly opened, an edict from the Vatican forbade the attendance of any Catholic.

Conversations on theological questions between groups of Catholic and Protestant scholars are today possible only with explicit permission to Catholics from their local bishops.

### What are the posibilities of ultimate Roman Catholic-Protestant union?

None whatever, so long as the Vatican holds to its claim of exclusive and absolute authority and insists that other Christian churches acknowledge that claim. Indeed, the present policies of the Vatican tend to separate Roman Catholics and Protestants still further and render any *rapprochement*, within the foreseeable future, increasingly remote.

### What is the most promising pathway to Christian unity?

It is not through the acceptance by all other churches of the exclusive claims of any one of them. Rather, it is through each church recognizing that its understanding of Christian truth, while important, is partial and needs to be completed by joining with those of other Christians to constitute a larger whole. This "principle of comprehension" is accepted by the official spokesmen of almost all non-Roman Christian bodies. At one of the earliest great modern church conferences on Christian unity, at Lausanne in 1927, this principle was unanimously set forth in words which have been reaffirmed repeatedly since:

> We therefore recognize that these several elements must all . . . have an appropriate place in the order of life of a reunited Church, and that each separate Communion, recalling the abun-

dant blessing vouchsafed to its ministry in the past, should gladly bring to the common life of the united Church its own spiritual treasures.

This statement is the accepted signpost to Christian unity among Protestants.

# What Is a Quaker?

## by RICHMOND P. MILLER

AMERICAN QUAKERISM split into two groups in 1827–28 because of differences concerning evangelical and "mystical" emphases. The more "evangelical" group became the Five Years Meeting; the more "liberal" group became the Friends General Conference.

The major difference between the branches of Quakerism probably lies in the services of worship. This article describes the distinctive practices followed in the so-called liberal group, in many conservative Meetings, and in numerous independent Meetings. These practices are fairly characteristic of Friends Meetings throughout the world. But it should be noted that some Quaker groups use "the pastoral system," in which an employed pastor conducts services which resemble those of most Protestant churches (except for the Lord's Supper and the celebration of baptism). There is acknowledgment among Friends of their diversities, but all branches of Quakerism meet and work amicably—in the American Friends Service Committèe, the Friends World Committee for Consultation, and world conferences.

Richmond P. Miller, vice-president of the Philadelphia Council of Churches, has been field secretary of the Philadelphia Yearly Meeting of the Religious Society of Friends since 1939. He is vice-president of the Friends Historical Association, a fellow of the National Council on Religion in Higher Education, and member of the Study Department of the World Council of Churches.

Mr. Miller was born in Reading, Pennsylvania, in 1902. He was graduated from Swarthmore College and attended Harvard for graduate studies. He has served on the faculty of Swarthmore College and was director of Religious Interests at the George School. He has been on the board of directors of the American Friends Service Committee, and on numerous other Quaker boards. He attended the Friends World Conference at Oxford, England, to celebrate the 300th anniversary of the founding of the Quaker movement.

Mr. Miller's writings have appeared in several magazines, newspapers, and anthologies.

## What does a Quaker believe?

A Quaker is a member of the Religious Society of Friends, a worldwide fellowship of those who believe that there is "that of God in every man." Quakers hold that the worship of God is the primary purpose of the religious life. For non-Friends, this is accomplished by receiving sacraments, performing rituals, listening to sermons, reading

*121*

from the Scriptures, singing sacred music. For Friends, group worship is a fellowship of the spirit—based on silent communion without any program, yet resulting in vocal prayer, "witness," testimony or exhortation. Quakers believe that God speaks to all men and women through the still, small inner voice. This was true not only in the past. God speaks also in the present; his revelation is continuing. That is the Quaker contribution to religious experience.

**What does "Quaker" mean?**

"Quaker" was the nickname given to the followers of George Fox in seventeenth-century England when, at a magistrate's trial in Derby, they trembled at the word of God. Early Quakers called themselves "Children of the Light" and "Friends in the Truth." They might have been styled "Seekers," for they were searching for religious truth. Quakers arose as a group in the century after Martin Luther and carried the Protestant Reformation to its logical conclusion.

**Do they consider themselves Protestants?**

Quakers consider themselves a "third way" of Christians' emphasizing fundamentals differently from Roman Catholics and Protestants. Roman Catholics emphasize Church authority, the hierarchy, and an absolute creed. Protestant denominations emphasize one or another interpretation of religion as found in the Holy Bible. But the Society of Friends puts its mark on religion as a fellowship of the Spirit, a movement which can and does grow, develop, and change because it has within it the inward power of expansion. To Friends, all those who do the will of the Father are brethren of Jesus in the Spirit.

**What are the basic tenets of Quaker faith?**

The faith of a Friend is simple and rests on absolute sincerity. Quakers believe that God can be approached and experienced by the individual directly—without any intermediary priest or preacher. God is experienced through the "Inward Light," which is the spirit of "Christ Within." From this contact, God's will is determined, direction is given for all human affairs, and the power to live the abundant life is shared. This is a universal grace. "The Quakers, of all Christian bodies, have remained nearest to the teaching and example of Christ," wrote the Anglican prelate Dean William Ralph Inge. Many Friends are embarrassed when such praise is poured upon them. After all, they are human followers of the "Way of Christ," and know they are fallible and weak in performance. But Friends know what kind of Christians they *ought* to be.

### Do the Quakers have a creed?

No, not a written or spoken formal creed. They do have deep and strong beliefs. The Society never requires of its members the acceptance of any formula of belief. Friends hold that the basis of religious fellowship is an inward, personal experience. The essentials of Quaker unity are the love of God and the love of man, conceived and practiced in the spirit of Jesus Christ. George Macaulay Trevelyan put it this way: "The finer essence of George Fox's queer teaching was surely this—that Christian qualities matter much more than Christian dogmas. No church or sect had ever made that its living rule before. To maintain the Christian quality in the world of business and domestic life, and to maintain it without hypocrisy, was the great achievement of these extraordinary people."

### What is the "Inward Light"?

The "Inward Light" is not conscience. It is what Quakers call "that of God" in every man. It instructs and transforms the conscience as the true guide of life. Most often it is termed the "Inner Light" or the "Light Within." It exists in all men and women. It resembles the doctrine of the Holy Spirit. But to Quakers, it is known directly, without any mediation by any prophet or priest. For Friends, it is the source of all reality in religion, leading immediately to the experience of God.

### Do the Friends have an ordained clergy?

From the beginning, Friends have believed that everyone has the potentiality to become a minister. There is no division between clergy and laity because both ideas are eliminated. The vocation of every Friend is to be a lay minister and to practice the free ministry of all laymen. (That includes women.) Elders and overseers are appointed to serve each meeting.

Elders are given the "oversight" of the religious meetings for worship, for marriage, and for memorial services at the time of death. All meetings have a recorder who is responsible for the careful keeping of all vital statistics. Overseers look after the pastoral care of the membership. In some meetings, the gift of public ministry leads to the recording of ministers.

## How do Quakers worship?

The "Meeting for Worship" is a form of church service without ritual or an ordained minister or outward sacraments or formal program. It is held in a meetinghouse without a steeple, stained-glass windows, altar, reredos, or organ.

Friends gather at the appointed time "on the basis of silence," without prearrangement. Out of their silent waiting may flow spiritual messages, vocal prayer, Bible reading, or ministry—from anyone who feels called to participate. After about an hour of worship, the meeting is broken by everyone shaking hands with the neighbor who sits beside him, following the lead of those Friends appointed to have oversight of the meeting who sit on the benches facing the meeting.

It should be emphasized that the form of Quaker worship and ministry is not prescribed or uniform. In some parts of the United States, Meetings for Worship differ from the description given above. Where Quaker Meetings follow a programed system, they are called "Pastoral Meetings."

## What is the "Meeting for Business"?

The affairs connected with organization are discussed at a "Meeting for Business," at another time than on First-day (Sunday) morning. Pure democracy is practiced in all decisions, which are recorded in minutes written by the clerk of the meeting. There is no vote. The clerk takes down "the sense of the meeting" after full discussion has reached agreement. The local meeting is the Monthly Meeting; groups in a particular district form a Quarterly Meeting; the Yearly Meeting is the inclusive body for all meetings in a region. In the United States and Canada, there are 28 Yearly Meetings comprising over 900 Monthly Meetings.

## What is meant by the Quaker "witness"?

An essential part of the Quaker tradition is that all members bear individual and group witness to their principles by the simplicity, integrity, uprightness, and directness they exhibit in personal life and in their dealing with all peoples. The outward expression of Quaker beliefs is found in group testimonies against war, for penal reform, against capital punishment; in opposition to slavery and all forms of discrimination and segregation; in efforts for better intercultural relations, a more Christian economic and social order, intelligent treatment of the mentally ill and equality for women, and in opposition to the use of alcohol and gambling.

**Do Quakers try to convert others to their faith?**

Friends are always alert to discover those who are in unity with them and nurture them until they are accorded full membership following a written request of the applicant to become a member.

New members are called "convinced." Those whose parents are Friends acquire membership by right of birth and are called "birthright" members.

**How did the Quaker movement begin?**

A schoolboy once wrote: "The Quakers are a peculiar people invented by Oliver Cromwell. They are a quiet people, do not fight, and never answer back. My father is a Quaker. My mother is not!" This is amusing but not true.

Quakerism sprang up in England's Lake District during the turbulent seventeenth century. It spread quickly after 1652. There were several sects which protested against the religious hierarchy, the domination of the church by the state, excessive formalism in doctrine, and elaborate rituals in religious ceremonies. Friends suffered imprisonment, mob violence, loss of property, and severe persecution. (In Massachusetts, they were banished or put to death.) Yet all this only fired them into a remarkable band of "publishers of Truth." It was a heroic period similar to the days of early Christian persecution by the Romans.

The great American philosopher William James wrote: "The Quaker religion which George Fox founded is something which it is impossible to overpraise. In a day of shams, it was a religion of veracity rooted in spiritual inwardness, and a return to something more like the original gospel truth than men had ever known in England. So far as our Christian sects today are evolving, they are simply reverting in essence to the position which Fox and the early Quakers so long ago assumed."

Among Friends who have won a high place in American life are William Penn, Herbert Hoover, John Woolman, Lucretia Mott, John Greenleaf Whittier, Sen. Paul H. Douglas and Vice-President Richard M. Nixon.

### What is meant by the "plain" language?

A characteristic of early Friends which has persisted through three centuries is the "plain" language—which means refusing to use "you," the plural form, in addressing one person. (This differentiated plain people from those of noble status in the seventeenth century.) Quakers went back to Biblical Christianity and used "thee" and "thou." Friends also replaced the customary names of the months and days of the week because of their pagan origins. Even today, they use "First-day" for Sunday or "Fourth-day" for Wednesday, "First Month" for January or "Third Month" for March. Use of the plain language is now generally confined to conversations among members of the Society of Friends and in the intimate family life.

### What is the "plain" dress?

The early Friends refused to doff their hats, as a sign either of honor or respect, except in prayer to God. For both of these customs, they suffered bitter ridicule and persecution. When William Penn, whose father was an admiral, a general, and a courtier, first visited the court after his conversion to Quakerism, he advanced to meet King Charles II with his conscience dictating that he keep his hat upon his head. The King, with a smile, removed his hat. Whereupon Penn asked with surprise, "Friend Charles, wherefore dost thou uncover thyself?" "Friend Penn," King Charles replied, "it is the custom of this place for only one man to wear a hat at a time."

"Hat honor" no longer prevails; Friends today follow custom in tipping their hats. But there are still some Friends who wear hats into meeting and take them off only when they rise to pray in the presence of the Lord. In like manner, Quaker simplicity in dress and color (gray for the women and black for the men) has largely disappeared —because of the disappearance of the trimmings and foppery which separated the plain people of God from "the world's people" in the seventeenth century. Some women Friends still wear plain dresses and sugar-scoop bonnets, while their men use plain gray suits, without lapels or useless buttons, no neckties and broad-brimmed plain hats.

### Why do Quakers object to swearing in courts?

Instead of swearing to the truth, Quakers affirm that they are telling the truth. The Quaker stand against judicial oaths has caused them great trouble throughout their history. The objection to swearing an oath was once the one way to catch Quakers and persecute them legally. Objection to swearing is in conformity with Biblical injunctions to "Swear not at all" and "Above all things, my brethren, swear not." Besides, swearing to the truth implies a double standard of truth: If one tells the truth *only* when under oath, then obviously a man's word is not good unless he is under oath. Quakers believe in telling the truth at all times. Today, laws permit affirmations in court, instead of the usual oath.

### How do Quakers get married?

Friends practice a simple wedding ceremony without music or ritual, held in connection with a meeting for worship. The bride and the groom marry themselves in the presence of God. Their families and their friends are witnesses. Permission is obtained from the meeting to secure "oversight" of the marriage (called "passing meeting"). In Pennsylvania and other states, a special marriage-license form certifies to a legal marriage signed by witnesses rather than an ordained minister or official.

After the legal license has been obtained, the couple go to the meetinghouse on the appointed wedding day. The bride and groom repeat their vows to each other. The certificate of marriage is read publicly. The certificate is signed by all who witnessed the marriage. Then follows a meeting for worship. A prayer may be offered, poetry recited, or a message given suitable to the occasion. Silent waiting bathes all those present. After the meeting, there is a reception for the newly married couple.

### Do Quakers permit divorce?

Divorce is contrary to the "Discipline of Friends." Marriages are promises to love, cherish, and obey until death. Since divorce is legal, however, there *are* divorces within the Society—but not nearly as frequently as would be expected statistically. Quakers have committees on family relationships and offer marriage counsel to deal constructively with family problems and to prevent family breakdown. Marriage study, education, advice, and Friendly interest apply to the entire membership—not only to those in marital difficulties.

### What is the Quaker position on birth control?

This is a matter for the individual conscience. Friends, like other Christians, have always regarded marriage as a continuing religious sacrament, not merely a civil contract. Education for marriage and parenthood has long been a concern of Quakers, particularly as part of their stand for the equality of women and the religious basis of all family relationships.

## What do Quakers believe about sin?

For over 300 years, the Quakers have pointed to the inherent goodness in men and women, instead of emphasizing the inheritance of sin from the fall of Adam and Eve as recorded in the Bible. In this, Friends oppose the views of both Catholics and the majority of Protestants. Roman Catholics hold that it is the high calling of the Church, through its sacraments, to save its members from sin. The majority of Protestants regard sin as the fundamental fact of man's life on earth and hold that the will of God is discovered through faith, not reason.

Quakers believe that while sin is a fact in life, it is best described as existing in a universe like a checkerboard of black (sin) and white (goodness )squares. But the black squares are imposed on the basic white squares, not the reverse. There is an "ocean of light over the ocean of darkness," George Fox said. To Friends, the term "original sin" overemphasizes the power of evil. Even when he is fallen, man still belongs to God, who continues to appeal to the goodness within him.

## What then is the solution to evil in the world?

The Quakers believe that evil is destroyed by "concern." Everywhere Quakers "have a concern"—to eliminate war, to make for righteousness in economic and political life, to treat all humans as equals on the basis of freedom, to stimulate education, to bear witness to the testimonies of integrity, simplicity, sincerity in every walk of life.

One of the first committees established by the Society was called the "meeting for sufferings." One of the prayers most often used by Quakers (written by John Wilhelm Rowntree) is this: "Thou, O Christ, convince us by Thy spirit; thrill us with Thy divine passion; drown our selfishness in Thy invading love; lay on us the burden of the world's sufferings; drive us forth with the apostolic fervor of the early church. So only can our message be delivered. Speak to the children of Israel that they go forward."

## What is the attitude of Friends toward Jesus?

Quakers have a common belief in the revelation of God in Christ.

There is a variety of points of view among Friends, but there is a universal witness (a common faith) that God expressed His love historically in Jesus of Nazareth, and eternally through the Spirit of Christ. To many Friends, these are two experiences of the same reality —the historical Jesus and the risen Christ within.

## Do Quakers believe Jesus was divine?

This is a difficult question to answer categorically for all Friends. Friends refer to the "Seed," the "Light of Christ," the "Inner Guide," the "Inner Light" as the external creative power of God, expressed supremely and uniquely in the supreme gift of God to man—Jesus Christ.

## Do Quakers believe in the Virgin Birth?

The question of the Virgin Birth does not seem as important a problem for Quakers as the meaning and teaching of Christ's life on earth and His continuing power to reveal Himself at all times and to all seekers.

## Do Quakers believe in the sacraments?

For Friends, there is no necessity for any ritual to establish relationship between man and God. Friends believe in all the sacraments but only in their inward and spiritual revelation of the Divine presence. All life is sacramental. At all times, and to all men and women, God is available to those who reverently wait upon Him.

## Do Friends baptize?

No. They do believe in the baptism of the Spirit but practice no form of baptism. At birth, the infant's name is recorded on the official books of the meeting to which his parents belong.

## What about heaven, hell, and purgatory?

Quakers consider these matters for individual interpretation. *The Book of Discipline, Faith and Practice* does not deal with these theological issues. Friends do believe in life after this life and usually refer to the funeral service of a deceased member as a "Memorial Meeting for Worship."

## What about the Trinity?

Again, there is wide freedom for personal opinion. It must be remembered that Quakerism is based on a religious way of life rather than accepted dogmas. The Quaker faith is a religion of experience. Whatever is known experimentally about God, the Holy Spirit, the Christ Within becomes the True Guide. Friends tend to believe in the immanence of God rather than His transcendence.

## What about the Bible?

Friends have always believed that the Truth is found in the Bible, rather than holding that what has been written is true *because* it is in the Bible. Quakers have always been students of the Bible, placing strong emphasis on its value and use. A Quaker scholar was a member of the committee that issued the American Standard Version of the Bible, and another Quaker, a New Testament scholar, served on the group that translated the new Revised Standard Version of the Bible.

## Are all Quakers pacifists?

No. Some Quakers have given up their pacifism and gone to war. But Quakers as a group hold that nonviolent forms of peacemaking are the only ways to solve international strife. William Penn maintained that it was "not fighting but suffering" to which Friends were called. The witness for peace is one of the most universal of all Quaker testimonies.

Quakers have always been amongst the conscientious objectors to war. Oliver Cromwell asked George Fox to fight with him in 1650 and Fox wrote in his *Journal*: "I told him I knew from whence all wars arose and that I lived in the virtue of that life and power that took away the occasion of all wars." During World War I, the right of conscientious objectors was not recognized and many Friends went to jail. The present Selective Service legislation establishes the right of conscientious objectors to be assigned to civilian service of national importance in lieu of military service.

## Do the Quakers have any substitute for a creed?

Yes—the "Queries." Originally, the Queries were a set of questions designed to encourage the faithfulness of the members in their religious life. It is the practice to answer one of the Queries in meeting each month and to report on all twelve at the annual Yearly Meeting.

Typical Queries are: Do your meetings give evidence that Friends come to them with hearts and minds prepared for worship? Are love and unity maintained among you? Do you manifest a forgiving spirit and a care for the reputation of others?

What are you doing as individuals or as a meeting: To aid those in need of material help? To insure equal opportunities in social and economic life for those who suffer discrimination because of race, creed, or social class? To understand and remove the causes of war and to develop the conditions and institutions of peace? To assure freedom of speech and of religion, and equal educational opportunities for all?

Do you frequently and reverently read the Bible and other religious literature? Are you punctual in keeping promises, just in the payment of debts, and honorable in all your dealings? In all your relations with others, do you treat them as brothers and equals?

## How is Quaker influence felt?

*Service* is the Quaker word which represents for many Friends what missionary activity does for the churches. It grows out of spiritual conviction. In social service, foreign relief, reconciliation, and mediation—both at home and abroad—Quakers carry on an enormous amount of activities around the globe. Friends won the Nobel Peace Award for 1947 and enjoy consultative status in the United Nations. The eight-pointed star of the American Friends Service Committee (and the Friends Service Council of London) is known all over Europe, in Israel, India, China, Japan, Korea, and Africa.

## How large is the Quaker movement?

There are 185,431 members of the Society of Friends all over the world. There are 117,783 Friends in the United States and Canada, and 20,839 in Great Britain. Over 900 separate Monthly Meetings are located in the United States. There are 54 Yearly Meetings all over the world.

## What message do Friends offer the world today?

In 1952, the Friends commemorated their 300th anniversary as a religious movement with a World Conference at Oxford, England. There, they dedicated themselves anew to God's will and purpose and to the "Way of Jesus Christ." At the conclusion of ten days of conference, 900 Quakers from 22 countries issued this message to persons everywhere:

"The Christian faith, which we believe is the hope of our troubled world, is a revolutionary faith. It is rooted in inward experience, but, wherever it is genuine, it leads to radical changes in the ways in which men live and act. We rejoice in the movements, appearing in many parts of the world at once, which are inspired by the desire for social justice, equal rights for all races and the dignity of the individual person. These changes can neither be achieved nor prevented by war. War leads to a vicious circle of hatred, oppression, subversive movements, false propaganda, rearmament and new wars. An armaments race cannot bring peace, freedom, or security. We call upon peoples everywhere to break this vicious circle, to behave as nations with the same decency as they would behave as men and brothers, to substitute the institutions of peace for the institutions of war.

"Let us join together throughout the world to grow more food, to heal and prevent disease, to conserve and develop the resources of the good earth to the glory of God and the comfort of man's distress. These are among the tasks to which in humility for our share in the world's shame, and in faith in the power of love, we call our own Society and all men and nations everywhere."

# What Is a Seventh-day Adventist?

## by ARTHUR S. MAXWELL

ARTHUR S. MAXWELL has been editor of *Signs of the Times,* the leading journal of the Seventh-day Adventists, for over eighteen years. He is the author of over sixty books, some of which (stories for children) have been translated into fourteen languages.

Mr. Maxwell was born in London in 1896. He attended Stanborough College in England, was manager of the Stanborough Press from 1925 to 1936, and served as editor of *Present Truth.*

He is the father of two daughters and four sons, three of whom are ordained ministers in the Seventh-day Adventist Church.

Among Mr. Maxwell's writings are *The Book that Changed the World, Our Wonderful Bible, Great Prophecies for Our Time, Christ and Tomorrow,* and *The Bible Story.*

### What is a Seventh-day Adventist?

A Seventh-day Adventist is one who, having accepted Christ as his personal Savior, walks in humble obedience to the will of God as revealed in the Holy Scriptures. A Bible-loving Christian, he seeks to pattern his life according to the teachings of this book, while looking for the imminent return of his Lord. He lives under a sense of destiny, believing it his duty to warn mankind that the end of the world is at hand.

### Are Seventh-day Adventists Protestants?

Yes. Like the reformers of the sixteenth century, Seventh-day Adventists believe that every individual may have immediate access to God by prayer—without the intervention of any priest, saint, or other ecclesiastical functionary.

They believe that their Church constitutes the nucleus of a twentieth-century Reformation, a world-wide revival of New Testament Christianity.

**How do Seventh-day Adventists differ from other Protestants?**

Most noticeably in their observance of Saturday, not Sunday, as the Sabbath. But they also differ from many (but not all) Protestants in their teaching concerning the nature of man, the state of the dead, and the manner of Christ's second coming.

Seventh-day Adventists claim that they are not inventors of new doctrines but recoverers of old truths—truths long eclipsed by the infiltration of pagan traditions and superstitions into the Christian Church.

**Why do Seventh-day Adventists observe Saturday as the Sabbath?**

Because God, in the beginning, set apart the seventh day of creation week as a perpetual memorial of His creative power. Saturday is the seventh day of the week. Sunday is the *first* day of the week.

In Exodus 20:8–11, it is written, "Remember the Sabbath day, to keep it holy. Six days shalt thou labor, and do all thy work: but the seventh day is the Sabbath of the Lord thy God: in it thou shalt not do any work, thou, nor thy son, nor thy daughter, thy manservant, nor thy maidservant, nor thy cattle, nor the stranger that is within thy gates: for in six days the Lord made heaven and earth, the sea, and all that in them is, and rested the seventh day: wherefore the Lord blessed the Sabbath day, and hallowed it."

It is distinctly stated of Christ that it was His "custom" to attend the synagogue on "the Sabbath day" (Luke 4:16). And after His crucifixion, His closest disciples were so loyal to His teaching and example they would not even embalm His body on the holy seventh day. Instead, "they . . . rested the Sabbath day, according to the commandment" (Luke 23:56).

As Seventh-day Adventists have never been able to find a single text in the Bible suggesting that Christ authorized a change of the Sabbath from the seventh day of the week to the first, they say, "What else can a true Christian do but follow the clear teaching of the Word?"

**How do Seventh-day Adventists know Saturday is the seventh day?**

By the calendar. Every calendar shows Saturday as the seventh day of the week. Two unquestionable pieces of evidence confirm this: First, the fact that Orthodox Jews, from time immemorial, have observed the seventh-day Sabbath on Saturday; and, second, millions of

Christians, for many centuries, have observed Sunday because Christ *rose* on the first day of the week.

## Do Seventh-day Adventists accept the Bible literally?

Yes. They believe that the original authors were inspired by God. As the Apostle Peter said, "Holy men of God spake as they were moved by the Holy Ghost."

Seventh-day Adventists, of course, know that there have been many translations of the Bible, but hold that the original intent of the inspired authors has come down unimpaired through the centuries. Because words change in meaning with the passage of time, occasional revisions of translations are desirable, but through them all the original message is clearly discernible and "the word of the Lord endureth forever."

## What do Seventh-day Adventists teach about the beginning of the world?

They believe God created the world by divine fiat, in six literal days.

They believe that the record of creation in the first chapter of Genesis is not fable but fact. They consider that if the omnipotent Creator could make billions of suns (which the astronomers claim to have seen circling through the immensities of space), it was no great problem for Him to call this one planet into existence.

The evidence to which geologists and paleontologists point to support their theory that the earth is millions of years old is regarded by Seventh-day Adventists as substantiating the Bible story of the Flood. That global catastrophe, they hold, affords a completely satisfactory explanation of all the fossils, buried coal beds, and oil-bearing strata.

Supporting this view are such Seventh-day Adventist scientists as Prof. George McCready Price and Dr. Frank Marsh.

## How did the Seventh-day Adventist movement start?

It grew out of the world-wide discussion in the early decades of the nineteenth century concerning the second advent of Christ. At that time, many godly scholars, in many countries and of many denominations, simultaneously came to the conclusion, from their study of Bible prophecy, that the coming of Christ was near. Between 1820 and 1830, more than 300 clergymen of the Church of England, and twice that number of Nonconformists, were advocating this belief.

In America, a similar advent movement began, supported by 200 leading clergymen—including Presbyterians, Baptists, Congregational-ists, Episcopalians, and Methodists. Led by William Miller, a farmer, they stirred America with the message that Christ would come in 1844. When He failed to come, the movement melted away. One of the smaller groups decided to restudy the prophecies and search for clearer light. In doing so, they caught the vision of a world to be *warned* before Christ could come again. Penniless but full of faith, this group set out to accomplish the task. Accepting the Sabbath truth from the Seventh-day Baptists, they became the nucleus of the Seventh-day Adventist movement, which now claims over 900,000 around the globe.

## Do Seventh-day Adventists believe in the Trinity?

They do. Reverently they worship Father, Son, and Holy Spirit, "three Persons in one God." And they do so because they believe this to be the teaching of the Bible concerning God in His relation to this world and the human race.

## Do Seventh-day Adventists believe in the Virgin Birth?

Most definitely. They hold that it is one of the vital truths of the Christian faith, foretold in the Old Testament and confirmed in the New.

## Do Adventists believe in baptism?

Yes. Heeding Christ's teaching that "he that believeth and is baptized shall be saved" (Mark 16:16), they require all who would enter the Church to be baptized by immersion, the method followed by the Church of New Testament times.

## Do Adventists teach that people must obey the Ten Commandments in order to be saved?

No. Salvation is by grace alone. There is only one way of salvation. That is faith in the atoning death of Jesus Christ.

No one can "work his way" into the kingdom of God. No degree of obedience, no works of penance, no amount of money entitles any-one to any divine favor. Nevertheless, "faith without works is dead."

Keeping the commandments is the result, the evidence, of salvation. It is a matter of love, not legal duty. "If ye love me," said Jesus, "keep my commandments" (John 14:15).

**What do Adventists believe about Christ's return?**

The word "Adventist" indicates their special concern for this phase of Christian teaching. From their study of the Bible, they have become convinced not only that Christ is coming but that He is coming soon. They believe He will come personally, exactly as He went away (Acts 1:11).

Christ's second coming will climax a sequence of stupendous events —political and religious—which will involve the entire population of the globe and mark the end of the world, or age, as we know it today. In that day, when "the Lord Himself shall descend from heaven with a shout, with the voice of the Archangel and with the trump of God," the graves of all God's children will be opened, the "dead in Christ" shall rise, and all true Christians alive at that moment will be "caught up together with them in the clouds, to meet the Lord in the air" (I Thessalonians 4:16–17).

The effect of Christ's coming upon unbelievers is described, Seventh-day Adventists believe, in Revelation 6, where they are pictured as fleeing from His presence, only to be destroyed by "the brightness of his coming" (II Thessalonians 2:8).

**Do Seventh-day Adventists believe in a millennium?**

Yes. They believe that the followers of Christ who are raised, or translated, at His second coming will live and reign "with Christ a thousand years" (Revelation 20:4). However, they believe this reign will take place in heaven, not on earth, which will remain a desolated, depopulated wilderness throughout this period.

At the close of the millennium, the earth will again become a scene of great activity, with the resurrection of the wicked, the return of the righteous from heaven, the setting up of the New Jerusalem on earth and the execution of final judgment upon the unrepentant (Revelation 20).

After that, Seventh-day Adventists believe, the earth will be purified by fire and re-created at the command of Christ into the eternal home of His redeemed. "The eyes of the blind shall be opened, and the ears of the deaf shall be unstopped" (Isaiah 35:5). "And there shall be no more death, neither sorrow nor crying, neither shall there be any more pain" (Revelation 21:4). Then all sorrows will be over, and all man's brightest hopes will be realized. This will be "heaven on·earth" at last, not only for Seventh-day Adventists but for all who love the Lord Jesus Christ in sincerity.

## What makes Adventists think Christ is coming soon?

The signs of the times. Notably, certain developments among the nations and in the social, economic, and religious life of the masses— including the invention of the hydrogen bomb. As never before, a great fear grips the nations—fear of war, fear of inflation, fear of atomic annihilation. And this fear is driving men, in their search for security, to combine into massive confederacies, as foreshadowed in Bible prophecies.

This tragic situation, Seventh-day Adventists believe, was predicted by Christ Himself when, enumerating the signs of His second coming, He said, "There shall be . . . upon the earth distress of nations, with perplexity; . . . men's hearts failing them for fear, and for looking after those things which are coming on the earth: for the powers of heaven shall be shaken. And then shall they see the Son of Man coming in a cloud with power and great glory" (Luke 21:25–27).

Seventh-day Adventists believe another striking sign is the amazing multiplication of inventions that have changed man's whole way of life. This unprecedented increase of knowledge, with multitudes running to and fro, was prophesied to occur in the "time of the end" (Daniel 12:4).

Still another sign is the moral collapse so evident in social and political life today. Everybody admits that the moral underpinnings of Western civilization are giving way. And while there is still much outward show of religion, there is little inward piety or spiritual power. This too, Seventh-day Adventists believe, was forecast by the Apostle Paul to happen in "the last days" (II Timothy 3).

## Do Seventh-day Adventists set a time for Christ to come?

No. Nor have they ever done so. They accept Christ's statement, "Of that day and hour knoweth no man, no, not the angels of heaven, but my Father only" (Matthew 24:36). However, they give special force to His declaration, "When ye shall see these things come to pass, know that it is nigh, even at the doors" (Mark 13:29).

## What is the Adventist position regarding divorce?

Briefly, it is the Biblical position, enunciated by Jesus Christ when He said, "Whosoever shall put away his wife, except it be for fornication, and shall marry another, committeth adultery: and whoso marrieth her which is put away doth commit adultery" (Matthew 19:9). Seventh-day Adventists believe that this counsel is very clear and that members who knowingly depart from it should not continue in the fellowship of the Church.

**What is the attitude of Adventists toward drinking and smoking?**

No Seventh-day Adventist drinks alcoholic beverages or smokes tobacco. They accept at face value Paul's statement that man's body is the "temple of the Holy Spirit." Believing this, they refrain from all harmful indulgences which might weaken their efficiency and the sincerity of their witness, as workers for God. They are also motivated by a regard for the example that true Christians should set before others who do not acknowledge Christ, and in particular, before children and youth.

**How many Seventh-day Adventists are there?**

At the close of December, 1953, the total number of baptized members in North America was 275,733; the world total was 924,822. In addition, many thousands have accepted most of the teachings of the Church but are awaiting baptism.

**Do Seventh-day Adventists have missionaries?**

Yes—all over the world. Their foreign mission budget for 1953 was $11,947,578. Throughout the world, they employ 39,762 full-time workers—17,840 in direct evangelistic service and 21,922 in publishing, medical, and educational institutions. They issue publications in 198 languages.

Seventh-day Adventists carry on a large health and medical work alongside their evangelistic activities. They have a chain of sanitariums, hospitals, and clinics in all the principal countries of the world. Patients treated annually total some 2,000,000.

**Are Adventists interested in welfare work?**

Very much. Most churches have a Dorcas Society, active in caring for local needy and in projects of wider significance. Since the close of World War II, Seventh-day Adventists have sent overseas, to the poor and needy of 41 countries, more than 1,500 tons of clothing and 2,000 tons of food.

An unusual phase of Seventh-day Adventists' welfare work is their interest in prisoners in state penitentiaries. Wherever arrangements can be made, they visit inmates, conduct religious services, distribute literature, and generally spread the hope of the Gospel.

### Do Adventists believe in religious liberty?

They certainly do. As champions of religious liberty, they fought—and helped to defeat—the calendar reformers before the League of Nations in 1931 and later. They are opposed to all religious legislation such as "blue" laws. They are ardent supporters of the principle of separation of church and state. They publish the quarterly *Liberty* magazine, devoted exclusively to the preservation and extension of religious liberty.

### Do Adventists believe in life after death?

Yes. But they hold that life comes only from Christ, the source of life. No one, they assert, can have eternal life apart from Christ. Man by himself is mortal, subject to death. Only Christ can make him immortal. And immortality, says the Bible, will not be conferred until the resurrection at the second coming of Christ in glory.

Seventh-day Adventists hold that the ancient supposition that people go to heaven or hell immediately upon death is an infiltration of pagan mythology into Christian theology. Bible teaching on this subject, they claim, is as clear as day—that the dead are asleep until the glorious return of Jesus Christ as King of Kings and Lord of Lords. Then, but not till then, will final rewards and punishments be meted out.

# What Is a Unitarian?

## by KARL M. CHWOROWSKY

KARL M. CHWOROWSKY is minister of the First Unitarian Church of Fairfield County in Westport, Connecticut. He is a member of the United World Federalists, the Unitarian Fellowship for Social Justice, the American Christian Palestine Committee, the American Civil Liberties Union, and the American Humanist Association.

Mr. Chworowsky was born in Riga, Russia, in 1887. His father was a Lutheran minister who came to the United States to take over a church in South Dakota, and who spent forty-five years in the ministry in various places in the Middle West.

Mr. Chworowsky attended Wartburg College and Wartburg Theological Seminary, an orthodox Lutheran institution in the Iowa District. He pursued graduate studies at the University of Wisconsin. He engaged in Lutheran religious activities for many years, serving as minister in the Evangelical Synod (now part of the Evangelical and Reformed Church) in Oconto, Wisconsin, from 1918 to 1921. He taught and acted as pastor at the College of the Evangelical Synod in Elmhurst, Illinois, where he became known for his work and interest in interfaith and interracial groups.

Mr. Chworowsky joined the Unitarian church in 1935. He served the first Unitarian church in Newburgh, New York, in 1936, and for twelve years was minister of the Unitarian Church of Flatbush in Brooklyn. He has written many articles, sermons, and reviews which have been reprinted in journals throughout the world.

## What is a Unitarian?

Unitarians are decidedly individualistic in their religion; they prefer to let every Unitarian speak for himself about his faith.

In general, a Unitarian is a religious person whose ethic derives primarily from that of Jesus, who believes in one God—not the Trinity—and whose philosophy of faith and life is founded upon the principles of freedom, reason and tolerance.

Unitarians are firm believers in "the Church Universal." They believe that this church includes all men and women, of every race, color, and creed, who seek God and worship him through *service* to their fellow man.

Membership in the Church Universal depends not upon the profession of a formal creed, but simply upon the honest desire in a person's heart "to do justly, to love kindness, and to walk humbly with thy God." The only thing that can destroy such membership is, in the words of the great American Unitarian William Ellery Channing, "the death of goodness in his own breast."

## Are Unitarians Christians?

If to be "a Christian" is to profess and sincerely seek to practice the religion of Jesus, so simply and beautifully given in the Sermon on the Mount, then Unitarians are Christians. Unitarians hold that the orthodox Christian world has forgotten and forsaken the real, human Jesus of the Gospels, and has substituted a "Christ" of dogmatism, metaphysics, and pagan philosophy.

Because Unitarians refuse to acknowledge Jesus as their "Lord and God," they are excluded from the National Council of the Churches of Christ. But their monthly journal is called *The Christian Register,* and many of them today prefer to be called "liberal Christians," or simply religious Liberals. The intolerance and prejudice of many Christians make it difficult at times for Unitarians to rejoice in the name "Christian."

Unitarians worship God as earnestly and reverently as those of any other faith or church. They worship "differently" because they believe that every individual has the right to approach his God in his own way, and that every religious community has the duty of creating such patterns of worship as best serve the needs of those who worship.

## How did the name "Unitarian" arise?

The roots of the Unitarian movement go back to the early years of the Christian Church—when those who disagreed with the developing "Christology" were active under such names as Ebionites, Samosatenians, Arians, or Photinians. This early form of Unitarianism was a movement of protest against the semi-pagan caricatures of the simple monotheism of Jesus and his first simple Jewish followers.

The name "Unitarian" was first used in the sixteenth century—for certain Protestant dissenters from the dogma of the Trinity. Francis David, Faustus Socinus, and Michael Servetus, who was burned at the stake in 1553 for his "Unitarian heresy" in John Calvin's Geneva, may be said to be responsible for the birth of modern Unitarianism. In 1568, King John Sigismund, the Unitarian ruler of Transylvania (Hungary), issued the first great edict for religious freedom in his land. By 1600 there were 425 Unitarian churches in that country.

Unitarianism came to America over 125 years ago, and has become a religious movement of wide reach and deep implications.

## What do Unitarians believe about the Bible?

The Scriptures occupy a position of high esteem and affection among Unitarians. This great book of religious prose, poetry, and drama is awarded a place of honor in every Unitarian church. Unitarian services usually include a reading or a sermon from Holy Writ. Divinity students, in their preparation for the Unitarian ministry, undergo a thorough training in the Bible. But it must be remembered that the use of the Bible by Unitarians differs from that in most churches. (See below.)

## Do Unitarians believe the Bible is divinely inspired and infallible?

No. The doctrine of "revelation," of the absolute and indisputable authority of the Bible, is alien to our faith and teaching. Unitarians hold the Bible very dear, but they reserve the prerogative of critical appreciation which is intimately related to liberty of conscience. These lines from James Russell Lowell express the Unitarian attitude:

> Slowly the Bible of the race is writ,
>     And not on paper leaves or leaves of stone;
> Each age, each kindred, adds a verse to it,
>     Texts of despair or hope, of joy or moan.
> While swings the sea, while mists the mountains shroud,
>     While thunder's surges burst on cliff and cloud,
> Still at the prophets' feet the nations sit.

## Do Unitarians hold the Bible to be "the Word of God"?

Yes, provided "the Word of God" means *every* revelation of truth, every unfolding of beauty, every voice of wisdom that human experience discovers in its slow progress toward clearer understanding, freedom, and the Good Life.

## What do Unitarians believe about Jesus?

Unitarians love the person and message of the great Galilean. They consider him one of the rarest of personalities that have walked among men. Jesus is one of the greatest religious teachers, and Unitarians endorse his prophetic preaching, his moral teaching, and his spiritual insight. But Unitarians of all times have stubbornly refused to "make a god" of one who was so utterly human in all his words and deeds, and who once even protested against being called "good."

### Do Unitarians deny the divinity of Christ?

Unitarians do not believe that Jesus is either the Messiah of Jewish hope or Christian fantasy. They do not believe he is "God incarnate" or "the Second Person in the Trinity" or the final arbiter at the end of time who "shall come to judge the quick and the dead."

On the authority of reason and common sense, and on the basis of research into the Bible, Unitarians are satisfied to look upon Jesus as a great and inspired moral and spiritual teacher. They see him as one whote stature grows with the ages, and whose words and example will remain the bread of life for those who hunger after truth, justice, and righteousness.

### Do Unitarians deny the Virgin Birth?

Unitarians repudiate the dogma or doctrine of the Virgin Birth.

### What do Unitarians teach about sin?

Unitarians recognize the evil in our world and man's responsibility for much of it. They do not agree with the Christian doctrine that holds that the disobedience of Adam ("original sin") has so completely incapacitated man for anything good that only God's "grace"— operating through a church and its rites and sacraments—can save him. Because of this total depravity of man, supposedly, God sent His only-begotten son into the world, to die for sinful men in order that . . . whosoever believeth on Him may have everlasting life.

Such doctrine Unitarians find offensive, unbiblical, even immoral. It is certainly inconsistent with the nature of God or the dignity of man, whom the Eternal One created in "the image of God" to love with "an everlasting love."

Unitarians believe that man has native capacities for both good and evil. His natural tendency for good can grow—through proper environment, effective education, and honest effort. Man, in appreciation of the Good Life, can achieve the stature of "the man of God."

### Do Unitarians believe in salvation?

Unitarians believe in "salvation by character." They hold that as man develops a society where moral values and spiritual insights are treasured, man will find the road that leads to peace, justice, and brotherhood.

Man at his best is the surest proof that he needs no God-man

Savior to die for him and for the sins of the world. He needs all the help that good education, noble example, and friendly cooperation can give him. God's help is not likely to come to those who cast all their burdens on the Lord. There is practical wisdom in the saying: "God helps those that help themselves." If man is to be "saved," the image of God within man will save him—here as well as hereafter.

### Do Unitarians baptize?

While many Unitarians do practice baptism of infants and, more rarely, of adults, they prefer to look upon baptism as an act of dedication which has only symbolic meaning. It is not considered a carrier of "forgiveness of sin" or of God's "special grace" towards sinners. Unitarians are horrified to know that in some churches baptism is supposed to wash away the stain of "original sin." They find it hard to discuss with restraint the teaching which apparently consigns unbaptized infants to perdition. You can become a Unitarian without being baptized, and you can remain a good Unitarian without sharing in the rite of Holy Communion.

### Do Unitarians observe Holy Communion?

Where Communion is observed in Unitarian churches it is a symbolic rite of remembrance and fellowship. It is intended to remind the participants of the Last Supper. For Unitarians, this is a ceremony in which the sharing of bread and wine in solemn fellowship of reverent memory and devotion brings back the inspiring image of him whose life was devoted to the establishment of peace and good will on earth. We do not believe that any supernatural power or "grace" resides in this sacrament, or that its observance automatically conveys any special spiritual gift, such as the forgiveness of sin. Communion remains for Unitarians a ceremony through which "the still, small voice" of faith and hope and love speaks to us.

### Do Unitarians believe in heaven and hell?

If by heaven you mean an abode of eternal light where the "saved and redeemed" enjoy everlasting bliss, and if by hell you mean the devil's eternal darkness where the wicked suffer unending torment and punishment—then Unitarians emphatically repudiate such beliefs.

Unitarians believe that evil defeats itself and that virtue is the reward of those who obey the laws of man and God. The idea that a

God of Love and Mercy would want to consign a human being, because of wrongdoing during a relatively brief spell of mortal existence, to eternal damnation, or that God will reward the mortal doers of good with everlasting happiness, appears to most Unitarians as absurd —entirely inconsistent with any moral concept of our Deity.

As regards our notion of heaven, these lines by Edwin Markham may indicate what many Unitarians believe:

> We men of Earth have here the stuff
> Of Paradise—we have enough!
> We need no other stones to build
> The Temple of the Unfulfilled— . . .
> Here on the paths of every-day—
> Here on the common human way
> Is all the stuff the gods would take
> To build a Heaven, to mold and make
> New Edens. Ours the stuff sublime
> To build Eternity in time.

A typical Unitarian statement on hell is: "Hell is man's failure to be and live up to his best. Hell is injustice, violence, tyranny, hatred, war, and everything that fits these Satanic categories. Let us fight these evil forces here and now to help create that Paradise of which the poets speak."

### Do Unitarians believe in immortality?

Unitarian attitudes to immortality vary widely. Some Unitarians hold views which closely approach traditional Judaism and Christianity; others admit to being humble agnostics as regards "life after death" or "life everlasting." Religious Liberals sometimes hold conceptions of immortality that are sympathetic to such Eastern religions as Hinduism and Buddhism. Socrates' noble sentiments about immortality, in the *Phaedo,* have captured the imagination of many who find them emotionally satisfying.

Unitarians believe that life goes on and that its tomorrow will be determined not by the arbitrary judgment of a tyrannical God, but by our actions here and now, according to God's eternal way.

### May a Unitarian believe what he pleases?

While Unitarians believe in freedom of conscience and freedom of choice in religion, they do not follow every wind of doctrine, or accept uncritically whatever they read or hear.

To believe, in the Unitarian sense, is to arrive at conviction through mental discipline and labor of the spirit and the heart. Dr. Charles Eliot, the late Unitarian president of Harvard University, called Unitarianism "a cheerful religion." It is cheerful because it represents the individual's victory over ignorance, over superstition, over fear and uncertainty.

**Do Unitarians believe in prayer?**

Of course they do. Some Unitarians prefer to call prayer "meditation" or "aspiration." But in their prayers and meditations, Unitarians do not pray "in the name of the Father and the Son and the Holy Ghost," nor do they commonly end their prayers in the name of Jesus. On the other hand, an observer will find that Unitarians fully appreciate the mood of heart and mind that finds expression in prayer.

**What is the Unitarian position on divorce and birth control?**

Unitarians recognize no specifically theological doctrines as regards divorce and birth control. These questions are referred to the individual's conscience, intelligence, and common sense. The church is always ready to offer counsel and advice in keeping with its ethical and spiritual ideals.

**How is the Unitarian Church organized?**

In Unitarian Church organization, "the congregational polity" prevails. The local church enjoys full self-determination in all matters and jealously guards its interests as an autonomous body, especially where efforts at federation and church union are concerned.

**Do Unitarian services differ from those in other churches?**

Some forms of Unitarian worship remind you of services in other Protestant churches. *Hymns of the Spirit,* the book of worship most commonly employed in Unitarian churches, contains orders of service, responsive readings, hymns, prayers, and other devotional material (but without "Trinitarian" reference) that may be found in the traditional Protestant books of public worship. Some old hymns have been altered in order to make their meaning fit into the accepted Unitarian pattern. In one city, a Unitarian church may have the atmosphere of a Lutheran or Episcopalian or Methodist service. In another, worship is characterized by the utmost simplicity. Unitarians employ many variations of the great human-divine theme of *religion* as expressed in meditation, music, and words.

**Do Unitarians try to make converts?**

No. Unitarians do not proselytize; they do not send out missionaries. They do, quietly and effectively, let people know who they are and what they stand for. "He that hath an ear, let him hear what the Spirit saith."

**How does one become a Unitarian?**

Not by baptism or confirmation or a rite. To become a Unitarian you must (1) feel within your own heart and mind the love of freedom of conscience; (2) recognize the demands of the voice of reason, challenging you to examine the truths you would incorporate into the texture of your personal faith; (3) understand the point of view of those who disagree with you, even those who will oppose what you hold dear as your religion.

It is your own mind and heart that make you a Unitarian—not what somebody else thinks, says, or does. Thus, you will enter into fellowship with other men and women who seek to worship God through truth, beauty, and goodness.

**What role have Unitarians played in American history?**

Many Unitarian names are in "The Hall of Fame" of New York University. Here among the immortal leaders of our republic, you will find Thomas Jefferson, John and John Quincy Adams, George Bancroft, William Cullen Bryant, William Ellery Channing, Ralph Waldo Emerson, Oliver Wendell Holmes, Henry W. Longfellow, James Russell Lowell, Horace Mann, Francis Parkman. Present-day Unitarians are proud of the distinguished humanitarian work of the Unitarian Service Committee as a practical application of their principle, "Service to Fellow Man." Whether you think of public schools or the abolition of slavery, of equal rights or peace, of the just demands of labor or the rights of minority groups, of penology or public health—in all these movements to make America truly "the land of the free," Unitarian men and women have given of their best efforts, their noblest devotion, and their creative imagination.

# What Is an Agnostic?

## by BERTRAND RUSSELL

BERTRAND RUSSELL, winner of the Nobel Prize in literature, is one of the most original, incisive, and significant minds of the twentieth century. Through more than forty books, Mr. Russell has made lasting contributions to many fields: philosophy, mathematics, logic, political thought, theories of education, social problems. His Nobel Prize citation called him one who has "constantly figured as a defender of humanity and freedom of thought."

Bertrand Arthur William Russell was born in 1872 at Ravenscroft, England, in a family which has played an important role in English history since the sixteenth century. (His grandfather was twice Prime Minister.) He became the third Earl Russell in 1931, when his older brother died, but does not choose to be addressed as Lord Russell.

Bertrand Russell's first intellectual loves were mathematics (he studied Euclid when he was eleven) and philosophy. He received an M.A. from Trinity College, Cambridge, and won international attention with *The Principles of Mathematics* (1903), in which he explored the relationship between mathematics, logic, and symbols. With Alfred North Whitehead, he wrote the monumental three-volume *Principia Mathematica*.

Russell has been active in political affairs for three decades. He was a member of the Fabian Society, an early advocate of women's suffrage, and once decided to stand for Parliament. (He was turned down by the Liberal Party because he was an avowed freethinker.) A pacifist and conscientious objector, he spent four months in an English prison during the First World War—and used the time to write his admirable *Introduction to Mathematical Philosophy*.

Mr. Russell has traveled widely and made many lecture tours throughout the United States. He has taught at Harvard University, the University of Chicago, the National University in Peking (China), the University of California at Los Angeles, and the College of the City of New York—where, it will be remembered, a storm of public protest revolved around him as "an enemy of religion and morality."

The insight, power, and originality of Russell's mind are suggested by a few of the writings for which he is famed:

*The Principles of Mathematics*
*Our Knowledge of the External World*
*Why Men Fight?*
*Roads to Freedom*
*The Problems of China*
*The ABC of Relativity*
*A Free Man's Worship*
*Education and the Social Order*
*Freedom and Organization*

*Human Knowledge: Its Scope and
   Limits
Mysticism and Logic
Marriage and Morals
The Conquest of Happiness
The Scientific Outlook
A History of Western Philosophy*
Among the many honors Mr. Russell has received are the Order of Merit; the Nicholas Murray Butler Medal of Columbia University; the Sylvester Medal of the Royal Society;
the de Morgan Medal of the London Mathematical Society.

Mr. Russell's literary style, celebrated for clarity and precision, has earned him a high place among the masters of English prose. When Russell was awarded the Nobel Prize in 1950, the Swedish Academy cited him as "one of our times' most brilliant spokesmen of rationality and humanity, and a fearless champion of free speech and free thought in the West."

### Are agnostics atheists?

No. An atheist, like a Christian, holds that we *can* know whether or not there is a God. The Christian holds that we can know there is a God; the atheist, that we can know there is not. The agnostic suspends judgment, saying that there arc not sufficient grounds either for affirmation or for denial. At the same time, an agnostic may hold that the existence of God, though not impossible, is very improbable; he may even hold it so improbable that it is not worth considering in practice. In that case, he is not far removed from atheism. His attitude may be that which a careful philosopher would have toward the gods of ancient Greece. If I were asked to *prove* that Zeus and Poseidon and Hera and the rest of the Olympians do not exist, I should be at a loss to find conclusive arguments. An agnostic may think the Christian God as improbable as the Olympians; in that case, he is, for practical purposes, at one with the atheists.

### Since you deny "God's law," what authority do you accept as a guide to conduct?

An agnostic does not accept any "authority" in the sense in which religious people do. He holds that a man should think out questions of conduct for himself. Of course, he will seek to profit by the wisdom of others, but he will have to select for himself the people he is to consider wise, and he will not regard even what they say as unquestionable. He will observe that what passes as "God's law" varies from time to time. The Bible says both that a woman must not marry her deceased husband's brother, and that, in certain circumstances, she must do so. If you have the misfortune to be a childless widow with an unmarried brother-in-law, it is logically impossible for you to avoid disobeying "God's law."

**How do you know what is good and what is evil? What does an agnostic consider a sin?**

The agnostic is not quite so certain as some Christians are as to what is good and what is evil. He does not hold, as most Christians in the past held, that people who disagree with the government on abstruse points of theology ought to suffer a painful death. He is against persecution, and rather chary of moral condemnation.

As for "sin," he thinks it not a useful notion. He admits, of course, that some kinds of conduct are desirable and some undesirable, but he holds that the punishment of undesirable kinds is only to be commended when it is deterrent or reformatory, not when it is inflicted because it is thought a good thing on its own account that the wicked should suffer. It was this belief in vindictive punishment that made men accept hell. This is part of the harm done by the notion of "sin."

**Does an agnostic do whatever he pleases?**

In one sense, no; in another sense, everyone does whatever he pleases. Suppose, for example, you hate someone so much that you would like to murder him. Why do you not do so? You may reply: "Because religion tells me that murder is a sin." But as a statistical fact, agnostics are not more prone to murder than other people, in fact, rather less so. They have the same motives for abstaining from murder as other people have. Far and away the most powerful of these motives is the fear of punishment. In lawless conditions, such as a gold rush, all sorts of people will commit crimes, although in ordinary circumstances they would have been law-abiding. There is not only actual legal punishment; there is the discomfort of dreading discovery, and the loneliness of knowing that, to avoid being hated, you must wear a mask even with your closest intimates. And there is also what may be called "conscience": If you ever contemplated a murder, you would dread the horrible memory of your victim's last moments or lifeless corpse. All this, it is true, depends upon your living in a law-abiding community, but there are abundant secular reasons for creating and preserving such a community.

I said that there is another sense in which every man does as he pleases. No one but a fool indulges every impulse, but what holds a desire in check is always some other desire. A man's anti-social wishes may be restrained by a wish to please God, but they may also be restrained by a wish to please his friends, or to win the respect of his community, or to be able to contemplate himself without disgust. But if he has no such wishes, the mere abstract precepts of morality will not keep him straight.

## How does an agnostic regard the Bible?

An agnostic regards the Bible exactly as enlightened clerics regard it. He does not think that it is divinely inspired; he thinks its early history legendary, and no more exactly true than that in Homer; he thinks its moral teaching sometimes good, but sometimes very bad. For example: Samuel ordered Saul, in a war, to kill not only every man, woman, and child of the enemy, but also all the sheep and cattle. Saul, however, let the sheep and cattle live, and for this we are told to condemn him. I have never been able to admire Elisha for cursing the children who laughed at him, or to believe (what the Bible asserts) that a benevolent Deity would send two she-bears to kill the children.

## How does an agnostic regard Jesus, the Virgin Birth and the Holy Trinity?

Since an agnostic does not believe in God, he cannot think that Jesus was God. Most agnostics admire the life and moral teachings of Jesus as told in the Gospels, but not necessarily more than those of certain other men. Some would place him on a level with Buddha, some with Socrates and some with Abraham Lincoln. Nor do they think that what He said is not open to question, since they do not accept any authority as absolute.

They regard the Virgin Birth as a doctrine taken over from pagan mythology, where such births were not uncommon. (Zoroaster was said to have been born of a virgin; Ishtar, the Babylonian goddess, is called the Holy Virgin.) They cannot give credence to it, or to the doctrine of the Trinity, since neither is possible without belief in God.

## Can an agnostic be a Christian?

The word "Christian" has had various different meanings at different times. Throughout most of the centuries since the time of Christ, it has meant a person who believed in God and immortality and held that Christ was God. But Unitarians call themselves Christians, although they do not believe in the divinity of Christ, and many people nowadays use the word God in a much less precise sense than that which it used to bear. Many people who say they believe in God no longer mean a person, or a trinity of persons, but only a vague tendency or power or purpose immanent in evolution. Others, going still further, mean by "Christianity" merely a system of ethics which, since they are ignorant of history, they imagine to be characteristic of Christians only.

When, in a recent book, I said that what the world needs is "love, Christian love, or compassion," many people thought this showed some change in my views, although, in fact, I might have said the same thing at any time. If you mean by a "Christian" a man who loves his neighbor, who has wide sympathy with suffering, and who ardently desires a world freed from the cruelties and abominations which at present disfigure it, then, certainly, you will be justified in calling me a Christian. And, in this sense, I think you will find more "Christians" among agnostics than among the orthodox. But, for my part, I cannot accept such a definition. Apart from other objections to it, it seems rude to Jews, Buddhists, Mohammedans and other non-Christians, who, so far as history shows, have been at least as apt as Christians to practice the virtues which some modern Christians arrogantly claim as distinctive of their own religion.

I think also that all who called themselves Christians in an earlier time, and a great majority of those who do so at the present day, would consider that belief in God and immortality is essential to a Christian. On these grounds, I should not call myself a Christian, and I should say that an agnostic cannot be a Christian. But, if the word "Christianity" comes to be generally used to mean merely a kind of morality, then it will certainly be possible for an agnostic to be a Christian.

**Does an agnostic deny that man has a soul?**

This question has no precise meaning unless we are given a definition of the word "soul." I suppose what is meant is, roughly, something nonmaterial which persists throughout a person's life and even, for those who believe in immortality, throughout all future time. If this is what is meant, an agnostic is not likely to believe that man has a soul. But I must hasten to add that this does not mean that an agnostic must be a materialist. Many agnostics (including myself) are quite as doubtful of the body as they are of the soul, but this is a long story taking one into difficult metaphysics. Mind and matter alike, I should say, are only convenient symbols in discourse, not actually existing things.

**Does an agnostic believe in a hereafter, in heaven or hell?**

The question whether people survive death is one as to which evidence is possible. Psychical research and spiritualism are thought by many to supply such evidence. An agnostic, as such, does not take a view about survival unless he thinks that there is evidence one way or the other. For my part, I do not think there is any good reason to believe that we survive death, but I am open to conviction if adequate evidence should appear.

Heaven and hell are a different matter. Belief in hell is bound up with the belief that the vindictive punishment of sin is a good thing, quite independently of any reformative or deterrent effect that it may have. Hardly any agnostic believes this. As for heaven, there might conceivably someday be evidence of its existence through spiritualism, but most agnostics do not think that there is such evidence, and therefore do not believe in heaven.

**Are you never afraid of God's judgment in denying Him?**

Most certainly not. I also deny Zeus and Jupiter and Odin and Brahma, but this causes me no qualms. I observe that a very large portion of the human race does not believe in God and suffers no visible punishment in consequence. And if there were a God, I think it very unlikely that He would have such an uneasy vanity as to be offended by those who doubt His existence.

**How do agnostics explain the beauty and harmony of nature?**

I do not understand where this "beauty" and "harmony" are supposed to be found. Throughout the animal kingdom, animals ruthlessly prey upon each other. Most of them are either cruelly killed by other animals or slowly die of hunger. For my part, I am unable to see any very great beauty or harmony in the tapeworm. Let it not be said that this creature is sent as a punishment for our sins, for it is more prevalent among animals than among humans. I suppose the questioner is thinking of such things as the beauty of the starry heavens. But one should remember that stars every now and again explode and reduce everything in their neighborhood to a vague mist. Beauty, in any case, is subjective and exists only in the eye of the beholder.

**How do agnostics explain miracles and other revelations of God's omnipotence?**

Agnostics do not think that there is any evidence of "miracles" in the sense of happenings contrary to natural law. We know that faith healing occurs and is in no sense miraculous. At Lourdes, certain diseases can be cured and others cannot. Those that can be cured at Lourdes can probably be cured by any doctor in whom the patient has faith. As for the records of other miracles, such as Joshua commanding the sun to stand still, the agnostic dismisses them as legends and points to the fact that all religions are plentifully supplied with such legends. There is just as much miraculous evidence for the Greek gods in Homer as for the Christian God in the Bible.

**There have been base and cruel passions, which religion opposes. If you abandon religious principles, could mankind exist?**

The existence of base and cruel passions is undeniable, but I find no evidence in history that religion has opposed these passions. On the contrary, it has sanctified them, and enabled people to indulge them without remorse. Cruel persecutions have been commoner in Christendom than anywhere else. What appears to justify persecution is dogmatic belief. Kindliness and tolerance only prevail in proportion as dogmatic belief decays. In our day, a new dogmatic religion, namely, communism, has arisen. To this, as to other systems of dogma, the agnostic is opposed. The persecuting character of present-day communism is exactly like the persecuting character of Christianity in earlier centuries. In so far as Christianity has become less persecuting, this is mainly due to the work of freethinkers who have made dogmatists rather less dogmatic. If they were as dogmatic now as in former times, they would still think it right to burn heretics at the stake. The spirit of tolerance which some modern Christians regard as essentially Christian is, in fact, a product of the temper which allows doubt and is suspicious of absolute certainties. I think that anybody who surveys past history in an impartial manner will be driven to the conclusion that religion has caused more suffering than it has prevented.

**What is the meaning of life to the agnostic?**

I feel inclined to answer by another question: What is the meaning of "the meaning of life"? I suppose what is intended is some general purpose. I do not think that life in general has any purpose. It just happened. But individual human beings have purposes, and there is nothing in agnosticism to cause them to abandon these purposes. They cannot, of course, be certain of achieving the results at which they aim; but you would think ill of a soldier who refused to fight unless victory was certain. The person who needs religion to bolster up his own purposes is a timorous person, and I cannot think as well of him as of the man who takes his chances, while admitting that defeat is not impossible.

## Does not the denial of religion mean the denial of marriage and chastity?

Here again, one must reply by another question: Does the man who asks this question believe that marriage and chastity contribute to earthly happiness here below, or does he think that, while they cause misery here below, they are to be advocated as means of getting to heaven? The man who takes the latter view will no doubt expect agnosticism to lead to a decay of what he calls virtue, but he will have to admit that what he calls virtue is not what ministers to the happiness of the human race while on earth. If, on the other hand, he takes the former view, namely, that there are terrestrial arguments in favor of marriage and chastity, he must also hold that these arguments are such as should appeal to an agnostic. Agnostics, as such, have no distinctive views about sexual morality. But most of them would admit that there are valid arguments against the unbridled indulgence of sexual desires. They would derive these arguments, however, from terrestrial sources and not from supposed divine commands.

## Is not faith in reason alone a dangerous creed? Is not reason imperfect and inadequate without spiritual and moral law?

No sensible man, however agnostic, has "faith in reason alone." Reason is concerned with matters of fact, some observed, some inferred. The question whether there is a future life and the question whether there is a God concern matters of fact, and the agnostic will hold that they should be investigated in the same way as the question, "Will there be an eclipse of the moon tomorrow?" But matters of fact alone are not sufficient to determine action, since they do not tell us what ends we ought to pursue. In the realm of ends, we need something other than reason. The agnostic will find his ends in his own heart and not in an external command. Let us take an illustration: Suppose you wish to travel by train from New York to Chicago; you will use reason to discover when the trains run, and a person who thought that there was some faculty of insight or intuition enabling him to dispense with the timetable would be thought rather silly. But no timetable will tell him that it is wise to travel to Chicago. No doubt, in deciding that it is wise, he will have to take account of further matters of fact; but behind all the matters of fact, there will be the ends that he thinks fitting to pursue, and these, for an agnostic as for other men, belong to a realm which is not that of reason, though it should be in no degree contrary to it. The realm I mean is that of emotion and feeling and desire.

**Do you regard all religions as forms of superstition or dogma? Which of the existing religions do you most respect, and why?**

All the great organized religions that have dominated large populations have involved a greater or less amount of dogma, but "religion" is a word of which the meaning is not very definite. Confucianism, for instance, might be called a religion, although it involves no dogma. And in some forms of liberal Christianity, the element of dogma is reduced to a minimum.

Of the great religions of history, I prefer Buddhism, especially in its earliest forms, because it has had the smallest element of persecution.

**Communism, like agnosticism, opposes religion. Are agnostics communists?**

Communism does not oppose religion. It merely opposes the Christian religion, just as Mohammedanism does. Communism, at least in the form advocated by the Soviet government and the Communist party, is a new system of dogma of a peculiarly virulent and persecuting sort. Every genuine agnostic must therefore be opposed to it.

**Do agnostics think that science and religion are impossible to reconcile?**

The answer turns upon what is meant by "religion." If it means merely a system of ethics, it can be reconciled with science. If it means a system of dogma, regarded as unquestionably true, it is incompatible with the scientific spirit, which refuses to accept matters of fact without evidence, and also holds that complete certainty is hardly ever attainable.

**What kind of evidence could convince you that God exists?**

I think that if I heard a voice from the sky predicting all that was going to happen to me during the next twenty-four hours, including events that would have seemed highly improbable, and if all these events then proceeded to happen, I might perhaps be convinced at least of the existence of some superhuman intelligence. I can imagine other evidence of the same sort which might convince me, but so far as I know, no such evidence exists.

# Can a Scientist Believe in God?

## by WARREN WEAVER

WARREN WEAVER, scientist, mathematician, and educator, has for over twenty years been director of the Division of Natural Sciences and Agriculture of the Rockefeller Foundation and is currently chairman of the board of the American Association for the Advancement of Science.

He was born in Reedsburg, Wisconsin, in 1894 and received his Ph.D. at the University of Wisconsin, where he was chairman of the Mathematics Department. He has been awarded an honorary LL.D. from his alma mater, and a Doctor of Science degree from the University of São Paulo, Brazil.

Mr. Weaver has had a distinguished career in the government service. During World War II, he was chief of the Applied Mathematics Panel of the National Research Defense Committee of the Office of Scientific Research and Development. He has served as a member of the War Department's Research Advisory Panel and was chairman of the Naval Research Advisory Committee. He is a member of the Board of Scientific Consultants of the Sloan-Kettering Institute for Cancer Research.

Mr. Weaver has received the U.S. Medal for Merit, is an officer of the Legion of Honor, and was awarded the King's Medal for Service in the Cause of Freedom. He has edited the compilation entitled *The Scientists Speak,* and is co-author of *The Electromagnetic Field* (with Max Mason), *Elementary Mathematical Analysis,* and *The Mathematical Theory of Communication* (with Claude Shannon).

### What is science?

It is the activity whereby man gains understanding and control of nature. It is practiced professionally and intensely by a few, but practiced to some degree by every person. It proceeds by observing and experimenting, by constructing theories and testing them; by discarding the theories that do not check with the facts, and by improving good theories into better ones. It is never perfect, never absolute, never final; but it is useful and it improves.

Not every scientist would accept this definition. Almost every scientist would want to change it a little, and a few would change it a lot. But, by and large, a scientist is ready to define science. He doesn't feel the need (as he would in trying to define religion) to qualify his statement by saying, "This is *my* kind of science—this is what science means to me."

## What is religion?

Religion is a highly personal affair. I can only tell you what *I* mean by the word.

Religion, to me, has two main aspects. It is, first and foremost, a guide to conduct. Second, it is the theory of the moral meaning of our existence.

Do not be surprised that this definition of religion involves a practical aspect, which touches every act of every day, and a more "intellectual" aspect, which comes into play relatively seldom. This double answer is to be expected from a scientist, as we shall see. And scientists are precisely the kind of people who should not be surprised if these two aspects are not "consistent" with each other.

Science tries to answer the question "How?" How do cells act in the body? How do you design an airplane that will fly faster than sound? How is a molecule of insulin constructed?

Religion, by contrast, tries to answer the question "Why?" Why was man created? Why ought I tell the truth? Why must there be sorrow or pain or death?

Science attempts to analyze how things and people and animals behave; it has no concern as to whether this behavior is good or bad, is purposeful or not. But religion is precisely the quest for such answers: whether an act is right or wrong, good or bad, and why.

I realize that when theologians define religion they emphasize more abstract considerations. They would probably say that "religion is the service and adoration of God" or "a system of faith and worship"; or that religion is primarily "an apprehension, awareness, or conviction of the existence of a supreme being . . . controlling man's destiny and nature's."

## How do you define God?

Some regard God in very human terms, as a father who is kind but nevertheless subject to spells of wrath. Others assign to God a lot of other human qualities (love, anger, sympathy, knowledge, etc.) but expand these qualities beyond human possibilities (limitless love, infinite wisdom, total knowledge, etc.). Still others take a mystical attitude toward the concept of God: God is a spirit, and it is not useful or possible to describe God in any other way.

I am sure that each of these ideas has well served different persons at different times. But my own concept of God is rather different.

The difficulty I find with the three conceptions of God just summarized is not that they are vague; not that they depend upon faith rather than reason; not that they may even involve contradiction. I think that vagueness is sometimes not only inevitable but even desirable; that faith, in certain realms of experience, is more powerful than logic. And scientists accept such contradictions more readily than most people think.

My difficulty with the views of God sketched above is simply that though they bring comfort on the emotional plane, they do not seem to bring satisfaction on the intellectual plane. When I take any such idea of God and try to work with it mentally, try to clarify it or think it through, I find myself getting confused or embarrassed, using words with which I am not fundamentally content, words which cover up difficulties rather than explain them. It therefore gratifies me to use additional ways of thinking about God—ways which seem to me intellectually satisfying, and consistent with the thinking I try to do along other lines—scientific or not. Indeed, it is these additional ways which very directly relate to scientific thinking and scientific theories. Let me illustrate this.

When I am troubled or afraid, when I am deeply concerned for those I love, when I listen to the hymns which go back to the loveliest memories of my childhood, then God is to me an emotional and comforting God—a protecting Father.

When I am trying to work out a problem of right and wrong, then God is a clear and unambiguous Voice, an unfailing source of moral standard. I do not in the least understand how these things happen; but I know perfectly well, if I listen to this Voice, what is the right thing to do. I have many times been uncertain which course of action would best serve a certain practical purpose; but I cannot think of a single instance in my life when, asking what was the really *right* thing to do, the answer was not forthcoming.

These two statements cover my everyday relation with God. I do not find it helpful—or necessary—to try to analyze these statements in logical terms. They state facts of *experience*. You can no more convince me that there is no such God than you can convince me that a table or a rock is not solid—in each case the evidence is simple, direct, and uniform.

As a scientist who is familiar with the detailed explanations of the atomic structure of, say, the table and the rock, it does not surprise me, nor disturb me, that these everyday concepts of God do not offer me detailed logical explanation. God on an intellectual plane (corresponding to the theoretical plane of the physicist) is something else.

That "something else," just as a scientist would expect, is very abstract: on the intellectual level, God is, to me, the name behind a consistent set of phenomena, all of which are recognizable in terms of moral purpose and which deal with the control of man's destiny. I shall explain this in greater detail in a moment.

## Can a scientist believe in God?

Some persons think that scientists simply can't believe in God. But I think scientists have unique advantages here—for scientists are precisely the persons who believe in the unseeable, the essentially undefinable.

No scientist has ever seen an electron. No scientist soberly thinks that anyone ever could. In fact, "electron" is simply the name for a set of things that happen under certain circumstances. Yet nothing is more "real" to a scientist than an electron. Chairs and tables and rocks—these are in fact not very "real" to a scientist, if he is thinking deeply. A table, viewed with the precise tools of the atomic physicist, is a shadowy, swirling set of electric charges, these electric charges themselves being very vague and elusive. So viewed, the table completely loses its large-scale illusion of solidity.

In fact, the modern scientist has two sets of ideas about the world, which he carries in his head simultaneously. He uses the simpler set of ideas when it works, and he falls back on the more fundamental set when necessary. The simpler set of ideas deals with large-scale objects —you, me, tables, chairs, rocks, mountains. For these large-scale objects, the scientist has a workaday set of ideas about solidity, location, reality, etc. In these everyday terms, a rock is solid and real because it hurts your toe when you kick it. You know how to measure where a star is and how it is moving. These ideas are extremely useful. If a scientist got up some morning without these workaday ideas, he couldn't even succeed in getting his shoes on. Indeed, he would never figure out how to get out of bed.

But the scientist also knows that all these large-scale ideas simply *do not stand up under close examination.* When he forces his thinking down to basic levels, a wholly new and strangely abstract set of ideas comes into play. Solids are not really solid. "Real objects" are not even composed, as physicists thought a half-century ago, of sub-microscopic atoms like billiard balls.

Consider the electron, for example. For a while physicists thought it was a particle. (You mustn't really ask what "particle" means, any more than you should ask just what it means when you say God has certain human characteristics.) Then physicists realized that electrons are wave motions. (Wave motions of *what*? Well, it isn't useful to ask this question, either.) Today, physicists think of electrons as being both (or either) particles or waves.

Further, you can't pin down this electron-object, whatever it is. If you ask the electron more and more insistently "Where *are* you?" you end up with less and less information about where it is going. Or, if you demand to know more and more accurately "Where are you *going*?" you end up with less and less information about where it *is*. I am not being facetious. Modern physics simply cannot tell both where a particle is and where it is going; it can answer one or the other, but not both.

Or suppose you carry out careful measurements and consult the best theories of physics to determine what an electron is going to do next. Well, it turns out that you can only say what it is *likely* to do next. Science can predict with great definiteness on large-scale, everyday sort of phenomena; but this definiteness fades away and vanishes as you proceed down the scale of size, to individual events. If a scientist is studying just two electrons, it turns out to be completely hopeless for him even to try to keep track of which is which.

All this may seem funny or ridiculous to you. But you had better not jump to unwise conclusions. Science may move on to more advanced views of the ultimate nature of things; but there is not the slightest promise that the "improved" view can be any less abstract. Most scientists, I think, have had to come to an entirely new concept of what "explaining," "understanding," or "defining" really mean. And this holds for science no less than religion.

To "explain" something used to mean that you described a strange situation in terms of more familiar situations; you "understand" the thing which was "explained" with more familiar ideas. But if you have any mental curiosity, you are bound to say "How about the more familiar ideas? Explain *them*!" And then you run into a real dead end. For any "explanation," however useful and however comforting, finally comes to rest on the *unfamiliar*—because when you get to the bottom step of an explaining process there simply are no terms which you can use to become "familiar" with the bottom step.

Let's take stock of where we are. I am trying to explain whether or not a scientist can believe in God. To do this, I am trying to explain the way scientists think. And we find that a scientist is, by his training, specially prepared to think about things in two ways: the everyday way, and a second way which is a deep, logical, restless, and detailed way. In this second way of thinking, the scientist is forced to live with very abstract ideas. He has come to feel their value and their inevitability. He has developed skepticism concerning easy answers or the "obvious" nature of events. He is the last to expect that an "ultimate explanation" is going to involve familiar ideas. He is convinced, moreover, that reality is not simply denseness or visibility, hardness or solidity. To the scientist, the real is simply what is *universally experienced*.

Does this sound abstract and difficult? Of course it does: The scientist knows that when he is pushed back to a point at which his thinking should begin, he is forced to deal with difficult abstractions. A scientist is just the one who should not say that an abstract concept of God results in an "unreal" God. For the scientist knows that the everyday reality of the table and the rock is an illusion, and that reality is in fact a very subtle, evasive, and somewhat abstract business.

A scientist does not accept ideas just because they are abstract or unreal. He raises a very basic question: "Does this definition *work* successfully?" "Electron" is only the name behind a set of phenomena, but essentially all physicists agree as to what these electron-phenomena are; and there is a high degree of agreement on the rules which govern electron-phenomena. If there is this kind of consistency, then a definition "works"—and the scientist finds it acceptable and satisfying.

Man has not attained the same universal agreement, or consistent explanations, for what can be called God-phenomena. Yet I accept the idea of God for three reasons: First, in the total history of man there has been a most impressive amount of general agreement about the existence (if not the details) of "God." This agreement is not so logically precise as the agreements about electrons; but far, far more people believe and have believed in God than believe or have ever believed in electrons.

Second, I know I cannot think through the realm of religious experience as satisfactorily as I can think through certain smaller and less important problems. The nuclear physicist today only has incomplete and contradictory theories. But the theories work pretty well, and represent the best knowledge we have on a very important subject.

Third, I accept two sets of ideas of God—the everyday concept of an emotional and intuitive God, and the intellectual concept of an abstract God—for the very solid reason that I find both of them personally satisfying. It does not at all worry me that these are two rather different sets of ideas: if an electron can be two wholly inconsistent things, it is a little narrow to expect so much less of God.

## Can a scientist believe the Bible?

I think that God has revealed Himself to many at many times and in many places. I think, indeed, that he keeps continuously revealing Himself to man today. Every new discovery of science is a further "revelation" of the order which God has built into His universe.

I believe that the Bible is the purest revelation we have of the nature and goodness of God. It seems to me natural, indeed inevitable, that the human record of divine truth should exhibit a little human frailty along with much divine truth. It seems to me quite unnecessary to be disturbed over minor eccentricities in the record.

There are, of course, sincere and earnest persons who find it necessary to place a literal interpretation on every word in the Bible, and who accept every statement as divinely revealed truth. This attitude seems to me to lead to both spiritual and intellectual poverty.

The reports of miraculous happenings in Biblical times seem to me more reasonably understandable as poetic exaggeration, as ancient interpretations of events which we would not consider miraculous today, or as concessions (on the part of Christian writers) to the problem of competing with the magical claims of other religions.

## Can a scientist believe in miracles?

Put a kettle of water on the stove. What happens? Does the water get hot and boil, or does it freeze? The nineteenth-century scientist would have considered it ridiculous to ask this question. But scientists today, aware of the peculiarities of modern physical theories, would say, "In the overwhelming proportion of the cases, the water will get hot and boil. But in one of a vast number of trials, it is to be expected that the water will *freeze* rather than boil."

Modern science recognizes the exceedingly rare possibility of happenings—like water freezing on a hot stove, or like a brick spontaneously moving upward several feet—which so contradict the usual order of events that they can be called "miracles." No one can logically hold that science rules out "miracles" as impossible.

If my religious faith required miracles, my scientific knowledge would not necessarily deny them. But my religious faith does not at all rest on the validity of ancient miracles. To me, God gains in dignity and power through manifestations of His reason and order, not through exhibitions of caprice.

**Can a scientist believe in "life after death"?**

Scientists are very heavily (but not exclusively, as some claim) influenced by evidence: If there is good evidence for a statement, they accept or believe the statement; if there is good evidence *against,* they reject. If it seems impossible to produce any evidence—either for or against a statement—then scientists tend to consider such statements as unprofitable matters of inquiry.

So far as I am concerned, "life after death" is a matter in which I can neither believe nor disbelieve. To date, at least, I have been too much interested in this life to feel any urge to indulge in pure speculation about another.

# Sixty-four Million Americans Do Not Go to Church:
# What Do They Believe?

## by JEROME NATHANSON

JEROME NATHANSON, chairman of the Board of Leaders of the New York Society for Ethical Culture, is director of the John L. Elliott Institute for Adult Education, a director of the American Ethical Union, a member of the board of trustees of the National Child Labor Committee, and a member of the board of directors of the International Humanist and Ethical Union.

Mr. Nathanson was born in Chicago in 1908. He was graduated from Cornell University and worked on the Yonkers *Herald* for several years. He received an M.A. at Columbia University and joined the staff of the New York Society for Ethical Culture in 1937. He was chairman of the National Committee on Federal Aid to Public Education from 1949 to 1952, and served as chairman of the Conference on the Scientific Spirit and the Democratic Faith from 1944 to 1947. He is a member of Phi Beta Kappa, the American Association of Arbitrators, and the American Philosophical Association.

Mr. Nathanson is the author of *John Dewey: The Reconstruction of the Democratic Life,* and *Forerunners of Freedom.* A contributor to various journals, he has also edited two books: *Science for Democracy* and *The Authoritarian Attempt to Capture Education.*

If anyone were to ask you how many Americans belong to a church or temple or synagogue, you would probably say, "Almost all." But the facts are startling. Actually, 64,000,000 Americans—40.5 per cent of the population—are not even *claimed* as church members. This figure is all the more remarkable if we remember that some denominations count as members not simply those who go to church but anyone who was baptized or who ever belonged to the group and subsequently left.

Why are so many Americans members of no church? Has religion failed them?

There is no simple answer. Many of those who do not belong to any church have taken the hard rather than the easy road, for they have withstood great pressure in order to stay out of groups it is so easy to join, and for which high approval from neighbors and community is given.

We all know that many people join a church out of habit, or out of respect for their parents, or for family tradition. Some do so in order to wear the badge of respectability, or get a testimonial to good character. Businessmen and professional men often prize the "contacts" they make in a church or a temple; their careers are helped if they conform to the community's values. Some parents want their children to have a religious education, even though they themselves feel no strong need for a formal faith. Other parents want their children to "belong," to do what others in the group do, to associate with the "right" people, to make a good marriage with a decent and moral spouse. In addition, in these terrible days of anxiety and fear—with war and annihilation hanging over our heads—millions upon millions, not knowing where to turn or whom to trust, attend religious services which promise inner peace, salvation, and life eternal. It is small wonder that ours is a day of a great religious revival.

The great majority of church-goers are undoubtedly sincere and devout; they believe in God, in morality, in the specific articles of their church's creed. But in the light of the variety of motives which lead people into church membership, we can see how many and how varied are the pressures which are brought to bear on those who do not join any church. Why, then, do so many millions stay away from our churches and the solace they offer, the hope they proffer? Is it because they are "bad" people? Surely not.

Many stay away from a church because of the denominational rivalries and bickering. Some dislike formal, elaborate rituals. And some (though they do not know it) follow the example of the noblest man our land has produced, Abraham Lincoln, who made this startling and little-known statement of his faith when he declared that he had never united himself to any church because he found difficulty in giving his assent, without mental reservations, to the long complicated statements of Christian doctrine which characterize their articles of belief and confessions of faith. "When any church will inscribe over its altar as its sole qualifications for membership the Savior's condensed statement of the substance of both the law and the gospel, 'Thou shalt love the Lord thy God with all thy heart, and with all thy soul, and with all thy strength, and with all thy mind; and thy neighbor as thyself'—that church will I join with all my heart and all my soul." *

Now the Americans who do not go to church are not without faith; nor is it true that life has neither meaning nor purpose for them. As Tennyson says:

> "There lives more faith in honest doubt,
> Believe me, than in half the creeds."

For some have a faith that resists conformity, that impels a man to face the problems of life and death and God and the hereafter for himself, that considers creeds or rituals an unnecessary part of true religious affirmation. Such a faith means a code of honor and decency and—above all—humane relations with other human beings. In one sense, the faith that finds belief and conduct enough—without church affiliation—is a logical development of the Protestant tradition. For deep in Protestantism is the powerful idea that there need be no intermediary between a man and God—no preacher or priest or rabbi, no liturgy, no ceremonials, no public demonstration of faith. Many of the 64,000,000 Americans who do not go to church would probably agree with John Lovejoy Elliott, who declared: "I have known many good men who believed in God. I have known many good men who did not believe in God. But I have never known a human being who was good who did not believe in man."

We must realize that the overwhelming majority of our 64,000,000 are not *anti*-religious. To be sure, some of them profess atheism openly —but they are a very small fraction of the total. And some are agnostics—those who say they simply do not *know* whether there is or is not a God, or a heaven and hell, or a life hereafter. They hold that to go to church without real conviction and unquestioning faith is hypocritical, a profanation of the religious idea. They may even quote Holy Scripture to support their stand: "Lord, I believe; help thou mine unbelief" (St. Mark, 9:24). And some follow the ringing words of Thomas Jefferson: "Fix reason firmly in her seat, and call to her tribunal every fact, every opinion. Question with boldness even the existence of a God; because, if there be one, he must more approve of the homage of reason, than that of blindfolded fear. . . . Your own reason is the only oracle given you by heaven, and you are answerable, not for the rightness, but uprightness of the decision."

* Deming, Henry Champion, *Eulogy of Abraham Lincoln.* (Hartford: A. N. Clark, 1865.)

For, strange though it may seem, most of the millions who do not go to church *are* religious. Many have a profound faith in God; they simply do not believe that any existing organized religion is a satisfactory expression of God's will. They cannot overlook the many differing conceptions of God—from Christianity to Buddhism and the other great religions of the East. The monotheism of Jews is not the same as the Trinitarian conception of Christians. The Protestant conception of man's relation to God is so different from the Catholic that it was one of Luther's chief reasons for revolting from Rome. Baptist conceptions of faith and worship differ as much from Episcopalian as Lutherans differ from Mormons.

For there are surely many conceptions of God: Matthew Arnold thought of God as the Power-not-ourselves which makes for good; William James believed in a limited but growing God, who needs our help in making the good more prevalent; Henri Bergson spoke of the creative force which expresses itself in the evolutionary process. Some scientists speak of a "cosmic consciousness" which gives meaning to existence. Some philosophers believe in an absolute moral law, embedded in the very structure of the universe. But how many of these conceptions are organized into a formal church with a rigid ritual and set ideas about sin or salvation?

We should remember that many people hold fast to a faith about which, intellectually, they are a little uneasy. Two six-year-olds were recently engaged in an earnest discussion of death. "When my mother dies," said the first, "she will go to heaven, and when I die I'll see her there."

"I don't think so," the other remarked.

"Oh, yes, I will. When I die an angel will come down to me. And when the angel brushes my cheek with its wing, then I'll go to heaven and see my mother."

"Do you *really* think that?" the second boy asked.

"Well, I don't really *think* it," came the rejoinder, "but I believe it."

Do the 64,000,000 Americans who refuse to "believe" in this way have anything in common—except the fact that they do not go to church? Yes. They share an important attitude—the idea that it is possible to be "religious," moral, decent, without joining a group and worshiping *en masse*. They believe the individual can get as close to the idea of God as any cleric or institution can bring him. They hold the high faith that men are responsible for what they do with their lives, how they think and live. They do not feel the need for "official" forgiveness or rituals or catechisms to make them men of virtue. They try to lead a life which is honorable, productive, satisfying, right, good —for *them.* (It may or may not be right or good for someone else.) A good life, to their minds, does not depend upon church attendance. They believe, as did some of the greatest men the human race has produced, that personal morality is not dependent on organized religion.

Is it bad for our country that so many Americans hold this independent attitude? The Founding Fathers did not think so: they created the First Amendment to the Constitution for the specific purpose of letting each man have the right to his own form of worship—or his own independence from religious groups.

The very richness and creativity of American life rests on the fact that people can and do think different thoughts, hold different beliefs, live in different ways. James Madison, "the Father of the Constitution," went so far as to say: "The best and only security for religious liberty in any society is a multiplicity of sects. Where there is such a variety of sects, there cannot be a majority of any one sect to oppress and persecute the rest."

Democracy means that people respect the rights of others, including *the right to be different*. Only dictatorships want everybody to think, feel, and act the same.

Are "bad" lives—immorality, crimes, anti-social conduct—greater among those who do not go to church than among church members? Not at all. Two social scientists, May and Hartshorne, in their *Studies in Deceit,* found a surprisingly high percentage of "dishonesty" among Sunday School graduates. The research of Negley K. Teeters and other sociologists has demonstrated that criminals are not found more often among non-churchgoers. The majority of Americans are identified with one church or another. The majority of criminals are identified with a church. It would be absurd to conclude that churches are responsible for delinquency and crime. But it is equally false to conclude that the failure to attend church is responsible. The facts do not support this.

Some people feel guilty because they do not belong to a church. Is there any reason for this? Of course there is. As children, they were taught to hold certain beliefs; but as they grew up they found that they no longer believed these things. This did not happen because they *wanted* to disbelieve or because they were "bad" people. It happened because their experiences and development and intelligence led them to question or doubt their earlier beliefs. Often they long for the sense of security they got from their childhood faith. Often they would *like* to believe again what they once accepted. But they cannot honestly do so, and they feel uneasy about "betraying" the good people who taught them what a good life means.

Yet they have done nothing wrong. On the contrary, they refuse to give lip service to what they do not really believe. They have the courage to stand up for their own faith. They honor their own convictions and try to maintain their own integrity. Just so did the Hebrew prophets speak to the people of Israel. Just so did Socrates defy the Athenians in his search for truth. Just so did Jesus assail all those who would sacrifice the spirit of love for the letter of the law.

No, the nonconformist need not feel guilty. He is following some of the greatest visions of the human spirit—to seek dignity without dogma.

Now when moral and religious questions are discussed in our country, we refer to the position of Catholics, Protestants, and Jews. That takes care of "the religious groups." The 64,000,000 Americans who are not members of a church or temple or synagogue are dismissed as of little importance. They live as individuals and are not united into any one group; *no one* speaks for them.

We must remember that when the "three faiths" have expressed themselves, we have *not* canvassed all sides of religious and moral questions. The real concern with living a good life represents the ground for unity between those who go to church and those who do not. This unity will not be achieved through discussions of theory or theology. It will be achieved through common *action* in behalf of common goals. Despite differences about the meaning of religion, all of us have a common stake in improving the health and education of our people, in developing the fullest talents of our children and youth, in lessening discrimination, in advancing welfare and security, in forwarding democracy, in striving for world peace and world unity.

Beyond this, there is an ancient vision which can be revived for our common benefit. For however each of us may make his peace with the universe, our faith in *man* expresses the vision of the human-ness, the humaneness, the humanity of man. It is the vision which speaks in the following prayer:

May I be no man's enemy, and may I be the friend of that which is eternal and abides. . . . May I never devise evil against any man; if any devise evil against me, may I escape . . . without the need of hurting him. May I love, seek, and attain only that which is good. May I wish for all men's happiness and envy none. . . . When I have done or said what is wrong, may I never wait for the rebuke of others, but always rebuke myself until I make amends. . . . May I win no victory that harms either me or my opponent. . . . May I reconcile friends who are wroth with one another. May I, to the extent of my power, give all needful help . . . to all who are in want. May I never fail a friend in danger. . . . May I respect myself. . . . May I always keep tame that which rages within me. . . . May I never discuss who is wicked and what wicked things he has done, but know good men and follow in their footsteps.

No, this is not the prayer of a Catholic priest, a Protestant minister, a Jewish rabbi, a Quaker teacher. These words are those of Eusebius, a "pagan" who lived some two thousand years ago.* In these words is the voice of man's best hope on earth.

* Quoted by Gilbert Murray, *Five Stages of Greek Religion* (1946), pp. 197–198, G. Watts & Co. (London).

# PART TWO

# FACTS AND FIGURES ON RELIGION IN THE UNITED STATES

# Doctrines and Beliefs

## 1. What Catholics, Jews, and Protestants Believe: A Comparison Chart *

### By STANLEY I. STUBER

Reprinted by permission from the February, 1954, issue of the *International Journal of Religious Education*. Reprints of this chart are available from the National Council of Churches, 79 E. Adams Street, Chicago 3, Illinois.

### GOD

**Protestants**

God is one; manifested as Father, Son and Holy Spirit. Protestants believe in a much more individual and direct approach to God than do Roman Catholics. More stress is placed on the love of God, as revealed in Christ, than in a God of law and justice.

**Roman Catholics**

Supreme Being, infinitely perfect, who made all things and keeps them in existence. God is the only one God, but has three divine Persons—Father, Son, and Holy Ghost. Revealed through Jesus Christ, the Son of God, who teaches through the Catholic Church.

**Jews**

One God, personal and universal, whose ways are beyond understanding, yet whose reality gives purpose to man and to the world. No one can serve as an intermediary between God and man.

### CHRIST

**Protestants**

Accept Christ as divine Son of God. Believe in direct, personal relationship, rather than through Church institutionalism, including Virgin Mary. He is elder brother, moral leader, as well as Messiah and Savior.

**Roman Catholics**

Christ is God made man. Born of the Virgin Mary, incarnation of God, atonement for sin, bodily resurrection. Second Person of Trinity. Both man and God. Salvation through his sacrifice on the Cross, manifested in the Mass.

**Jews**

Many accept Jesus as a child of God, as a Jew, and as a prophet or inspired teacher, with no supernatural powers. They do not accept the Divinity and Atonement of Christ.

### ONE TRUE RELIGION

**Protestants**

Protestantism has never claimed to be the one and only true religion; but that Christ is the only true way to salvation—not the Church. Recognize Roman Catholics and members of the Eastern Orthodox churches as Christians. Desire the same recognition from others.

**Roman Catholics**

"We know that the Catholic Church is the one true Church established by Christ because it alone has the marks of the true Church." (One, holy, universal, apostolic.) "We know that no other church but the Catholic Church is the true Church of Christ because no other church has these four marks." (*Catechism of Christian Doctrine*)

* The statements listed here are drawn by the author from authentic sources within the faiths concerned, and represent the analysis of each faith by authorities within that faith, not the opinion of one about the others.

## Jews

Jews do not claim that their religion alone is the true one. They are content that others have their own faith, as long as it has elements of decency, kindliness, justice, and integrity. However, Jews regard *Judaism* as the only religion for Jews.

## CHURCH

**Protestants**

Protestants believe that the Church belongs to all true Christians, and is a community of forgiven sinners. Christ the only head. Voluntary attendance and financial support. Make a difference between Kingdom of God and the Church as an institution.

**Roman Catholics**

Christ founded the Roman Catholic Church. It is the Body of Christ. The congregation of all baptized persons united in the same faith, sacrifice, sacraments, pope and bishops. Peter the first pope. Chief attributes of the Church: authority, infallibility, indefectibility. Saving institution represented in papacy and priesthood.

**Jews**

Jews are permitted to attend Christian churches as visitors, not as worshipers. They have their own synagogues and temples. These are self-governing. Most Jews will join interfaith services when Bible readings, prayers, hymns are acceptable to all concerned.

## CHURCH MEMBERSHIP

**Protestants**

No one is automatically born into the Protestant faith. Baptism the usual way to membership. Both infant and adult baptism practiced. Infant baptism followed by confirmation. Stress is placed upon active, not formal, membership.

**Roman Catholics**

Baptism is the gateway to the Church. Each remains a member (from infancy) so long as he professes the "one true faith"; does not withdraw through schism or heresy, or is not excommunicated.

**Jews**

Jews are born into Judaism. Converts accepted upon commitment to faith. (Circumcision the outward sign for males.) Confirmation personal recognition of membership.

## BIBLE

**Protestants**

Accept Old and New Testaments as inspired, but not *Aprocrypha*. Individual right of interpretation. Final authority for faith and life.

**Roman Catholics**

Inspired Word of God. Interpreted by the Church, which preceded it. 72 books, including *Apocrypha*. Not sufficient guide; tradition of Church added.

**Jews**

Accept the Old Testament, but not the *Apocrypha* or New Testament. First five books of Moses, called *Torah*, are considered basic to the faith. Wide range of interpretation.

## SACRAMENTS

**Protestants**

Two: Baptism and the Lord's Supper. Wide variation of meaning, from a saving sacrament to mere symbol. Protestants are not "sacramentalists."

**Roman Catholics**

Seven: Baptism, Confirmation, Holy Eucharist, Penance, Extreme Unction, Holy Orders, Matrimony. All instituted by Christ and all give grace.

**Jews**

No sacraments, but many rites and ceremonies such as circumcision, Bar Mitzvah, confirmation. Reject all imagery.

## PRAYER

**Protestants**

Honor is paid to saints, but prayers never directed to them. Emphasis placed upon direct approach to God through prayer. No beads or rosary used. Informal, individual prayers encouraged. Worship must be in spirit and in truth.

**Roman Catholics**

Largely formal prayers not only for themselves personally, but for others (such as those in purgatory). Prayers through Virgin Mary and saints. Use of the rosary as aid to prayer. Not all prayers answered.

**Jews**

Great stress placed upon prayer: petitions, adoration, confession of sin, expression of joyful fellowship, thanksgiving. Found both in daily personal devotions and in public worship.

## SIN

**Protestants**

Original sin through Adam usually accepted, and plan of salvation through Christ's death on the Cross. All in need of redemption. But salvation comes through Christ and not Church; forgiveness comes from Christ and not through priest.

**Roman Catholics**

Original sin due to Adam's "fall." Baptism removes this, but sins after baptism must be removed through penance and absolution of the priest. Sins are carefully catalogued, along with penalties.

**Jews**

Recognize two kinds of sin: against man; against God. Must seek forgiveness of the first from those sinned against. Sin against God expiated by "a return to God."

## HEAVEN and HELL

**Protestants**

Believe in both heaven and hell, but not purgatory. Wide differences in interpretation. General belief in some form of punishment for sin, and eternal reward for righteousness.

**Roman Catholics**

Accept literal heaven and hell, plus temporal place of punishment known as purgatory.

**Jews**

Most Jews no longer accept any literal conception of heaven and hell. More concerned with leading a good life in this world, rather than reward or punishment in the next (which they do not reject).

## EVANGELISM

**Protestants**

A basic principle and practice with Protestants, linked closely to church extension, world missions, and salvation.

**Roman Catholics**

Mostly conducted by the priesthood, although laity now being encouraged to be evangelists and win converts.

**Jews**

Not a proselytizing religion, although sincere converts are welcomed.

## CONFESSION

**Protestants**

Confession of sins directed to Christ. He alone has power of forgiveness (along with God). Counseling services of pastors now encouraged, but no absolution.

**Roman Catholics**

All must go to confession. Confession tied directly to penance and power of priest to forgive sins.

**Jews**

Confess sins directly to God. Have no intermediary. Day of Atonement on collective as well as individual basis. Personal confession also before marriage and just prior to death.

## MARRIAGE

**Protestants**

While secular (civil) marriage contract is recognized, the sacredness of the marriage bond is stressed. Love basis of marriage. Beautiful ceremony either at home or church the usual practice.

**Roman Catholics**

A sacrament binding a baptized man and a baptized woman for life. Parties actually perform ceremony, conferring on each other the sacrament.

**Jews**

Marriage much more than a personal matter; part of entire Jewish community. Usually elaborate marriage rites and symbols.

## DIVORCE

**Protestants**

Divorce is allowed under certain conditions such as adultery and wilful desertion, but is held as a last resort. Will remarry the innocent party.

**Roman Catholics**

Not allowed. Separation permitted. Annulment, when there has been "no true marriage," is sometimes granted.

## Jews
Divorce is permitted when living together is intolerable. Emphasis on reconciliation and better understanding.

## BIRTH CONTROL

### Protestants
Not thought of as a sin. Permitted when not abused. May be employed for health purposes.

### Roman Catholics
Not permitted under any circumstances by any artificial means, and birth prevention is considered a grave sin.

### Jews
Permitted and even advocated when it is for the welfare of all concerned.

## INDIVIDUAL RESPONSIBILITY

### Protestants
Individual supreme; salvation a very personal matter. Priesthood of all believers stressed. Nothing can be substituted for personal responsibility.

### Roman Catholics
Roman Catholicism stresses individual responsibility for sin and salvation, but power is placed in Church and priesthood —not in the individual.

### Jews
All Jews completely free as individuals. Rabbis have no authority over individuals. No religious hierarchy.

## SOCIAL RESPONSIBILITY

### Protestants
While salvation is thought of as an individual affair, Protestants have always applied their faith in good works to all areas of life. Have responsibility to community. Along with missions goes the desire to build as much of the Kingdom of God into the world as possible.

### Roman Catholics
Parents responsible for well-being of children. Taught to love country and obey all laws. Charity basic principle. Social teaching of Pope Leo XIII now championed by Church.

### Jews
Have a marked sense of community relationships and service. Charity basic tenet. Inspired by Old Testament prophets. Human rights, freedom, and equality paramount in Jewish practice.

## 2. Comparison of Religious Beliefs: 15 American Denominations

### Prepared by ROBINETTE NIXON and BARBARA J. KAPLAN

This summary-comparison of religious beliefs (of the fifteen denominations whose creeds have been presented in the main body of this book) is designed solely as a cross-reference aid.

The material which follows is not to be construed as representing official doctrine—except where the articles in *Look* Magazine, from which these extracts are taken, were themselves approved by a denomination. Nor does this summary attempt to include the variations in creed and practice of groups within any individual denomination.

The material has been arranged by points of creed or practice: under each point, the position of the religious groups is listed in alphabetical order.

### THE BIBLE

**Baptists.** All Baptists believe in the inspiration of the Bible, but only the extreme fundamentalists accept it literally or regard it as infallible in every detail. All Baptists accept the Bible as infallible in religious teachings and as a trustworthy record of the progressive revelation of God, climaxed by the supreme revelation of Himself in Jesus

Christ. No official dogma prescribes how an individual Baptist shall interpret the Bible.

**Catholics.** The Church is the divinely appointed custodian of the Bible and has the final word on what is meant in any specific passage. The Church guards orthodoxy (including interpretation of the Scriptures) and passes down essential Christian tradition from one generation to another.

**Christian Scientists.** Each person, of any religion, can find what is satisfying to him as the spiritual meaning in the Bible. But Christian Scientists feel that Mary Baker Eddy's book, *Science and Health with Key to the Scriptures,* offers the complete spiritual meaning of the Bible.

**Congregationalists.** The Bible reveals God in a way which will never be superseded. Christ shows that God is love; all subsequent knowledge, imparted to men by God through the Scriptures, merely elaborates this fundamental truth. Congregationalists apply methods of science to Bible study; thus, they feel they know what God is saying in the Bible better than their fathers who lived in a pre-scientific age.

**Disciples of Christ.** Disciples share the common Protestant belief that the Bible (except for the Apocryphal Books) is the inspired Word of God, written at different times under the inspiration of the Holy Spirit. Many Disciples accept the New Testament as a third and purely Christian dispensation, following the Old Testament which represents two dispensations.

Fundamentalist Disciples accept the Authorized Version of the Bible as the final and infallible word of God. The liberals believe newer translations and studies of inspired scholars have thrown new light on many passages of the Scriptures.

**Episcopalians.** The Holy Scriptures are the great source and testing ground of Christian doctrine. But the Episcopal Church does not hold to the literal inerrancy of Scripture. The Bible is considered sacred for its general inspiration, as the record of God's revelation.

**Jehovah's Witnesses.** The Bible is followed all the way, not half the way. The Hebrew and Greek Scriptures are considered entirely consistent and practical for our day.

**Jews.** Orthodox Jews accept the Bible as the revealed Will of God. Reform Jews accept as binding only the moral laws of the Bible. Conservative Jews follow the pattern of traditional Judaism but regard it as an evolving, ever-growing religion.

**Lutherans.** God's Word is recorded in the Bible, but the Word itself is a living, active thing through which the Holy Spirit stirs us to growth in understanding and obedience to God's will.

**Methodists.** Methodists look upon the Bible as a library of inspired books containing the progressive revelation of God. They believe in the "open Bible" and encourage the individual to read it for himself, leaving him free to make his own interpretation under the guidance of the Holy Spirit.

**"Mormons."** The Bible is basic to "Mormon" belief. The King James version is used officially and is believed "to be the word of God as far as it is translated correctly." (8th Article of Faith.) The Book of Mormon is a complementary work accepted by "Mormons" as scripture.

**Presbyterians.** Presbyterians believe the Scriptures of the Old and New Testaments to be the Word of God and "the only infallible rule of faith and practice," and that they are the source of those truths by which men live. They believe that God spoke through men whose minds and hearts He had touched. They therefore emphasize inspired men, not inspired words.

**Quakers.** Friends have always believed that the Truth is found in the Bible, rather than holding that what has been written is true *because* it is in the Bible.

**Seventh-day Adventists.** Seventh-day Adventists accept the Bible literally and believe that the authors were inspired by God. There have been many translations but the original intent of the authors has come down unimpaired through the centuries, the original message is clearly discernible, and "the word of the Lord endureth forever." The record of creation in the first chapter of Genesis is considered not fable but literal fact.

**Unitarians.** The doctrine of "revelation," of the absolute and indisputable authority of the Bible, is alien to Unitarian faith and teaching. Unitarians hold the Bible very dear, but they reserve the prerogative of critical appreciation.

## CREED

**Baptists.** There is no single, official creed. The nearest statement is the so-called "Grand Rapids Affirmation," adopted by the American Baptist Convention on May 23, 1946. It resolves that faith be reaffirmed in the New Testament as a divinely inspired record and therefore an all-sufficient rule of faith and practice. It also calls all

its churches to the common task of sharing the whole Gospel with the whole world.

**Catholics.** The chief articles of faith are summed up in the creeds. There are four great creeds: The Apostles', the Nicene, the Athanasian, and that of Pius IV. Equally essential to Catholic belief are the doctrines and dogmas proclaimed infallibly true by the teaching authority of the Church— e.g., the Immaculate Conception of the Blessed Virgin Mary, her assumption into heaven after death, the real presence of Jesus Christ in the Blessed Sacrament, and so forth.

**Christian Scientists.** Christian Scientists have no formal creed. They have six brief religious tenets to which all members of the Church of Christ, Scientist, subscribe. (These are found in *Science and Health with Key to the Scriptures,* by Mary Baker Eddy.)

**Congregationalists.** Each particular congregation is accustomed to write its own creed. A few churches use the Apostles' Creed.

**Disciples of Christ.** Disciples of Christ have no creed but Christ and no doctrines save those which are found in the New Testament or are reasonably to be inferred therefrom.

**Episcopalians.** Basic Episcopalian beliefs are affirmed in the Apostles' Creed and the Nicene Creed.

**Jehovah's Witnesses.** The Witnesses have no creed. They follow the Bible completely.

**Jews.** There is no formal creed. However, the *Talmud* speaks of three central principles in life: Torah—or learning; service of God; and the performance of good deeds, or charity. This represents the core of Judaism.

**Lutherans.** Lutheran teachings are based on the common Christian faith described in the New Testament and first summarized in the Apostles' Creed.

**Methodists.** Methodists are not required to sign any formal creed. Those joining the church are asked to affirm allegiance to Christ and the New Testament faith.

**"Mormons."** Basic Latter-day Saint beliefs are to be found in the "Mormon" Articles of Faith.

**Presbyterians.** The Westminster Confession of Faith is the creed of English-speaking Presbyterians. Most adherents accept also the Nicene and Apostles' Creeds.

**Quakers.** There is no written or formal creed. Serving as a substitute are the "Queries," a set of questions designed to encourage the faithfulness of the members in their religious life.

**Seventh-day Adventists.** Seventh-day Adventists do not make use of a formal creed. They hold certain fundamental beliefs based, they claim, upon the Bible.

**Unitarians.** Unitarians have no formal creed. Individualistic, they prefer to let every Unitarian speak for himself about his faith.

## BAPTISM

**Baptists.** Baptism is by immersion. It is limited to adults and to such children as have reached an age when they can understand the meaning of the ceremony. Baptists look upon immersion as realistic symbolism, through which the life of sin is buried and the new life of faith emerges.

**Catholics.** Baptism restores supernatural life. Without that life, man does not have the capacity to enjoy heaven. Adults may gain the life of grace by an act of perfect contrition or pure love of God ("baptism of desire"). Infants are incapable of such an act of the will; unbaptized babies cannot go to heaven but in their state of limbo do not suffer in any way.

**Christian Scientists.** Baptism means purification from all material sense and is not practiced in the material form.

**Congregationalists.** Baptism is the rite by which the Church takes a child or an adult to itself. The mode is usually "sprinkling," though other forms may be used if desired.

**Disciples of Christ.** Baptism is by immersion as an act of obedience and surrender, a symbol of the death, burial, and resurrection of the Lord Jesus. Only those who are adult enough to know what they are doing when they stand up to confess Christ are baptized.

**Episcopalians.** All who are baptized (whether by Episcopalian or other baptism, provided it is with water and in the name of the Holy Trinity) are members of the Church of Christ. Even those who are not actually baptized, but by intention would be baptized if they were able, are believed to be "saved."

**Jehovah's Witnesses.** Baptism is complete submersion. It is not for infants but for persons of responsible age who have the ability to learn.

**Jews.** In traditional Judaism, baptism is required only for those converted from another faith.

**Lutherans.** In baptism a person is born into the Kingdom of God and becomes an heir of salvation.

**Methodists.** Baptism is usually by sprinkling. It is a sign not only of profession but also of regeneration, or a new birth. The church assumes responsibility for her baptized children and awaits the time when they will be mature enough to appreciate and assume for themselves the vows made at baptism.

**"Mormons."** Baptism is by immersion and performed by those having authority. It is only for those who have become "accountable" for their actions, by the age of eight years and over.

**Presbyterians.** Ordinarily performed by sprinkling, this rite is an outward symbol of inward regeneration. While baptism is urgently recommended, it is not held to be necessary for salvation. It is customary to baptize children, but those children who die without baptism are not excluded from heaven.

**Quakers.** Friends believe in baptism of the Spirit but practice no form of baptism. At birth, the infant's name is recorded on the official books of the meeting to which his parents belong.

**Seventh-day Adventists.** All who would enter the Church are required to be baptized by immersion, the method followed by the Church of New Testament times.

**Unitarians.** While many Unitarians do practice baptism of infants and, more rarely, of adults, they prefer to look upon baptism as an act of dedication which has only symbolic meaning. It is possible to become a Unitarian without being baptized.

## LORD'S SUPPER

**Baptists.** Sacraments are regarded by Baptists as simple, dignified ordinances with no supernatural significance and no sacramental value. The Communion Service is usually observed on the first Sunday of the month.

**Catholics.** Catholics believe that Christ is truly and substantially present in the Eucharist, body and soul, humanity and divinity, after the priest pronounces the words of consecration in the Mass. The whole substance of the bread becomes the Body of Christ, the whole substance of the wine becomes the Blood of Christ.

**Christian Scientists.** A Communion Service is held in all branch Churches of Christ, Scientist, twice a year. The communion celebrated is wholly spiritual, without visible elements of bread and wine.

**Congregationalists.** The Holy Communion is the ritual meal at which Christ is the host, and through which the Church's faith is confirmed and increased.

**Disciples of Christ.** Disciples hold to the weekly observance of the Lord's Supper. Communion is never omitted from the Sunday service.

**Episcopalians.** Holy Communion, or Holy Eucharist, is the chief service of worship in the Episcopal Church, though it may not always have chief place in the Sunday service. "The Sacrament of the Lord's Supper was ordained for the continual remembrance of the sacrifice of the death of Christ, and of the benefits which we receive thereby."

**Jehovah's Witnesses.** Witnesses celebrate the Memorial of Christ's death annually on the day corresponding to *Nisan* 14 of the Jewish calendar—the day Christ instituted the celebration. They consider it unscriptural to celebrate this occasion more often than once a year.

**Jews.** Jews cannot accept the principle of incarnation. A cardinal tenet of Judaism is that God is purely spiritual; He admits no human attributes.

**Lutherans.** The Lord's Supper is an encounter of the believer with the living Lord, who is truly present in the Holy Communion to forgive sins and renew the spiritual life of believers. But no physical change takes place in the bread and wine.

**Methodists.** Methodists do not regard the Lord's Supper as the "real presence" of Christ in body and soul. God is a spirit; the body of Christ is given, taken, and eaten only in a "heavenly and spiritual manner."

**"Mormons."** The sacrament of the Lord's Supper is administered in a simple manner "in remembrance" of the Savior and as witness that "they are willing to keep His commandments."

**Presbyterians.** Christ is spiritually and not physically present in Holy Communion. The Sacrament is only a commemoration of the sacrifice of Christ.

**Quakers.** There is no necessity for any ritual to establish relationship between man and God. Friends believe in all the Sacraments but only in their inward and spiritual revelation of the Divine presence.

**Seventh-day Adventists.** Seventh-day Adventists celebrate the Lord's Supper in their churches about once a quarter. The consecrated bread and wine are regarded as symbols of Christ's body and blood and "show forth the Lord's death till He come."

**Unitarians.** Communion in Unitarian churches is a symbolic rite of remembrance and fellowship. No supernatural power of "grace" resides in this sacrament, nor does its observance automatically convey any special spiritual gift.

## THE TRINITY

**Baptists.** The doctrine of the Trinity is accepted by Baptists, who leave its sublime mystery to interpretation by theologians.

**Catholics.** Catholics believe in one God, in whom there are three Divine Persons co-equal in all things. The doctrine of the Holy Trinity is a central mystery of the Catholic faith.

**Christian Scientists.** By the Trinity, Christian Scientists mean the unity of Father, Son, and Holy Spirit, but do not accept the Trinity as three persons in one. Life, Truth and Love are "the triune Principle called God."

**Congregationalists.** Congregationalists believe fully in the Holy Trinity.

**Disciples of Christ.** Disciples are not bothered by speculation about the Holy Trinity and the nature of a triune God. They baptize into the name of the Father, Son, and Holy Spirit, as Christ commanded. They believe that the Holy Spirit is the Comforter promised in the New Testament, but they do not worry over its constitution or the nature of its operations, accepting its guidance as constantly enlarging the horizons of Christian thought.

**Episcopalians.** In light of man's experience of God's working in the world, it is seen that God *is* as He *reveals* Himself. He is Creative Reality (God the Father); He is Expressive Act (God the Son); He is Responsive Power (God the Holy Spirit). He is one God experienced in a "trinitarian" fashion.

**Jehovah's Witnesses.** Witnesses believe that Jehovah God and Christ Jesus are two distinct persons and are not combined with a so-called "Holy Ghost" in one godhead called a Trinity.

**Jews.** Jews do not accept the divinity of Christ and therefore cannot accept the concept of the Trinity. The Lord is One.

**Lutherans.** Lutherans believe in the Trinity as one God in three personalities.

**Methodists.** The meaning of the Trinity is not fully understood. The doctrine is the expression of the three aspects in our experience of God: the Creator, the Father; the historical personality of Christ, the Son; a pervading and continuing presence and power in our lives, the Holy Spirit. The Trinity is also the formula for understanding the personality of God. God is Love, Love must have an object. Before Creation God must have loved Christ. The divine activity linking the Father with the object of his love is the Holy Spirit.

**"Mormons."** The Latter-day Saint accepts the Godhead as three literal, distinct personalities: God the Father; His Son, Jesus the Christ (who is one with the Father in purpose and in thought, but separate from Him in physical fact); and the Holy Ghost, a Personage of Spirit. This interpretation is derived from literal scriptural language.

**Presbyterians.** Presbyterians think of God not as three individuals, but as three manifestations of One.

**Quakers.** There is wide freedom for personal opinion regarding the Trinity.

Friends tend to believe in the immanence of God rather than His transcendence.

**Seventh-day Adventists.** Seventh-day Adventists worship Father, Son, and Holy Spirit—"three Persons in one God."

**Unitarians.** Unitarians do not believe in the Trinity but in one God.

## VIRGIN BIRTH

**Baptists.** A great majority undoubtedly accept the Virgin Birth. A substantial minority do not. Since Baptists have no authoritarian creed to control their faith and practice, each local parish has the right to decide whether or not to make acceptance of the doctrine of the Virgin Birth a condition of church membership.

**Catholics.** Catholics believe in the Virgin Birth and believe that Mary remained a virgin throughout her life.

**Christian Scientists.** Christian Scientists accept completely the Virgin Birth.

**Congregationalists.** Probably the majority do not accept the doctrine of the Virgin Birth; undoubtedly many do. The fact of Christ, and not the manner in which he was born, is held to be of dominant importance.

**Disciples of Christ.** It is probable that about ninety-nine per cent believe in the Virgin Birth; it is possible that others have doubts. There is no ecclesiastical or denominational authority that can declare one belief to be orthodox and reject the other as heretical.

**Episcopalians.** The creeds and the liturgy of the Episcopal Church assert the traditional belief that Jesus was born of Mary without human father. There is disagreement within the

Church, not on the *theological* meaning of the Virgin Birth, but on its biological detail. Most Episcopalians probably accept it as literally true; some regard it as symbolic in character.

**Jehovah's Witnesses.** Witnesses believe that Jesus was born miraculously, a virgin birth in fulfillment of the prophecy of Isaiah 7:14.

**Jews.** Jews do not believe in the doctrine of the Virgin Birth.

**Lutherans.** Lutherans affirm the Apostles' Creed as a basic summary of belief, including "born of the Virgin Mary." However, Lutherans do not go on to the extra-Biblical doctrines regarding the perpetual virginity of Mary.

**Methodists.** The great majority accept the Virgin Birth literally. Some would distinguish the biological aspects from the theological implications. As long as a Methodist believes in the Deity of Christ, it is not necessary for him to believe that Christ was begotten without a human father.

**"Mormons."** The Latter-day Saint accepts the miraculous conception of Jesus the Christ.

**Presbyterians.** A majority of Presbyterians undoubtedly believe in the Virgin Birth. Some find a symbolic rather than a physical meaning in the accounts of the birth of Jesus.

**Quakers.** The question of the Virgin Birth does not seem as important a problem for Quakers as the meaning and teaching of Christ's life on earth and His continuing power to reveal Himself at all times and to all seekers.

**Seventh-day Adventists.** Seventh-day Adventists accept the Virgin Birth as one of the vital truths of the Christian faith, foretold in the Old Testament and confirmed in the New.

**Unitarians.** Unitarians repudiate the dogma or doctrine of the Virgin Birth.

## HEAVEN and HELL

**Baptists.** Most Baptists believe in some form of life beyond the grave. Ideas range from a nebulous, indefinable existence to a definite place, like a city of golden streets or a region of everlasting torment. Some Baptists find it difficult to reconcile the fact of an all-merciful God with endless punishment for sins committed within the short span of a lifetime on earth.

**Catholics.** Heaven is both a place and a state of being. The state consists essentially in seeing God "face to face." We have no knowledge of the place beyond the fact that it exists. Hell is both a place and a state of punishment. Purgatory exists to purge those souls who are not yet pure enough for heaven but have not died in a state of serious (mortal) sin.

**Christian Scientists.** Christian Scientists believe in heaven and hell but not in a geographical sense. In the words of Mrs. Eddy: "The sinner makes his own hell by doing evil, and the saint his own heaven by doing right."

**Congregationalists.** Heaven and hell are not viewed as places of bliss and torment. God's justice cannot be escaped; it will be heaven to be with God and hell to be without him.

**Disciples of Christ.** Practically all Disciples believe in the immortality of the soul and in a blissful reunion hereafter for all the faithful who have died in the Lord. Many doubtless believe in a literal paradise and hell. Many others are content to leave the details of future rewards and punishments in the hands of Divine mercy. Disciple faith in general is a matter of deep personal conviction.

**Episcopalians.** Heaven is a state in which the vision of God is enjoyed in a "life of perfect service" of God; hell is alienation from God. Episcopalians do not believe in a physical heaven or hell; these are "states of being."

**Jehovah's Witnesses.** Hell is a place of rest, in hope of resurrection, not an inescapable place of torture. Heaven is the habitation of spirit creatures. The reward of spiritual life with Christ Jesus in heaven for men on earth is limited to exactly 144,000. The rest of mankind who gain life in God's new world will live forever in the paradise earth. The Devil and the willfully wicked will be permanently destroyed.

**Jews.** Jews believe in the immortality of the soul—an immortality whose nature is known only to God—but they no longer accept the literal idea of heaven and hell.

**Lutherans.** Those who live and die in faith in Christ will live with Him eternally, freed from the limitations of time and space. Predictions about this eternal life must necessarily be in picture language, for it is beyond the range of finite minds. Naïve descriptions of heaven and hell are inadequate, but victory over death is the certain destiny of God's people.

**Methodists.** Methodists believe in divine judgment after death. Goodness will be rewarded and evil punished. Concepts of heaven and hell vary from the concrete idea of golden streets and fiery furnaces to the more prevalent spiritual idea that heaven is the realm where the redeemed keep company with God and His Risen Son and hell is the state where such fellowship is absent.

**"Mormons."** Heaven is looked to and lived for as a real place of eternal progress, with endless association with loved ones, with families and friends. For those wilfully indifferent to their opportunities on earth, the knowledge that they have fallen short of their highest possible happiness will be part of the punishment of the "hell" of hereafter.

**Presbyterians.** Heaven and hell are not only places; they are also states of mind and character. The Bible and human experience teach us that we are living in a moral universe; therefore, sin carries its own appropriate penalty, and righteousness is its own reward, including the vision of God.

**Quakers.** Friends consider heaven and hell as matters for individual interpretation. They do, nonetheless, believe in life after this life.

**Seventh-day Adventists.** The ancient supposition that people go to heaven or hell immediately upon death is held to be an infiltration of pagan mythology into Christian theology. The dead are merely asleep until the glorious return of Christ. Then and only then will final rewards and punishments be meted out.

**Unitarians.** The idea that a God of Love and Mercy would want to consign a human being to eternal damnation because of wrongdoing during a relatively brief spell of mortal existence, or that God will reward the mortal doers of good with everlasting happiness appears to most Unitarians as entirely inconsistent with any moral concept of our Deity. Unitarians repudiate literal interpretations of heaven and hell as places of eternal bliss or damnation.

## SIN and SALVATION

**Baptists.** Every true believer in Christ as personal Savior is saved—without the intervention of preacher or church. The confession of sin is a personal matter between the individual and God. Each individual must give evidence of his personal redemption by faith, good works and the Christian way of life.

**Catholics.** Catholics believe in original sin and in the possibility of a man's damning himself for all eternity by deliberately and knowingly disobeying the law of God. Catholics believe that men are saved by faith and good works. Salvation comes through the Church but is not limited to visible members of the Church, in the case of those who are invincibly ignorant of the Church's divine authority.

**Christian Scientists.** Sin is the belief in the real existence of a mind or minds other than the Divine Mind, God. Christian Scientists hold that sin is unreal. If the sinner knew this, his capacity for sinning would be destroyed. Salvation consists of being saved from the illusions and delusions of mortal sense—the sense of being capable of becoming sick and dying.

**Congregationalists.** Sin is opposition or indifference to the will of God. God, however, is willing to forgive. When a person repents in faith, God accepts him—then he need have no fear of any future in this world or the next. He is "saved."

**Disciples of Christ.** Disciples, as a rule, reject the doctrine of original sin, but most believe we are all sinful creatures unless and until redeemed by the saving sacrifice of the Lord Jesus.

**Episcopalians.** In man, sinner because he is ridiculously proud and self-centered, there is no real "health"; by fellowship with God in Christ, he is brought into the sphere of healthy and whole life. Salvation, therefore, means that one is given the wholeness which is God's will for man, and is delivered from arrogance and selfishness. Salvation has to do not only with the "hereafter" but also with man's present earthly existence.

**Jehovah's Witness.** Sin is lawlessness. The human race was born in sin because Adam and Eve rebelled against God and His law. Salvation is only possible through the ransom sacrifice of Christ Jesus. It will come to those who conform to the conditions upon which it is offered. All must accept Christ Jesus and obey. Those who believe will be saved but the wicked will be destroyed.

**Jews.** Judaism does not accept the doctrine of original sin. Nor can Judaism accept the principle of vicarious atonement—the idea of salvation *through* Christ. Every man is responsible for his own salvation. Jews approach God —each man after his own fashion— without a mediator.

**Lutherans.** Sin is the word describing the situation of all people as disobedient to God. Sin is not specific wrongdoing (this is the result of sin), but the basic condition of our personality. Salvation is a gift from God; even the desire for salvation comes from God, and only God can save human beings.

**Methodists.** When men truly and earnestly repent of their sins, God forgives them. Man's salvation comes by faith and through the grace of God. Salvation means not only security in heaven after death but a present experience of God's grace and power.

**"Mormons."** "Salvation," according to Latter-day Saints, is universal. However, "exaltation" (with the highest eternal opportunities) must be earned by obedience to laws, ordinances, and commandments of the Kingdom.

**Presbyterians.** God pardons our sins and accepts us, not for any merit of our own, but because of our faith in the perfect obedience of Christ and His sacrificial death. Forgiveness, grace, and salvation are obtained through a direct personal relationship to God. Salvation is not earned by good works but is the gift of God. Good works are the *fruits* of salvation, evidence that we are growing in grace and in the knowledge of Christ.

**Quakers.** Friends point to the inherent goodness in men and women, instead of emphasizing the inheritance of sin. The term "original sin" overemphasizes the power of evil. Even when he is fallen, man still belongs to God, who continues to appeal to the goodness within him.

**Seventh-day Adventists.** Salvation is by grace alone. Keeping the commandments is the result, the evidence of salvation.

**Unitarians.** Unitarians recognize the evil in our world and man's responsibi'ity for much of it. They do not believe in original sin. Man has native capacities for both good and evil. His natural tendency for good can grow through proper environment, effective education, and honest effort. Unitarians believe in "salvation by character." If a man is to be "saved," the image of God within man will save him—here as well as hereafter.

## DIVORCE

**Baptists.** Baptists do not approve of divorce except on grounds of adultery. But there is no regulation among Baptist churches regarding divorce. Each clergyman depends on his conscience in deciding whether or not to officiate at the marriage of divorced persons.

**Catholics.** The Church does not recognize any absolute divorce between a couple who are validly married, where one or the other would be free to marry again. Separation from bed and board may be approved.

**Christian Scientists.** The Church of Christ, Scientist, takes no doctrinaire position on such social questions as divorce, but leaves its members free to work out their salvation on the basis of their highest understanding of moral and spiritual law.

**Congregationalists.** Though the churches have never made a joint official pronouncement on divorce, they frown upon current divorce habits of Americans. They do not oppose legal divorce after a couple has been "spiritually" divorced.

**Disciples of Christ.** There is no central church authority on this subject. Some ministers and congregations oppose any remarriage of divorced persons. Others will remarry the innocent party to a divorce obtained on the ground of adultery. Others, perhaps a majority, believe that divorce has become a legal function of the State and will remarry anyone to whom the civil government accords the right of remarriage.

**Episcopalians.** In America, the "canons" (church law) do not recognize divorce but do provide a number of grounds for annulment. A bishop may permit a divorced person to remarry if certain conditions are met.

**Jehovah's Witnesses.** Divorce may be obtained only on the ground of marital unfaithfulness.

**Jews.** Divorce is permitted when love and harmony have ceased to exist between a man and a woman, and their marriage has become empty and meaningless.

**Lutherans.** Following the New Testament, Lutherans agree that adultery and desertion may be grounds for divorce. They feel that Christians should not legislate general principles to apply to all cases; every case must be considered individually.

**Methodists.** No Methodist minister should remarry a divorced person whose mate is living and unmarried, unless the person is the innocent party to a divorce on the grounds of adultery or other vicious conditions invalidating the marriage vow.

**"Mormons."** Divorce is deplored and discouraged. "Temple divorces" (as distinguished from civil divorces) may be granted only by the president of the Church, for serious cause, including infidelity.

**Presbyterians.** Divorce is permitted to the innocent party on scriptural grounds (adultery), and that party may remarry. Divorce is also permitted in cases of willful desertion. In cases of doubt, the minister can consult his Presbytery's Committee on Divorce. However, no minister may remarry persons who have been divorced less than twelve months.

**Quakers.** Divorce is contrary to the "Discipline of Friends." Friends' Meetings are urged not to permit weddings of divorced persons as long as one of the divorced couple is still alive.

**Seventh-day Adventists.** Seventh-day Adventists follow the Biblical position that adultery is the only possible ground for divorce.

**Unitarians.** Unitarianism recognizes no specifically theological doctrines as regards divorce. It is referred to the individual's conscience, intelligence, and common sense. The church is always ready to offer counsel and advice in keeping with its ethical and spiritual ideals.

## BIRTH CONTROL

**Baptists.** No parish Baptist Church and no ecclesiastical convention of Baptists has ever by resolution expressed approval or disapproval of birth control. Most Baptists would resent and repudiate such a resolution as an unwarranted intrusion into the private life of husband and wife.

**Catholics.** The Church is opposed to birth control in the belief that artificial contraception is against the law of God and that because it is immoral, it cannot be employed as a means, even to a good end. Birth prevention is regarded as an evil in itself—circumstances cannot change it into something morally good or indifferent. "Natural" birth control—the so-called rhythm theory—is permitted (as the Pope recently stated) in cases where undue medical or economic hardship makes family limitation imperative.

**Christian Scientists.** Married couples are free to follow their own judgment as to having children and as to the number they will have.

**Congregationalists.** There is no official statement on birth control from the churches. In general, Congregationalists believe that the use by man of the brains which God has given him to invent means of preventing conception is not contrary to God's will.

**Disciples of Christ.** A majority of Disciple ministers believe that birth control is justifiable under certain circumstances. In general, Disciples are content to leave such matters to the individual consciences of husband and wife.

**Episcopalians.** When birth control is practiced without selfish motives, it is permissible.

**Jehovah's Witnesses.** Birth control is regarded as an entirely personal matter.

**Jews.** The Jewish religion has traditionally been opposed to birth control when practiced for purely selfish reasons. It sanctions birth control if pregnancy represents a health hazard or if previous children have been born defective; modern Judaism extends this to cases of extreme poverty, inadequate living conditions.

**Lutherans.** There is no general objection to birth control. It can be sinful and selfish either to have an overabundance of children without considering the responsibilities involved or to avoid parenthood completely.

**Methodists.** The General Conference of the Methodist Church has never made an official pronouncement on birth control. Statements by individual leaders suggest that prevailing opinion approves the use of contraceptives by lawfully married couples when in the interest of the mothers' health and the children's welfare. The ultimate reason must be unselfish.

**"Mormons."** The Church advocates rearing large families; birth control, as commonly understood, is contrary to its teachings.

**Presbyterians.** The Presbyterian Church does not legislate for its people on personal issues. Nothing in the Church's teaching can be construed as forbidding an intelligent, conservative, and unselfish employment of birth control.

**Quakers.** Birth control is a matter for the individual conscience. Education for marriage and parenthood has long been a concern of Quakers.

**Seventh-day Adventists.** Seventh-day Adventists, as a denomination, have never taken an official position on the matter of birth control.

**Unitarians.** Unitarianism recognizes no specifically theological doctrines regarding birth control. This question is referred to the individual's conscience, intelligence, and common sense.

## PROPAGATION OF THE FAITH

**Baptists.** The historic Baptist view holds that *every* church member and every professing Christian is an evangelist. Throughout their history, Baptists have engaged in very active missionary effort at home and abroad.

**Catholics.** The Catholic Church from its very beginning has sent out missionaries to all nations to make known to all men the Gospel of Christ and incorporate them into His Church. Catholicism is a world-wide religion meant for all men of all races at all times.

**Christian Scientists.** The Church of Christ, Scientist, engages in no formal missionary activities. However, its Board of Lectureship, its periodicals, and its radio programs are important elements in its preaching of the gospel to all men.

**Congregationalists.** Missionary work is carried on in the name of Christianity through preaching of the Gospel. It is not carried on to propagate Congregationalism *per se*.

**Disciples of Christ.** Disciples of Christ

invite but do not proselytize. An offer of fellowship to any adult who wishes to take his stand by the Cross of the Risen Lord is given at the close of Sunday morning service.

**Episcopalians.** The Church has been active in propagation of the faith, carrying missionary work throughout the world.

**Jehovah's Witnesses.** Witnesses believe they have the most urgent message of all time and believe they must preach to people around the world before this generation passes away. Witnesses enter people's homes to try to convert them and they distribute literature on street corners.

**Jews.** Modern Judaism is not a proselytizing creed.

**Lutherans.** Lutherans believe that Christians are under compulsion to seek to convert all people to the Christian faith. This is a matter of doctrinal conviction.

**Methodists.** Methodists put much emphasis on missionary expansion and evangelistic sharing of the Gospel.

**"Mormons."** Missionaries have been active since the 1830's in proselytizing.

**Presbyterians.** Presbyterianism is a decidedly missionary faith. The central core of the missionary effort is evangelistic.

**Quakers.** Friends do not try to make converts; they discover those who are in unity with them and nurture them until they are accorded full membership following a written request of the applicant to become a member.

**Seventh-day Adventists.** Seventh-day Adventists have missionaries all over the world and publications are issued in 198 languages. Seventh-day Adventists carry on a large health and medical work alongside their evangelistic activities.

**Unitarians.** Unitarians do not proselytize and do not send out missionaries.

## CHURCH ORGANIZATION

**Baptists.** Baptists have no hierarchy, no centralized control of religious activity, no headquarters' "oversight" of churches or liturgies, practices or regulations. The local parish church is a law unto itself.

**Catholics.** The Catholic Church describes itself as "the visible society founded by Jesus Christ and consisting of members throughout the world who are united by the same Faith, particularly the same Sacraments, and in spiritual matters accept the supreme authority of the Bishop of Rome (the Pope), the successor of Saint Peter." The Pope is assisted by the College of Cardinals. The Church is divided into bishoprics. Each Catholic lives under the jurisdiction of a bishop or archbishop, appointed by the Pope. Each bishopric is divided into parishes and each parish is directed by a pastor appointed by the bishop. Side by side with the parochial clergy are members of the religious orders (who may be priests, simple monks, or nuns) who engage in a variety of activities under the ultimate direction of the hierarchy.

**Christian Scientists.** Christian Science has no ordained clergy or personal pastors. There is no personal preacher in a Christian Science service; texts are read aloud by a first and second reader. A Christian Science practitioner is one who prays for those who ask his prayers in their behalf. To be registered as a public practitioner, one must be approved by the Mother Church, the First Church of Christ, Scientist, in Boston, Massachusetts.

**Congregationalists.** Congregationalists have county and state associations of churches and a national association— the General Council; but these have no power over the internal life of any of the congregations. The freedom of the congregation is inviolable. No minister beloved by his people can be removed by external pressure. No church can be disbanded except by the wish of its people.

**Disciples of Christ.** The average Disciple church is administered by a pastor, an Official Board of Elders and Deacons, and perhaps representatives of the Christian Women's Fellowship. Elders look after the spiritual welfare of members; deacons manage incidental business. All matters of fundamental importance must ultimately be decided by the congregation as a whole.

**Episcopalians.** There are three orders of ministry: bishops, priests, and deacons. There are also many orders of monks and nuns. In the United States there are parishes with elected laymen to represent the congregation; dioceses with the "convention" under which the bishop and his clergy carry on the Church's work; a general convention which meets every three years and represents the entire American Church. Neither bishops nor parish clergy have any autocratic rights; all must cooperate with the laity.

**Jehovah's Witnesses.** Jehovah's Witnesses are a society or body of ministers, for the public ceremony of water immersion identifies one as a minister of God. Boys and girls are invited to preach. Ministers at national headquarters and in the field are voluntary workers. The world-wide members of the Society elect seven ministers as a board of directors; the board chooses one director as president. Clerical garb is never used.

**Jews.** There is no religious hierarchy in Judaism. The authority of the rabbi is based not on his position but upon his learning. In Orthodox practice, the rabbi rarely leads in services; the cantor conducts worship. Any well-informed layman may rise to the pulpit to lead the congregation in prayer. The modern rabbi is responsible for religious education, for worship in the synagogue, for ceremonials surrounding birth, confirmation, marriage, and death, and for pastoral guidance. Judaism is essentially a family religion; the home is often regarded as a fitting place of worship.

**Lutherans.** Church conventions, which elect presidents and other officials, are the main instruments of authority in the American churches. The foundation of this authority is in the congregations themselves. Each congregation owns its own church building or other property and is self-governing in all of its local affairs. Men are çalled to the office of the ministry by God through the congregations, and if they cease to perform the functions of their office they cease to be ministers.

**Methodists.** The Methodist Church in America parallels rather uniquely the pattern of American government. The executive branch consists of a Council of Bishops elected by jurisdictional conferences composed of ministers and laymen. Each bishop presides over an area. The bishops appoint the ministers of individual parishes. The legislative power is vested in a General Conference which meets every four years and is composed of both clergy and laymen in equal numbers. Delegates are democratically elected by an annual conference and on a proportional basis. The supreme judicial power rests in a Judicial Council whose members and qualifications are determined by the General Conference of the church.

**"Mormons."** The Church has a strong central organization with a First Presidency of three presiding high priests followed in order by the Council of the Twelve Apostles (with assistants); a patriarch, the First Council of the Seventy; also a Presiding Bishopric who preside over the Aaronic Priesthood. Geographically, the Church is divided into "stakes" and "wards" (somewhat resembling the diocese and parishes), and "missions."

**Presbyterians.** The people govern the Church through elected representatives. The layman has a prominent role in the Presbyterian Church. All property is vested in laymen—not in ministers or bishops. Laymen are eligible for the highest office (moderator) in each court. The courts are the Session, made up of the elders and ministers who have supreme authority in the spiritual matters of the local church; the Presbytery, which has oversight of all congregations within its prescribed area; the Synod, composed of ministers and representative elders from congregations within a specified number of Presbyteries; and the General Assembly, which is the court of final appeal and representative of the whole church.

**Quakers.** Friends do not have an ordained clergy. They believe that everyone has the potentiality to become a minister. There is no division between clergy and laity because both ideas are eliminated. Elders and overseers are appointed to serve each meeting. Elders are given the "oversight" of the religious meetings for worship, for marriage, and for memorial services

at time of death. Overseers look after the pastoral care of the membership. All meetings have a recorder who is responsible for the careful keeping of all vital statistics.

**Seventh-day Adventists.** Seventh-day Adventists have developed a global organization, comprising twelve divisions, directed by the General Conference. Each of these twelve divisions is made up of several union conferences, which in turn are made up of local conferences, each consisting of a group of churches. Lay members elect officers of their local churches and appoint delegates to local conferences for the election of their officers.

**Unitarians.** Unitarians practice a congregational form of government. There is no authority above the congregation itself. It sets aside a man to be the minister; the act of setting aside is regarded as ordination. Once ordained in this manner, the minister remains ordained throughout his life and can move from one congregation to another.

## POSITION REGARDING OTHER RELIGIONS

**Baptists.** Baptists are staunch believers in the historic Baptist principle of full, complete, unrestricted religious freedom and demand it for other religions just as zealously as for themselves.

**Catholics.** American Catholics believe in and practice religious tolerance. However, Catholics believe that theirs is the only true religion.

**Christian Scientists.** The Christian Scientist does not feel superior to the adherents of any denomination. Every man is free to demonstrate the efficacy of his own faith; each is entitled to encouragement in his pursuit of spiritual objectives.

**Congregationalists.** Congregationalists believe in cooperation among the Christian denominations and encourage exchanges of ideas with Jewish groups. In any community they oppose religious isolationism and denominational exclusiveness.

**Disciples of Christ.** Disciples do not believe theirs is the only true religion; they do believe it is most nearly in accord with the practices of the early Christian churches. They never doubt the right of any man to go directly to God, by prayer, for guidance in all problems of conscience. They have no sense of rivalry among the denominations.

**Episcopalians.** The Church is Christ's instrument for fulfilling His purpose in the world and the means by which His continuing presence is made available. Of that one Church, Episcopalians believe they are a part; they have never claimed they are the *only* part.

**Jehovah's Witnesses.** Witnesses believe that theirs is the only true faith and that there is only one way to gain salvation. They do not believe that the majority of people will meet the strict requirements of true faith.

**Jews.** Jews do not presume to judge the honest worshiper of any faith. "The righteous of *all* nations are worthy of immortality."

**Lutherans.** Lutherans believe there is only one church, but it is not any visible institution. It consists of all the congregations of believers which rightly teach the Gospel and administer the Sacraments. Lutherans are eager for better understanding and cooperation among Christians everywhere.

**Methodists.** Methodist leaders encourage tolerance and understanding toward all other religious bodies.

**"Mormons."** The "Mormon" believes his is the "right way." The Church of Jesus Christ of Latter-day Saints affirms it is the "restored" Church of Jesus Christ, with the same authority, organization, and ordinances that Jesus established on earth but which were lost by centuries of change and apostasy.

**Presbyterians.** Presbyterians believe that every man has the right to choose and practice the faith that he personally accepts.

**Quakers.** To Friends, all those who do the will of the Father are brethren of Jesus in the Spirit. In their attitude toward other religions, Friends have considered that they are members of one household in the family of God.

**Seventh-day Adventists.** Seventh-day Adventists are ardent champions of religious liberty. They are opposed to all religious legislation such as "blue" laws and support the principle of separation of church and state.

**Unitarians.** Unitarians are firm believers in the "Church Universal," which includes all men and women of every race, color, and creed who seek God and worship Him through service to their fellow man. Every individual has the right to approach God in his own way; every religious community has the duty of creating such patterns of worship as best serve the needs of those who worship.

By ROBERT WINSTON CARDEN, Professor, Schreiner Institute, Kerrville, Texas

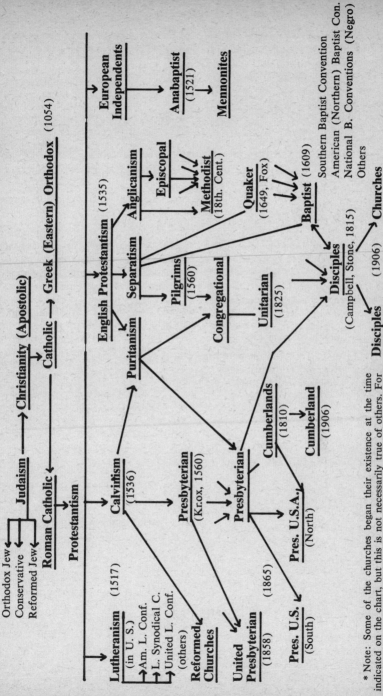

* Note: Some of the churches began their existence at the time indicated on the chart, but this is not necessarily true of others. For example, the Roman Catholic and the Eastern (Greek) branch split in A.D. 1054, but both churches, of course, existed before that time. Likewise the Anglican Church (Church of England) did not originate in A.D. 1535, but it was in that year that it pulled out from the authority of Rome.

# Church Membership

## 1. National Statistics on Church Membership, Number of Churches, and the Ordained Clergy

From the 1955 *Yearbook of American Churches*, BENSON Y. LANDIS, ed., New York: National Council of the Churches of Christ in the U. S. A., 1954. pp. 253–260 and pp. 266–272.

The figures furnished and here tabulated are mainly for the calendar year 1953, or for a fiscal year ending in 1953. The methods used in this compilation are more fully described below.

### Church Membership

The reports on church membership received from official statisticians of religious bodies reveal a total membership of 94,842,845 persons in 255 bodies in 1953, compared with a total of 92,277,129 persons in 1952, published in the previous *Yearbook*. These figures are for the continental United States, i.e., the 48 states and the District of Columbia.

*The total number of church members* is equal to over 59.5 per cent of the population in the continental United States. This is the highest proportion of the population ever reported to be on the church rolls.

*The gain* of 2,565,716 persons is equal to 2.8 per cent for the year. The number of Protestants reported increased 3.0 per cent over the previous annual total. The number of Roman Catholics increased 4.0 per cent.

A portion of the 2,565,716 gain in membership over the 1953 *Yearbook*

figure is accounted for by the fact that five Protestant bodies with a combined membership of 195,804 reported this year for the first time.

Between 1952 and 1953, the estimated population of continental United States increased 1.7 per cent.

There are 294,359 local churches reported in 1953, compared with 285,277 in 1952. The gain is equal to 1.5 per cent.

Of 268 religious bodies listed, there are 255 reports of church membership and 255 reports of the number of local churches. There are 16 bodies for which the gains reported are for a period of two years, or more.

An analysis of the latest information in six major groups reveals the following:

### Church Membership, by Religious Groups

|  | Number of Members |
|---|---:|
| Buddhist | 63,000 |
| Old Catholic and Polish National Catholic | 366,088 |
| Eastern Orthodox | 2,100,171 |
| Jewish | 5,000,000 |
| Roman Catholic | 31,476,261 |
| Protestant | 55,837,325 |
| Total | 94,842,845 |

## Number of Churches, by Religious Groups

| | Number of Churches |
|---|---|
| Buddhist | 48 |
| Old Catholic and Polish National Catholic | 256 |
| Eastern Orthodox | 1,340 |
| Jewish | 3,990 |
| Roman Catholic | 20,618 |
| Protestant | 268,107 |
| **Total** | 294,359 |

There are also Muslims in the United States, but no statistical reports are available. Informal estimates are cited in the directory of religious bodies in the *Yearbook*.

The Protestant church membership was equal to 58.9 per cent of all church members in 1953—the same as in 1952, and also about the same as in 1906. It seems that the major religious groups have developed in about the same relation to each other during the last 50 years. The data for 1926–53 are more fully discussed below.

A recital of these trends and data

gives rise to the usual questions about definitions of membership. The Roman Catholics count all baptized persons, including infants. The Jews regard as members all Jews in communities having congregations. The Eastern Orthodox Churches include all persons in their nationality or cultural groups. Most Protestant bodies count only the persons who have attained full membership, and previous estimates have indicated that all but a small minority of these are over 13 years of age. However, many Lutheran bodies and the Protestant Episcopal Church now report all baptized persons, and not only those confirmed.

The Church of Christ, Scientist, did not furnish membership figures because of a regulation of that body that forbids "the numbering of people and the reporting of such statistics for publication." In the Census of Religious Bodies, 1936, published by the U. S. Bureau of the Census, there were reported 268,915 members of the Church of Christ, Scientist.

The table on church membership follows:

## CHURCH MEMBERSHIP AND CLERGY STATISTICS

Mainly for the Calendar Year 1953 or a Fiscal Year Ending in 1953

| Name of Religious Body | Year | No. of Churches Reported | Inclusive Church Membership | Number of Pastors Having Charges | Total Number of Ordained Persons |
|---|---|---|---|---|---|
| **ADVENTIST BODIES:** | | | | | |
| Advent Christian Church | 1953 | 406 | 30,737 | 314 | 432 |
| Church of God (Abrahamic Faith) | 1940 | 79 | 5,295 | No report | |
| Life and Advent Union | 1953 | 3 | 315 | 3 | 8 |
| Primitive Advent Christian Church | 1953 | 13 | 476 | 7 | 27 |
| Seventh-day Adventists | 1953 | 2,835 | 260,742 | 2,246 | 2,084 |
| African Orthodox Church | 1953 | 30 | 7,000 | 30 | 90 |
| Amana Church Society | 1953 | 7 | 819 | 23 | None |
| American Ethical Union | 1953 | 19 | 5,265 | 13 | 23 |
| American Evangelical Christian Churches | No report | | | | |

## CHURCH MEMBERSHIP AND CLERGY STATISTICS

| Name of Religious Body | Year | No. of Churches Reported | Inclusive Church Membership | Number of Pastors Having Charges | Total Number of Ordained Persons |
|---|---|---|---|---|---|
| American Rescue Workers.......... | 1952 | 23 | 1,240 | 23 | 30 |
| Apostolic Overcoming Holy Church of God.......................... | 1951 | 300 | 75,000 | 850 | No data |
| Assemblies of God................. | 1953 | 6,400 | 370,118 | 6,400 | 7,641 |
| Associated Gospel Churches......... | No report | | | | |
| Bahá'í Faith....................... | No report | | | | |
| BAPTIST BODIES: | | | | | |
| American Baptist Convention........ | 1952 | 6,531 | 1,557,816 | 5,500 | 6,000 |
| Southern Baptist Convention........ | 1953 | 29,481 | 7,883,708 | 23,992 | 27,747 |
| National Baptist Convention, U.S.A., Inc. ........................... | 1953 | 24,415 | 4,526,847 | 18,964('52) | 27,005 |
| National Baptist Convention of America ............................. | 1953 | 11,136 | 2,606,510 | No data | 27,800 |
| American Baptist Association........ | 1951 | 2,105 | 286,691 | No report | |
| Baptist General Conference of America ......................... | 1953 | 362 | 49,981 | 315 | 442 |
| Christian Unity Baptist Association.. | 1953 | 13 | 622 | 7 | 13 |
| Conservative Baptist Association of America ......................... | No report | | | | |
| Duck River (and Kindred) Associations of Baptists................... | 1952 | 326 | 9,720 | No data | 151 |
| Evangelical Baptist Church, Inc., Gen. Conf. ........................... | 1952 | 31 | 2,200 | 22 | 37 |
| Free Will Baptists ................. | 1953 | 4,200 | 425,000 | 3,000 | 6,500 |
| General Baptists ................... | 1953 | 688 | 52,382 | 600 | 1,050 |
| General Six-Principle Baptists....... | 1944 | 3 | 280 | No report | |
| Independent Baptist Church of America ............................. | 1952 | 3 | 50 | 5 | 4 |
| National Baptist Evangelical Life and Soul Saving Assembly of U.S.A. ... | 1951 | 264 | 57,674 | 128 | 137 |
| National Primitive Baptist Convention of the U.S.A. ............... | 1952 | 1,019 | 80,000 | 600 | 750 |
| North American Baptist Association.. | 1953 | 1,591 | 160,000 | 1,300 | 1,425 |
| North American Baptist General Conference ......................... | 1953 | 274 | 45,121 | 272 | 356 |
| Primitive Baptists ................. | 1950 | 1,000 | 72,000 | No report | * |
| Regular Baptists ................... | 1936 | 266 | 17,186 | No report | |
| Separate Baptists .................. | 1952 | 86 | 6,435 | 42 | 93 |
| Seventh-day Baptist General Conference ............................. | 1953 | 65 | 6,257 | 31 | 66 |
| Seventh-day Baptists (German 1728). | 1951 | 3 | 150 | 2 | 4 |
| Two-Seed-in-the-Spirit Predestinarian Baptists ......................... | 1945 | 16 | 201 | No report | |
| United Baptists .................... | 1953 | 444 | 43,782 | 341 | 872 |
| United Free Will Baptist Church.... | 1952 | 836 | 100,000 | 915 | 784 |
| Bible Protestant Church............. | 1953 | 34 | 2,134 | 26 | 31 |
| BRETHREN (GERMAN BAPTISTS): | | | | | |
| Brethren Church (Ashland, Ohio).... | 1953 | 109 | 18,610 | 85 | 158 |
| Brethren Church (Progressive)....... | 1952 | 137 | 20,828 | 133 | 249('51) |
| Church of the Brethren............. | 1953 | 1,028 | 190,263 | 841 | 3,103 |
| Church of God (New Dunkards).... | 1953 | 8 | 611 | 8 | 5 |
| Old German Baptist Brethren........ | 1953 | 31 | 4,000('52) | 31 | 187 |
| Plymouth Brethren ................. | 1936 | 664 | 25,806 | No report | |

## CHURCH MEMBERSHIP AND CLERGY STATISTICS

| Name of Religious Body | Year | No. of Churches Reported | Inclusive Church Membership | Number of Pastors Having Charges | Total Number of Ordained Persons |
|---|---|---|---|---|---|
| BRETHREN (RIVER): | | | | | |
| Brethren in Christ.................. | 1953 | 112 | 5,950 | 112 | 343 |
| Old Order or Yorker Brethren...... | 1936 | 7 | 291 | No report | |
| United Zion Church................ | 1951 | 15 | 1,008 | 20 | 43 |
| Buddhist Churches of America....... | 1953 | 48 | 63,000 | 42 | 62 |
| Catholic Apostolic Church.......... | 1936 | 7 | 2,577 | No report | |
| Christ Unity Science Church........ | 1953 | 4,481 | 1,581,286 | 4,971 | 5,019 |
| Christadelphians ................... | 1950 | 115 | 3,755 | No report | |
| Christian and Missionary Alliance.... | 1952 | 928 | 56,097 | 922 | 851 |
| Christian Catholic Church.......... | No report | | | | |
| Christian Nation Church............ | 1953 | 40 | 600 | 40 | 20 |
| Christian Union ................... | 1938 | 220 | 15,400 | No report | |
| Christ's Sanctified Holy Church...... | 1952 | 30 | 550 | 16 | 45 |
| Church of Christ (Holiness), U.S.A.. | 1953 | 142 | 7,786 | 87 | 165 |
| Church of Christ, Scientist.......... | No statistics furnished | | | | |
| Church of Eternal Life............. | 1940 | 2 | 113 | No report | |
| CHURCHES OF GOD: | | | | | |
| Church of God (Cleveland, Tenn.).. | 1953 | 2,615 | 131,623 | 2,556 | 1,387 |
| Church of God (Anderson, Ind.).... | 1953 | 2,051 | 113,698 | 1,731 | 2,600 |
| Church of God (Seventh-day)....... | 1951 | 15 | 2,000 | No report | |
| The (Original) Church of God, Inc.. | 1952 | 75 | 6,000 | 50 | 155 |
| The Church of God................ | 1953 | 1,723 | 66,293 | 1,505 | 2,055 |
| The Church of God (Seventh-day), Denver, Colo. ................... | 1953 | 110 | 3,500 | 61 | 48 |
| The Church of God of Prophecy..... | 1953 | 1,100 | 31,956 | 1,000 | 700 |
| Evangelistic Church of God........ | 1953 | 12 | 774 | 7 | 17 |
| Church of God and Saints of Christ.. | 1953 | 214 | 35,126 | No report | |
| Church of God in Christ............ | 1953 | 3,600 | 338,304 | 3,200 | 5,250 |
| Church of Illumination............. | 1945 | 7 | 5,000 | No report | |
| Church of Our Lord Jesus Christ of the Apostolic Faith, Inc.......... | 1952 | 175 | 50,000 | 160 | 185 |
| Church of the Gospel .............. | 1953 | 5 | 55 | 4 | 3 |
| Church of the Nazarene............. | 1953 | 3,826 | 249,749 | 3,725 | 4,886 |
| The Church of Revelation........... | 1953 | 9 | 3,490 | 9 | 36 |
| Churches of Christ................. | 1953 | 15,000 | 1,500,000 | 12,000 | 15,500('52) |
| Churches of Christ in Christian Union. | 1953 | 182 | 10,200 | 200 | 269 |
| Churches of God, Holiness.......... | 1953 | 34 | 23,000 | 28 | 40 |
| Churches of God in N.A., Inc. (General Eldership) ............. | 1950 | 380 | 32,352 | 168 | 254 |

## CHURCH MEMBERSHIP AND CLERGY STATISTICS

| Name of Religious Body | Year | No. of Churches Reported | Inclusive Church Membership | Number of Pastors Having Charges | Total Number of Ordained Persons |
|---|---|---|---|---|---|
| **CHURCHES OF THE LIVING GOD:** | | | | | |
| Church of the Living God (Christian Workers for Fellowship) | 1952 | 5 | 65 | 7 | 10 |
| House of God, which is the Church of the Living God, the Pillar and Ground of the Truth, Inc. | 1936 | 119 | 4,838 | No report | |
| **CHURCHES OF THE NEW JERUSALEM:** | | | | | |
| General Convention of the New Jerusalem in the U.S.A. | 1953 | 63 | 4,219 | 37 | 58 |
| General Church of the New Jerusalem | 1953 | 5 | 1,677 | 15 | 25 |
| Congregational Christian Churches... | 1953 | 5,573 | 1,283,754 | 3,256 | 5,816 |
| Congregational Holiness Church | 1953 | 132 | 4,170 | 125 | 250 |
| Disciples of Christ, International Convention | 1953 | 7,864 | 1,847,954 | 5,085 | 8,035('52) |
| Divine Science Church | 1953 | 28 | 7,107 | 23 | No data |
| **EASTERN CHURCHES:** | | | | | |
| Albanian Orthodox Church in America | 1953 | 13 | 12,500 | 13 | 13 |
| American Carpatho-Russian Orthodox Greek Catholic Church | 1953 | 58 | 75,000 | 44 | 50 |
| American Catholic Church (Syro-Antiochian) | 1953 | 34 | 4,165 | 51 | 59 |
| The American Holy Orthodox Catholic Apostolic Eastern Church | 1953 | 24 | 2,700 | 20 | 25 |
| The American Orthodox Church | No report | | | | |
| Apostolic Episcopal Church | 1947 | 46 | 7,086 | No report | |
| Armenian Apostolic Orthodox Church of America | 1951 | 57 | 130,000 | 45 | 45 |
| Assyrian Orthodox Church | 1951 | 4 | 3,300 | 4 | 4 |
| Bulgarian Eastern Orthodox Church.. | 1953 | 20 | 4,670 | 7 | 8 |
| Church of the East and of the Assyrians | 1952 | 10 | 3,200 | 8 | 38 |
| Eastern Orthodox Catholic Church in America | Included in the Russian Orthodox Church Outside Russia | | | | |
| Greek Archdiocese of North and South America | 1953 | 325 | 1,000,000 | 375 | 375 |
| Holy Orthodox Church in America (Eastern Catholic and Apostolic).. | 1953 | 4 | 1,300('44) | 4 | 10 |
| Romanian Orthodox Episcopate of America | 1953 | 55 | 50,000 | 35 | 40 |
| The Russian Orthodox Catholic Church, Archdiocese of the Aleutian Islands and North America | No report | | | | |
| The Russian Orthodox Church Outside Russia | 1951 | 91 | 55,000 | 150 | 224 |
| The Russian Orthodox Greek Catholic Church of North America | 1953 | 326 | 440,000 | 304 | 339 |
| Serbian Eastern Orthodox Church... | 1953 | 53 | 100,000 | 63 | 65 |
| Syrian Antiochian Orthodox Church.. | 1953 | 80 | 100,000 | 80 | 90 |
| Ukrainian Orthodox Church of America | 1951 | 47 | 40,250 | 34 | 50 |
| Ukrainian Orthodox Church of U.S.A. | 1953 | 93 | 71,000 | 84 | 102 |
| Ecclesia of Christ | No report | | | | |

## CHURCH MEMBERSHIP AND CLERGY STATISTICS

| Name of Religious Body | Year | No. of Churches Reported | Inclusive Church Membership | Number of Pastors Having Charges | Total Number of Ordained Persons |
|---|---|---|---|---|---|
| Evangelical and Reformed Church... | 1953 | 2,735 | 765,335 | 1,832 | 2,539 |
| Evangelical Congregational Church.. | 1953 | 166 | 28,450 | 130 | 149 |
| Evangelical Free Church of America (merged with Evangelical Free Church Association)............ | 1953 | 342 | 28,000 | 394 | 468 |
| Evangelical Mission Covenant Church of America ..................... | 1953 | 476 | 52,085 | 395 | 508 |
| Evangelical United Brethren Church.. | 1953 | 4,347 | 727,549 | 2,833 | 3,438 |
| EVANGELISTIC ASSOCIATIONS: | | | | | |
| Apostolic Christian Church (Nazarene) .......................... | 1952 | 30 | 1,500 | 90 | 11 |
| Apostolic Christian Church of America ....................... | 1953 | 58 | 7,669 | 163 | 25 |
| Apostolic Faith Mission ............ | 1936 | 17 | 2,288 | 2('50) | 2('50) |
| The Christian Congregation......... | 1953 | 87 | 9,987 | 85 | 102 |
| Church of Daniel's Band........... | 1951 | 4 | 200 | 4 | 10 |
| Church of God (Apostolic)......... | 1953 | 26 | 381 | 21 | 71 |
| Church of God as Organized by Christ ........................... | 1938 | 14 | 2,192 | No report | |
| Metropolitan Church Association.... | 1951 | 20 | 800 | 20 | 61 |
| Missionary Bands of the World, Inc. | 1953 | 11 | 237 | 11 | 26 |
| Missionary Church Association....... | 1953 | 78 | 6,497 | 75 | 144 |
| Pillar of Fire ...................... | 1948 | 61 | 5,100 | No report | |
| Federated Churches ............... | 1936 | 508 | 88,411 | No report | |
| Fire-Baptized Holiness Church....... | 1940 | 300 | 6,000 | No report | |
| Fire-Baptized Holiness Church (Wesleyan) ..................... | 1953 | 46 | 1,000 | 46 | 69 |
| Free Christian Zion Church of Christ .......................... | 1952 | 734 | 18,975 | 624 | 698 |
| FRIENDS: | | | | | |
| Central Yearly Meeting of Friends... | 1953 | 9 | 554 | 9 | 30 |
| The Five Years Meeting of Friends.. | 1952 | 499 | 69,419 | 371 | 613 |
| Ohio Yearly Meeting of Friends Church (Independent)............ | 1953 | 83 | 6,067 | 83 | 164 |
| Oregon Yearly Meeting of Friends Church ......................... | 1953 | 52 | 4,753 | 52 | 145 |
| Pacific Yearly Meeting of Friends.... | 1953 | 17 | 912 | No report | |
| Primitive Friends .................. | Included in Rel. Soc. of Friends (Philadelphia and Vicinity) | | | | |
| Religious Society of Friends (Conservative) ...................... | 1953 | 24 | 2,011 | 5 | 6 |
| Religious Society of Friends (General Conference) ................ | 1952 | 150 | 19,543 | 2 | None |
| Religious Society of Friends (Kansas Yearly Meeting) ................ | 1952 | 85 | 8,103 | No report | |
| Religious Society of Friends (Philadelphia and Vicinity) ............ | 1953 | 50 | 6,114 | None | None |
| Holiness Church of God, Inc........ | 1953 | 25 | 535 | 25 | 26 |
| House of David ................... | 1953 | 1 | 150 | 12 | 10 |
| Independent Churches .............. | 1936 | 384 | 40,276 | No report | |

## CHURCH MEMBERSHIP AND CLERGY STATISTICS

| Name of Religious Body | Year | No. of Churches Reported | Inclusive Church Membership | Number of Pastors Having Charges | Total Number of Ordained Persons |
|---|---|---|---|---|---|
| Independent Fundamental Churches of America | 1946 | 650 | 65,000 | No report | |
| Independent Negro Churches | 1936 | 50 | 12,337 | No report | |
| International Church of the Foursquare Gospel | 1953 | 579 | 81,590 | 579 | 1,706 |
| ITALIAN: | | | | | |
| Christian Church of North America | 1953 | 175 | 17,000 | 143 | 191 |
| Jehovah's Witnesses* | No statistics furnished | | | | |
| Jewish Congregations | 1953 | 3,990 | 5,000,000 | 2,680 | 3,550('50) |
| Kodesh Church of Immanuel | 1936 | 9 | 562 | No report | |
| LATTER-DAY SAINTS: | | | | | |
| Church of Christ, Temple Lot | 1951 | 25 | 2,275 | No report | |
| Church of Jesus Christ (Bickertonites) | 1953 | 36 | 1,916 | 36 | 177 |
| Church of Jesus Christ (Cutlerites) | 1953 | 1 | 16 | None | 3 |
| Church of Jesus Christ of Latter-day Saints | 1952 | 2,348 | 1,077,285 | No report | |
| Church of Jesus Christ of Latter-day Saints (Strangites) | 1952 | 6 | 200 | No report | |
| Reorganized Church of Jesus Christ of Latter-day Saints | 1953 | 692 | 131,781 | 692 | 8,750 |
| Liberal Catholic Church | 1953 | 9 | 3,500 | 9 | 34 |
| Lithuanian National Catholic Church | 1951 | 3 | 5,672 | 3 | 3 |
| LUTHERAN: | | | | | |
| American Evangelical Lutheran Church | 1953 | 89 | 21,106 | 75 | 117 |
| Church of the Lutheran Brethren of America | 1952 | 40 | 3,929 | 42 | 58 |
| Evangelical Lutheran Church in America (Eielsen Synod) | 1953 | 12 | 1,535 | 4 | 5 |
| Finnish Apostolic Lutheran Church of America | 1953 | 57 | 6,567 | 17 | 22 |
| Finnish Evangelical Lutheran Church (Suomi Synod) | 1953 | 164 | 31,853 | 65 | 87 |
| Icelandic Evangelical Lutheran Synod of America | Statistics included in United Lutheran Church in America | | | | |
| Independent Lutheran Churches | 1949 | 12 | 1,465 | 9 | 9 |
| National Evangelical Lutheran Church | 1953 | 60 | 7,148 | 28 | 25 |
| Protestant Conference (Lutheran) | 1947 | 22 | 3,253 | No report | |
| United Lutheran Church in America | 1953 | 3,991 | 2,061,004 | 3,099 | 3,971 |
| *American Lutheran Conference—* | | | | | |
| American Lutheran Church | 1952 | 1,891 | 767,261 | 1,438 | 1,826 |
| Augustana Evangelical Lutheran Church | 1953 | 1,196 | 493,085 | 801 | 1,049 |
| Evangelical Lutheran Church | 1952 | 2,503('51) | 888,634 | 1,172 | 1,612 |

*Jehovah's Witnesses do not keep membership records; but officials of the Watch Tower Bible and Tract Society report that 580,498 preachers are active throughout the world. According to their official doctrine, they are a society of ministers. After a Witness has prepared himself by study and engaged in the public ceremony of water immersion, he is considered a minister of God.

## CHURCH MEMBERSHIP AND CLERGY STATISTICS

| Name of Religious Body | Year | No. of Churches Reported | Inclusive Church Membership | Number of Pastors Having Charges | Total Number of Ordained Persons |
|---|---|---|---|---|---|
| Lutheran Free Church.............. | 1953 | 341 | 65,904 | 145 | 225 |
| United Evangelical Lutheran Church. | 1952 | 166 | 48,955 | 170 | 201 |
| *Lutheran Synodical Conference of N. A.—* | | | | | |
| Lutheran Church—Missouri Synod... | 1953 | 4,592 | 1,850,100 | 3,725 | 4,817 |
| Evangelical Lutheran Joint Synod of Wisconsin and Other States...... | 1952 | 837 | 316,839 | 650 | 700 |
| Norwegian Synod of the American Evangelical Lutheran Church..... | 1953 | 73 | 11,625 | 50 | 68 |
| Slovak Evangelical Lutheran Church.. | 1952 | 59 | 20,562 | 47 | 7 |
| Negro Missions ................... | 1952 | 65 | 8,126 | 32 | 38 |
| **MENNONITE BODIES:** | | | | | |
| Church of God in Christ (Mennonite) | 1952 | 32 | 3,828 | 28 | 71 |
| Conference of the Evangelical Mennonite Church ................. | 1953 | 21 | 2,062 | 17 | 24 |
| Conservative Amish Mennonite Church ........................ | 1953 | 31 | 4,842 | 17 | 93 |
| Evangelical Mennonite Brethren..... | 1953 | 15 | 2,000 | 24 | 44 |
| General Conference Mennonite Church ........................ | 1953 | 187 | 36,170 | 177 | 360 |
| Hutterian Brethren ............... | 1953 | 25 | 2,324 | 39 | 29 |
| Krimmer Mennonite Brethren Conf... | 1950 | 9 | 1,593 | 9 | 67 |
| Mennonite Brethren Church of N.A.. | 1952 | 59 | 10,359 | 59 | 128 |
| Mennonite Church ................ | 1953 | 498 | 63,016 | 758 | 1,246('52) |
| Old Order Amish Mennonite Church. | 1953 | 203 | 15,435 | 400 | 725 |
| Old Order (Wisler) Mennonite Church ........................ | 1953 | 30 | 3,786 | 30 | 66 |
| Reformed Mennonite Church........ | 1953 | 16 | 685 | 21 | 23 |
| Stauffer Mennonite Church......... | 1953 | 2 | 220 | 5 | 7 |
| Unaffiliated Conservative Amish Mennonite Church .............. | 1953 | 20 | 2,034 | 45 | 59 |
| Unaffiliated Mennonite Congregations .......................... | Statistics included in statistics for Mennonite Church | | | | |
| United Missionary Church.......... | 1953 | 192 | 9,556 | 177 | 201 |
| **METHODIST BODIES:** | | | | | |
| African Methodist Episcopal Church. | 1951 | 5,878 | 1,166,301 | 5,878 | 7,089 |
| African Methodist Episcopal Zion Church ........................ | 1952 | 3,160 | 760,158 | 1,800 | 2,500 |
| African Union First Colored Methodist Protestant Church, Inc....... | 1953 | 33 | 5,000 | 33 | 40 |
| Colored Methodist Episcopal Church. | 1951 | 2,469 | 392,167 | 1,820 | 1,631 |
| Congregational Methodist Church.... | 1949 | 160 | 11,189 | 160 | 198 |
| Congregational Methodist Church of U.S.A. ........................ | 1952 | 140 | 6,500 | 125 | 135 |
| Cumberland Methodist Church...... | 1953 | 4 | 60 | 4 | 5 |
| Evangelical Methodist Church....... | No report | | | | |
| Free Methodist Church of N.A...... | 1953 | 1,268 | 51,952 | 1,250 | 1,991 |
| Holiness Methodist Church......... | 1953 | 24 | 675 | 24 | 30 |
| Independent A.M.E. Denomination.. | 1940 | 12 | 1,000 | No report | |
| Independent Fundamental Methodist Church ........................ | 1953 | 14 | 476 | 13 | 15 |
| Lumber River Annual Conference of the Holiness Methodist Church.... | 1953 | 7 | 570 | 5 | 6 |
| The Methodist Church............. | 1953 | 39,780 | 9,151,524 | 23,015 | 25,907 |
| New Congregational Methodist Church ........................ | 1936 | 25 | 1,449 | No report | |
| Primitive Methodist Church, U.S.A.. | 1953 | 90 | 12,217 | 66 | 63 |
| Reformed Methodist Union Episcopal Church ................... | 1952 | 39 | 16,000 | 39 | 42 |

## CHURCH MEMBERSHIP AND CLERGY STATISTICS

| Name of Religious Body | Year | No. of Churches Reported | Inclusive Church Membership | Number of Pastors Having Charges | Total Number of Ordained Persons |
|---|---|---|---|---|---|
| Reformed New Congregational Methodist Church .............. | 1936 | 8 | 329 | No report | |
| Reformed Zion Union Apostolic Church ......................... | 1953 | 52 | 13,500 | 27 | 35 |
| Southern Methodist Church......... | 1953 | 50 | 6,500 | 27 | 13 |
| Union American Methodist Episcopal Church ..................... | 1936 | 71 | 9,369 | No report | |
| Wesleyan Methodist Church of America ....................... | 1953 | 971 | 34,9⁵5 | 971 | 1,320 |
| MORAVIAN BODIES: | | | | | |
| Bohemian and Moravian Brethren... | 1953 | 2 | 230 | 1 | 2 |
| Evangelical Unity of the Czech-Moravian Brethren in N. A....... | 1952 | 32 | 5,143 | 8 | 8 |
| Moravian Church in America (Unitas Fratrum) ....................... | 1953 | 152 | 51,276 | 122 | 144 |
| Muslims .......................... | No report | | | | |
| National David Spiritual Temple of Christ Church Union (Inc.), U.S.A. ......................... | 1953 | 63 | 43,744 | 63 | 176 |
| New Apostolic Church of N.A., Inc. | 1953 | 149 | 10,100 | 149 | 526 |
| OLD CATHOLIC CHURCHES: | | | | | |
| American Catholic Church, Archdiocese of N. Y................ | 1947 | 20 | 8,435 | No report | |
| North American Old Roman Catholic Church ..................... | 1953 | 52 | 85,500 | 52 | 90 |
| Old Catholic Church in America.... | 1940 | 28 | 6,274 | No report | |
| Open Bible Standard Churches, Inc.. | 1953 | 260 | 26,000 | 260 | 501 |
| PENTECOSTAL ASSEMBLIES: | | | | | |
| Calvary Pentecostal Church, Inc..... | 1944 | 35 | 20,000 | No report | |
| Emmanuel Holiness Church......... | 1953 | 41 | 902 | 36 | 58 |
| International Pentecostal Assemblies. | 1952 | 96 | 5,000 | 85 | 137 |
| Pentecostal Assemblies of the World, Inc. ..................... | 1951 | 600 | 50,000 | 500('50) | 650('50) |
| Pentecostal Church of God of America ......................... | 1953 | 550 | 38,000 | 550 | 1,117 |
| Pentecostal Fire-Baptized Holiness Church ......................... | 1953 | 50 | 894 | 40 | 67 |
| The Pentecostal Holiness Church.... | 1953 | 1,045 | 43,943 | 983 | 1,452 |
| United Pentecostal Church......... | 1952 | 1,100 | 125,000 | 1,100 | 1,300 |
| Pilgrim Holiness Church............ | 1953 | 969 | 30,952 | 944 | 1,619 |
| Polish National Catholic Church of America ....................... | 1951 | 156 | 265,879 | 147 | 147 |
| PRESBYTERIAN BODIES: | | | | | |
| Associate Presbyterian Church of N. A. ........................... | 1953 | 5 | 400 | 4 | 4 |
| Associate Reformed Presbyterian Church (General Synod).......... | 1953 | 146 | 27,171 | 105 | 107 |
| Bible Presbyterian Church.......... | No report | | | | |
| Colored Cumberland Presbyterian Church ......................... | 1944 | 121 | 30,000 | No report | |
| Cumberland Presbyterian Church.... | 1953 | 1,014 | 83,307 | 550 | 706 |

## CHURCH MEMBERSHIP AND CLERGY STATISTICS

| Name of Religious Body | Year | No. of Churches Reported | Inclusive Church Membership | Number of Pastors Having Charges | Total Number of Ordained Persons |
|---|---|---|---|---|---|
| Orthodox Presbyterian Church...... | 1953 | 71 | 8,357 | 55 | 97 |
| Presbyterian Church in the U.S...... | 1953 | 3,778 | 756,866 | 2,148 | 3,071 |
| Presbyterian Church in the U.S.A... | 1953 | 8,320 | 2,492,504 | 5,215('52) | 9,643 |
| Reformed Presbyterian Church in N. A. (General Synod).......... | 1953 | 11 | 1,279 | 5 | 8 |
| Reformed Presbyterian Church of N. A. (Old School) ............. | 1953 | 75 | 6,475 | 60 | 94 |
| United Presbyterian Church of N. A. | 1953 | 831 | 228,718 | 619 | 929 |
| Protestant Episcopal Church........ | 1952 | 7,215 | 2,550,831 | 4,963('51) | 6,961 |
| REFORMED BODIES: | | | | | |
| Christian Reformed Church ......... | 1953 | 429 | 186,526 | 334 | 401 |
| Free Magyar Reformed Church in America ........................ | 1951 | 20 | 7,189 | 16 | 20 |
| Reformed Church in America........ | 1953 | 787 | 197,616 | 724 | 958 |
| Reformed Episcopal Church......... | 1953 | 69 | 8,567 | 62 | 80 |
| Roman Catholic Church............ | 1953 | 20,618 | 31,476,261 | 15,835 | 45,271 |
| Salvation Army ................... | 1953 | 1,342 | 235,559 | No data | 5,108 |
| The Schwenkfelder Church......... | 1950 | 5 | 2,400 | 5 | 5 |
| Social Brethren .................... | 1951 | 22 | 1,001 | 18 | No data |
| SPIRITUALISTS: | | | | | |
| International General Assembly of Spiritualists ..................... | 1952 | 182 | 157,000 | 204 | 170 |
| National Spiritual Alliance of the U.S.A. ........................ | 1953 | 21 | 1,010 | 21 | 37 |
| National Spiritualist Association of Churches ....................... | 1953 | 245 | 7,637 | 180 | 218 |
| Triumph the Church and Kingdom of God in Christ .................. | 1953 | 500 | 5,000('52) | 387 | 900 |
| Unitarian Churches ................ | 1953 | 355 | 86,129 | 413 | 503 |
| UNITED BRETHREN BODIES: | | | | | |
| United Brethren in Christ ......... | 1953 | 316 | 20,014 | 167 | 127 |
| United Christian Church............ | 1953 | 14 | 603 | 9 | 12 |
| United Holy Church of America, Inc. ........................... | 1953 | 376 | 26,560 | 353 | 382 |
| Universalist Church of America..... | 1953 | 404 | 73,194 | 236 | 457 |
| Vedanta Society ................... | 1951 | 11 | 1,200 | No report | |
| Volunteers of America.............. | 1953 | 186 | 25,860 | 290 | 290 |
| Totals: (268 bodies, 255 reporting membership, 212 reporting clergy). | | 294,359 | 94,842,845 | 207,618 | 338,250 |

## 2. Catholic Population in the United States: by States and Ecclesiastical Divisions

From the General Summary of Statistics, supplement to *The Official Catholic Directory*, 1954, P. J. KENEDY & SONS, publishers, New York.

*Note:* These statistics are compiled for archdioceses and dioceses. Dioceses which cross state lines are indicated by a dagger (†). The divisions under each state represent archdioceses indicated by an asterisk (*), or dioceses, not cities. Bold face indicates totals.—Ed.

| State and Ecclesiastical Divisions | Number of Catholics | State and Ecclesiastical Divisions | Number of Catholics |
|---|---|---|---|
| **†Alabama** | **83,079** | **Indiana** | **483,351** |
| Mobile (also comprises | | *Indianapolis | 147,000 |
| West Florida) | 83,079 | Evansville | 62,726 |
| **†Arizona** | **176,000** | Fort Wayne | 227,174 |
| Tucson | 176,000 | Lafayette | 46,451 |
| **Arkansas** | **40,335** | **Iowa** | **371,331** |
| Little Rock | 40,335 | *Dubuque | 151,654 |
| **California** | **2,483,411** | Davenport | 76,585 |
| *Los Angeles | 984,370 | Des Moines | 54,792 |
| *San Francisco | 825,000 | Sioux City | 88,300 |
| Monterey-Fresno | 277,042 | **Kansas** | **206,516** |
| Sacramento | 209,231 | *Kansas City | 82,550 |
| San Diego | 187,768 | Dodge City | 23,168 |
| **Colorado** | **240,529** | Salina | 42,692 |
| *Denver | 145,829 | Wichita | 58,106 |
| Pueblo | 94,700 | **Kentucky** | **246,018** |
| **Connecticut** | **976,614** | *Louisville | 139,417 |
| *Hartford | 608,428 | Covington | 72,000 |
| Bridgeport | 243,668 | Owensboro | 34,601 |
| Norwich | 124,518 | **Louisiana** | **898,450** |
| **†Delaware** | **36,932** | *New Orleans | 516,105 |
| Wilmington | 36,932 | Alexandria | 60,345 |
| **†District of Columbia** | **210,318** | Lafayette | 322,000 |
| *Washington | 210,318 | **Maine** | **229,792** |
| **†Florida** | **131,000** | Portland | 229,792 |
| St. Augustine | | **†Maryland** | **347,615** |
| (East Florida) | 131,000 | *Baltimore | 347,615 |
| **Georgia** | **35,696** | **Massachusetts** | **2,263,619** |
| Savannah-Atlanta | 35,696 | *Boston | 1,426,319 |
| **Idaho** | **31,511** | Fall River | 235,383 |
| Boise | 31,511 | Springfield | 325,129 |
| **Illinois** | **2,387,873** | Worcester | 276,788 |
| *Chicago | 1,815,976 | **Michigan** | **1,540,527** |
| Belleville | 93,279 | *Detroit | 1,075,000 |
| Joliet | 108,571 | Grand Rapids | 126,708 |
| Peoria | 161,441 | Lansing | 115,439 |
| Rockford | 82,428 | Marquette | 94,599 |
| Springfield | 126,178 | Saginaw | 128,781 |

| State and Ecclesiastical Divisions | Number of Catholics | State and Ecclesiastical Divisions | Number of Catholics |
|---|---|---|---|
| **Minnesota** | **697,997** | **Oklahoma** | **83,212** |
| *St. Paul | 393,009 | Oklahoma City and Tulsa | 83,212 |
| Crookston | 32,935 | **Oregon** | **128,383** |
| Duluth | 91,064 | *Portland | 112,497 |
| St. Cloud | 97,784 | Baker | 15,886 |
| Winona | 83,205. | **Pennsylvania** | **2,953,613** |
| **Mississippi** | **56,317** | *Philadelphia | 1,250,469 |
| Natchez | 56,317 | Altoona | 142,579 |
| **Missouri** | **594,358** | Erie | 183,663 |
| *St. Louis | 475,000 | Greensburg | 181,575 |
| Kansas City | 85,000 | Harrisburg | 130,938 |
| St. Joseph | 34,358 | Pittsburgh | 720,166 |
| **Montana** | **132,475** | Scranton | 344,223 |
| Great Falls | 52,475 | **Rhode Island** | **465,178** |
| Helena | 80,000 | Providence | 465,178 |
| **Nebraska** | **214,051** | **South Carolina** | **22,322** |
| *Omaha | 132,531 | Charleston | 22,322 |
| Grand Island | 36,772 | **South Dakota** | **112,370** |
| Lincoln | 44,748 | Rapid City | 30,200 |
| **Nevada** | **29,000** | Sioux Falls | 82,170 |
| Reno | 29,000 | **Tennessee** | **53,301** |
| **New Hampshire** | **190,303** | Nashville | 53,301 |
| Manchester | 190,303 | †**Texas** | **1,507,642** |
| **New Jersey** | **.1,850,128** | *San Antonio | 300,187 |
| *Newark | 1,123,607 | Amarillo | 57,031 |
| Camden | 178,610 | Austin | 97,269 |
| Paterson | 175,795 | Corpus Christi | 500,000 |
| Trenton | 372,116 | Dallas | 86,340 |
| †**New Mexico** | **283,095** | †El Paso | 148,271 |
| *Santa Fe | 240,000 | Galveston | 318,544 |
| †Gallup | 43,095 | **Utah** | **30,937** |
| **New York** | **4,562,296** | Salt Lake City | 30,937 |
| *New York | 1,316,170 | **Vermont** | **111,006** |
| Albany | 319,157 | Burlington | 111,006 |
| Brooklyn | 1,443,848 | †**Virginia** | **109,413** |
| Buffalo | 695,048 | Richmond | 109,413 |
| Ogdensburg | 131,467 | **Washington** | **266,135** |
| Rochester | 327,516 | *Seattle | 185,000 |
| Syracuse | 284,090 | Spokane | 49,635 |
| **North Carolina** | **33,686** | Yakima | 31,500 |
| Belmont Abbey | 855 | †**West Virginia** | **97,504** |
| Raleigh | 32,831 | Wheeling | 97,504 |
| **North Dakota** | **139,385** | **Wisconsin** | **1,068,999** |
| Bismarck | 60,424 | *Milwaukee | 494,241 |
| Fargo | 78,961 | Green Bay | 231,496 |
| **Ohio** | **1,577,868** | La Crosse | 156,199 |
| *Cincinnati | 375,000 | Madison | 108,549 |
| Cleveland | 607,412 | Superior | 78,514 |
| Columbus | 121,360 | **Wyoming** | **48,304** |
| Steubenville | 52,266 | Cheyenne | 48,304 |
| Toledo | 221,830 | | |
| Youngstown | 200,000 | | |

## 3. Jewish Population in the United States: by States and Cities

From ALVIN CHENKIN and BEN B. SELIGMAN in the 1954 *American Jewish Year Book,* MORRIS FINE, ed., Vol. 55, New York: The American Jewish Committee, and Philadelphia: the Jewish Publication Society of America, pp. 3–4.

At the time of writing (August, 1953), the Jewish population in the United States could be estimated at over 5,000,000.

There had been some guesses in the past that the American Jewish population had passed the 5,000,000 mark; but this was the first time that the compilation of estimates, from the vast majority of communities with Jewish populations, presented a basis for this belief.

This over-all estimate was based on the list of Jewish populations for more than 700 communities containing the bulk of American Jewry as well as a projection for communities not represented on that list, either because they failed to report or because they had fewer than 100 Jews. This list is the second revision of the compilation of estimates originally published in the *American Jewish Year Book,* 1949 (Vol. 50) and subsequently modified for the *Year Book,* 1951 (Vol. 52).

In evaluating the current estimates, it must be remembered that there simply was no other source in the United States capable at the time of writing of providing estimates that could be more accurate or up to date. In 1926 and 1936 the United States Bureau of the Census conducted decennial censuses of religious bodies. However, no such census had been taken in 1946, for lack of a Congressional appropriation.

### a) State Totals

*Note: State totals* are estimates, based on the communities reporting a Jewish population of 100 or more in the *American Jewish Year Book,* 1954 (Vol. 55), pp. 8–12.—Ed.

| State | Population |
| --- | --- |
| Alabama | 8,644 |
| Arizona | 9,300 |
| Arkansas | 2,370 |
| California | 441,058 |
| Colorado | 16,900 |
| Connecticut | 87,899 |
| Delaware | 6,500 |
| District of Columbia | 35,000 |
| Florida | 71,133 |
| Georgia | 17,130 |
| Idaho | 120 |
| Illinois | 339,963 |
| Indiana | 21,418 |
| Iowa | 9,395 |
| Kansas | 1,243 |
| Kentucky | 9,822 |
| Louisiana | 13,984 |
| Maine | 7,102 |
| Maryland | 80,233 |
| Massachusetts | 200,978 |
| Michigan | 82,990 |
| Minnesota | 35,999 |
| Mississippi | 2,560 |
| Missouri | 69,770 |
| Montana | 306 |
| Nebraska | 7,450 |
| Nevada | 720 |
| New Hampshire | 3,361 |
| New Jersey | 257,313 |
| New Mexico | 1,095 |
| New York | 2,546,097 |
| North Carolina | 4,128 |
| North Dakota | 932 |
| Ohio | 151,521 |
| Oklahoma | 4,254 |
| Oregon | 6,930 |
| Pennsylvania | 363,833 |
| Rhode Island | 23,220 |
| South Carolina | 3,639 |
| South Dakota | 473 |
| Tennessee | 13,855 |
| Texas | 50,946 |
| Utah | 1,440 |
| Vermont | 1,280 |
| Virginia | 22,863 |
| Washington | 11,188 |
| West Virginia | 5,588 |
| Wisconsin | 37,346 |
| Wyoming | 500 |
| **U.S. Total** | **5,091,789** |

**b) Jewish Population in Order of Size in 15 Leading U. S. Cities**

Extracted from the 1954 *American Jewish Year Book,* Morris Fine, ed., Vol. 55, New York: The American Jewish Committee, and Philadelphia: the Jewish Publication Society of America, pp. 8–12.

(Estimate based on communities reporting Jewish population of 100 or more.)

| City | Jewish Population | |
|------|------------------:|---|
| New York, N.Y. | 2,294,000 | |
| Chicago, Ill. | 325,000 | (1950) |
| Los Angeles, Calif. | 325,000 | |
| Philadelphia, Pa. | 245,000 | |
| Boston, Mass. | 140,000 | |
| Cleveland, Ohio | 85,000 | |
| Baltimore, Md. | 78,000 | |
| Detroit, Mich. | 72,000 | |
| Newark, N.J. | 56,800 | |
| Miami, Fla. | 55,000 | |
| Pittsburgh, Pa. | 54,000 | (1948) |
| San Francisco, Calif. | 51,000 | |
| St. Louis, Mo. | 48,000 | |
| District of Columbia | 35,000 | |
| Milwaukee, Wisc. | 30,000 | |

# 4. Protestant Population in the U.S.

## a) A Note on Protestant Statistics

By DAVID W. BARRY, Executive Director, Central Department of Research and Survey, National Council of the Churches of Christ in the U.S.A.

The only available statistics on total membership of religious bodies in the United States are those compiled annually by the National Council of Churches and published in its *Yearbook of American Churches*. Certain limitations of these statistics must be understood if they are to be properly interpreted.

1. They refer to the *continental United States* only, although many of the church bodies reported actually have churches and members elsewhere in North and South America, in Africa and Asia, and other parts of the world.

2. They are based on official reports from the headquarters of the various religious bodies, and no attempt is made to go behind these reports to check their accuracy. Some, obviously, are estimates; personal contacts with some denominations have revealed that a number of them do not compile such reports from actual records

of membership of local churches reported to a central office each year.

3. The basis of reporting "membership" is quite different from one church body to another. The Roman Catholics count all baptized persons, including infants. Some Protestant bodies, notably the Protestant Episcopal Church and many Lutheran churches, do the same. Most Protestant churches, however, count only the persons who have attained full membership, of whom only a small minority are less than 13 years of age. Jews regard as members all Jews in communities where congregations are organized, and the Eastern Orthodox churches usually include all persons in their respective nationality or cultural groups.

These facts help explain the difficulty of making analyses of the geographic distribution of church members in the United States. The table showing the distribution of membership of 14 Protestant churches which belong to the National Council includes all the major member churches of that agency which actually have such statistics to report. The membership involved here is about 22,000,000 "full" members, or members the great majority of whom are 13 years of age or over. If it included the entire "baptized" membership of the Lutheran and Protestant Episcopal Churches on the list, the total would be about 24,000,000.

There are actually about 54,000,000 Protestant church members in the United States. Who are the remaining 30 million? In rounded figures, they consist of the following groups:

| | |
|---|---|
| Southern Baptists | 7,900,000 |
| Negro Baptists (do not report such data) | 7,200,000 |
| Negro Methodists (do not report such data) | 2,300,000 |
| Lutheran Synodical Conference (Missouri Synod and associated bodies) | 2,200,000 |
| Christ Unity Science Church (no data so far as we know) | 1,600,000 |
| Churches of Christ (no such data, although they are beginning to set up records) | 1,500,000 |
| Latter-day Saints (6 bodies— maintain such records, but we do not have them) | 1,200,000 |
| 195 other smaller Protestant bodies (which may or may not keep such records) | 6,100,000 |
| Total | 30,000,000 |

### b) Southern Baptist Convention: Membership Figures by States (1953)

From the Department of Survey, Statistics and Information of the Southern Baptist Convention, Nashville, Tennessee.

*Note:* The Southern Baptist Convention is the second largest Protestant denomination in the United States. It is a legally organized denomination with a membership of 7,873,044 individuals and 29,481 churches (as of 1953).

The Southern Baptist Convention was formed in 1845 by a group of Baptists in the South who broke away from the General Missionary Convention (a national Baptist body) over the question of slavery.

Not all Baptist churches in the South belong to the Southern Baptist Convention; nor are all the members of the Convention from the South.

Affiliated churches are found in California, Oregon, and Washington.—Ed.

| State | Number of Southern Baptists |
|---|---|
| Alabama | 581,443 |
| Arizona | 22,148 |
| Arkansas | 265,478 |
| California | 61,096 |
| District of Columbia | 32,186 |
| Florida | 330,346 |
| Georgia | 739,755 |
| Illinois | 118,646 |
| Kansas | 12,614 |
| Kentucky | 572,543 |
| Louisiana | 323,158 |
| Maryland | 34,016 |
| Mississippi | 413,514 |
| Missouri | 380,629 |
| New Mexico | 58,673 |
| North Carolina | 758,207 |
| Oklahoma | 379,861 |
| Oregon-Washington | 8,139 |
| South Carolina | 419,855 |
| Tennessee | 665,982 |
| Texas | 1,318,942 |
| Virginia | 375,813 |
| *Total*, Southern Baptist Convention in U.S. | 7,873,044 |

## c) The 30 Constituent Bodies of the National Council of the Churches of Christ in the U.S.A.

From the 1955 *Yearbook of American Churches*, BENSON Y. LANDIS, ed., New York: The National Council of the Churches of Christ in the U.S.A., 1954, p. 275.

*Note:* The National Council of the Churches of Christ in the U.S.A. is a cooperative agency of thirty Protestant and Eastern Orthodox denominations.

It represents about 35,000,000 church members in approximately 143,500 local congregations.

The Council was organized in December, 1950, as a merger of 12 interdenominational agencies, among which were the Federal Council of Churches of Christ in America, the Home Missions Council of North America, the Foreign Missions Conference, and the International Council of Religious Education—Ed.

|  | Year | Number of Churches | Inclusive Membership | Pastors Having Charges |
|---|---|---|---|---|
| African Methodist Episcopal Church.... | 1951 | 5,878 | 1,166,301 | 5,878 |
| African Methodist Episcopal Zion Church | 1952 | 3,160 | 760,158 | 1,800 |
| American Baptist Convention.......... | 1952 | 6,531 | 1,557,816 | 5,500 |
| American Evangelical Lutheran Church.. | 1953 | 89 | 2,106 | 75 |
| Augustana Evangelical Lutheran Church | 1953 | 1,196 | 493,085 | 801 |
| Church of the Brethren............... | 1953 | 1,028 | 190,263 | 841 |
| Colored Methodist Episcopal Church  .. | 1951 | 2,469 | 392,167 | 1,820 |
| Congregational Christian Churches...... | 1953 | 5,573 | 1,283,754 | 3,256 |
| Disciples of Christ, International Convention ...................... | 1953 | 7,864 | 1,847,954 | 5,085 |
| Evangelical and Reformed Church...... | 1953 | 2,735 | 761,335 | 1,832 |
| Evangelical United Brethren Church.... | 1953 | 4,347 | 727,549 | 2,833 |
| Evangelical Unity of the Czech-Moravian Brethren in North America.......... | 1952 | 32 | 5,143 | 8 |
| Greek Archdiocese of North and South America ......................... | 1953 | 325 | 1,000,000 | 375 |
| Moravian Church in America (Unitas Fratum) ......................... | 1953 | 152 | 51,276 | 122 |
| National Baptist Convention of America | 1953 | 11,136 | 2,606,510 | 27,800* |
| National Baptist Convention, U.S.A., Inc. | 1953 | 24,415 | 4,526,847 | 18,964 |
| Presbyterian Church in the U.S........ | 1953 | 3,778 | 756,866 | 2,148 |
| Presbyterian Church in the U.S.A....... | 1953 | 8,320 | 2,492,504 | 5,215 |
| Protestant Episcopal Church........... | 1952 | 7,215 | 2,550,831 | 4,963 |
| Reformed Church in America.......... | 1953 | 787 | 197,616 | 724 |
| Religious Society of Friends (Philadelphia and Vicinity) ..................... | 1953 | 50 | 6,114 | None |
| Romanian Orthodox Episcopate of America .............................. | 1953 | 55 | 50,000 | 35 |
| Seventh Day Baptist General Conference | 1953 | 65 | 6,257 | 31 |
| Syrian Antiochian Orthodox Church.... | 1953 | 80 | 100,000 | 80 |
| The Five Years Meeting of Friends..... | 1952 | 499 | 69,419 | 371 |
| The Methodist Church................ | 1953 | 39,780 | 9,151,524 | 23,015 |
| The Russian Orthodox Greek Catholic Church of North America........... | 1953 | 326 | 440,000 | 304 |
| Ukrainian Orthodox Church of America | 1951 | 47 | 40,250 | 34 |
| United Lutheran Church in America.... | 1953 | 3,991 | 2,061,004 | 3,099 |
| United Presbyterian Church of N.A..... | 1953 | 831 | 228,718 | 619 |
| TOTAL ...................... |  | 142,754 | 35,542,367 | 117,628 |

* This is the total number of ordained persons. The number of pastors having charges is not available.

### d) MEMBERSHIP FIGURES, BY STATES, AFFILIATED WITH THE NATIONAL

From the Central Department of Research and Survey of the

| States | American Baptist Convention (1952) | Augustana Lutheran Church (1953) | Church of the Brethren (1953) | Congregat'l Christian Churches (1953) | Disciples of Christ (1953) | Evangelical and Reformed Church (1953) | Evangelical United Brethren Church (1953) |
|---|---|---|---|---|---|---|---|
| Alabama | — | — | — | 5,795 | 11,110 | 422 | — |
| Arizona | 6,532 | 498 | — | 3,277 | 5,620 | 4 | — |
| Arkansas | — | — | 295 | 190 | 16,527 | 259 | — |
| California | 163,065 | 12,294 | 7,994 | 79,922 | 87,993 | 3,180 | 8,245 |
| Colorado | 29,691 | 3,618 | 1,519 | 17,558 | 21,694 | 2,386 | 7,313 |
| Connecticut | 29,914 | 11,543 | — | 118,249 | 376 | 1,861 | 123 |
| Delaware | 2,342 | — | 1,241 | 647 | 6,138 | — | — |
| Washington, D.C. | 31,972 | 611 | — | 4,882 | 6,139 | 1,225 | — |
| Florida | — | 2,094 | 458 | 8,453 | 17,907 | 391 | 1,462 |
| Georgia | — | — | 458 | 4,344 | 27,136 | — | — |
| Idaho | 9,017 | 1,094 | 756 | 3,792 | 9,948 | 124 | — |
| Illinois | 116,545 | 55,980 | 5,411 | 91,872 | 155,158 | 78,075 | 47,336 |
| Indiana | 111,905 | 4,720 | 18,330 | 23,264 | 194,589 | 40,381 | 85,795 |
| Iowa | 35,067 | 20,520 | 4,096 | 42,626 | 80,321 | 19,417 | 22,091 |
| Kansas | 72,005 | 8,754 | 5,550 | 18,407 | 98,716 | 5,064 | 31,269 |
| Kentucky | — | — | — | 665 | 136,454 | 12,274 | 540 |
| Louisiana | — | — | 213 | 1,612 | 6,294 | 4,114 | — |
| Maine | 37,043 | 503 | — | 33,535 | 376 | — | 123 |
| Maryland | — | 442 | 12,541 | 2,103 | 6,138 | 20,479 | — |
| Massachusetts | 95,344 | 13,831 | — | 196,011 | 376 | 267 | 123 |
| Michigan | 53,672 | 18,318 | 3,033 | 68,933 | 18,394 | 21,588 | 19,871 |
| Minnesota | 15,335 | 98,287 | 789 | 37,514 | 3,850 | 11,551 | 14,902 |
| Mississippi | — | — | — | 131 | 9,177 | 98 | — |
| Missouri | — | 1,836 | 1,990 | 9,573 | 164,953 | 42,345 | 3,537 |
| Montana | 5,771 | 1,602 | 948 | 8,523 | 5,589 | 370 | 1,117 |
| Nebraska | 17,143 | 11,755 | 776 | 21,965 | 29,817 | 7,743 | 13,538 |
| Nevada | 1,784 | — | — | 156 | 411 | — | — |
| New Hampshire | 13,813 | 432 | — | 30,327 | 376 | — | 123 |
| New Jersey | 55,725 | 3,391 | 843 | 20,051 | 892 | 4,449 | 6,607 |
| New Mexico | — | — | 465 | 979 | 4,933 | — | 1,116 |
| New York | 173,892 | 12,396 | 843 | 83,827 | 13,367 | 29,755 | 7,137 |
| North Carolina | — | — | 753 | 29,223 | 60,770 | 14,627 | — |
| North Dakota | 3,045 | 4,517 | 190 | 9,727 | 3,850 | 5,022 | 7,774 |
| Ohio | 98,068 | 2,391 | 21,647 | 84,586 | 155,375 | 108,600 | 149,668 |
| Oklahoma | 1,599 | — | 465 | 2,558 | 99,092 | 648 | 3,410 |
| Oregon | 15,911 | 3,092 | 673 | 11,048 | 40,957 | 1,453 | — |
| Pennsylvania | 118,027 | 9,013 | 48,687 | 18,976 | 45,636 | 198,561 | 201,655 |
| Rhode Island | 23,287 | 3,860 | — | 12,037 | 376 | — | 122 |
| South Carolina | — | — | 754 | 269 | 5,233 | — | — |
| South Dakota | 6,861 | 4,039 | 788 | 16,422 | 2,113 | 2,197 | — |
| Tennessee | — | — | 2,266 | 1,260 | 38,128 | 259 | 6,075 |
| Texas | — | 3,730 | 678 | 1,822 | 126,599 | 12,210 | 1,326 |
| Utah | 2,599 | 628 | — | 1,542 | 760 | — | — |
| Virginia | 646 | — | 33,266 | 22,680 | 59,079 | 3,300 | 21,242 |
| Vermont | 10,159 | 475 | — | 27,202 | 376 | — | 122 |
| Washington | 31,357 | 8,685 | 2,524 | 21,200 | 31,682 | 625 | 11,221 |
| West Virginia | 136,539 | — | 4,580 | — | 29,085 | 1,839 | 26,972 |
| Wisconsin | 26,301 | 10,623 | 2,367 | 47,853 | 4,984 | 48,154 | 25,594 |
| Wyoming | 5,840 | 620 | — | 2,904 | 2,758 | 1,529 | — |

* This survey includes only denominations of 100,000

## OF 14 OF THE 30 DENOMINATIONS
## COUNCIL OF CHURCHES *

National Council of the Churches of Christ in the U.S.A.

| The Methodist Church (1950) | Presbyterian Church in the U.S. (Southern) (1953) | Presbyterian Church in the U.S.A. (Northern) (1953) | Protestant Episcopal Church (1952) | Reformed Church in America (1953) | United Lutheran Church in America (1953) | United Presbyterian Church of North America (1953) | Totals |
|---|---|---|---|---|---|---|---|
| 304,439 | 33,524 | 2,360 | 14,602 | — | 655 | — | 372,907 |
| 19,224 | — | 12,976 | 7,380 | — | 2,013 | — | 59,524 |
| 193,117 | 21,695 | — | 7,322 | —. | 91 | — | 239,496 |
| 230,081 | — | 178,401 | 101,914 | 3,163 | 15,472 | 10,123 | 901,847 |
| 66,214 | — | 35,948 | 18,693 | 494 | 3,248 | 3,663 | 212,039 |
| 49,226 | — | 3,045 | 68,195 | — | 8,648 | 1,300 | 292,480 |
| 41,834 | — | — | 9,603 | — | 2,087 | — | 63,892 |
| 44,788 | — | 22,958 | 31,969 | — | 4,930 | — | 149,474 |
| 167,616 | 54,386 | 13,660 | 40,928 | — | 3,775 | — | 311,130 |
| 354,936 | 57,110 | — | 21,645 | — | 4,897 | — | 470,526 |
| 20,035 | — | 9,237 | 4,198 | — | 188 | 1,167 | 59,556 |
| 466,165 | — | 170,000 | 55,344 | 11,334 | 49,388 | 12,103 | 1,314,711 |
| 354,235 | — | 89,752 | 13,714 | 2,177 | 19,560 | 2,152 | 960,574 |
| 279,297 | — | 80,588 | 11,015 | 15,418 | 17,097 | 10,586 | 638,139 |
| 214,249 | — | 59,606 | 16,425 | — | 7,286 | 6,167 | 543,498 |
| 204,876 | 25,991 | 16,048 | 14,906 | 247 | 4,477 | — | 416,478 |
| 122,698 | 25,959 | — | 18,668 | — | — | — | 179,558 |
| 30,281 | — | 3,045 | 9,329 | — | — | — | 114,235 |
| 191,126 | — | 38,894 | 42,086 | — | 38,374 | — | 352,183 |
| 101,669 | — | 3,045 | 97,064 | — | 1,368 | 1,301 | 510,399 |
| 229,056 | — | 103,015 | 63,487 | 35,682 | 9,754 | 6,151 | 650,954 |
| 105,192 | — | 60,331 | 26,531 | 3,379 | 19,760 | — | 397,421 |
| 224,028 | 31,335 | — | 10,443 | — | 596 | — | 275,808 |
| 260,220 | 22,897 | 67,043 | 24,313 | — | 4,198 | — | 602,905 |
| 22,685 | — | 12,419 | 6,626 | 69 | 1,057 | — | 66,776 |
| 115,860 | — | 47,090 | 11,342 | 1,469 | 27,312 | 2,951 | 308,761 |
| 1,909 | — | — | 2,129 | — | 199 | — | 6,588 |
| 19,086 | — | 3,045 | 10,483 | — | — | — | 77,685 |
| 175,256 | — | 173,316 | 99,346 | 42,895 | 35,203 | 9,200 | 627,174 |
| 29,904 | — | 11,678 | 8,238 | 453 | 1,140 | — | 58,906 |
| 424,371 | — | 284,362 | 268,182 | 63,831 | 89,031 | 9,201 | 1,460,195 |
| 416,116 | 133,657 | — | 31,214 | — | 31,783 | — | 718,143 |
| 18,103 | — | 12,746 | 3,011 | 458 | 2,075 | — | 70,518 |
| 544,088 | — | 202,222 | 60,809 | 432 | 76,790 | 33,080 | 1,537,756 |
| 192,033 | 5,703 | 41,060 | 10,433 | 201 | 891 | 1,257 | 359,350 |
| 43,762 | — | 31,769 | 18,619 | — | 2,432 | 1,930 | 171,676 |
| 540,997 | — | 406,612 | 147,555 | 1,624 | 392,223 | 101,212 | 2,230,778 |
| 11,857 | — | 3,045 | 31,334 | — | — | 1,301 | 87,219 |
| 221,967 | 56,029 | 9,167 | 21,198 | — | 22,298 | — | 336,915 |
| 35,667 | — | 15,461 | 11,294 | 2,818 | 133 | — | 97,793 |
| 343,098 | 52,954 | 31,071 | 21,255 | — | 3,529 | 1,034 | 500,929 |
| 656,447 | 92,212 | 42,992 | 67,716 | — | 6,471 | — | 1,012,203 |
| 3,669 | — | — | 2,705 | — | — | — | 11,903 |
| 360,068 | 113,060 | — | 55,346 | — | 15,666 | — | 684,354 |
| 22,150 | — | 3,045 | 7,128 | — | — | 654 | 71,311 |
| 67,649 | — | 54,700 | 23,592 | 845 | 4,254 | 3,671 | 262,005 |
| 233,659 | 30,372 | 16,857 | 11,866 | — | 5,396 | 695 | 497,860 |
| 109,266 | — | 49,430 | 27,787 | 6,629 | 42,318 | 1,302 | 402,518 |
| 11,222 | — | 6,853 | 7,938 | — | 369 | — | 40,033 |

or over which publish state membership statistics.

## e) LUTHERAN MEMBERSHIP

Statistics provided by HELEN KNUBEL, Secretary
based on figures from the 1953

### THE NATIONAL LUTHERAN COUNCIL *
(organized 1918)

| States | United Luth. Ch. in Amer. (1918) | Evang. Luth. Ch. (1946) | American Luth. Ch. (1930) | Augustana Luth. Ch. (1918) | Lutheran Free Church (1897) | United Evang. Luth. Ch. (1918) |
|---|---|---|---|---|---|---|
| Alabama | 1,072 | — | 1,147 | — | — | — |
| Arizona | 3,485 | 170 | 1,614 | 706 | — | — |
| Arkansas | 276 | — | 294 | — | — | — |
| California | 33,519 | 21,844 | 22,765 | 17,897 | — | 4,995 |
| Colorado | 5,625 | 1,932 | 6,102 | 5,254 | — | 618 |
| Connecticut | 16,311 | — | — | 14,858 | — | — |
| Delaware | 3,944 | — | — | — | — | — |
| District of Columbia | 9,634 | — | 2,054 | 814 | — | — |
| Florida | 6,987 | — | 2,614 | 2,909 | — | — |
| Georgia | 9,010 | — | — | — | — | — |
| Idaho | 395 | 2,393 | 2,408 | 1,655 | — | — |
| Illinois | 105,025 | 33,115 | 43,325 | 77,880 | 432 | 1,496 |
| Indiana | 38,060 | — | 15,058 | 6,607 | — | 139 |
| Iowa | 35,303 | 74,651 | 81,180 | 28,502 | 163 | 12,060 |
| Kansas | 15,653 | 843 | 8,679 | 11,752 | 555 | 240 |
| Kentucky | 8,335 | — | 142 | — | — | — |
| Louisiana | — | — | 1,290 | — | — | — |
| Maine | — | 343 | — | 703 | — | 549 |
| Maryland | 85,609 | — | 18,666 | 664 | — | — |
| Massachusetts | 3,241 | 725 | — | 18,636 | — | 140 |
| Michigan | 20,342 | 5,786 | 59,750 | 26,154 | 1,047 | 1,103 |
| Minnesota | 37,024 | 289,386 | 49,459 | 142,952 | 33,789 | 5,241 |
| Mississippi | 1,329 | — | 52 | — | — | — |
| Missouri | 8,749 | — | 2,480 | 2,517 | — | 218 |
| Montana | 2,167 | 30,137 | 756 | 2,702 | 450 | 1,122 |
| Nebraska | 55,741 | 3,581 | 27,497 | 16,111 | 344 | 4,378 |
| Nevada | 397 | — | — | — | — | — |
| New Hampshire | — | 370 | — | 533 | — | — |
| New Jersey | 80,738 | 2,092 | — | 4,792 | — | — |
| New Mexico | 2,215 | — | — | — | — | — |
| New York | 204,072 | 10,053 | 13,510 | 18,687 | 93 | 934 |
| North Carolina | 58,357 | — | 2,738 | — | — | — |
| North Dakota | 4,737 | 115,659 | 24,607 | 6,750 | 12,113 | 1,373 |
| Ohio | 150,359 | 818 | 149,533 | 3,256 | — | — |
| Oklahoma | 1,578 | — | 1,414 | — | — | 137 |
| Oregon | 5,232 | 10,085 | 6,764 | 4,770 | 999 | 1,350 |
| Pennsylvania | 796,914 | 288 | 24,798 | 12,186 | — | — |
| Rhode Island | — | — | — | 5,089 | — | — |
| South Carolina | 40,168 | — | — | — | — | — |
| South Dakota | 307 | 80,662 | 15,731 | 5,672 | 1,948 | 759 |
| Tennessee | 7,037 | — | — | — | — | — |
| Texas | 11,472 | 4,725 | 68,198 | 5,304 | — | — |
| Utah | — | — | — | 970 | — | 156 |
| Vermont | — | — | — | 623 | — | — |
| Virginia | 31,212 | 186 | 2,717 | — | — | — |
| Washington | 11,034 | 30,476 | 14,345 | 14,509 | 3,732 | — |
| West Virginia | 11,311 | — | 5,153 | — | — | — |
| Wisconsin | 75,492 | 167,004 | 89,004 | 15,710 | 7,678 | 11,946 |
| Wyoming | 989 | 715 | — | 988 | — | — |
| **Totals** | **2,000,457**** | **888,039** | **765,844** | **479,112** | **63,343** | **48,954** |

* The National Lutheran Council is the U. S. A. Committee of the Lutheran World Federation.

# FIGURES: BY STATES

for Research of the National Lutheran Council,
yearbooks of various Lutheran bodies.

## THE EVANGELICAL LUTHERAN SYNODICAL CONFERENCE OF NORTH AMERICA
### (organized 1871)

| Suomi Synod (1918) | American Evang. Luth. Ch. (1953) | Missouri Synod (1847) | Wisconsin Synod (1850) | Slovak Synod (1902) | Negro Missions | Total |
|---|---|---|---|---|---|---|
| — | — | 3,337 | — | — | 3,279 | 8,825 |
| — | — | 1,370 | 6,277 | — | — | 13,622 |
| — | — | 5,971 | — | — | — | 6,541 |
| 723 | 1,383 | 87,971 | 255 | — | — | 191,352 |
| — | 121 | 20,930 | 1,796 | — | — | 42,378 |
| 115 | 635 | 13,108 | — | — | — | 45,027 |
| — | — | 1,011 | — | — | — | 4,955 |
| — | — | 3,168 | — | — | — | 15,670 |
| — | — | 8,991 | — | 240 | 358 | 22,099 |
| — | — | 896 | — | — | 47 | 9,953 |
| — | — | 6,542 | 59 | — | — | 13,452 |
| 1,100 | 1,382 | 263,893 | 4,167 | 4,713 | — | 536,528 |
| — | — | 85,967 | — | 1,119 | — | 146,950 |
| — | 4,516 | 93,823 | 889 | — | — | 331,087 |
| — | 148 | 43,376 | — | — | — | 81,246 |
| — | — | 2,919 | — | — | — | 11,396 |
| — | — | 12,984 | — | — | 2,252 | 16,526 |
| 216 | 187 | 282 | — | — | — | 2,280 |
| — | — | 17,238 | — | — | 257 | 122,434 |
| 1,806 | — | 9,005 | — | — | — | 33,553 |
| 13,528 | 2,553 | 181,852 | 34,196 | 26 | — | 346,337 |
| 4,969 | 2,788 | 161,459 | 58,429 | 843 | 18 | 786,357 |
| 21 | 43 | 1,211 | — | — | 86 | 2,742 |
| — | — | 114,695 | — | 870 | — | 129,529 |
| — | 468 | 9,290 | 363 | — | — | 47,455 |
| — | 1,572 | 82,075 | 6,404 | — | — | 197,703 |
| — | — | 1,687 | — | — | — | 2,084 |
| — | — | 659 | — | — | — | 1,562 |
| — | 509 | 25,062 | — | 1,780 | — | 114,973 |
| — | — | 2,370 | — | — | — | 4,585 |
| 841 | 532 | 105,507 | — | 492 | — | 354,721 |
| — | — | 8,926 | — | — | 1,633 | 71,654 |
| 100 | 25 | 25,397 | 2,199 | — | — | 192,960 |
| 3,902 | — | 68,710 | 2,460 | 4,249 | — | 383,287 |
| — | — | 14,454 | — | — | — | 17,583 |
| 658 | 262 | 18,512 | 248 | — | — | 48,880 |
| 615 | — | 24,114 | — | 3,755 | — | 862,670 |
| — | — | 1,494 | — | — | — | 6,583 |
| — | — | 562 | — | — | 33 | 40,763 |
| 528 | 843 | 28,764 | 10,004 | — | — | 145,218 |
| — | — | 3,719 | — | — | — | 10,756 |
| — | 154 | 56,355 | — | 77 | — | 146,285 |
| — | — | 1,397 | — | — | — | 2,523 |
| — | — | 424 | — | — | — | 1,047 |
| — | — | 4,059 | — | 211 | 147 | 38,532 |
| 275 | 833 | 21,931 | 2,034 | — | — | 99,169 |
| 22 | — | 272 | — | — | — | 16,758 |
| 505 | 1,249 | 197,341 | 186,987 | 874 | — | 753,790 |
| 8 | — | 5,030 | 72 | — | — | 7,802 |
| 29,932 | 20,263 | 1,850,100 | 316,839 | 19,249 | 8,110 | 6,490,182** |

** To these figures should be added 32,799—members of four small groups: the Norwegian Synod (which is affiliated with the Evangelical Lutheran Synodical Conference), and three small independent groups: Lutheran Brethren, Finnish Apostolic Church, Eielsen Synod.

**f) Quaker Membership in Yearly Meetings in the United States—December, 1953**

From the Philadelphia Yearly Meeting of Friends, Friends Central Bureau, Philadelphia, Pennsylvania.

| Yearly Meetings (Affiliations) [1] | Member- ship |
|---|---|
| Baltimore [2] (Five Years Meeting) | 1,151 |
| Baltimore [2] (Friends General Conference) | 2,135 |
| California (Five Years Meeting) | 6,441 |
| Central (Independent) | 554 |
| Illinois (Friends General Conference) | 655 |
| Indiana (Five Years Meeting) | 14,075 |
| Indiana (Friends General Conference) | 558 |
| Iowa (Five Years Meeting) | 6,757 |
| Iowa (Conservative) | 836 |
| Kansas (Independent) | 8,397 |
| Nebraska (Five Years Meeting) | 1,855 |
| New England (Independent) | 3,248 |
| New York (Five Years Meeting) | 4,184 |
| New York (Friends General Conference) | 3,534 |
| North Carolina (Conservative) | 200 |
| North Carolina (Five Years Meeting) | 13,847 |
| Ohio (Independent) | 6,434 |
| Ohio (Conservative) | 913 |
| Oregon (Independent) | 4,753 |
| Pacific (Independent) | 1,000 |
| Philadelphia Arch Street [3] (Independent) | 4,547 |
| Philadelphia Race Street [3] (Friends General Conference) | 11,079 |
| Western [4] (Five Years Meeting) | 12,603 |
| Western [4] (Conservative) | 50 |
| Wilmington [5] (Five Years Meeting) | 5,052 |
| United Arch and Race Street | 1,367 |
| New Meetings [6] (Independent) | 794 |
| Total Reported in the Continental U.S. | 117,119 |

[1] *Five Years Meetings* are groups of Yearly Meetings which convene every five years. *Friends General Conference* is a group of six Yearly Meetings which convenes every two years.

*Independents* are separate Yearly Meetings not connected with any other groups. *Conservatives* are Yearly Meetings which keep in contact with each other through correspondence but not through general conferences.

[2] Includes Maryland, District of Columbia, Virginia.

[3] Includes Pennsylvania, New Jersey, Delaware, Maryland.

[4] Indiana groups.

[5] Includes Illinois and Kentucky.

[6] New Meetings are monthly meetings not yet associated with Yearly Meetings.

**g) Seventh-day Adventist Church Membership in the 48 States, December 31, 1953**

From the General Conference of Seventh-day Adventists, Takoma Park, Washington, D.C.

| State | No. of Churches | Member- ship |
|---|---|---|
| Alabama | 4 | 3,301 |
| Arizona | 31 | 1,932 |
| Arkansas | 25 | 1,779 |
| California | 37 | 54,551 |
| Colorado | 319 | 6,358 |
| Connecticut | 66 | 749 |
| Delaware | 16 | 428 |
| District of Columbia | 8 | 1,428 |
| Florida | 87 | 8,924 |
| Georgia | 45 | 4,017 |
| Idaho | 51 | 3,655 |
| Illinois | 80 | 6,878 |
| Indiana | 79 | 5,336 |
| Iowa | 65 | 3,726 |
| Kansas | 67 | 4,108 |
| Kentucky | 36 | 2,507 |
| Louisiana | 28 | 2,478 |
| Maine | 26 | 1,364 |
| Maryland | 43 | 6,815 |
| Massachusetts | 35 | 4,168 |
| Michigan | 174 | 14,783 |
| Minnesota | 73 | 4,425 |
| Mississippi | 39 | 1,976 |
| Missouri | 60 | 4,826 |
| Montana | 29 | 1,736 |
| Nebraska | 58 | 4,698 |
| Nevada | 5 | 486 |
| New Hampshire | 8 | 557 |
| New Jersey | 50 | 3,072 |
| New Mexico | 26 | 1,196 |
| New York | 112 | 11,256 |
| North Carolina | 55 | 4,406 |
| North Dakota | 57 | 2,532 |
| Ohio | 102 | 8,549 |
| Oklahoma | 61 | 4,053 |
| Oregon | 110 | 15,163 |
| Pennsylvania | 110 | 7,586 |
| Rhode Island | 6 | 567 |
| South Carolina | 26 | 1,414 |
| South Dakota | 34 | 1,749 |
| Tennessee | 67 | 6,893 |
| Texas | 107 | 8,622 |
| Utah | 6 | 372 |
| Vermont | 15 | 661 |
| Virginia | 53 | 3,606 |
| Washington | 109 | 13,355 |
| West Virginia | 31 | 1,712 |
| Wisconsin | 85 | 4,792 |
| Wyoming | 23 | 1,174 |
| Total | 2,839 | 260,719 |

## 5. Church Membership and Population Trends

From the 1955 *Yearbook of American Churches*, BENSON Y. LANDIS, ed., New York: The National Council of the Churches of Christ in the U.S.A., 1954, pp. 288–290.

The annual compilation on church membership . . . can best be understood by comparison with figures for previous years. In this section, available church statistics for earlier years are summarized.

*Proportion of Church Members in the Population*

Throughout the history of the United States, the proportion of church members in the total population has risen. Data for a century are given below. In 1850, 16 per cent of the population were recorded on the church membership rolls. By 1950, 57 per cent of the people were so reported. In 1953, the percentage was 59.5.

Prior to the Census of Religious Bodies, 1926, the basis of reporting members in a number of religious bodies was different from that followed in 1926 and since. For example, prior to 1926 a few bodies reported only heads of families as members; and a few other bodies at about that time began reporting as members all baptized persons, including infants, instead of only adults. *Thus the figures in the table for 1920 and prior years are not on the same basis as those in 1930 and following years.*

It is apparent that the gains officially reported were at a more rapid rate from 1940 on than during the preceding two decades. The figures themselves obviously do not tell the reasons. But there is statistical evidence that the people turned to the churches in 1940–53 to a greater extent than during the 20's or the 30's.

### Church Membership as Percentage of Population

| | |
|---|---|
| 1850 | 16% |
| 1860 | 23% |
| 1870 | 18% |
| 1880 | 20% |
| 1890 | 22% |
| 1900 | 36% |
| 1910 | 43% |
| 1920 | 43% |
| 1930 | 47% |
| 1940 | 49% |
| 1950 | 57% |
| 1953 | 59.5% |

Sources: H. C. Weber, *Yearbook of American Churches, 1933;* for succeeding years, studies by the Editor of statistics on church membership appearing in *Yearbook of American Churches,* and population data from U.S. Bureau of the Census.

*Inclusive Membership of Religious Bodies*

The number of church members of all faiths increased from 54,576,346 in 1926 to 86,830,490 in 1950, and 94,842,845 in 1953.

During the same period the population of the continental United States increased from 117,136,000 in 1926 to 159,017,000 in 1953.

The figures for 1950 and 1953 appearing in the table below include estimates of the number of persons in the armed forces serving overseas, since the church members among those in the armed services are undoubtedly included on the rolls of their home churches.

For a comparison of the trends, see tables below. The gains of the churches have been far more rapid than the increase in the population.

### Total Number of Members—All Religious Bodies

| | |
|---|---|
| 1926 | 54,576,346 |
| 1940 | 64,501,594 |
| 1950 | 86,830,490 |
| 1953 | 94,842,845 |

Sources: *Census of Religious Bodies, 1926; Yearbook of American Churches* for other years.

### Estimated Population of Continental United States

| | |
|---|---|
| 1926 | 117,136,000 |
| 1940 | 131,669,000 |
| 1950 | 151,132,000 |
| 1953 | 159,017,000 |

Sources: 1926, an estimate by the Editor of this *Yearbook;* U.S. Bureau of the Census for other years, that of 1953 being an estimate of the Bureau; figures for 1950 and 1953 include an estimate of the number in the armed forces overseas.

#### Members per Church Increasing

Since 1926, the average membership per local church (parish, congregation) of all religious bodies has been increasing. In 1926 the figure was 235; by 1950, it was 304; and by 1953, 322.

Comparing 1926 and 1953, the increase was 37 per cent.

### Average Number of Members per Church—All Religious Bodies

| Year | Number |
|---|---|
| 1926 | 235 |
| 1936 | 262 |
| 1940 | 265 |
| 1945 | 249 |
| 1950 | 304 |
| 1953 | 322 |

Sources: *Census of Religious Bodies,* U.S. Bureau of the Census, for 1926 and 1936; *Yearbook of American Churches,* for succeeding years.

## 6. Comparison of Protestant and Catholic Membership Figures

From the 1955 *Yearbook of American Churches,* BENSON Y. LANDIS, ed., New York: The National Council of the Churches of Christ in the U.S.A., 1954, pp. 290–291.

#### Protestant and Roman Catholic Comparisons

No precise comparison is possible between Protestant and Roman Catholic figures. Most Protestant churches enumerate as members persons who have attained full membership, usually at age 13. Probably 90 to 95 per cent of Protestant members are over 13 years of age. Roman Catholics regard all baptized persons, including children, as members.

Since 1926, the total membership of Protestant churches increased from 31,511,701 to 50,079,578 in 1950, and 55,837,325 in 1953. Comparing figures for 1953 with those of 1926, there was an increase of 77.2 per cent (see below).

Protestants were 27 per cent of the total population of the continental United States in 1926; 33.8 per cent in 1950; and 35.1 per cent in 1953.

The membership of the Roman Catholic Church increased from 18,-605,003 persons in 1926 to 28,634,878 in 1950, and 31,476,261 in 1953. From 1926 to 1953 it increased 69.2 per cent.

**Membership of All Protestant Bodies**

| 1926 | 31,511,701 |
|------|-----------|
| 1940 | 37,814,606 |
| 1950 | 51,079,578 |
| 1953 | 55,837,325 |

**Protestants as Percentage of Total Population**

| 1926 | 27.0% |
|------|-------|
| 1940 | 28.7% |
| 1950 | 33.8% |
| 1953 | 35.1% |

**Membership of the Roman Catholic Church**

| 1926 | 18,605,003 |
|------|-----------|
| 1940 | 21,284,455 |
| 1950 | 28,634,878 |
| 1953 | 31,476,261 |

**Roman Catholics as Percentage of Total Population**

| 1926 | 16.0% |
|------|-------|
| 1940 | 16.1% |
| 1950 | 18.9% |
| 1953 | 19.8% |

## 7. Church Membership for Persons 13 Years of Age and Over

From the 1952 *Yearbook of American Churches,* BENSON Y. LANDIS, ed., New York: National Council of the Churches of Christ in the U.S.A., 1952, pp. 258–259.

*Membership 13 Years and Over*

The estimated membership of persons 13 years of age and over in the continental United States increased from about 45,200,000 persons in 1926 to about 71,276,000 persons in 1950.

Comparing the membership with the estimated population, one finds a marked gain in the so-called "adult membership" (13 years of age and over) between 1940 and 1950. In 1940, about 507 persons over 13 years of age out of every 1,000 people in this bracket were church members; in 1950, about 637 persons over 13 years of age in every 1,000 in this bracket were church members.

**Membership of Churches, 13 Years of Age and Over, Compared with Population, 13 Years of Age and Over Continental United States**

|  | Estimated Church Membership 13 Years and Over | Estimated Population 13 Years and Over | Members per 1,000 Population 13 Years and Over |
|------|------|------|------|
| 1926 | 45,200,000 | 85,900,000 | 527 |
| 1940 | 52,400,000 | 103,200,000 | 507 |
| 1950 | 71,276,000 | 111,900,000 | 637 |

Sources: Estimates by the Editor of the *Yearbook,* based on *Census of Religious Bodies, 1926,* and estimated population of that year. For 1940 and 1950, estimates from reports of church membership appearing in *Yearbook of American Churches,* compared with U.S. Census data on population.

# 8. Catholic Vital Statistics

From the General Summary of Statistics, supplement to *The Official Catholic Directory*, 1954, P. J. Kenedy & Sons, publishers, New York.

| State | Total Baptisms | Infant Baptisms | Convert Baptisms | Marriages | Deaths |
|---|---|---|---|---|---|
| Alabama | 3,900 | 2,853 | 1,047 | 797 | 707 |
| Arizona | 9,133 | 8,512 | 621 | 1,636 | 1,331 |
| Arkansas | 1,406 | 1,041 | 365 | 393 | 123 |
| California | 98,689 | 87,280 | 11,409 | 18,929 | 18,614 |
| Colorado | 13,917 | 12,558 | 1,359 | 2,514 | 2,342 |
| Connecticut | 29,919 | 28,507 | 1,411 | 8,235 | 8,225 |
| Delaware | 2,744 | 2,466 | 278 | 769 | 497 |
| District of Columbia | 11,430 | 9,685 | 1,745 | 2,852 | 1,883 |
| Florida | 8,322 | 7,225 | 1,097 | 1,510 | 1,586 |
| Georgia | 2,321 | 1,797 | 524 | 511 | 352 |
| Idaho | 2,228 | 1,795 | 433 | 445 | 351 |
| Illinois | 78,533 | 68,781 | 9,752 | 20,730 | 22,761 |
| Indiana | 22,065 | 18,674 | 3,391 | 5,125 | 4,608 |
| Iowa | 17,945 | 15,551 | 2,394 | 3,925 | 3,920 |
| Kansas | 10,898 | 9,108 | 1,790 | 2,356 | 1,843 |
| Kentucky | 10,789 | 9,509 | 1,280 | 2,533 | 2,797 |
| Louisiana | 34,127 | 32,006 | 2,121 | 8,509 | 7,779 |
| Maine | 8,400 | 7,706 | 694 | 2,276 | 2,249 |
| Maryland | 13,053 | 11,539 | 1,514 | 3,869 | 3,481 |
| Massachusetts | 70,123 | 66,630 | 3,493 | 21,054 | 22,879 |
| Michigan | 63,238 | 56,440 | 6,798 | 16,765 | 12,251 |
| Minnesota | 31,909 | 28,920 | 2,989 | 7,125 | 6,398 |
| Mississippi | 3,462 | 2,881 | 581 | 637 | 503 |
| Missouri | 24,004 | 19,838 | 4,166 | 5,792 | 5,761 |
| Montana | 5,196 | 4,554 | 642 | 939 | 1,282 |
| Nebraska | 10,253 | 8,787 | 1,466 | 2,240 | 2,002 |
| Nevada | 886 | 741 | 145 | 541 | 171 |
| New Hampshire | 6,257 | 5,831 | 426 | 1,853 | 2,068 |
| New Jersey | 59,097 | 55,461 | 3,636 | 17,093 | 15,728 |
| New Mexico | 10,565 | 10,075 | 490 | 1,943 | 1,758 |
| New York | 178,556 | 167,002 | 11,554 | 50,139 | 46,796 |
| North Carolina | 2,468 | 1,859 | 609 | 473 | 161 |
| North Dakota | 6,813 | 6,170 | 643 | 1,443 | 1,169 |
| Ohio | 63,142 | 55,700 | 7,442 | 15,080 | 16,049 |
| Oklahoma | 4,460 | 3,122 | 1,338 | 845 | 960 |
| Oregon | 7,333 | 5,974 | 1,359 | 1,396 | 1,270 |
| Pennsylvania | 100,344 | 91,207 | 9,137 | 29,124 | 29,724 |
| Rhode Island | 12,097 | 11,616 | 481 | 3,697 | 3,823 |
| South Carolina | 1,723 | 1,303 | 420 | 334 | 180 |
| South Dakota | 5,133 | 4,450 | 683 | 1,391 | 828 |
| Tennessee | 3,578 | 2,685 | 893 | 739 | 538 |
| Texas | 67,918 | 64,329 | 3,589 | 10,187 | 8,373 |
| Utah | 1,742 | 1,532 | 210 | 280 | 210 |
| Vermont | 4,591 | 4,159 | 432 | 1,282 | 1,190 |
| Virginia | 6,233 | 5,284 | 949 | 1,254 | 764 |
| Washington | 13,295 | 11,282 | 2,013 | 2,682 | 2,810 |
| West Virginia | 3,951 | 3,112 | 839 | 1,028 | 1,079 |
| Wisconsin | 44,865 | 40,545 | 4,320 | 11,006 | 10,263 |
| Wyoming | 1,935 | 1,660 | 275 | 330 | 351 |

## 9. Number of Churches in the U.S. by City

Condensed from the *1954 Information Please Almanac,* Dan Golenpaul Associates, New York, N.Y., pp. 171, 192–208.

| City | Protestant | Roman Catholic | Jewish | Other | Total |
|------|-----------|---------------|--------|-------|-------|
| Atlanta, Ga. | | | | | 480+[1] |
| Baltimore, Md. | 482[2] | 72 | 57 | | 611 |
| Birmingham, Ala. | 491 | 26 | 3 | | 520 |
| Boston, Mass. | 183 | 73 | 40 | 74 | 370 |
| Buffalo, N. Y. | 268 | 82 | 16 | 34 | 400 |
| Chicago, Ill. | 1,725 | 299 | 170 | | 2,194 |
| Cincinnati, Ohio | | | | | 505[1] |
| Cleveland, Ohio | 377 | 118 | 36 | 6 | 537 |
| Columbus, Ohio | 256 | 36 | 5 | | 297 |
| Dallas, Texas | | | | | 500[1] |
| Denver, Colo. | 289 | 42 | 16 | | 347 |
| Des Moines, Iowa | 184 | 13 | 4 | | 201 |
| Detroit, Mich. | 850[3] | 181 | 38 | | 1,069 |
| Dist. of Columbia | 425 | 36 | 12 | 4 | 477 |
| Hartford, Conn. | 94 | 14 | 6 | | 114 |
| Houston, Texas | | | | | 500+[1] |
| Indianapolis, Ind. | | | | | 515[1] |
| Jersey City, N. J. | 96 | 39 | 17 | 45 | 197 |
| Los Angeles, Calif. | | | | | 1,700[1] |
| Memphis, Tenn. | 419[2] | 16 | 6 | | 441 |
| Miami, Fla. | | | | | 235[1] |
| Milwaukee, Wis. | | | | | 396[1] |
| Minneapolis, Minn. | | | | | 465[1] |
| New Bedford, Mass. | 53 | 23 | 3 | | 79 |
| New Orleans, La. | | | | | 600+[1] |
| New York, N. Y. | 1,418 | 525 | 1,330 | | 3,273 |
| Newark, N. J. | 159 | 41 | 32 | 57 | 289 |
| Oklahoma City, Okla. | 280[4] | 13 | 2 | 5 | 300[4] |
| Philadelphia, Pa. | 876[2] | 137 | 124 | | 1,137 |
| Pittsburgh, Pa. | 778 | 204 | 8 | | 990 |
| Portland, Maine | | | | | 80[1] |
| Portland, Ore. | 400 | 37 | 10 | 2[5] | 449 |
| Providence, R. I. | 94 | 31 | | | 125 |
| Richmond, Va. | 201 | 13 | 5 | 74 | 293 |
| Rochester, N. Y. | 128 | 38 | 19 | 22 | 207 |
| St. Louis, Mo. | | | | | 1,043[1] |
| Salt Lake City, Utah | | 8 | 4 | 173[6] | 185 |
| San Francisco, Calif. | | | | | 353[1] |
| Seattle, Wash. | 254 | 27 | 7 | | 288 |
| Syracuse, N. Y. | 76 | 23 | 8 | 8 | 115 |

[1] No breakdown by creed given     [4] Approximate
[2] Includes Protestant and Other   [5] Buddhist
[3] Metropolitan area               [6] Includes 135 "Mormon" temples

## 10. Value of New Construction of Religious Buildings

From the 1955 *Yearbook of American Churches*, BENSON Y. LANDIS, ed., New York: National Council of the Churches of Christ in the U.S.A., 1954, pp. 299–300.

Estimates of the annual value of new construction of religious buildings, 1920–1952 inclusive, are found in *Statistical Supplement*, May, 1953, *Construction and Building Materials*, published by the U.S. Department of Commerce, Washington.

The published figures follow:

| Year | Value |
|------|-------|
| 1920 | $ 55,000,000 |
| 1921 | 71,000,000 |
| 1922 | 103,000,000 |
| 1923 | 117,000,000 |
| 1924 | 130,000,000 |
| 1925 | 165,000,000 |
| 1926 | 177,000,000 |
| 1927 | 179,000,000 |
| 1928 | 168,000,000 |
| 1929 | 147,000,000 |
| 1930 | 135,000,000 |
| 1931 | 87,000,000 |
| 1932 | 45,000,000 |
| 1933 | 22,000,000 |
| 1934 | 21,000,000 |
| 1935 | 28,000,000 |
| 1936 | 34,000,000 |
| 1937 | 44,000,000 |
| 1938 | 51,000,000 |
| 1939 | 48,000,000 |
| 1940 | 59,000,000 |
| 1941 | 62,000,000 |
| 1942 | 31,000,000 |
| 1943 | 6,000,000 |
| 1944 | 11,000,000 |
| 1945 | 26,000,000 |
| 1946 | 76,000,000 |
| 1947 | 126,000,000 |
| 1948 | 251,000,000 |
| 1949 | 360,000,000 |
| 1950 | 409,000,000 |
| 1951 | 452,000,000 |
| 1952 | 399,000,000 |
| 1953* | 474,000,000 |

* The 1953 figure was published in 1954 in a supplement to the 1953 publication cited above.

## 1. The Catholic Clergy: Summary

From the General Summary of Statistics, supplement to *The Official Catholic Directory*, 1954, P. J. Kenedy & Sons, publishers, New York.

| *Hierarchy* | *Number in U.S.* |
|---|---|
| Cardinals | 4 |
| Archbishops | 29 |
| Bishops | 163 |
| *Total* | 196 |

| *Clergy* | |
|---|---|
| Abbots | 36 |
| Priests, Diocesan [1] | 28,573 |
| Priests, Religious [2] | 16,698 |
| *Total* | 45,307 |

*Brothers and Sisters*

> *Note:* Catholic Brothers and Catholic Sisters are not considered part of the ordained clergy. Brothers, for instance, cannot conduct church services, lead the Mass, or administer sacraments.—Ed.

| | |
|---|---|
| Brothers | 8,603 |
| Sisters | 153,573 |
| *Total* | 162,176 |

[1] *Diocesan priests* are ordained ministers who function under the immediate supervision of the bishop of their diocese and are ordained for the work of the diocese.—Ed.

[2] *Religious priests* are ordained members of orders and communities. They live under the supervision of the head of the religious community to which they belong. They are ordained to carry out the special work to which the community has been dedicated: education, care of the sick, contemplation, propagating the faith, and so on. In the U.S. (as of 1954) there are 88 religious orders of priests, 36 religious orders of brothers, and approximately 275 religious orders of women.—Ed.

## 2. Hierarchy and Clergy of the Catholic Church by States

From the General Summary of Statistics, supplement to *The Official Catholic Directory*, 1954, P. J. Kenedy & Sons, publishers, New York.

| State | Cardinals | Archbishops | Bishops | Abbots | Diocesan Priests | Religious Priests |
|---|---|---|---|---|---|---|
| Alabama | | | 1 | 2 | 139 | 180 |
| Arizona | | | 2 | | 80 | 79 |
| Arkansas | | | 2 | 1 | 115 | 43 |
| California | 1 | 1 | 8 | | 1,351 | 951 |
| | (Los Angeles) | | | | | |
| Colorado | | 1 | 3 | 1 | 216 | 190 |
| Connecticut | | 1 | 3 | | 737 | 234 |
| Delaware | | | 1 | | 72 | 57 |
| District of Columbia | | 1 | 4 | | 176 | 230 |
| Florida | | 1 | 1 | 1 | 144 | 78 |
| Georgia | | 1 | 2 | 1 | 48 | 102 |
| Idaho | | | 1 | | 65 | 17 |
| Illinois | 1 | | 7 | 3 | 2,085 | 1,753 |
| | (Chicago) | | | | | |
| Indiana | | 1 | 4 | 1 | 651 | 393 |
| Iowa | | 2 | 4 | 1 | 861 | 112 |
| Kansas | | 1 | 4 | 1 | 399 | 297 |
| Kentucky | | 1 | 2 | 1 | 403 | 158 |
| Louisiana | | 1 | 4 | 2 | 407 | 480 |
| Maine | | | 2 | | 249 | 99 |
| Maryland | | 1 | 1 | | 253 | 425 |
| Massachusetts | | 1 | 4 | 1 | 1,941 | 1,264 |
| Michigan | 1 | | 5 | | 1,232 | 499 |
| | (Detroit) | | | | | |
| Minnesota | | 1 | 5 | 1 | 977 | 287 |
| Mississippi | | | 1 | | 78 | 82 |
| Missouri | | 1 | 5 | 1 | 741 | 677 |
| Montana | | | 2 | | 189 | 44 |
| Nebraska | | 1 | 2 | | 404 | 131 |
| Nevada | | | 1 | | 54 | 6 |
| New Hampshire | | | 1 | 1 | 230 | 111 |
| New Jersey | | 1 | 3 | 2 | 1,134 | 597 |
| New Mexico | | 1 | 1 | 1 | 150 | 148 |
| New York | 1 | 1 | 21 | 1 | 4,004 | 2,336 |
| | (New York) | | | | | |
| North Carolina | | | 2 | 1 | 120 | 90 |
| North Dakota | | 1 | 2 | 1 | 228 | 60 |
| Ohio | | 2 | 7 | 1 | 1,705 | 836 |
| Oklahoma | | | 1 | 2 | 140 | 88 |
| Oregon | | 1 | 1 | 2 | 182 | 167 |
| Pennsylvania | | 2 | 10 | 1 | 2,878 | 1,204 |
| Rhode Island | | | 1 | | 372 | 168 |
| South Carolina | | | 1 | | 61 | 31 |
| South Dakota | | | 2 | | 210 | 82 |
| Tennessee | | | 1 | | 90 | 28 |
| Texas | | 1 | 8 | | 610 | 636 |
| Utah | | | 2 | 1 | 41 | 34 |
| Vermont | | | 1 | | 145 | 54 |
| Virginia | | | 3 | | 139 | 101 |
| Washington | | 1 | 2 | 1 | 230 | 272 |
| West Virginia | | | 2 | | 101 | 51 |
| Wisconsin | | 1 | 6 | 3 | 1,271 | 664 |
| Wyoming | | | 1 | | 45 | 9 |
| Totals | 4 | 29 | 163 | 36 | 28,573 | 16,698 |

### 3. Women in the Ministry

From the 1955 *Yearbook of American Churches*, BENSON Y. LANDIS, ed., New York: National Council of the Churches of Christ in the U.S.A., 1954, p. 299.

Since the publication of the 1953 *Yearbook*, the Bureau of the Census has published figures reporting 6,777 women clergymen, or 4.1 per cent of the total number of clergymen, which was 168,419, according to the population census of 1950. The figures are for all religious bodies of all faiths, and there is no breakdown.

A study of available *published* reports, appearing in *Information Service*, May 31, 1952, revealed 5,791 ordained or licensed women ministers of whom 2,896 were pastors of local churches. Of the pastors reported, about one-tenth were in communions affiliated with the National Council of Churches. A precise count could not be made, and the data were limited to the denominations publishing data. The figures could not be compared directly with any other compilation. It appears that 63 religious bodies ordain women, while a total of 77 bodies ordain or license. Seven of these "give women special status of some sort."

For a later discussion, "Women Ministers Today," see *Information Service*, National Council of Churches, March 6, 1954.

### 4. Ministers' Annual Salaries

From the 1955 *Yearbook of American Churches*, BENSON Y. LANDIS, ed., New York: National Council of the Churches of Christ in the U.S.A., 1954, pp. 291–295.

#### A Preliminary Inquiry

The inquiry has mainly to do with the three religious bodies that have published data on average salaries from 1939 through 1952, the latest year for which data were available. These are the Congregational Christian Churches, the Protestant Episcopal Church, and the United Presbyterian Church. Despite the fact that information for the period is found for only these three denominations, the *trends* are probably of general significance.

A main purpose of the inquiry is to report on trends in purchasing power of ministers' salaries, and to consider how this compares with some other groups in the population. No attempt is made here fully to evaluate the adequacy of the salaries, and it is recognized that salaries are not *total income*. Many clergymen receive an undetermined amount of fees for services, and many are furnished with living quarters. Of the three religious bodies considered, only the Protestant Episcopal figures include actual rental value of dwellings furnished, or an estimate figured at 15 per cent of the salary.

**Table 1.**

**Average Annual Salaries of Ministers in Three Denominations Compared with the "Real" Value of their Salaries for the Period 1939 to 1952.**

| Year | CONGREGATIONAL CHRISTIAN | | UNITED PRESBYTERIAN | | PROTESTANT EPISCOPAL | |
|------|--------------------------|--------------|---------------------|--------------|----------------------|--------------|
| | Average Annual Salary | "Real" Salary[1] | Average Annual Salary | "Real" Salary[1] | Average Annual Salary | "Real" Salary[1] |
| 1939 | $1,769 | $1,769 | $1,979 | $1,979 | $2,725 | $2,725 |
| 1940 | 1,774 | 1,760 | 2,020 | 2,004 | 2,750 | 2,728 |
| 41 | 1,961 | 1,853 | 2,046 | 1,934 | 2,775 | 2,623 |
| 42 | 1,884 | 1,606 | 2,119 | 1,806 | 2,830 | 2,413 |
| 43 | 1,969 | 1,583 | 2,176 | 1,749 | 2,900 | 2,331 |
| 44 | 2,082 | 1,646 | 2,200 | 1,739 | 3,030 | 2,395 |
| 1945 | 2,140 | 1,654 | 2,303 | 1,780 | 3,160 | 2,442 |
| 46 | 2,268 | 1,617 | 2,400 | 1,711 | 3,350 | 2,388 |
| 47 | 2,640 | 1,644 | 2,691 | 1,676 | 3,575 | 2,226 |
| 48 | 2,813 | 1,627 | 2,914 | 1,685 | 3,625 | 2,097 |
| 49 | 2,894 | 1,690 | 3,070 | 1,793 | 3,900 | 2,278 |
| 1950 | 2,921 | 1,689 | 3,188 | 1,844 | 4,060 | 2,348 |
| 51 | 3,174 | 1,700 | 3,421 | 1,832 | 4,225 | 2,263 |
| 52 | 3,313 | 1,734 | 3,709 | 1,941 | 4,391 | 2,298 |

[1] The figures in this column have been calculated to take into account the decline in the value of the dollar since 1939. The figures in this column are called "1939 dollars" in the text.

SOURCES OF SALARY DATA:

    a. Yearbooks of the Congregational Christian Churches, 1939 to 1952.

    b. Minutes of the General Assembly of the United Presbyterian Church, 1939 to 1952.

    c. Protection Points, Volume 17, No. 2, November, 1952, Bulletin issued by Pension Fund of the Protestant Episcopal Church. (Salaries shown for ministers of this denomination include "a rental value of rectory, when supplied the clergyman rent-free, figured as one-sixth of the cash stipend. When the rent is paid by the parish for quarters not owned by the parish the full rent figure is used.") Data for 1952 by correspondence with the Pension Fund.

The abbreviated table above indicates an increase in the average salaries of ministers in these bodies, in terms of current dollars, 1939 through 1952, but a decrease in "1939 dollars." In other words, when account is taken of the decline in the purchasing power of the dollar, the purchasing power of the ministers' salaries was less in 1952 than in 1939.

This is in striking contrast to published figures of persons engaged in all grades and skills in manufacturing, services, and government employment. In these vocations, average earnings increased in terms of current dollars and of "1939 dollars."

In the Congregational Christian Churches, the average salary advanced from $1,769 in 1939 to $3,313 in 1952; but in terms of "1939 dollars," the 1952 salary was equal to only $1,734.

In the United Presbyterian Church, the average salary advanced from $1,979 in 1939, to $3,709 in 1952; but in terms of "1939 dollars," the 1952 salary was equal to only $1,941.

In the Protestant Episcopal Church, the average salary increased from $2,725 in 1939 to $4,391 in 1952; but in "1939 dollars," the 1952 salary was equal to only $2,298.

See Table 1.

**Table 2.**

**Average Annual Earnings of Full-time Employes in Selected Occupational Groups Compared with the "Real" Value of their Earnings for the Period 1939 to 1952.**

| Year | Manufacturing Average Annual Earnings | Manufacturing "Real" Earnings | Services Average Annual Earnings | Services "Real" Earnings | Government & Government Enterprises Average Annual Earnings | Government & Government Enterprises "Real" Earnings |
|------|------|------|------|------|------|------|
| 1939 | $1,363 | $1,363 | $ 943 | $ 943 | $1,339 | $1,339 |
| 1940 | 1,432 | 1,421 | 949 | 941 | 1,349 | 1,338 |
| 41 | 1,653 | 1,562 | 1,016 | 960 | 1,392 | 1,316 |
| 42 | 2,023 | 1,725 | 1,131 | 964 | 1,653 | 1,409 |
| 43 | 2,349 | 1,888 | 1,337 | 1,075 | 1,813 | 1,457 |
| 44 | 2,517 | 1,990 | 1,519 | 1,201 | 1,958 | 1,548 |
| 1945 | 2,517 | 1,945 | 1,669 | 1,290 | 2,097 | 1,621 |
| 46 | 2,517 | 1,794 | 1,870 | 1,333 | 2,364 | 1,685 |
| 47 | 2,793 | 1,739 | 2,002 | 1,247 | 2,568 | 1,599 |
| 48 | 3,039 | 1,758 | 2,111 | 1,221 | 2,786 | 1,611 |
| 49 | 3,093 | 1,807 | 2,168 | 1,266 | 2,882 | 1,683 |
| 1950 | 3,303 | 1,910 | 2,214 | 1,281 | 3,045 | 1,761 |
| 51 | 3,611 | 1,934 | 2,342 | 1,254 | 3,121 | 1,672 |
| 52 | 3,809 | 1,993 | 2,483 | 1,299 | 3,272 | 1,712 |

SOURCES:

*National Income 1951 Edition*, U.S. Department of Commerce, Bureau of Foreign and Domestic Commerce, Office of Business Economics, Table 26, pp. 184–185 for years 1939–1950.

*Survey of Current Business*, February, 1953, Table 4, Employment Payrolls and Average Annual Earnings by Major Industrial Divisions, 1951 and 1952, p. 9. Later data from subsequent issues of *Survey of Current Business*.

In manufacturing, the average annual earnings increased from $1,363 in 1939 to $3,809 in 1952; and the 1952 earnings, in "1939 dollars," were equal to $1,993.

In employment in services, average annual earnings increased from $943 in 1939 to $2,483 in 1952; and the 1952 earnings, in "1939 dollars," were equal to $1,299.

In government employment, average annual earnings increased from $1,339 in 1939 to $3,272 in 1952; and the 1952 earnings, in "1939 dollars," were equal to $1,712.

See Table 2.

**Census Data on Clergymen's Incomes**

The incomes of clergymen of all faiths, based on a 20 per cent sample, as given by persons in the course of the Census of Population, 1950, have been published by the Bureau of the Census in Volume II, *Characteristics of the Population*, Part 1, U.S. Summary, Table 129 (Superintendent of Documents, Government Printing Office, 1953. $3.75). The figures are for the calendar year 1949. Data on incomes of members of many other vocations are also published.

The median income reported by *male clergymen* for 1949 was $2,412. Eighty-five per cent of the clergymen reported an income of less than $4,000 for 1949. Presumably the figure was given in terms of cash, not including rental value of living quarters which are furnished for many clergymen, since the enumerators asked for a figure with no qualifications. Possibly, there are also included persons giving their main calling as clergymen who also have other occupations.

The figures for males in certain groups are as follows:

| Occupation | Median Income, 1949 |
|---|---|
| Accountants and Auditors | $4,002 |
| Architects | 5,580 |
| Artists and Art Teachers | 2,360 |
| Authors, Editors and Reporters | 4,469 |
| *Clergymen* | *2,412* |
| Dentists | 6,232 |
| Engineers, Civil | 4,518 |
| Lawyers and Judges | 6,257 |
| Musicians and Music Teachers | 3,189 |
| Pharmacists | 4,246 |
| Physicians and Surgeons | 8,115 |
| Social, Welfare, and Recreation Workers | 3,186 |
| Teachers | 3,456 |
| | |
| Bakers | 2,917 |
| Barbers | 2,370 |
| Blacksmiths | 2,701 |
| Bookkeepers | 2,847 |
| Bus drivers | 3,116 |
| Farmers and Farm Managers | 1,455 |
| Laborers, in manufacturing | 2,217 |
| Longshoremen | 2,501 |
| Mail Carriers | 3,465 |
| Operators, Manufacturing | 2,671 |
| Sailors and Deck Hands | 2,376 |
| Waiters | 2,154 |

# Religious Education

## 1. Sunday and Sabbath Schools

From the 1955 *Yearbook of American Churches*, BENSON Y. LANDIS, ed., New York: National Council of the Churches of Christ in the U.S.A., 1954, p. 290.

The total number of Sunday and Sabbath schools in all religious bodies increased from 184,686 in 1926 to 246,240 in 1950, and 262,084 in 1953. (The term Sabbath schools is used to designate the schools of those bodies that observe the Sabbath on Saturday.)

The total enrollment in schools in all religious bodies increased from 23,206,374 persons in 1926 to 29,775,357 in 1950, and 35,389,466 in 1953. Between 1926 and 1953 the gain was 52.5 per cent.

### Sunday and Sabbath Schools of All Religious Bodies

|  | Number of Schools | Total Enrollment |
|---|---|---|
| 1926 ......... | 184,686 | 23,206,374 |
| 1941–42 ...... | 213,424 | 24,100,710 |
| 1950 ......... | 246,240 | 29,775,357 |
| 1953 ......... | 262,084 | 35,389,466 |

Sources: *1926 Census of Religious Bodies;* following years, compilations published in *Yearbook of American Churches.*

## 2. Church-affiliated Day Schools

From the 1955 *Yearbook of American Churches*, BENSON Y. LANDIS, ed., New York: National Council of the Churches of Christ in the U.S.A., 1954, p. 297.

In 1952, there were about 3,000 Protestant church-affiliated day schools with about 187,000 children enrolled, compared with about 2,000 schools and 110,000 pupils in 1937. These were nursery, kindergarten, and elementary schools. The figures appeared in *Information Service,* National Council of Churches, May 3, 1952. Later figures have not been available.

*The Official Catholic Directory,* 1952, New York, reported 2,692,706 pupils in 8,358 elementary parochial schools in the Roman Catholic Church, at that time an all-time high for that body. Later figures for Roman Catholics are found in subsequent annual issues of the *Directory.*

## 3. Catholic Education Statistics: Summary

From the General Summary of Statistics, supplement to *The Official Catholic Directory*, 1954, P. J. Kenedy & Sons, publishers, New York.

| Educational Institution | Number in U. S. | Number of Students |
|---|---|---|
| Diocesan Seminaries | 76 | 15,048 |
| Seminaries, Religious, or Scholasticates | 379 | 18,400 |
| Catholic Colleges and Universities | 250 | 210,920[1] |
| High Schools, Diocesan and Parochial | 1,536 | 375,099 |
| High Schools, Private | 830 | 227,900 |
| Elementary Schools, Parochial | 8,493 | 2,992,318 |
| Elementary Schools, Private | 541 | 91,243 |

| Educational Institution | Number in U. S. | Number of Students |
|---|---|---|
| Orphanages and Infant Asylums | 332 | 36,528 |
| Protective Institutions | 177 | 20,418 |
| Total | 12,614 | 3,987,874 |
| Special Religious Instruction Classes for Public School Pupils | 35,729 | 1,946,143 |
| Total under Catholic Instruction | | 5,934,017 |

[1] Includes non-Catholic as well as Catholic college students.

Key:

*Diocesan seminaries* train for the priesthood of individual dioceses.

*Religious seminaries* train priests for religious and monastic orders.

*Scholasticates* are places where candidates for priesthood pursue their studies before entry into major seminaries.

*Diocesan high schools* are schools supported by the diocese.

*Parochial high schools* are schools supported by the parish.

*Private high schools* are those which charge tuition.

*Elementary parochial schools: see* parochial high schools.

*Private elementary schools: see* private high schools.

## 4. Catholic Education:

From the General Summary of Statistics, supplement to *The Official Catholic*

| State | Diocesan Seminaries (No. of students) | | Religious Seminaries or Scholasticates (No. of students) | | Catholic Colleges and Universities (No. of students) | |
|---|---|---|---|---|---|---|
| Alabama | | | 4 | (229) | 3 | (1,237) |
| Arizona | | | | | 1 | (86) |
| Arkansas | 1 | (51) | 1 | (38) | 1 | (28) |
| California | 7 | (833) | 23 | (1,117) | 13 | (8,886) |
| Colorado | 1 | (60) | 1 | (7) | 3 | (1,270) |
| Connecticut | 1 | (183) | 7 | (289) | 6 | (1,834) |
| Delaware | | | 2 | (33) | | |
| District of Columbia | 1 | (7) | 39 | (1,358) | 6 | (13,271) |
| Florida | | | 1 | (8) | 1 | (372) |
| Georgia | | | 1 | (12) | | |
| Idaho | | | | | | |
| Illinois | 4 | (1,139) | 22 | (1,364) | 14 | (19,315) |
| Indiana | 1 | (99) | 12 | (1,608) | 6 | (7,452) |
| Iowa | 4 | (173) | 5 | (209) | 8 | (3,160) |
| Kansas | | | 4 | (198) | 8 | (2,505) |
| Kentucky | 1 | (68) | 4 | (139) | 9 | (2,763) |
| Louisiana | 3 | (182) | 3 | (226) | 4 | (3,853) |
| Maine | | | 2 | (156) | 3 | (232) |
| Maryland | 3 | (205) | 7 | (376) | 6 | (2,640) |
| Massachusetts | 2 | (441) | 39 | (1,438) | 11 | (12,057) |
| Michigan | 4 | (716) | 7 | (229) | 8 | (10,348) |
| Minnesota | 4 | (393) | 6 | (265) | 8 | (5,070) |
| Mississippi | | | 2 | (153) | | |
| Missouri | 3 | (593) | 15 | (941) | 9 | (9,950) |
| Montana | 1 | (22) | | | 2 | (937) |
| Nebraska | | | 1 | (14) | 3 | (2,928) |
| Nevada | | | | | | |
| New Hampshire | | | 7 | (243) | 4 | (1,180) |
| New Jersey | 1 | (236) | 12 | (537) | 5 | (8,591) |
| New Mexico | 1 | (60) | 3 | (58) | 2 | (620) |
| New York | 11 | (822) | 53 | (2,582) | 24 | (33,217) |
| North Carolina | | | 1 | (12) | 3 | (302) |
| North Dakota | | | 1 | (32) | 1 | (30) |
| Ohio | 6 | (541) | 20 | (1,153) | 11 | (12,368) |
| Oklahoma | 1 | (20) | 2 | (14) | 2 | (71) |
| Oregon | 1 | (75) | 2 | (245) | 3 | (1,557) |
| Pennsylvania | 2 | (431) | 19 | (1,068) | 20 | (19,322) |
| Rhode Island | 1 | (109) | 3 | (63) | 3 | (1,794) |
| South Carolina | | | | | | |
| South Dakota | | | 1 | (7) | 2 | (350) |
| Tennessee | | | | | 2 | (454) |
| Texas | 3 | (157) | 10 | (398) | 7 | (3,235) |
| Utah | | | 1 | (28) | 1 | (109) |
| Vermont | | | 5 | (68) | 2 | (876) |
| Virginia | | | 3 | (78) | 1 | (100) |
| Washington | 1 | (112) | 3 | (207) | 5 | (4,583) |
| West Virginia | | | | | | |
| Wisconsin | 4 | (909) | 22 | (1,188) | 14 | (11,933) |
| Wyoming | | | | | | |

# Statistics by State

*Directory*, 1954, P. J. Kenedy & Sons, publishers, New York.

| Diocesan and Parochial High Schools (No. of students) | | Private High Schools (No. of students) | | Elementary Schools, Parochial (No. of students) | | Elementary Schools, Private (No. of students) | |
|---|---|---|---|---|---|---|---|
| 16 | (2,786) | 3 | (421) | 65 | (13,180) | 1 | (48) |
| 4 | (1,223) | 3 | (303) | 34 | (10,516) | 4 | (498) |
| 7 | (597) | 9 | (976) | 46 | (5,611) | 6 | (753) |
| 54 | (20,117) | 48 | (14,577) | 389 | (160,057) | 36 | (7,194) |
| 14 | (3,563) | 5 | (920) | 60 | (18,727) | 1 | (112) |
| | | | | | | | |
| 12 | (3,495) | 11 | (3,259) | 120 | (53,513) | 6 | (566) |
| 3 | (605) | 3 | (971) | 25 | (8,717) | 4 | (504) |
| 12 | (2,237) | 16 | (3,823) | 63 | (27,245) | 10 | (1,596) |
| 14 | (2,383) | 9 | (1,411) | 68 | (19,525) | 5 | (985) |
| 5 | (272) | 5 | (1,086) | 29 | (8,007) | 2 | (419) |
| | | 5 | (385) | 15 | (2,575) | 5 | (717) |
| 75 | (18,708) | 72 | (38,367) | 719 | (240,565) | 10 | (2,075) |
| 21 | (8,133) | 11 | (2,442) | 174 | (73,041) | | |
| 111 | (9,796) | 12 | (2,862) | 261 | (48,968) | 4 | (479) |
| 26 | (4,392) | 10 | (1,415) | 182 | (27,861) | 1 | (65) |
| | | | | | | | |
| 42 | (5,576) | 24 | (5,785) | 186 | (43,695) | 16 | (1,494) |
| 53 | (7,132) | 34 | (8,616) | 184 | (71,952) | 34 | (7,127) |
| 9 | (2,062) | 7 | (881) | 53 | (20,207) | 7 | (434) |
| 11 | (1,166) | 14 | (6,610) | 96 | (44,733) | 8 | (1,653) |
| 96 | (25,792) | 36 | (7,948) | 344 | (153,986) | 39 | (5,344) |
| | | | | | | | |
| 124 | (30,934) | 20 | (9,109) | 409 | (166,141) | 10 | (2,225) |
| 52 | (10,152) | 16 | (4,220) | 289 | (84,489) | 6 | (730) |
| 25 | (1,906) | 3 | (391) | 43 | (8,124) | 4 | (600) |
| 39 | (11,593) | 25 | (6,394) | 331 | (84,185) | 13 | (1,827) |
| 13 | (2,269) | 1 | (121) | 40 | (9,799) | 4 | (740) |
| | | | | | | | |
| 34 | (4,579) | 8 | (2,313) | 124 | (22,992) | 7 | (1,163) |
| 1 | (156) | | | 4 | (1,449) | | |
| 14 | (3,228) | 5 | (342) | 51 | (20,586) | 7 | (775) |
| 53 | (17,882) | 33 | (7,228) | 343 | (166,346) | 20 | (3,314) |
| 12 | (1,655) | 8 | (773) | 57 | (14,082) | 11 | (1,832) |
| | | | | | | | |
| 136 | (44,392) | 126 | (43,546) | 868 | (451,712) | 67 | (11,219) |
| 5 | (252) | 6 | (355) | 45 | (5,884) | 6 | (698) |
| 5 | (1,196) | 11 | (944) | 37 | (9,045) | 14 | (2,121) |
| 92 | (31,376) | 32 | (10,484) | 568 | (200,925) | 19 | (3,459) |
| 25 | (1,753) | 9 | (816) | 65 | (9,405) | 7 | (992) |
| | | | | | | | |
| 6 | (1,387) | 13 | (2,263) | 59 | (14,593) | 12 | (1,714) |
| 126 | (55,954) | 54 | (9,246) | 841 | (321,878) | 41 | (6,253) |
| 11 | (3,973) | 8 | (1,803) | 87 | (33,293) | 5 | (1,284) |
| 2 | (525) | 2 | (194) | 22 | (4,359) | 1 | (272) |
| 14 | (1,619) | 1 | (168) | 45 | (9,005) | 4 | (485) |
| | | | | | | | |
| 12 | (1,739) | 4 | (769) | 48 | (10,324) | 5 | (388) |
| 27 | (3,367) | 43 | (8,621) | 260 | (71,535) | 45 | (11,144) |
| 2 | (287) | 1 | (89) | 4 | (1,507) | 1 | (107) |
| 6 | (1,345) | 5 | (741) | 24 | (9,490) | 3 | (784) |
| 12 | (1,627) | 8 | (896) | 42 | (17,623) | 8 | (1,101) |
| | | | | | | | |
| 13 | (2,304) | 18 | (3,694) | 70 | (25,126) | 11 | (2,020) |
| 13 | (1,936) | 4 | (195) | 46 | (8,200) | 4 | (252) |
| 69 | (13,983) | 21 | (6,895) | 481 | (133,886) | 4 | (516) |
| 2 | (224) | | | 8 | (2,850) | | |

## 5. Jewish School Enrollment

The following chart was prepared by C. Morris Horowitz, statistician of the American Association for Jewish Education, and is taken from a pamphlet reprint of the article "Trends and Developments in American Jewish Education" by Dr. Uriah Zevi Engelman in the 1953 *American Jewish Year Book*, Morris Fine, ed., Vol. 54, New York: The American Jewish Committee, and Philadelphia: The Jewish Publication Society of America.

**Estimated Jewish School Enrollment, Spring 1952**

| Type of School | No. of Pupils | Per Cent of Total Enrollment |
|---|---|---|
| Weekday Afternoon Hebrew School.. | 123,577 | 36.8% |
| All Day School.... | 23,500 | 7.0% |
| Yiddish School ... | 13,000 | 3.8% |
| Sunday School ... | 176,007 | 52.4% |
| Total .......... | 336,084 | 100% |

## 6. Trends and Developments in American Jewish Education *

### By Dr. Uriah Engelman

From the 1953 *American Jewish Year Book,* Morris Fine, ed., Vol. 54, New York: The American Jewish Committee, and Philadelphia: The Jewish Publication Society of America, pp. 118–119.

For the third consecutive year, Jewish school enrollment in the Sunday and weekday afternoon Hebrew schools was recorded according to congregational and noncongregational auspices.

**Growth of Jewish School Enrollment 1948–52**

| Year | Weekday School Enrollment [1] | | | Sunday School Enrollment [2] | | | Total Enrollment | | |
|---|---|---|---|---|---|---|---|---|---|
| | Number | Per Cent of Total | Per Cent Annual Change | Number | Per Cent of Total | Per Cent Annual Change | Number | Per Cent of Total | Per Cent Annual Change |
| 1952..... | 160,077 | 47.6 | +13.3 | 176,007 | 52.4 | +10.0 | 336,084 | 100 | +11.1 |
| 1951..... | 141,278 | 47.2 | + 6.3 | 157,974 | 52.8 | +21.0 | 302,454 | 100 | +13.4 |
| 1950..... | 132,642 | 50.4 | + 8.6 | 130,574 | 49.6 | + 1.4 | 266,609 | 100 | + 4.2 |
| 1949..... | 122,109 | 48.7 | + 3.0 | 128,719 | 51.3 | + 6.5 | 255,865 | 100 | + 6.9 |
| 1948..... | 118,502 | 49.5 | — | 120,896 | 50.5 | — | 239,398 | 100 | — |

[1] The term "weekday school" includes the weekday afternoon Hebrew, Yiddish, and the all-day schools.

[2] Includes 5,037 enrolled in released-time classes in 1949; 3,393 in 1950; 3,202 in 1951; and 3,000 in 1952.

The total recorded enrollment under all auspices in the 140 communities was 123,392 pupils: 63.4 per cent were found in Sunday schools and 36.6 per cent in afternoon weekday Hebrew schools. The proportion enrolled under Orthodox congregational auspices in these communities was 17.1 per cent; under Reform auspices, 30.2 per cent; under Conservative auspices, 35.1 per

* During the past two years there has been a yearly increase of close to 10 per cent in Jewish school enrollment in the United States.

cent; and under noncongregational auspices, 16.6 per cent. Most of the noncongregational schools were Orthodox-oriented, though not under Orthodox congregational auspices.

Of the children attending Orthodox congregational schools, 45.5 per cent attended weekday afternoon schools, and 54.5 per cent Sunday schools; of those attending Conservative congregational schools, 41.9 per cent were in weekday schools and 58.1 per cent in Sunday schools; of those attending Reform congregational schools, 10.0 per cent attended on weekday afternoons, and 90.0 per cent on Sunday and Saturday mornings; of the noncongregational school enrollment, 62.9 per cent were in the weekday afternoon schools and 37.1 per cent in Sunday schools.

## 7. How Religion of Parents Is Related to Education

From *Youth Tell Their Story* by Howard M. Bell, American Council on Education, Washington, D.C., 1938, p. 195, as reprinted in *Marriage and the Family* by Meyer Nimkoff, Boston: Houghton Mifflin Company, 1947, p. 267.

### Percentage of Youth Graduating from High School

| Religious Affiliation of Parents | Percentage of Youth Graduating from High School |
|---|---|
| Jewish | 65% |
| Protestant | 40% |
| Mixed | 38% |
| All | 37% |
| Catholic | 28% |
| None | 25% |

The percentage of youths in each religious group who graduated from high school. Based on a representative sample of more than 13,000 youths in the State of Maryland in 1936. Rather marked variation in the schooling of youths of different religious backgrounds suggests that group tradition as well as income is a factor. It is not to be implied that the study measured only the religious factor.

# Public Opinion Polls

## 1. A Comparison of the Theological Beliefs of Ministers and Theological Students

### By GEORGE HERBERT BETTS *

In 1929, George Herbert Betts published *The Beliefs of 700 Ministers* (Abingdon Press).

Mr. Betts asked fifty-six questions of ministers and theological students. The first group of ministers contained 50 Baptists, 50 Congregationalists, 30 Episcopalians, 49 Evangelicals, 105 Lutherans, 111 Methodists, 63 Presbyterians, and 43 from 13 other denominations.

The following questions and figures are taken from Mr. Betts's fifty-six, and the percentage is based on **500 ministers** and 500 students—Ed.

**"Do you believe . . .**

|  | Yes | No | ? |
|---|---|---|---|
| "That the creation of the world occurred in the manner and time recorded in Genesis? | | | |
| **Percentages Ministers** | **47** | **48** | **5** |
| Percentages Students | 5 | 89 | 6 |

"That God is three distinct persons in one?

| | Yes | No | ? |
|---|---|---|---|
| **Percentages Ministers** | **80** | **13** | **7** |
| Percentages Students | 44 | 35 | 21 |

"That God occasionally sets aside law, thus performing a miracle?

| | Yes | No | ? |
|---|---|---|---|
| **Percentages Ministers** | **68** | **24** | **8** |
| Percentages Students | 24 | 60 | 16 |

"That the inspiration that resulted in the writing of the Bible is different from that of other great religious literature?

| | Yes | No | ? |
|---|---|---|---|
| **Percentages Ministers** | **70** | **25** | **5** |
| Percentages Students | 26 | 68 | 6 |

|  | Yes | No | ? |
|---|---|---|---|
| "That the Bible is wholly free from legend or myth? | | | |
| **Percentages Ministers** | **38** | **55** | **7** |
| Percentages Students | 4 | 95 | 1 |

"That the principles of criticism and evaluation applied to other literature and history should be applied to the Bible?

| | Yes | No | ? |
|---|---|---|---|
| **Percentages Ministers** | **67** | **28** | **5** |
| Percentages Students | 88 | 7 | 5 |

"That the New Testament is the absolute and infallible standard by which all religious creeds or beliefs among men should be judged as to their truth and validity?

| | Yes | No | ? |
|---|---|---|---|
| **Percentages Ministers** | **77** | **20** | **3** |
| Percentages Students | 33 | 55 | 12 |

"That Jesus was born of a virgin without a human father?

| | Yes | No | ? |
|---|---|---|---|
| **Percentages Ministers** | **71** | **19** | **10** |
| Percentages Students | 25 | 51 | 24 |

"That while upon earth Jesus possessed and used the power to restore the dead to life?

| | Yes | No | ? |
|---|---|---|---|
| **Percentages Ministers** | **82** | **9** | **9** |
| Percentages Students | 45 | 27 | 28 |

"That after Jesus was dead and buried he actually rose from the dead, leaving the tomb empty?

| | Yes | No | ? |
|---|---|---|---|
| **Percentages Ministers** | **84** | **12** | **4** |
| Percentages Students | 42 | 31 | 27 |

"That heaven exists as an actual place or location?

| | Yes | No | ? |
|---|---|---|---|
| **Percentages Ministers** | **57** | **28** | **15** |
| Percentages Students | 11 | 69 | 20 |

* Reprinted by permission of Harlan C. Betts.

| | Yes | No | ? |
|---|---|---|---|
| "That hell exists as an actual place or location? | | | |
| Percentages Ministers | 53 | 34 | 13 |
| Percentages Students | 11 | 76 | 13 |

"That the Devil exists as an actual being?

| | Yes | No | ? |
|---|---|---|---|
| Percentages Ministers | 60 | 33 | 7 |
| Percentages Students | 9 | 82 | 9 |

"That there is a continuance of life after death?

| | Yes | No | ? |
|---|---|---|---|
| Percentages Ministers | 97 | 1 | 2 |
| Percentages Students | 89 | 4 | 7 |

"In the resurrection of the body?

| | Yes | No | ? |
|---|---|---|---|
| Percentages Ministers | 62 | 33 | 5 |
| Percentages Students | 18 | 69 | 13 |

"That there will be one final day of judgment for all who have lived upon earth?

| | Yes | No | ? |
|---|---|---|---|
| Percentages Ministers | 60 | 32 | 8 |
| Percentages Students | 17 | 77 | 16 |

"That all men, being sons of Adam, are born with natures wholly perverse, sinful, and depraved?

| | Yes | No | ? |
|---|---|---|---|
| Percentages Ministers | 53 | 43 | 4 |
| Percentages Students | 13 | 80 | 7 |

"That prayer has the power to change conditions in nature—such as drought?

| | Yes | No | ? |
|---|---|---|---|
| Percentages Ministers | 64 | 25 | 11 |
| Percentages Students | 21 | 57 | 22 |

"That prayer for others directly affects their lives whether or not they know that such prayer is being offered?

| | Yes | No | ? |
|---|---|---|---|
| Percentages Ministers | 83 | 8 | 9 |
| Percentages Students | 58 | 17 | 25 |

"That God now acts upon, or operates in, human lives through the agency and person of the Holy Spirit?

| | Yes | No | ? |
|---|---|---|---|
| Percentages Ministers | 94 | 5 | 1 |
| Percentages Students | 82 | 7 | 11 |

"That, regardless of creed or personal belief, persons who love God and do justly with their fellow men are worthy of acceptance into the Christian Church?"

| | Yes | No | ? |
|---|---|---|---|
| Percentages Ministers | 56 | 39 | 5 |
| Percentages Students | 85 | 11 | 4 |

## 2. The Religious Faiths of the American People

From GEORGE GALLUP, American Institute of Public Opinion (Dec. 9, 1944).

The survey asked these questions:

*"Have you attended a religious service within the past four weeks?"*

Fifty-eight per cent of those questioned said they had, while 42 per cent had not.

*"Do you, personally, believe in a God?"*

Ninety-six per cent said they did, one per cent said they did not, and another three per cent said they were undecided.

*"Do you believe there is a life after death?"*

Seventy-six per cent said "yes," 13 per cent "no," and 11 per cent expressed themselves as undecided.

| | Yes | No | Undec. |
|---|---|---|---|
| M. Atl. | 95% | 2% | 3% |
| E. Cent. | 97 | 1 | 2 |
| W. Cent. | 97 | 1 | 2 |
| South | 98 | 1 | 1 |
| Mountain | 98 | 1 | 1 |
| Pac. Coast | 93 | 1 | 6 |
| Farmers | 97 | 1 | 2 |
| Towns under 10,000 | 98 | 1 | 1 |
| 10,000–100,000 | 94 | 2 | 4 |
| 100,000 & over | 94 | 2 | 4 |
| Men | 95 | 1 | 4 |
| Women | 97 | 1 | 2 |
| Age 20–29 | 93 | 3 | 4 |
| 30–49 | 97 | 1 | 2 |
| 50 & over | 97 | 1 | 2 |

### Belief in God

| | Yes | No | Undec. |
|---|---|---|---|
| N. Eng. | 94% | 1% | 5% |

### Belief in Life after Death

| | Yes | No | No Opin. |
|---|---|---|---|
| N. Eng. | 68% | 16% | 16% |
| M. Atl. | 69 | 18 | 13 |

|            | Yes | No | No Opin. |
|------------|-----|----|----------|
| E. Cent.   | 77% | 14% | 9% |
| W. Cent.   | 85  | 7  | 8 |
| South      | 91  | 2  | 7 |
| Mountain   | 87  | 9  | 4 |
| Pac. Coast | 63  | 14 | 23 |
| Farmers    | 85  | 6  | 9 |
| Towns under 10,000 | 81 | 8 | 11 |
| 10,000–100,000 | 72 | 15 | 13 |
| 100,000 & over | 69 | 18 | 13 |
| Men        | 73  | 14 | 13 |
| Women      | 79  | 11 | 10 |
| Age 20–29  | 70  | 17 | 13 |
| 30–49      | 76  | 13 | 11 |
| 50 & over  | 79  | 10 | 11 |

A comparison with a poll taken in 1936 shows that there has been a 12 point increase in the number of persons believing in a life after death.

**Do You Personally Believe in a God?**

| Yes | No | Undec. |
|-----|----|--------|
| 96% | 1% | 3% |

**Do You Believe There Is a Life after Death?**

| Yes | No | No Opin. |
|-----|----|----------|
| 76% | 13% | 11% |

Polling the country on various religious issues, the Gallup Poll finds that although Americans believe in God and a large majority think there is a life after death, some 30 million people haven't been to church even once during the past month.

## 3. Church Attendance—by Faiths and Geographical Regions

From ELMO ROPER—NBC Survey (June, 1952)

**"Do you belong to a church, or do you have one you go to?"**

|  | Number of Respondents # | % | Church attendance Yes % | No % | No answer % |
|--|--------|---|------|------|------|
| Total sample | 3,015 | 100 | 84 | 12 | 4 |
| *Religion:* | | | | | |
| Protestant | 1,987 | 100 | 91 | 8 | 1 |
| Catholic | 646 | 100 | 93 | 4 | 3 |
| Jewish | 98* | 100 | 67 | 31 | 2 |
| Other | 71* | 100 | 84 | 13 | 3 |
| None | 137 | 100 | 4 | 95 | 1 |
| *Geographic Region:* | | | | | |
| Northeast | 854 | 100 | 84 | 11 | 5 |
| Midwest | 915 | 100 | 88 | 9 | 3 |
| South | 847 | 100 | 89 | 9 | 2 |
| Far West | 399 | 100 | 69 | 25 | 6 |

* Percentages based on less than 100 cases are often unreliable.

## 4. 8 out of 10 U.S. Adults Are Church Members

From GEORGE GALLUP, American Institute of Public Opinion (July 20, 1954).

*"Are you a member of a church?"*

|  | Per Cent | Total Number |
|---|---|---|
| Yes | 79% | 81,000,000 |
| No | 21 | 21,000,000 |
|  | 100% | 102,000,000 |

|  | Yes | No |
|---|---|---|
| South | 85% | 15% |
| Far West | 65 | 35 |
| Over 500,000 | 73 | 27 |
| 100,000–500,000 | 84 | 16 |
| 10,000–100,000 | 83 | 17 |
| Under 10,000 | 78 | 22 |
| Farm | 77 | 23 |

Two factors must be borne in mind in connection with these figures. One is that they represent only adults and thus do not include church members under 21 years of age.

The second is that some people claim they are members of a church, but they may not actually belong now to any given parish.

### Church Members

|  | Yes | No |
|---|---|---|
| NATIONAL | 79% | 21% |
| Men | 75 | 25 |
| Women | 83 | 17 |
| 21–29 years | 78 | 22 |
| 30–49 years | 80 | 20 |
| 50 years and over | 78 | 22 |
| College | 83 | 17 |
| High School | 81 | 19 |
| Grade School | 73 | 27 |
| Prof. & Bus. | 83 | 17 |
| White-Collar | 82 | 18 |
| Farmers | 77 | 23 |
| Manual Workers | 77 | 23 |
| New England | 85 | 15 |
| Mid-Atlantic | 80 | 20 |
| East Central | 75 | 25 |
| West Central | 82 | 18 |

### Attendance Record of Church Members

How many church members attended church on the average Sunday during the first half of 1954? How many non-church members attended?

More than half of all adult church members—55 per cent—had attended church.

Of those persons who are not members of a church, one person in nine —11 per cent—attended church.

Seventy-eight per cent of Catholics had attended.

Forty-eight per cent of Protestants had attended.

Thirty-one per cent of persons of the Jewish faith reached in the survey had attended.

Among the four largest Protestant denominations, . . . the best attendance record [was that of] the Baptists, followed in order by Methodists, Lutherans, and Presbyterians.

This happens to be the order of these four in size. It also happens to be the order in terms of per cent attending church.

## 5. Church Attendance on Typical Sabbath

From GEORGE GALLUP, American Institute of Public Opinion (Mar. 26, 1954).

*"Did you happen to go to church (or synagogue) during the last seven days?"*

The results nationwide:

| Yes | No |
|---|---|
| 47% | 53% |

Here are the results by religious affiliation:

| | Attended | Did Not Attend |
|---|---|---|
| Protestant | 40% | 60% |
| Catholic | 72 | 28 |

| | Attended | Did Not Attend |
|---|---|---|
| East | 52% | 48% |
| Midwest | 45 | 55 |
| South | 48 | 52 |
| Far West | 37 | 63 |

Church attendance increases, the survey finds, after people reach the age of 30. The proportion of those between 21 and 29 who went to church during the period covered by the survey was 43 per cent as compared to 48 per cent of those between the ages of 30 and 49, and 49 per cent of those who are 50 and over.

The results for the different areas of the country:

Women have a higher attendance record than men do; exactly half of the women interviewed said they had been in the previous week, only 44 per cent of the men had been to church during that period.

Church attendance is highest among the white-collar group and lowest among the manual workers. Fifty per cent of the farmers interviewed had been to church in the last week.

## 6. Church Attendance Up 9,000,000 in 4 Years

From GEORGE GALLUP, American Institute of Public Opinion (July 17, 1954).

Four years ago, an Institute survey found 39 per cent of the total adult population at that time attended church—or some 38,000,000.

Fifteen years ago, 34 per cent of the 1939 adult population attended—or some 34,000,000. Approximately 4,500 adults were asked in a coast-to-coast sampling survey:

*"Did you, yourself, happen to attend church in the last seven days?"*

The results below show, first, the percentage replies for each survey and then apply those percentages to the total number of adults on the basis of the 102 million estimated U.S. population 21 years of age and older.

### Attend Church Last Week?

| | Per Cent | Total Number |
|---|---|---|
| Early March | 47% | 48,000,000 |
| Early May | 47 | 48,000,000 |
| Mid-June | 45 | 46,000,000 |
| AVERAGE | 46 | 47,000,000 |

Similar Institute surveys in earlier years, conducted at one point of time only, show the following trend comparisons. Again, the percentages have been applied to the total adult population:

| Adult Millions | Per Cent | Total Number |
|---|---|---|
| Feb., 1939 (83) | 41% | 34,000,000 |
| Nov., 1940 (85) | 37 | 31,000,000 |
| May, 1942 (87) | 36 | 31,000,000 |
| May, 1947 (94) | 45 | 42,000,000 |
| Apr., 1950 (97) | 39 | 38,000,000 |
| July, 1954 (102) | 46 | 47,000,000 |

It must be remembered that survey figures are for *adults only* who claim to have attended church during the seven days preceding the time of the survey.

Church attendance increases after people pass the age of 30, the survey finds. The proportion of those between the ages of 21 to 29 who attended was 42 per cent, compared to 48 per cent of those in the age group 30 to 49 and 46 per cent of those aged 50 and over.

Women are found to be better

church-goers than men. Exactly half (50 per cent) of the women interviewed said they had been to church in the previous week, while only 42 per cent of the men had attended.

Attendance is highest among white-collar families and lowest among manual workers.

College people are better in attendance than those who did not go beyond high school or grammar school.

By city size, the largest proportion of church-goers is found among residents of cities between 10,000 and 100.000 population.

Here is the table giving these facts:

|  | Yes | No |
|---|---|---|
| NATIONAL | 46% | 54% |
| Men | 42 | 58 |
| Women | 50 | 50 |

|  | Yes | No |
|---|---|---|
| 21 to 29 years | 42% | 58% |
| 30 to 49 years | 48 | 52 |
| 50 years and over | 46 | 54 |
| College | 51 | 49 |
| High School | 47 | 53 |
| Grade School | 42 | 58 |
| Prof. & Bus. | 48 | 52 |
| White-Collar | 50 | 50 |
| Farmers | 47 | 53 |
| Manual Workers | 44 | 56 |
| New England | 53 | 47 |
| Mid-Atlantic | 51 | 49 |
| East Central | 40 | 60 |
| West Central | 47 | 53 |
| South | 50 | 50 |
| Far West | 35 | 65 |
| Over 500,000 | 45 | 55 |
| 100,000–500,000 | 48 | 52 |
| 10,000–100,000 | 51 | 49 |
| Under 10,000 | 43 | 57 |
| Farm | 46 | 54 |

## 7. One out of Three U.S. Adults Attends Church

From GEORGE GALLUP, American Institute of Public Opinion (April 7, 1950).

*"Did you happen to go to church (or synagogue) during the last seven days?"*

The results below show, first, the percentage replies in the survey and then apply these percentages to the total number of adults on the basis of the 96 million estimated U.S. population over 21 years of age.

### Attend Church Last Week?

|  | Per Cent | Total Number |
|---|---|---|
| Yes | 39% | 37,400,000 |
| No | 61% | 58,600,000 |
|  | 100% | 96,000,000 |

Twice as many of those who classified themselves as Catholics reported church attendance during the period of the survey as persons who classified themselves as Protestants.

|  | Attended | Did Not Attend |
|---|---|---|
| Protestant | 33% | 67% |
| Catholic | 62 | 38 |

Here are the results by age:

| Age | Attended | Did Not Attend |
|---|---|---|
| 21–29 | 31% | 69% |
| 30–49 | 41 | 59 |
| 50 & over | 42 | 58 |

Women have a much higher attendance record than men do, as the following table shows:

|  | Attended | Did Not Attend |
|---|---|---|
| Men | 34% | 66% |
| Women | 44 | 56 |

[The survey on church attendance was conducted among a balanced cross-section of the nation's 96 million adults by the Institute's new "time-place" sampling method. which utilizes area sampling techniques.]

## 8. Religion and Politics

From ELMO ROPER—NBC Survey.

**"Which of these groups do you feel is doing the most good for the country at the present time? (Card shown respondent.) Which one the least good?"**

|  | Sept. 1942 | Dec. 1943 | June 1946 | June 1947 | Oct. 1948 | Sept. 1953 |
|---|---|---|---|---|---|---|
| *Doing most good:* | % | % | % | % | % | % |
| Religious leaders | 18 | 26 | 32 | 33 | 34 | 40 |
| Government leaders | 28 | 24 | 13 | 15 | 11 | 18 |
| Business leaders | 19 | 17 | 18 | 19 | 20 | 10 |
| Labor leaders | 6 | 7 | 10 | 11 | 12 | 8 |
| Congress | 6 | 10 | 7 | 7 | 4 | 5 |
| Don't know and no answer | 24 | 21 | 21 | 18 | 19 | 21 |
| *Doing least good:* |  |  |  |  |  |  |
| Religious leaders | 7 | 6 | 5 | 4 | 4 | 4 |
| Government leaders | 3 | 5 | 9 | 9 | 12 | 6 |
| Business leaders | 6 | 6 | 8 | 10 | 6 | 9 |
| Labor leaders | 36 | 36 | 35 | 43 | 31 | 31 |
| Congress | 12 | 13 | 15 | 14 | 27 | 8 |
| Don't know and no answer | 36 | 35 | 28 | 22 | 21 | 42 |

*Note:* Percentages add to more than 100 because some respondents gave more than one answer.

## 9. Church Leaders and Politics

From ELMO ROPER—NBC Survey (June, 1952).

a) **"Regardless of how you intend to vote this year, would you say in the past you have usually found yourself agreeing with or disagreeing with the leaders of your church on candidates for public offices?"**

Asked of respondents who belong to a church—84% of total sample:

| | Total asked this question 100% |
|---|---|
| Usually agreed | 25% |
| Usually disagreed | 4% |
| They don't favor candidates (volunteered) | 39% |
| Don't know and no answer | 32% |

b) **"Which do you think the leaders of your church will probably favor for President this year—the Democrats or the Republicans?"**

Asked of respondents who belong to a church and who answered other than "most leaders of their church don't favor candidates for public office"— 51% of total sample:

| | Total asked this question 100% |
|---|---|
| Democrats | 12% |
| Republicans | 23% |
| They don't favor candidates | 5% |
| Don't know and no answer | 60% |

c) **"Have you ever talked politics with any of the leaders in your church?"**

Asked of respondents who belong to a church—84% of total sample:

| | Total asked this question 100% |
|---|---|
| Yes | 13% |
| No | 86% |
| No answer | 1% |

## 10. Political Influence of Organizations

From ELMO ROPER—NBC Survey (May, 1952).

"Here is a list of some groups and organizations that aren't directly connected with any political party. Are there any of these groups whose ideas you expect to be good on candidates running for office?"

| | Total sample |
|---|---|
| Number of respondents | 2,997 (100%) |
| The National Ass'n of Manufacturers | 6% |
| The CIO Labor Union | 7% |
| The AFL Labor Union | 9% |
| The American Legion | 23% |
| The League of Women Voters | 17% |
| The officials of your church | 22% |
| Prominent Southerners who have supported states' rights (Like Russell, Byrnes, Byrd) | 5% |
| The National Association for the Advancement of Colored People | 8% |
| The National Grange | 5% |
| The Farm Bureau Federation | 10% |
| None or don't know | 38% |
| No answer | 3% |

*Note:* Percentages add to more than 100 because some respondents gave more than one answer.

## 11. Predictions on Church Attendance in Future

From GEORGE GALLUP, American Institute of Public Opinion (Dec. 24, 1949).

"Do you, yourself, think any of the following things are likely to happen in the next 50 years? Do you think people in this country will go to church more often or less often than they do now?"

Interest in religion generally tends to increase with age. Perhaps that is the reason for the difference in attitude between those under 30 and those over 30 questioned in today's survey.

The vote:

| | | Age 21–29 | 30–49 | 50 & over |
|---|---|---|---|---|
| More often | 39% | 34% | 41% | 41% |
| Less often | 32 | 40 | 30 | 28 |
| No change | 21 | 19 | 23 | 20 |
| No opinion | 8 | 7 | 6 | 11 |

## 12. Attitudes on Intermarriage

From GEORGE GALLUP, American Institute of Public Opinion (Dec. 27, 1951).

"Do you think two young people in love who are of different religious faiths—Protestant, Catholic, or Jewish—should get married, or not?"

The national vote:

54% say they should
35% say they should not
11% express no opinion

Persons between the ages of 21 and 29 approve by more than 2-to-1,

whereas those over the age of 50 are closely divided in their opinions, as the following table shows.

| | 21–29 Years | 30–49 Years | 50 Years & over |
|---|---|---|---|
| Should | 65% | 55% | 47% |
| Should not | 25 | 34 | 42 |
| No opinion | 10 | 11 | 11 |
| | 100% | 100% | 100% |

"What chance do you think a marriage between young people of different religious faiths has of being successful—a good chance or a poor chance?"

38% say a good chance
53% say a poor or only fair chance
9% are undecided

Again, the attitude differs sharply by ages. Nearly half of the young people, 46 per cent, think a marriage of mixed religions has a good chance for success, while 44 per cent give it only a fair or a poor chance, with the remainder undecided.

In both the middle-aged and elderly group, on the other hand, only about one-third see a favorable outlook for such marriages.

**"Would you object to a son or daughter of yours marrying a person** of a different religious faith from yours, or not?"

33% say they would
58% say they would not
9% are undecided

Those who classify themselves as Protestants vote 52 to 37 per cent that persons of different religions should marry, with 11 per cent undecided.

Among Catholics the division is 59 to 32 per cent, with 9 per cent undecided.

As for the chances of success in such marriages, 42 per cent of Catholics take a favorable view, while 51 per cent say that the chances are poor or only fair and the rest are undecided.

Among Protestants the vote is 37 per cent good, 54 per cent poor or fair, and the remainder undecided.

## 13. Protestants and Church Unity

From GEORGE GALLUP, American Institute of Public Opinion (April 28, 1950).

**"A committee of church people in the U.S. is studying a plan whereby all Protestant churches in this country would join to form a single Protestant church. What is your feeling about an idea of this kind—would you be in favor of it or opposed to it?"**

(A closely similar question was put to the public in 1937 and again in 1948 by the Institute.)

### Vote of Protestants

|  | 1937 | 1948 | Today |
|---|---|---|---|
| Favor | 40% | 42% | 50% |
| Oppose | 51 | 47 | 39 |
| No opinion | 9 | 11 | 11 |
|  | 100% | 100% | 100% |

In this survey this second question was asked of the entire sample:

**"What do you think would be the attitude of your own church on the question of forming a single Protestant church in America—do you believe your church would favor that plan or oppose it?"**

### Protestants Only

| | |
|---|---|
| Church would favor | 28% |
| Church would not favor | 45 |
| No opinion | 27 |
| | 100% |

## 14. How Many Can Name First Four Books of New Testament?

From GEORGE GALLUP, American Institute of Public Opinion (Mar. 30, 1950).

"Will you tell me the names of any of the first four books of the New Testament of the Bible—that is, the first four Gospels?"

Named 4 Gospels correctly...... 35%
Named 3 correctly.............. 4
Named 2 correctly.............. 4
Named 1 correctly.............. 4
——
47%
Could not name *any*............ 53
——
100%

Americans are put to shame by the British when it comes to remembering the names of the Gospels.

A survey by the British Institute of Public Opinion found that three out of every five (61 per cent) were able to rattle off Matthew, Mark, Luke, and John and one in seven could name some.

But one-fourth of the British adults could not name any, as compared to more than half in the United States.

The British survey found young people more ignorant about the names of the Gospels than older people, with one-third unable to name any of the four books. A similar situation was found in the American survey. Here are the results by age:

### By Age:

| | 21–29 Years | 30–49 Years | 50 Years & over |
|---|---|---|---|
| Named all four Gospels .... | 26% | 36% | 39% |
| Named one, two, or three | 16 | 13 | 10 |
| Could not name *any* ....... | 58 | 51 | 51 |
| | 100% | 100% | 100% |

The American survey found that knowledge of the Gospels is a function of degree of school education, as follows:

### By Education:

| | College | High School | Grade School |
|---|---|---|---|
| Named all four Gospels ....... | 59% | 36% | 27% |
| Named one, two, or three....... | 11 | 14 | 11 |
| Could not name *any* .......... | 30 | 50 | 62 |
| | 100% | 100% | 100% |

## 15. Revision of Bible—Controversy

From GEORGE GALLUP, American Institute of Public Opinion (Dec. 26, 1952).

The new revised Bible, which modernizes the language used in the King James Version, has brought a mixture of praise and criticism from clergymen and lay members of the Protestant churches.

An Institute survey found that two out of every three persons (67 per cent) have heard or read about the new Bible and that 28 per cent approve of it, while 22 per cent disapprove and the rest have no opinion.

"Do you plan to buy a copy of the new Bible?"

A total of 4 per cent said they had already bought a copy—a figure which checks closely with sales to date.

Another 19 per cent, or nearly one out of every five, said they intended to buy a copy.

Nearly two persons out of every three questioned in the survey say they have read some part of the Bible at home within this last year. Here are the figures:

**"Have you, yourself, read any part of the Bible at home within the last year?"**

| Yes | No |
|-----|-----|
| 67% | 33% |

Of all sections of the country, the South shows the highest proportion of Bible readers—81 per cent. The New England and Middle Atlantic sections showed the lowest—59 per cent.

## 16. Opinions on Revised Bible

From GEORGE GALLUP, American Institute of Public Opinion (Dec. 25, 1952).

**"Have you heard or read about the changes in wording in the new revised edition of the Bible?"**

The vote:

| Yes | No |
|-----|-----|
| 67% | 33% |

Those who said "yes" were then asked:

**"From what you have heard or read, do you approve or disapprove of the changes in wordings which have been made in the new edition of the Bible?"**

| | |
|---|---|
| Approve ..................... | 28% |
| Disapprove .................... | 22 |
| No opinion ................... | 17 |
| Have not heard or read about it.. | 33 |
| | 100% |

Persons with the greatest amount of formal education are more likely to approve of the revised Bible than are persons with a limited education.

| | College | High School | Grade School |
|---|---|---|---|
| Approve ........ | 47% | 31% | 15% |
| Disapprove ..... | 20 | 21 | 24 |
| No opinion ..... | 17 | 19 | 14 |
| Have not heard or read about it... | 16 | 29 | 47 |
| | 100% | 100% | 100% |

Women are more inclined to approve of the new Bible than men are.

Protestants questioned in the survey had much more favorable views of the new Bible, from what they have heard or read about it, than Catholics had.

Among Protestants the vote was: approve 32 per cent, disapprove 24 per cent, and no opinion 17 per cent. Twenty-seven per cent had not heard or read about the new Bible.

Among Catholics the vote divides: approve 19 per cent, disapprove 18 per cent, and no opinion 17 per cent. Forty-six per cent had not heard or read about the new Bible.

## 17. International Poll: Belief in God and the After-Life

From GEORGE GALLUP, American Institute of Public Opinion (Jan. 9, 1948).

Eleven nations [were] covered:

### "Do you, personally, believe in God?"

The vote:

| | Yes | No | Don't know |
|---|---|---|---|
| Brazil | 96% | 3% | 1% |
| Australia | 95 | 5 | — |
| Canada | 95 | 2 | 3 |
| U. S. | 94 | 3 | 3 |
| Norway | 84 | 7 | 9 |
| Finland | 83 | 5 | 12 |
| Holland | 80 | 14 | 6 |
| Sweden | 80 | 8 | 12 |
| Denmark | 80 | 9 | 11 |
| France | 66 | 20 | 14 |

The vote in France according to political party affiliation shows these revealing differences:

| | Yes | No | Don't know |
|---|---|---|---|
| Communists | 17% | 64% | 19% |
| Socialists | 50 | 29 | 21 |
| Union of Left | 62 | 18 | 20 |
| R.P.F. (Gaullists) | 88 | 5 | 7 |
| M.R.P. | 92 | 5 | 3 |
| P.R.L. | 93 | 7 | — |

In England the question was put in a somewhat different way, with the following results:

### "Which of these statements comes closest to your belief?"

A. There is a personal God ... 45%  ⎫
B. There is some sort of spirit or vital force which controls life ... 39  ⎬ 84%
 ⎭
C. I am not sure there is any sort of God or life force ... 16

### "Do you believe in life after death?"

| | Yes | No | No Opin. |
|---|---|---|---|
| Canada | 78% | 9% | 13% |
| Brazil | 78 | 18 | 4 |
| Norway | 71 | 15 | 14 |
| Finland | 69 | 11 | 20 |
| U. S. | 68 | 13 | 19 |
| Holland | 68 | 26 | 6 |
| Australia | 63 | 20 | 17 |
| France | 58 | 22 | 20 |
| Denmark | 55 | 27 | 18 |
| Sweden | 49 | 17 | 34 |
| Britain | 49 | 27 | 24 |

Everyone [in the United States] was asked: "How do you imagine life after death to be?"

The principal replies:

1. Complete happiness, joy, peace, quiet.

2. Reward for virtue, punishment for sin; heaven or hell.

3. Dreamlike, disembodied, inanimate, spiritual.

4. As described in the Bible.

Faith in God diminishes as people get away from nature and the outdoors. For example, in the city of Copenhagen, Denmark, 17 per cent, or one person in every six, does not believe in God's existence. In the rural Danish countryside, only 4 per cent deny God.

Faith in God varies by age. In the United States fewer young people believe in God than older people, although the difference is not as great as in some other countries. In Denmark one in four under the age of 35 years either denies God's existence or expresses doubts. But among people over 50 years of age, one in 12 doubts or denies.

## 18. Three of Every 100 Families Give 10 per cent of Annual Income to Church

From GEORGE GALLUP, American Institute of Public Opinion (April 3, 1953).

The survey results, projected on an estimated 50 million U. S. family units today (including adult single-person families) would indicate that there are about 1½ million families who tithe—that is, give 10 per cent of their annual income to the Church.

**"Do you know of anyone in your community who tithes—that is, gives 10 per cent of his annual income to the Church?"**

A total of 3 per cent volunteered the answer that they themselves, or their husbands, tithed.

Of the remainder, 27 per cent said they knew of someone in their community who tithed, while 70 per cent did not know of anyone.

The custom of tithing today is found to be relatively more wide-spread in the South than in any other geographical section.

A total of 5 per cent of Southern respondents said they, or their husbands, believed in tithing. In addition, 48 per cent said they knew of someone in their community who tithed.

Adults in the heavily populated New England and Middle Atlantic states were, on the other hand, least aware of the practice of tithing.

One interesting aspect of the survey is the fact that the percentage of those who say they themselves tithe is uniform in all age groups—young, middle-aged, and old.

The survey also finds proportionately more manual worker families who believe in tithing than is the case in other major occupational groups.

# Church Holy Days and Religious Observances

## 1. Calendar and Description of Religious Observances: All Faiths

Compiled from the following sources: the *Information Please Almanac, 1954*, Dan Golenpaul Associates, New York, N.Y., pp. 499–501; the *School Calendar; indicating Holidays and Holy Days,* prepared by Community Relations Service, The American Jewish Committee, 386 Fourth Avenue, New York 16, N.Y.

*Note*: In determining church holidays, both the lunar and the solar calendars are used. Dates determined by the lunar calendar are generally *movable*; those determined by the solar calendar are *fixed*. Movable holidays are indicated by an asterisk (*).—Ed.

**New Year's Day**—Jan. 1—Protestant and Catholic Holy Day. Ecclesiastically the New Year celebrates the Feast of Circumcision.

**Feast of Epiphany**—Jan. 6—Falls the twelfth day after Christmas and commemorates the manifestation of Jesus as the Son of God, as represented by the adoration of the Magi, the baptism of Jesus, and the miracle of the wine at the marriage feast at Cana. Epiphany originally marked the beginning of the carnival season preceding Lent, and the evening (sometimes the eve) is known as Twelfth Night.

**\*Shrove Tuesday**—Falls the day before Ash Wednesday and marks the end of the carnival season, which once began on Epiphany but is now usually celebrated the last three days before Lent. In France, the day is known as Mardi Gras (Fat Tuesday), and Mardi Gras celebrations are also held in several American cities, particularly in New Orleans. The day is sometimes called Pancake Tuesday by the English because of the need of using up fats which were prohibited during Lent.

**\*Ash Wednesday**—The first day of the Lenten season, which lasts forty days. Having its origin sometime before A.D. 1000, it is a day of public penance and is marked in the Roman Catholic Church by the burning of the palms blessed on the previous Palm Sunday. With his thumb, the priest then marks a cross upon the forehead of each worshiper. The Anglican Church and a few Protestant groups in the United States also celebrate the day, but generally without the use of ashes.

**\*Purim (Feast of Esther)**—The Biblical Book of Esther is read in the synagogue and there is general merry-making in the home. Gifts are exchanged and also distributed to the poor.

**\*Palm Sunday**—Is observed the Sunday before Easter to commemorate the

249

entry of Jesus into Jerusalem. The procession and the ceremonies introducing the benediction of palms probably had their origin in Jerusalem.

*Holy Week—All the days of the week preceding Easter have special connotation as they relate to the events of the last days in Jesus' life. Beginning with Palm Sunday, each of these days takes on a special importance.

*Holy Thursday (in Holy Week)—This day is marked by the Sacrament of Holy Communion in remembrance of the Last Supper which Jesus had with His disciples.

*Good Friday—This day commemorates the Crucifixion, which is retold during services from the Gospel according to St. John. A feature in Roman Catholic churches is the Mass of the Presanctified: there is no Consecration, the Host having been consecrated the previous day. The eating of hot cross buns on this day is said to have started in England.

*Easter Sunday—Observed in all Christian churches, Easter is a principal feast of the ecclesiastical year, and commemorates the Resurrection of Jesus. It is celebrated on the first Sunday after the full moon which occurs on or next after March 21 and is therefore celebrated between March 22 and April 25 inclusive. This date was fixed by the Council of Nicaea in 325.

*First Day of Passover (*Pesach*)— (*Nisan* 15)—The Feast of the Passover, also called the Feast of Unleavened Bread, commemorates the escape of the first-born of the Jews from the Angel of Death, who took from the Egyptians their first-born, thus fulfilling the prophecy of Moses. As the Jews fled Egypt, they ate unleavened

bread, and from that time the Jews have allowed no leavening in the houses during Passover, bread being replaced by matzoth.

*Second Day of Passover.

*Conclusion and Last Day of Passover (8th Day).

*Greek Orthodox Palm Sunday— Commemorates the triumphal entry of Jesus into Jerusalem. First day of Greek Orthodox Holy Week.

*Greek Orthodox Holy Thursday— Commemorates the Last Supper at which Jesus instituted the Sacrament of Holy Communion.

*Greek Orthodox Holy Friday (Good Friday)—Commemorates the Passion and Crucifixion of Jesus.

*Greek Orthodox Easter.

*Ascension Day—Took place in the presence of His Apostles 40 days after the Resurrection of Jesus. It is traditionally held to have occurred on Mount Olivet in Bethany.

*Pentecost (Whitsunday)—This day commemorates the descent of the Holy Ghost upon the Apostles fifty days after the Resurrection. The sermon by the Apostle Peter, which led to the baptism of 3,000 who professed belief, originated the ceremonies that have since been followed. "Whitsunday" is believed to have come from "white Sunday" when, among the English, white robes were worn by those baptized on the day.

*First Day of Shabuoth (Hebrew Pentecost)—(*Sivan* 6)—This festival, sometimes called the Feast of Weeks, or of Harvest, or of the First Fruits, falls fifty days after Passover and originally celebrated the end of the seven-week grain-harvesting season.

In later tradition, it also celebrated the giving of the Law to Moses on Mt. Sinai, and both aspects have come down to the present.

**\*Fast of Ab** (*Tishah B'ab*)—A day of mourning in memory of the destruction of the Temple.

**Feast of the Assumption**—Aug. 15— The principal feast of the Blessed Virgin, this holy day commemorates two events: the happy departure of Mary from this life and the assumption of her body into heaven.

**\*First Day of Rosh Hashanah** (Jewish New Year)—(*Tishri* 1)—This day marks the beginning of the Jewish year and opens the Ten Days of Penitence, closing with Yom Kippur.

**\*Yom Kippur** (Day of Atonement)— (*Tishri* 10)—This day marks the end of the Ten Days of Penitence that began with Rosh Hashanah and is the holiest day of the Jewish year. It is described in Leviticus as the "Sabbath of Sabbaths," and synagogue services begin the preceding sundown, resume the following morning, and continue through the day to sundown.

**\*First Day of Sukkoth** (Feast of Tabernacles)—(*Tishri* 15)—This festival, also known as the Feast of the Ingathering, originally celebrated the fruit harvest; the name comes from the booths or tabernacles in which the Jews lived during the harvest, although one tradition traces it to the shelters used by the Jews in their wandering through the wilderness. During the festival, many Jews build small huts in their back yards or on the roofs of houses.

**\*Eighth Day of the Feast of Tabernacles**—This marks the climax of the Jewish Holy Day season. Prayers for rain are recited in the synagogue.

**\*Simhath Torah** (Rejoicing of the Law)—The Reading of the Law is concluded and re-commenced. Gaiety is the characteristic mood of the day combined with a spirit of reverence.

**Reformation Day**—Oct. 31—The date which is regarded as the beginning of the Protestant Reformation observed in many Protestant churches.

**All Saints Day**—Nov. 1—A Holy Day of Obligation. Commemorates all the lesser saints as well as all holy men and martyrs whose record has not survived.

**\*First Sunday in Advent**—Advent is the season in which the faithful must prepare themselves for the advent of the Savior on Christmas. The four Sundays before Christmas are marked by special church services.

**Feast of the Immaculate Conception**— Dec. 8—Catholic Holy Day of Obligation. Celebrating Mary's privilege of freedom from sin from the first moment of her conception as the child of St. Joachim and St. Anne.

**\*First Day of Hanukkah** (Festival of Lights)—(*Kislev* 25)—This festival was instituted by Judas Maccabaeus in 165 B.C. to celebrate the purification of the Temple of Jerusalem, which had been desecrated three years earlier by Antiochus Epiphanes, who set up a pagan altar and offered sacrifices to Zeus Olympius. In Jewish homes, a light is lighted the first night, and on each succeeding night of the eight-day festival, another is lighted to commemorate the rededication of the Temple by the Maccabees and the miracle of the consecrated oil that burned for eight days.

**Christmas** (Feast of the Nativity)— Dec. 25—A most important and widely celebrated holiday of the Christian year, it is observed as the anniversary of the birth of Jesus. Christmas customs are centuries old. The mistletoe, for example, comes from the Druids, who, in hanging the mistletoe, hoped for peace and good fortune. Use of such plants as holly comes from the ancient belief that such plants blossomed at Christmas.

Comparatively recent is the Christmas tree, first set up in Germany in the seventeenth century, and the use of candles on trees developed from the belief that candles appeared by miracle on the trees at Christmas. Colonial Manhattan Islanders introduced the name Santa Claus, a corruption of the Dutch name for the fourth-century Asia Minor St. Nicholas.

## 2. Tables of Movable Holidays: Christian and Jewish

Adapted from the *Information Please Almanac, 1954*, Dan Golenpaul Associates, New York, N.Y., p. 501.

### Movable Holidays, 1955 to 1963

#### CHRISTIAN

| Year | Ash Wed. | Easter | Pentecost | 1st Sun. Advent |
|------|----------|--------|-----------|-----------------|
| 1955 | Feb. 23 | Apr. 10 | May 29 | Nov. 27 |
| 1956 | Feb. 15 | Apr. 1 | May 20 | Dec. 2 |
| 1957 | Mar. 6 | Apr. 21 | June 9 | Dec. 1 |
| 1958 | Feb. 19 | Apr. 6 | May 25 | Nov. 30 |
| 1959 | Feb. 11 | Mar. 29 | May 17 | Nov. 29 |
| 1960 | Mar. 2 | Apr. 17 | June 5 | Nov. 27 |
| 1961 | Feb. 15 | Apr. 2 | May 21 | Dec. 3 |
| 1962 | Mar. 7 | Apr. 22 | June 10 | Dec. 2 |
| 1963 | Feb. 27 | Apr. 14 | June 2 | Dec. 1 |

Shrove Tuesday: 1 day before Ash Wednesday.
Palm Sunday: 7 days before Easter.
Maundy Thursday: 3 days before Easter.
Good Friday: 2 days before Easter.

Holy Saturday: 1 day before Easter.
Ascension Day: 10 days before Pentecost.
Trinity Sunday: 7 days after Pentecost.
Corpus Christi: 11 days after Pentecost.

#### JEWISH

| Year | Purim | 1st day Passover | 1st day Shabuoth | 1st day Rosh Hashanah | Yom Kippur | 1st Day Sukkoth | Simhath Torah | 1st Day Hanukkah |
|------|-------|------------------|------------------|-----------------------|------------|-----------------|---------------|------------------|
| 1955 | Mar. 8 | Apr. 7 | May 27 | Sept. 17 | Sept. 26 | Oct. 1 | Oct. 9 | Dec. 10 |
| 1956 | Feb. 26 | Mar. 27 | May 16 | Sept. 6 | Sept. 15 | Sept. 20 | Sept. 28 | Nov. 29 |
| 1957 | Mar. 17 | Apr. 16 | June 5 | Sept. 26 | Oct. 5 | Oct. 10 | Oct. 18 | Dec. 18 |
| 1958 | Mar. 6 | Apr. 5 | May 25 | Sept. 15 | Sept. 24 | Sept. 29 | Oct. 7 | Dec. 7 |
| 1959 | Mar. 24 | Apr. 23 | June 12 | Oct. 3 | Oct. 12 | Oct. 17 | Oct. 25 | Dec. 26 |
| 1960 | Mar. 13 | Apr. 12 | June 1 | Sept. 22 | Oct. 1 | Oct. 6 | Oct. 14 | Dec. 14 |
| 1961 | Mar. 2 | Apr. 1 | May 21 | Sept. 11 | Sept. 20 | Sept. 25 | Oct. 3 | Dec. 3 |
| 1962 | Mar. 20 | Apr. 19 | June 8 | Sept. 29 | Oct. 8 | Oct. 13 | Oct. 21 | Dec. 22 |
| 1963 | Mar. 10 | Apr. 9 | May 29 | Sept. 19 | Sept. 28 | Oct. 3 | Oct. 11 | Dec. 11 |

Length of Jewish holidays (O = Orthodox, C = Conservative, R = Reform):

Passover: O & C, 8 days (holy days: first 2 and last 2); R, 7 days (holy days: first and last).
Shabuoth: O & C, 2 days; R, 1 day.
Rosh Hashanah: O & C 2 days; R, 1 day.
Yom Kippur: All groups, 1 day.
Sukkoth: All groups, 7 days (holy days: O & C, first 2; R, first only). O & C observe two additional days: Shemini Atsereth (Eighth Day of the Feast) and Simhath Torah (Rejoicing of the Law). R observes Shemini Atsereth but not Simhath Torah.
Hanukkah: All groups, 8 days.
NOTE: All holidays begin at sundown on the evening before the date given.

## 3. Catholic Holy Days, Observances, and Feasts

### a) "Holy Days of Obligations for the United States"

From the *National Catholic Almanac, 1955,* St. Anthony's Guild, Paterson, New Jersey.

Every Catholic who has attained the age of reason, and is not prevented by sickness or other sufficient cause, is obliged to rest from servile work and attend Holy Mass on the following days:

All Sundays of the year.
The Circumcision of Our Lord (New Year's Day), January 1.

The Ascension of Our Lord, [40 days after Easter].
The Assumption of the Blessed Virgin Mary, August 15.
All Saints' Day, November 1.
The Immaculate Conception of the Blessed Virgin Mary (Patronal Feast of the United States), December 8.
Christmas, the Nativity of Our Lord, December 25.

### b) Principal Catholic Devotions

From the *National Catholic Almanac, 1955,* St. Anthony's Guild, Paterson, New Jersey.

**Angelus, The,** commemorates the Incarnation of Christ. It consists of three versicles, three Hail Marys, and a special prayer, and recalls the announcement to Mary by the Archangel Gabriel that she was chosen to be the Mother of Christ, her acceptance of the divine will, and the Incarnation. The practice of reciting the Hail Mary in honor of the Incarnation was introduced by the Franciscans in 1263. The Regina Caeli, commemorating the joy of Mary at Christ's Resurrection, replaces the Angelus during the Easter season.

**Benediction** is a short exposition of the Blessed Sacrament for adoration by the faithful. At the close of the exposition, the priest makes the Sign of the Cross with the Blessed Sacrament over the people. Benediction closes with recitation of the Divine Praises.

**Enthronement of the Sacred Heart, The,** in the home is the acknowledgment of the sovereignty of Jesus Christ over the Christian family, expressed by installation of an image or picture of the Sacred Heart in a place of honor, accompanied by a prescribed act of consecration. **Night adoration** in the home, which consists of one hour of adoration once a month between the hours of 9 P.M. and 6 A.M. by one or more persons, or even the entire family, is connected with the Enthronement, though distinct from it. Its purpose is to make reparation for the sins of families.

**First Friday** devotion is the practice of receiving Holy Communion on the first Friday of nine consecutive months in honor of the Sacred Heart of Jesus and in reparation for sin. Christ promised the grace of final penitence to those who would make the nine First Fridays.

**First Saturday** devotion had its origin in the promise of Mary at Fatima in 1917 to obtain the graces necessary to salvation for those who, besides going to confession, would on the first Saturday of five consecutive months receive Holy Communion, recite five decades of the Rosary, and meditate on the mysteries for fifteen minutes.

**Five Wounds, The,** of Christ are honored as the channels through which His Precious Blood flowed for the redemption of mankind.

**Forty Hours Adoration, The,** is the solemn exposition of the Blessed Sacrament for forty hours, in memory of the time Christ's Body lay in the tomb, and for the purpose of making reparation for sin and begging God's graces. The devotion, which includes the celebration of special Masses, the holding of processions and recitation of the Litany of the Saints, was first instituted in Milan in 1534.

**Immaculate Heart of Mary, The,** devotion was first propagated by St. John Eudes (d. 1680), and was revived and increased after the apparitions of Mary at Fatima in 1917. In keeping with her expressed wishes there, Pope Pius XII consecrated the world to the Immaculate Heart of Mary in 1942; three years later he extended the feast of this title to the universal Church. Recitation of the Rosary and observance of the five First Saturdays are elements of this devotion. (See above.)

**Infant Jesus of Prague, The,** devotion began in the early seventeenth century in Prague, Bohemia. Princess Polixena of Prague presented the Carmelites there with a statue of the Infant which was lost and forgotten when war and persecution befell the city. After recovery of the statue some years later devotions were instituted and became widespread.

The **Little Office of the Blessed Virgin** consists of psalms, lessons, hymns, and prayers in honor of the Blessed Virgin, arranged in seven hours like the divine office. The Little Office was probably written about the middle of the eighth century. It is recited by most religious communities of women, other religious, and many lay persons.

**Miraculous Medal, The,** devotion owes its origin to apparitions made by Mary to St. Catharine Laboure in 1830. In the course of the apparitions the Blessed Virgin revealed the form and elements of the Miraculous Medal, which was first struck in 1832. Wearing of the medal is indulgenced. Devotion to Mary under the title of Our Lady of the Miraculous Medal is widespread. The feast of this title is observed Nov. 27.

**Mother of Sorrows, The,** devotion consists of the recitation of approved prayers, a sermon on the Blessed Virgin, the Via Matris and Benediction of the Most Blessed Sacrament. The **Via Matris,** or Stations of the Cross of Our Sorrowful Mother, represents her seven Sorrows.

**Precious Blood, The,** devotion honors the Blood of Christ as the price of His redemption of mankind. The feast is observed July 1.

**Rosary, The,** is a form of prayer in honor of our Lady made up of a series of ten "Hail Marys" or decades, each beginning with an "Our Father" and ending with a "Glory be to the Father." The Apostles' Creed and the Hail, Holy Queen are also recited in the Rosary. The complete Rosary is made up of fifteen decades. While reciting the prayers of each decade a person meditates on **Mysteries of the Rosary,** which commemorate events in the life of Mary and Christ. The mysteries are **Joyful**—Annunciation, Visitation, Nativity of Christ, Presentation, Finding of the Christ Child in the

Temple; **Sorrowful**—Agony in the Garden, Scourging at the Pillar, Crowning with Thorns, Carrying the Cross, Crucifixion; **Glorious**—Resurrection, Ascension, Descent of the Holy Spirit upon the Apostles, Assumption, Coronation of Mary as Queen of Heaven. Rosary beads are used to aid in counting the prayers without distraction. Recitation of the Rosary is highly indulgenced. A common practice is the recitation of five decades daily. The Blessed Virgin confirmed the efficacy of this devotion by an appearance to St. Dominic in the thirteenth century when he was preaching in opposition to the Albigensian heresy.

**Sacred Heart, The,** devotion is directed to the humanity of Christ which is personally united with His divinity. In adoring the Heart of Christ, persons adore Christ Himself. The devotion was revealed by Christ to St. Margaret Mary Alacoque in the seventeenth century. He asked that a feast of reparation (now the feast of the Sacred Heart) be instituted. The Holy Hour and the Communion of Reparation on the first Friday of each month are special manifestations of the devotion. Christ made the **12 Promises of the Sacred Heart** to St. Margaret Mary: I will give them all the graces necessary in their state of life.—I will establish peace in their homes.—I will comfort them in all their afflictions —I will be their secure refuge during life and above all in death.—I will bestow abundant blessing upon all their undertakings.—Sinners shall find in My Heart the source and the infinite ocean of mercy.—By devotion to My Heart tepid souls shall grow fervent.—Fervent souls shall quickly mount to high perfection.—I will bless every place where a picture of My Heart shall be

set up and honored.—I will give to priests the gift of touching the most hardened hearts.—Those who promote this devotion shall have their names written in My Heart, never to be blotted out.—I will grant the grace of final penitence to those who communicate on the first Friday of nine consecutive months. (*See* Enthronement of, above.)

**Seven Sorrows** or **Seven Dolors** of the Blessed Virgin Mary is a form of prayer in honor of the seven Sorrows: prophecy of Simeon, flight into Egypt, loss of Jesus in the temple of Jerusalem, meeting Jesus on the way to Calvary, crucifixion, removal of the sacred Body from the Cross, burial of Jesus. Seven Hail Marys are said during a meditation on each of these Sorrows. A chaplet of beads is used to count the prayers.

**Stations of the Cross, The,** is a series of meditations on the sufferings endured by Christ during His Passion. The subjects of the meditations: Jesus is condemned to death by Pilate, Jesus carries His Cross, Jesus falls the first time, Jesus meets His Mother Mary, Simon of Cyrene helps Jesus carry the Cross, Veronica wipes the face of Jesus, Jesus falls the second time, Jesus speaks to the women of Jerusalem, Jesus falls the third time, Jesus is stripped of His garments, Jesus is nailed to the Cross, Jesus dies upon the Cross, Jesus is taken down from the Cross, Jesus is buried in the tomb. Depictions of these scenes (pictures or sculptured-pieces surmounted by crosses) are mounted in most churches and chapels. The person making the Way of the Cross passes in succession before each of these stations, pausing at each for the required meditations. Pilgrims to the Holy Land make the Stations by visiting places at which these events of the Passion occurred. The Stations of the Cross is highly indulgenced.

Those at sea, prisoners, the sick, residents of pagan countries, and others who are unable to make the Stations in their ordinary form, may gain all the indulgences provided they hold in their hand a crucifix blessed for this purpose **(Stations Crucifix)**, and recite with the proper sentiments Our Father, Hail Mary, and Glory once for each Station, five times in honor of the Wounds of our Lord, and once for the Pope's intention.

Those whose grave bodily infirmity prevents their making even the shorter Way of the Cross described above, may gain all the indulgences if they contritely kiss, or at least fix their eyes upon, a crucifix blessed for this purpose, and recite if possible some short prayer or ejaculation in memory of the Passion and Death of Christ.

**Three Hours' Agony, The,** is a devotion practiced on Good Friday in memory of the three hours Christ hung upon the Cross. It usually begins at twelve o'clock, when Christ was nailed to the Cross, includes prayers, hymns, and meditations upon His sufferings and His seven last words, and ends at three o'clock, the hour of His death.

**Vespers and Compline** are parts of the Divine Office which must be said daily by priests, men in major orders, and solemnly professed religious.

The order of Vespers is as follows: (1) five psalms, each with an antiphon; (2) capitulum, or little chapter; (3) a hymn; (4) versicle and response; (5) the Magnificat, with its antiphon; (6) the prayer; (7) conclusion, after which comes an anthem to the Blessed Virgin. There are four anthems, sung according to the season.

The order of Compline is as follows: (1) Confiteor, followed by three psalms with antiphon; (2) hymn "Te Lucis ante Terminum"; (3) a little chapter, with responses; (4) the canticle of Simeon, "Nunc Dimittis"; (5) the prayer, "Visita, Quaesumus"; (6) one of the four anthems used at Vespers.

### c) Principal Catholic Feasts

From the *National Catholic Almanac, 1955*, St. Anthony's Guild, Paterson, New Jersey.

**The Circumcision,** Jan. 1, commemorates the circumcision of Christ eight days after His birth, according to the Jewish law, His initiation into the Jewish religion, and His reception of the name Jesus which Archangel Gabriel had made known to Mary at the Annunciation. It is a holy day of obligation in the U.S.

**The Epiphany,** Jan. 6, commemorates Christ's manifestation of Himself to the Gentiles as represented by the Three Kings of the East who, guided by a star, came to adore Him in His infancy. It also marks Christ's manifestations of Himself near the beginning of His public life, when He was baptized by John the Baptist and when He performed His first recorded miracle at the marriage feast in Cana.

**The Purification,** Feb. 2, commemorates the purification of the Blessed Mother forty days after the birth of Christ and the presentation of Christ in the Temple according to the prescriptions of Lev. 12:2–8; Ex. 13:2. The feast is also called **Candlemas,** because candles for use during the year are blessed on this day and commemoration is made of the fact that Christ is, in the words of Simeon, "A light to the revelation of the Gentiles and the glory of His people Israel."

**Ash Wednesday,** first day of the penitential season of Lent, is so called because of the blessing of ashes and their use to remind the faithful: "Remember, man, that thou art dust and unto dust thou shalt return." The priest says these words as, with ashes, he makes the sign of the cross on each person's forehead.

**The Annunciation,** Mar. 25, commemorates the announcement by the Archangel Gabriel to Mary that she was to become the Mother of Christ, the Second Person of the Blessed Trinity made Man.

## HOLY WEEK AND EASTER

**Palm Sunday,** the first day of Holy Week, commemorates Christ's triumphant entry into Jerusalem. It receives its name from the palm branches which the people spread under the feet of Jesus, crying out, "Hosanna to the Son of David! Blessed is He Who comes in the name of the Lord!" On this day palms are blessed and distributed to the faithful.

**Holy Thursday,** or **Maundy Thursday,** occurs in Holy Week and commemorates the institution of the Holy Eucharist by Christ at the Last Supper the night before He died. There is only one Mass in each church on this day; white vestments are used because of the joyful commemoration, but at the same time there are certain signs of the mourning proper to Holy Week, such as the silencing of the bells. The celebrant consecrates two Hosts, one of which he receives, while the other is placed in a chalice and carried in solemn procession to an altar prepared for Its reception, called the **Altar of Repose or Repository.** Here It remains for the adoration of the faithful until Good Friday when It is taken back to the high altar and received by the priest at the Communion in the Mass of the Presanctified. After the procession of the Blessed Sacrament on Holy Thursday, the altars are stripped to recall the fact that Christ was stripped of His garments. Then follows the washing of the feet, known as the "Mandatum," from the first word of the antiphon recited during the ceremony; whence the name "Maundy" Thursday. Christ washed the feet of the Apostles at the Last Supper.

**Good Friday** commemorates the Passion and Crucifixion of Christ. The liturgy is in every way of an exceptional character, befitting the day of the Great Atonement. The distinctive feature is the **Mass of the Presanctified,** in which there is no Consecration, the Host having been consecrated in the Mass the day before. The service consists of (1) lessons from Holy Scripture and prayers, terminating with the chanting of the Passion; (2) solemn supplication for all conditions of men; (3) veneration of the Holy Cross; (4) procession of the Blessed Sacrament from the Repository and the priest's Communion, or the Mass of the Presanctified proper.

**Holy Saturday** is the day before Easter. During the eighth century the custom began of anticipating the Saturday night liturgy, which originally continued into Easter day and hence is full of the Resurrection spirit. This explains the joyous character of the Mass, and the fact that the history of the Resurrection is sung in the Gospel. The ceremonies begin early in the morning with the blessing of the new fire and the Paschal Candle, which is followed by the reading of the twelve prophecies. The priest then goes in procession to bless the baptismal font, and the water is scattered toward the four quarters of the world to indicate the catholicity of the Church and the world-wide efficacy of her sacraments. Solemn High Mass is then sung, white vestments are used, flowers and candles are set upon the altar, statues are unveiled, the organ is heard, and the bells, silent since Holy Thursday, are joyfully rung. Lent ends officially at noon on this day.

**Easter Sunday** or **The Resurrection** commemorates Christ's rising from the dead by His own power on the third day after His Crucifixion. The feast occurs on the first Sunday after the first full moon after the vernal equinox, or March 21.

**The Invention** or **Finding of the Holy Cross,** May 3, commemorates the finding of the true Cross by St. Helena, in 326, after it had been hidden by the infidels and buried for 180 years.

**The Patronage of St. Joseph,** on the third Wednesday after Easter, honors St. Joseph as the Patron of the Universal Church. St. Joseph is also commemorated by a special feast observed on Mar. 19.

**The Ascension,** forty days after Easter, commemorates Christ's Ascension into heaven from Mount Olivet, in the presence of His Blessed Mother and His Apostles and disciples. It is a holy day of obligation in the U.S.

**Pentecost** or **Whitsunday,** fifty days after Easter, commemorates the descent of the Holy Spirit upon the Apostles, in the form of fiery tongues. It is the birthday of the Catholic Church. The word "Pentecost" means "fiftieth." The name Whitsunday recalls the white garments worn by catechumens who were admitted to baptism on the eve of Pentecost.

**Trinity Sunday,** the first Sunday after Pentecost, commemorates the mystery of One God in Three Divine Persons.

**Corpus Christi,** the Thursday after Trinity Sunday, is the feast day of the Holy Eucharist, on which special honor is paid to Christ truly present in this sacrament under the appearances of bread and wine. The purpose of the feast is to make reparation for sins committed against the Blessed Sacrament and to kindle devotion to the Eucharist. Solemn ceremonies include a procession of the Blessed Sacrament, which may be held on the following Sunday.

**Sacred Heart,** the Friday after the Octave of Corpus Christi, commemorates the love of the God-Man Christ for men. An act of reparation is recited in all churches on this feast.

**SS. Peter and Paul,** June 29, honors the Prince of the Apostles and the great Apostle of the Gentiles who were both martyred on this day at Rome.

**The Precious Blood,** July 1, honors the Blood of Christ shed for the redemption of mankind.

**The Visitation,** July 2, commemorates Mary's visit to her cousin St. Elizabeth after the Annunciation.

**The Assumption,** Aug. 15, commemorates the taking into heaven of the Blessed Virgin, soul and body, at the end of her life on earth. It is a holyday of obligation in the U.S.

**The Immaculate Heart of Mary,** Aug. 22, honors the Blessed Virgin and commemorates the consecration of the world to her Immaculate Heart by Pope Pius XII in 1942. The feast also urges remembrance of the message of Our Lady of Fatima.

**The Nativity of the Blessed Virgin,** Sept. 8, commemorates the birth of Mary.

**The Exaltation of the Holy Cross,** Sept. 14, commemorates the recovery of the Cross from the Persians by Heraclius, King of Judea.

**St. Michael** or **Michaelmas,** Sept. 29, honors the Archangel Michael, prince of the angels and patron of the Church.

**Christ the King,** the last Sunday of October, commemorates the Kingship of Christ and His rule over the world.

**All Saints,** Nov. 1, honors all the saints in heaven, especially those who have no set feasts during the year. It is a holy day of obligation in the U.S.

**All Souls' Day,** Nov. 2, is a day set apart for the Church to pray for all the faithful departed in purgatory. All priests may say three Masses on this day.

**The Presentation of the Blessed Virgin Mary,** Nov. 21, commemorates Mary's presentation in the Temple of Jerusalem by her parents, SS. Joachim and Anne.

**The Immaculate Conception,** Dec. 8, commemorates the preservation of the Blessed Virgin from the stain of original sin from the moment of her conception. It is the patronal feast of the U.S. and a holy day of obligation.

**Christmas** or **The Nativity,** Dec. 25, commemorates the birth of Christ. It is a holy day of obligation. Priests may say three Masses on this day.

### d) Formula for Unified Regulations on Fast and Abstinence

[The regulations below are the official text submitted to Catholics. These regulations were drawn from the report of the Bishop's Committee on Fast and Abstinence, and were submitted to the Catholic hierarchy at the annual meeting in Washington, D.C., November 14–16, 1951.]

**Regulations on Fast and Abstinence**
To foster the spirit of penance and of reparation for sin, to encourage self-denial and mortification, and to guide her children in the footsteps of Our Divine Savior, Holy Mother Church imposes by law the observance of fast and abstinence.

In accordance with the provisions of Canon Law, as modified through the use of special faculties granted by the Holy See, we herewith publish the following regulations:

#### On Abstinence
Everyone over 7 years of age is bound to observe the law of abstinence.

Complete abstinence is to be observed on Fridays, Ash Wednesday, the Vigils of the Assumption and Christmas, and on Holy Saturday morning. On days of complete abstinence meat and soup or gravy made from meat may not be used at all.

Partial abstinence is to be observed on Ember Wednesdays and Saturdays and on the Vigils of Pentecost and All Saints. On days of partial abstinence meat and soup or gravy made from meat may be taken only *once* a day at the principal meal.

#### On Fast
Everyone over 21 and under 59 years of age is also bound to observe the law of fast.

The days of fast are the weekdays of Lent, Ember Days, the Vigils of Pentecost, the Assumption, All Saints and Christmas.

On days of fast only one full meal is allowed. Two other meatless meals, sufficient to maintain strength, may be taken according to each one's needs; but together they should not equal another full meal. Meat may be taken at the principal meal on a day of fast except on Fridays, Ash Wednesday and the Vigils of the Assumption and Christmas.

Eating between meals is not permitted; but liquids, including milk and fruit juices, are allowed.

When health or ability to work would be seriously affected, the law does not oblige. In doubt concerning fast or abstinence, a parish priest or confessor should be consulted.

We earnestly exhort the faithful during the periods of fast and abstinence to attend daily Mass; to receive Holy Communion often; to take part more frequently in exercises of piety; to give generously to works of religion and charity; to perform acts of kindness toward the sick, the aged and the poor; to practice voluntary self-denial especially regarding alcoholic drink and worldly amusements; and to pray more frequently, particularly for the intentions of the Holy Father.

## 4. Jewish Holidays

### By MORDECAI SOLTES

Extracts from a pamphlet. Revised and reprinted, 1952, The National Jewish Welfare Board, New York, N.Y.

A distinguishing characteristic of the Jewish religion is its emphasis on conduct and character rather than on belief, faith, or dogma. Judaism is synonymous with life and its ceremonial expression therefore embraces cultural and sociological as well as ritualistic elements. This is true particularly of the symbols and customs associated with the observance of the holidays which afford the Jew an opportunity to relive symbolically, yet vividly, significant experiences of his ancestors, and to commemorate their historic struggles for a fuller and richer life.

The Jewish calendar differs from the secular in that the former is based on the revolutions of the moon around the earth (lunar), while the latter is solar in character. The day begins and ends with sunset. The day preceding the Sabbath or a Jewish holiday is designated as *Ereb Shabbat* and *Ereb Yom Tob.*

There are twelve months in a normal year consisting of 29 or 30 days each, and their Hebrew names are: *Nisan* (falls about April), *Iyar* (May), *Sivan* (June), *Tammuz* (July), *Ab* (August), *Elul* (September), *Tishri* (October), *Heshvan* (November), *Kislev* (December), *Tebet* (January), *Shebat* (February), *Adar* (March). In a leap year, which occurs seven times in nineteen years, i.e., the third, sixth, eighth, eleventh, fourteenth, seventeenth and nineteenth, a thirteenth month is added, known as *Adar Sheni, Second Adar.* By means of this additional month, the lunar year (consisting of 354 days) is periodically brought into conformity with the solar year (365 days).

## Rosh Hashanah

*Rosh Hashanah* (lit., "head of the year") is observed in the beginning of the seventh month (*Tishri*), as the Jewish New Year.

*Nisan* is regarded as the first month of the Jewish calendar, and all the festivals are arranged according to this reckoning.

The first of *Tishri* marks the anniversary of the creation of the world, which occurred, according to tradition over 5,700 years ago. Hence Jewish chronology begins the year with this day.

The name *"Rosh Hashanah"* does not occur in the Bible. Instead, it is referred to as the Day of the Blowing of the Trumpet, the Day of Memorial or Remembrance, and the Memorial of the Blowing of the *Shofar*.

It is also considered the Day of Judgment (*Yom Hadin*), when all mankind is judged by the Creator, and the fate of each individual is inscribed in the Book of Life.

*Rosh Hashanah* inaugurates the Ten Days of Penitence, the most solemn season in the Jewish calendar, which has been set apart for retrospection and self-examination.

The observance of the High Holy Days is characterized by a feeling of solemnity. Jews generally abstain from their daily occupations and participate in communal worship.

The home customs and ceremonies also reflect concern over the fate for the New Year. In addition to the recital of the *Kiddush* (the sanctification prayer) and the kindling of the festive lights, a piece of sweet apple is dipped in honey on the eve of *Rosh Hashanah*, the person performing this symbolic act saying, "May it be God's will to grant us a good and sweet year." The bread, too, is dipped in honey, symbolizing the hope that, as the bread is sweet, so may the experiences during the approaching year be only of the most pleasant.

On the second night some kind of fruit is tasted which has not yet been eaten during the year, and an appropriate benediction is recited.

An outstanding feature of the Synagogue Service is the blowing of the *Shofar*, which serves to intensify the spirit of reverence and contributes toward the creation of an atmosphere of solemnity.

Sixty to one hundred distinct sounds, arranged in various combinations, are blown, the exact number varying with different congregations.

The *Shofar* is blown during the morning Service before the Scroll is returned to the Holy Ark, and during the Additional Service.

If the first day of *Rosh Hashanah* falls on a Sabbath, the blowing of the *Shofar* is usually deferred to the second day.

The *Shofar* is made of the horn of a ram, or of some other clean animal, except a cow or an ox.

In the afternoon of the first day of *Rosh Hashanah* (if it does not fall on a Sabbath), pious Jews assemble along the banks of a stream, river, or seashore, and recite verses from the prophets and appropriate prayers.

The Sabbath which falls during the ten days of repentance is called *"Shabbat Shubah,"* (the Sabbath of Repentance), because the prophetic portion read at the morning Service, which is taken from Hosea, begins with the word, *"Shubah"* (literally, Return). It is an exhortation to Israel to return to God.

The penitential days reach their culmination on the Day of Atonement (*Yom Kippur*), which is ushered in on the eve of the tenth of *Tishri*, and is regarded as the most sacred day in the Jewish year. It is frequently referred to as the Sabbath of Sabbaths.

In conformity with the Biblical injunction, "Ye shall afflict your souls," it is customary to abstain from all food and drink from sunset on the eve of the Day of Atonement until the beginning of night of the following day.

A large taper, sufficient to burn throughout the twenty-four hours of the fast, is kindled on the eve of *Yom Kippur,* in memory of the departed ones.

It is deemed appropriate to wear white shrouds on this solemn day, since white is a symbol of purity. The High Priest, in ancient times, wore white garments on *Yom Kippur.*

### Yom Kippur—Synagogue Service

The Evening Service of the Day of Atonement is preceded by the chanting of *Kol Nidre* (literally "all vows") which is repeated three times. It is a formal abrogation of all vows made under the influence of great emotional strain, and is intended to guard against oaths which may remain unfulfilled through negligence or forgetfulness.

This dispensation from vows refers only to those which an individual voluntarily assumes for himself alone, and concerns his relation to his conscience and Heavenly Judge. No oath or promise involving another person, a community, or a court of justice is implied in the *Kol Nidre.*

The ritual of the Day of Atonement is replete with petitions for forgiveness for sins committed by all the worshipers present. In the "Confessions," transgressions are enumerated of which a particular individual may not be guilty. The prayers for pardon are uttered in behalf of all Israel.

According to Jewish tradition, a person will not be forgiven on the Day of Atonement for any sins committed against a fellow being unless he rights the wrong and makes amends to the individual involved.

### Sukkoth, the Festival of Booths or Tabernacles

*Sukkoth* is the third of the three pilgrimage feasts—the other two being *Pesach* and *Shabuoth*—on which Jews from all parts of Palestine used to make pilgrimages to the Temple in Jerusalem.

This festival was originally pastoral in nature and occurred during the time of the fruit harvest. It was also generally observed as thanksgiving at the completion of the entire harvest, "for the bounties of nature during the previous year."

*Sukkoth* are temporary structures, especially built either in the yard or on the roof of a home, for the festival, and serve as a protection against the sun. They are not covered from above with board, but with detached branches, sparsely laid, "to allow the stars to shine through the roof."

The construction and decoration of the *Sukkah* are usually family functions. The mother blesses the candles and the father and children recite the *Kiddush* and sometimes partake of their meals in the *Sukkah.*

The *Sukkah* is the emblem of the *Galut* (Exile)—a temporary dwelling, dependent upon God's protection.

During the Spanish Inquisition, when to be found observing the Jewish religion meant death, the Jews used to build subterranean *Sukkoth*, so anxious were they to perform the precept of "dwelling in a *Sukkah.*"

### Hanukkah, the Festival of Dedication

*Hanukkah* is one of the two minor festivals, the observance of which is not enjoined in the Pentateuch. It was instituted by the early Rabbis for the purpose of strengthening the Jewish historic consciousness.

Hanukkah commemorates the successful struggle for religious liberty carried on by a small band of Israelites, led by the brave Maccabees, against the vast army of their Syrian oppressors, under the leadership of Antiochus, which culminated in the recapture of Jerusalem and the rededication of the Holy Temple (165 B.C.).

The celebration of *Hanukkah* begins on the twenty-fifth day of *Kislev*, the day on which the Temple was consecrated anew to the service of God, and lasts for eight days, because the ceremony of rededication and festivities continued for that length of time.

This holiday is also called the Feast of Lights or Illumination, since it is customary to kindle the *Hanukkah* lamp throughout the eight days of the festival. One light is kindled on the first night, and an additional one is lit on each succeeding evening until the last day, when eight lights are burned, exclusive of the *"Shamas,"* which is a special candle used in lighting the others. ("Thus do the pious grow in the service of praise and duty from strength to strength.")

Little yellow wax candles or wells of oil with threads folded together are used, as a rule, and the lamp is generally placed on the window sill or in some other conspicuous place where it may be seen from the outside. (Symbol of freedom.)

Because it is not permitted to do any work by the light of the *Hanukkah* candles, it has become customary to indulge in games, riddles, and other pastimes, especially during the evenings of the festival.

*Purim* is one of the minor historical

festivals of the Jewish calendar, and occurs on the 14th day of *Adar*. Its observance is based on the narrative recorded in one of the five small Biblical Scrolls or *Megillot*, known as the Book of Esther.

The events associated with the Feast of *Purim* occurred in Persia during the reign of Ahasuerus (Xerxes, 485–464 B.C.). Haman, haughty Prime Minister and arch anti-Semite, plotted to exterminate the entire Jewish people because a Jew, Mordecai, refused to bow down to him. His sinister designs were frustrated by the timely intervention of Queen Esther. The observance of this festival was ordained by the Great Men of the Synod, of which Mordecai was said to have been a member.

It is customary to read *Megillat Esther* (the Scroll of Esther) in the synagogue and at home on the eve of the *Purim* festival, as well as on the following morning. Because of the important part played by Esther, women are required to attend the *Purim* Service. Whenever the Reader mentions the name of Haman, the children are permitted to stamp their feet, whirl their "greggers" or rattles, and resort to other noise-making devices.

Two important customs prevalent on this holiday are the giving of alms to the poor and the mutual exchange of presents between friends and relatives. The latter custom gave rise to the interesting character known as the *"Shalah Manot Tregger"* (the messenger who carried the gifts from home to home on *Purim*).

Exuberant joy is the keynote of the *Purim* festival. It is marked by unbounded festivity and offers opportunities for participation of both parents and children in the domestic celebration. Special dainties and sweets are consumed, including the triangular cakes known as *Haman Taschen* (Haman's hat). All kinds of merry-making are indulged in, culminating in the evening with the jovial party, at which all the members of the household are gathered.

Masquerading by both young and old has been a general practice on this holiday. Companies of amateurs (*Purim Shpieler*) used to go from house to house to dance, sing, and produce episodes of the *Purim* story, usually concluding with the comic ditty, *"Heint is Purim, morgen is ois, git uns a groshen, und varft uns arois."* ("Today is *Purim*, tomorrow is not, give us a penny, and throw us out.")

### Pesach, the Festival of Freedom

Passover (*Pesach*) is associated with the birth of the Jewish nation, the redemption of its ancestors from Egyptian bondage (1200 B.C.)—an epoch-making event in the early history of its people.

*Pesach* also marked the early barley harvest in Palestine, when the Jewish farmers used to make a pilgrimage to the Temple in Jerusalem to offer sacrifices upon the altar.

During the Passover festival week Jews abstain from partaking of leavened bread or of any food prepared with leaven. Special sets of utensils and dishes are used, and *Matzoth* or unleavened cakes are eaten, as a reminder of the Israelites' hurried departure from Egypt, when they had to bake their bread in haste, without permitting the dough to rise. It is customary for the head of the household to search for *"hometz"* or "leaven" on the evening preceding the festival, and to remove or burn it the following morning.

A special service known as the *Pesach Seder* is conducted at home on the first two evenings of the Passover festival. *"Seder"* means "order," and refers to the order of the service arranged. It is considered a holy and solemn occasion and one of the most beautiful Jewish ceremonies.

The symbols included in the *"Seder"* are arranged in a special dish, and consist of the following: three *Matzoth*, bitter herbs (*Marror*), other vegetables—parsley, celery, lettuce (*Karpas*), salt water, a combination made of nuts, apples, raisins, and wine (*Haroset*), a roasted lamb bone (*Z'roa*), and a roasted egg.

Four cups of wine are drunk by every member of the family seated around the table, during the *Seder* service.

The *Haggadah* (literally, narrative), which contains the special ritual service of the evening, the story of Israel's Exodus from Egypt, as well as some folk songs and ditties (*Had Gadya, Addir Hu,* etc.), is read aloud and sung.

Various phases of the *Seder* have been introduced primarily for the benefit of the children: They ask the "Four Questions" to which the narrative of the *Haggadah* is a reply.

A special goblet or a cup of wine is prepared for Elijah, the Prophet, mysterious emissary of hope and faith, and a child opens the door to admit the eagerly-awaited guest.

*Matzoth* recalls the haste which characterized our ancestors' deliverance from Egyptian slavery. The Bible also calls the *Matzoth* "Bread of Affliction," reminding us of the affliction of the Israelites while under Pharaoh's yoke. Thus the unleavened bread is a symbol of both slavery and freedom.

*Marror* symbolizes the bitter hardships endured in Egypt.

*Haroset* resembles the brick and mortar used in Egypt (Exodus I, 14).

*Roasted Shank Bone and Egg.* In

the Temple days, the offering of the *paschal* lamb on the evening of Passover was an annual institution, which was observed with great detail. Some of the elements included in this ceremony have been retained in the *Seder* service, the roasted shank bone and egg on the *Seder* plate, symbolizing the *paschal* and festival offerings, respectively.

### Shabuoth, the Festival of Weeks

*Shabuoth* (literally "Weeks") falls on the sixth day of *Sivan*, the third month of the Jewish calendar, which is exactly seven weeks after *Pesach*. It is the second of the three major festivals of the Jewish year, the other two being *Pesach*, which precedes, and *Sukkoth,* which follows it. Together they are known as the *Shalosh Regalim,* or the Three Pilgrimage Feasts.

Originally *Shabuoth* was observed as an agricultural feast, and marked the beginning of the wheat harvest. Later, *Shabuoth* served to commemorate an important event in the early history of our people—the proclamation of the Ten Commandments at Mount Sinai. Since the destruction of the Temple, when the Jews ceased to be primarily an agricultural people, the historical aspect has assumed greater significance.

*Shabuoth* is observed one day in Palestine and for two days by all pious Jews in other countries. It is called by the following names, each of which suggests a different phase of its significance or refers to some ceremony in its celebration: Pentecost, *Hag Ha-Kazir* ("Feast of Harvest"), *Yom Ha-Bikhurin* ("Day of First Fruits"), and *Z'man Matan Toratenu* ("Season of the giving of Our Law").

*Pesach* marks the time when Israel received its *physical* freedom, while *Shabuoth* commemorates the occasion when Israel received *spiritual* freedom, the consummation of the purpose for which Israel was led forth from Egyptian bondage.

It is customary to display greens and to decorate the synagogue and home with flowers, plants, and even trees. The greens serve to commemorate the harvest festival of former times and to symbolize the freshness of the verdure which covered Mount Sinai, when the Law was given to Israel.

Another custom which is usually followed is that of partaking of dairy food. Special cheese cakes (*Blintzes*) are eaten as significant of the Torah, which is compared in the Bible to milk.

The Scroll of Ruth is read in the synagogue at the *Shabuoth* services, because the story of Ruth embracing Judaism and the charming description of agricultural life in ancient Palestine, particularly the treatment accorded the poor during the harvest season, furnish a proper background for the *Shabuoth* festival. Another reason is that King David, who was a descendant of Ruth, was born and passed away, according to tradition, on this holiday.

Pious Jews stay up until midnight or during the entire first night of *Shabuoth,* devoting their time in the synagogue to the study and reading of excerpts from the Pentateuch, Prophets, and Rabbinic literature. These selections have been assembled and arranged in a collection called *"Tikkun Shabuoth."*

### Tishah B'Ab

*Tishah B'Ab,* the ninth day in the Hebrew month of *Ab,* is observed as a fast day. It marks the anniversary of the destruction of the First and Second Temples in Jerusalem by the Babylonians under Nebuchadnezzar (586 B.C.) and the Romans under

Titus (70 A.D.), respectively, and the loss of Jewish independence.

Other sad episodes in the life of the Jewish people are associated with this mournful day, among them the suppression of Bar Kokhba's revolt by the Romans in 135 A.D., and the expulsion of the Jews from Spain in 1492.

Grief is the keynote of *Tishah B'Ab,* and the traditional mourning code governs this day. Pious Jews refrain from eating, drinking, bathing, or participating in festive occasions, from sunset to sunset, following the *Taanit S'udah* (the last repast before the fast), and study only melancholy phases of the Torah, such as the Book of Job, the prophecies of misfortune in Jeremiah, the laws of mourning, and similar subjects which tend to sadden the heart.

Some of the external features of the synagogue are brought into consonance with the gloomy character of the day. Thus, the curtain in front of the Holy Ark is removed, the latter being draped in black or remaining bare. Worshipers remove their shoes and seat themselves on boxes, low stools, or turned-over chairs or benches, as do mourners observing *Shib'ah* (seven days of mourning for the deceased). The *talit* (prayer shawl) and *tefillin* (phylacteries) are put on at the afternoon Service, instead of in the morning, and all prayers and scriptural readings are chanted in a low tone, with a weeping intonation.

In the synagogue *Tishah B'Ab* is ushered in at the Evening Service with the reading of the prophet Jeremiah's Book of Lamentations, in depressed, mournful tones. This also constitutes the central feature of the Service the following morning, when, in addition, the *Kinot,* a collection of plaintive hymns of poetic beauty, heartrending dirges and laments are chanted.

## Sabbath

The observance of the Sabbath is a fundamental precept of Judaism, and for thousands of years has exerted a dominant influence in Jewish life. The admonition to set aside a weekly day of rest from labor is included among the Ten Commandments ("Remember the Seventh day, to keep it holy"), and applies alike to masters, servants, and beasts of burden.

The Sabbath is ushered in at the home Friday before sunset with the kindling of candles by the housewife, with an appropriate benediction and ceremony, and at the synagogue with the recital of the *Kabbalat Shabbat* (welcoming the Sabbath) prayers.

While observant Jews refrain from carrying on their usual work or business on the Sabbath, the traditional rest on that holy day does not imply mere idleness, but rather a change in occupation. Invested by Scripture with a uniquely religious connotation, the Sabbath is dedicated to physical and spiritual relaxation and replenishment. Biblical readings, discussions of contemporary Jewish affairs, the study of *The Ethics of The Fathers,* and other intellectual activities are indulged in, which are in accord with the religious nature of the Sabbath and reflect a reverential concern for its sanctity. On the other hand, strenuous, excessive, or boisterous exercise, mourning, fasting, weeping, and other practices which would detract from the quiet contemplation, dignified cheerfulness, and pleasure that should characterize the Sabbath, are scrupulously avoided.

Among the Sabbath ceremonies which contribute towards the creation of a distinctive atmosphere in the home and synagogue are the recital of the *Kiddush* (Sanctification) prayer over sacramental wine or Sabbath white bread before the Friday evening and Sabbath noon repasts, and the *Habdalah* (distinction) blessings at the conclusion of the Sabbath, the singing of Sabbath hymns and melodies at the family table, attendance of public Services, central features of which are the reading of the weekly portion of the Pentateuch, as well as a corresponding selection from the Prophets, and a discourse by the Rabbi. In recent decades it has become customary to conduct, in addition, late Friday evening Services and Forums.

## 5. Dates of Jewish Holidays and Fast Days * (1955-63)

| Jewish Year | | 1955–6 5716 | 1956–7 5717 | 1957–8 5718 | 1958–9 5719 | 1959–60 5720 | 1960–1 5721 | 1961–2 5722 | 1962–3 5723 |
|---|---|---|---|---|---|---|---|---|---|
| ROSH HASHANAH (New Year) | | Sept. 17–18 | Sept. 6–7 | Sept. 26–27 | Sept. 15–16 | Oct. 3–4 | Sept. 22–23 | Sept. 11–12 | Sept. 29–30 |
| YOM KIPPUR (Day of Atonement) | | Sept. 26 | Sept. 15 | Oct. 5 | Sept. 24 | Oct. 12 | Oct. 1 | Sept. 20 | Oct. 8 |
| SUKKOTH (Tabernacles) | | Oct. 1–2 | Sept. 20–21 | Oct. 10–11 | Sept. 29–30 | Oct. 17–18 | Oct. 6–7 | Sept. 25–26 | Oct. 13–14 |
| SH'MINI AZERET (The Eighth day of Solemn Assembly) | | Oct. 8 | Sept. 27 | Oct. 17 | Oct. 6 | Oct. 24 | Oct. 13 | Oct. 2 | Oct. 20 |
| SIMHATH TORAH (Rejoicing in the Law) | | Oct. 9 | Sept. 28 | Oct. 18 | Oct. 7 | Oct. 25 | Oct. 14 | Oct. 3 | Oct. 21 |
| HANUKKAH (Festival of Dedication) | | Dec. 10–17 | Nov.29 –Dec.6 | Dec. 18–25 | Dec. 7–14 | Dec.26 –Jan.2 | Dec. 14–21 | Dec. 3–10 | Dec. 22–29 |
| HAMISHAH ASAR BI-SHEVAT (Jewish Arbor Day) | 1955 Feb. 7 | 1956 Jan. 28 | 1957 Jan. 17 | 1958 Feb. 5 | 1959 Jan. 24 | 1960 Feb. 13 | 1961 Feb. 1 | 1962 Jan. 20 | 1963 Feb. 9 |
| PURIM (Feast of Lots) | Mar. 8 | Feb. 26 | Mar. 17 | Mar. 6 | Mar. 24 | Mar. 13 | Mar. 2 | Mar. 20 | Mar. 10 |
| PESACH (Passover) | Apr. 7–14 | Mar. 27 –Apr. 3 | Apr. 16–23 | Apr. 5–12 | Apr. 23–30 | Apr. 12–19 | Apr. 1–8 | Apr. 19–26 | Apr. 9–16 |
| LAG BA'OMER (33rd day of the Omer) | May 10 | Apr. 29 | May 19 | May 8 | May 26 | May 15 | May 4 | May 22 | May 12 |
| SHABUOTH (Feast of Weeks) | May 27–28 | May 16–17 | June 5–6 | May 25–26 | June 12–13 | June 1–2 | May 21–22 | June 8–9 | May 29–30 |
| TISHAH B'AB (Ninth Day of Ab) | July 28 | July 17 | Aug. 6 | July 26 | Aug. 13 | Aug. 2 | July 22 | Aug. 9 | July 30 |

* From *The Jewish Holidays*, by Mordecai Soltes, The National Jewish Welfare Board, New York, 1952.

# Sociological Data on Religion

## 1. Marriage and Divorce

### a) Religious Affiliation and Marital Success

From *Building a Successful Marriage*, Landis and Landis, 2nd Edition. Copyright 1953 by Prentice-Hall, Inc., New York, pp. 321–323.

Research studies show that in general the presence of a religious faith is associated with more favorable chances for marital success. Burgess and Cottrell found more favorable adjustment in marriage among those who were regular in their religious observances.[1] Our study of 409 couples showed regular church attendance to be associated with happiness in marriage. In reporting on the happy and the unhappy married men among the group in his study, Terman says, "Unfavorable attitudes toward religion characterize more of the unhappy men. Happily married men are a distinct majority among those . . . who believe it essential that children have religious instruction."[2]

Terman also found that too strict religious training was almost as bad as none at all.

Studies covering approximately 25,000 marriages showed that there were three times as many marital failures among those with no religious affiliation as among those within given religions. In marriages between persons of different religions, religion is frequently a disruptive factor, yet the failure rate of marriages of mixed religions is generally lower than that among marriages where there is no religion.

In comparing divorced and happily married couples, Locke found a larger percentage of the happily married couples had had a church wedding, were church members, and were active in Sunday school and church attendance, both before and during marriage. He suggests that being a church member is not only a mark of a conventional person but also of a sociable person, and both characteristics are associated with good marital adjustment.[3]

#### Agreement on Religious Expression and Happiness in Marriage.

| Agreement | Very Happy | Happy | Average |
|---|---|---|---|
| Excellent ..... | 65% | 26% | 9% |
| Good ........ | 45 | 41 | 14 |
| Fair or poor... | 33 | 33 | 34 |

Agreement on religion was closely associated with happiness in marriage among 544 couples who were in the early years of marriage.

[1] E. W. Burgess and L. S. Cottrell, *Predicting Success or Failure in Marriage*, p. 123. New York: Prentice-Hall, Inc., 1939.

[2] Lewis Terman, *Psychological Factors in Marital Happiness*, p. 164. New York: McGraw-Hill Book Company, Inc., 1939.

[3] Harvey J. Locke, *Predicting Adjustment in Marriage*, pp. 239–241. New York: Henry Holt and Company, 1951.

## b) Church Attendance and Marital Happiness

From *Building a Successful Marriage*, Landis and Landis, 2nd edition. Copyright 1953 by Prentice-Hall Inc., New York, p. 328.

### Church Attendance and Happiness in Marriage.

|  | Very Happy | Happy | Average |
|---|---|---|---|
| Regularly ..... | 54% | 34% | 12% |
| Occasionally or never ....... | 43 | 36 | 21 |

Of 409 couples married successfully for a number of years, those who were regular in their church attendance had higher happiness ratings than those who attended church only occasionally or never.

## c) Church Weddings and Marital Adjustment

From *Predicting Success or Failure in Marriage* by Burgess and Cottrell, New York: Prentice-Hall, Inc., 1939, p. 126, as reprinted in *Building a Successful Marriage,* Landis and Landis, 2nd edition, p. 326. Copyright 1953 by Prentice-Hall, Inc., New York.

### Marital Adjustments

[adapted from chart]

| Place Married | Poor | Fair | Good |
|---|---|---|---|
| Church or Parsonage | 23% | 27% | 50% |
| Home ............ | 35 | 26 | 39 |
| Elsewhere . ....... | 36 | 29 | 35 |

People who were married in a church had happier marriages than those who were not. It does not necessarily follow that if all people were married in churches marriages in general would be happier. People who choose to have church weddings may also have other factors in their backgrounds which make them better "bets" in marriage.

## d) Catholic-Protestant Marriages

From *Leakage from a Catholic Parish* by Gerald J. Schnepp, Washington: Catholic University of America Press, 1942, as reprinted in *Marriage and the Family* by Meyer Nimkoff, Boston: Houghton Mifflin Company, 1947, p. 448.

Of every 10 children whose parents were both Catholics:

6 married a Catholic
3 married a non-Catholic
1 married without the approval of the Church

### Frequency of Catholic-Protestant Marriages

These data for 702 children, only a small sample, in one large parish on the Atlantic seaboard where both parents were Catholic, suggest that such intermarriage is probably not uncommon in areas of mixed population. Where only one of the parents was a Catholic, the proportion of mixed marriages was about 50 per cent greater. The association of children of different faiths in the public schools and neighborhood is thought to be an important reason for the high percentages of intermarriage.

## e) Birth Control and Religion

From *The Facts of Life from Birth to Death* by Louis I. Dublin, 1951, pp. 21–23. Reprinted by permission of The Macmillan Company, New York. **What indication is there of the extent to which contraception is practiced, and of its success?**

Data for the United States as a whole are lacking, but the situation undoubtedly varies widely within the country. In the selected group of native white Protestant couples included in the Indianapolis survey, it was found that about nine-tenths used contraception to control not only the number of their children but also their spacing. Success in either prevention or postponement of a first or second pregnancy was reported by about half of the couples. After the third pregnancy about nine-tenths of the couples succeeded in the attempts to prevent another pregnancy.

**Does the effective practice of contraception vary with the social-economic status of the family?**

It has been frequently noted that the fertility of families in the higher social-economic classes is less than that of families lower in the scale. According to the findings among the selected Protestant families in the Indianapolis survey, a large part of such differences reflects the greater success of the more favored classes in planning their family size. However, among those families that planned both the number and spacing of their children, there was a tendency for the size of the family to increase with rise in the social-economic scale.

**What proportion of couples succeed in having just the size of family they wanted?**

About three-quarters of the Protestant families in the Indianapolis survey reported that they had just the number of children they wanted, while one-quarter had more than they wanted. If these proportions are any indication at all for the country, it is apparent that the course of the birth rate is influenced largely by factors that bear upon the desires of the family.

**What is the time interval desired between the birth of children into the family?**

Almost three-quarters of the couples in the Indianapolis survey thought the first child should come within two or three years following marriage. The same interval was considered desirable by about five-sixths of the couples for the spacing between successive children. However, these expressions of opinion did not conform to the actual happenings in families. Those stating that they planned both the number and spacing of their children reported greater intervals than the expressed opinion; the others reported shorter intervals.

**f) Studies on Divorce and Desertion**
Note by Leo Rosten

Many studies have been made of divorce and desertion, according to the religious affiliation of husbands and wives, but authoritative statistics, based on large samples, are relatively scarce.

The reader's attention is directed to an interesting study by Thomas P. Monahan and William M. Kephart in the *American Journal of Sociology,* March, 1954 (pp. 454–465), entitled, "Divorce and Desertion by Religious and Mixed-Religious Groups."

Monahan and Kephart analyzed over 1,300 cases in Philadelphia for marriages, divorces, and separations. Some highlights of that study may be given here:

Protestants in Philadelphia (and in three areas studied by other scholars —Maryland, Washington, and Michigan) show a higher incidence of divorce than Catholics.

Divorce is increasing among the Catholic population.

Catholics figure in a disproportionately high number of desertions and non-support cases.

Jews appear least often (of the three major religious groups) in both the divorce and desertion categories.

Mixed-religious marriages are *not* a factor in desertion—but do appear to account for a higher percentage of divorces.

Monahan and Kephart concluded that "the sizable proportion of divorces among Catholics . . . is surprising. A prior or present divorce for both parties was found in many of the Catholic-Catholic marriages in Philadelphia's desertion cases . . ." Further: ". . . while Catholics were found to contribute less than their share of divorce" they appear "much more frequently than their relative number in the population" in desertion cases.

The findings of Monahan and Kephart and other sociologists are not presented as definitive or conclusive. All studies in this area suffer from the paucity of information available. As Monahan and Kephart say: "If the major religious denominations in this country took a public position on the desirability of statistical compilations, and if all persons could be assured that statements would be held in strictest confidence, the subtle resistance of some classes to answering a purely informational inquiry on religious affiliation or preference would dissipate. We could, then, in time develop a sound understanding of many of the religious aspects of family life in the United States."

## 2. Religion and Suicide

a) From "To Be or Not to Be," by Louis I. Dublin, New York: Smith and Haas, 1933, pp. 116–117, 119–121.

To gain any estimate of the influence of religious persuasion on the suicide rate, we must observe the suicide mortality of various religious groups living, as nearly as possible, under the same economic, political, and climactic conditions. In the United States we do not record religious faith on the standard certificate of death. We are, therefore, forced to rely upon European figures for our data. It is worthy of note, however, that Dr. Stearns in his study of 167 suicides [1] found that 77 were Protestants, 54 Catholics, and 4 Jews, the religion of the remainder being unknown. Traditionally the Jewish people have very low suicide rates. In New York City the mortality from suicide among the more than two million Jews is considerably lower than it is for the total population. Among New York Jewry in 1925 the crude rate was 10.5 [2] per 100,000, while for the entire population of the city it was 15.9.[3]

A most striking fact is that among all three religious faiths suicide frequency has increased considerably—although the amount of increase has not been uniform in the different provinces. In Prussia great increases have taken place in all three faiths, but notably among the Jewish population. Among these people suicide was more

[1] Albert Warren Stearns, "Suicide in Massachusetts," *Mental Hygiene*, October, 1921.

[2] "Jewish Communal Survey of Greater New York," New York Bureau of Jewish Social Research, 1928.

[3] New York State Department of Health Annual Report, 1925.

than eleven times as prevalent during 1925 as during the earlier years 1849 to 1855. The Catholic rate during the latter period was almost two and three-quarters times as high as in the early period, while among Protestants the recent rate was only one and three-quarters times as high as the early rate.

The increase in suicide among the Jews has attracted considerable attention among students of the problem. Dr. Frederick L. Hoffman [4] gives the following suicide statistics taken from the *Zeitschrift für Demographie und Statistik der Juden* for the Jewish population in Prussia:

> 1908–1913—32.2 per 100,000
> 1914–1918—34.9 per 100,000
> 1919–1923—41.6 per 100,000

During the years given, the Jewish suicide death rates were higher than those of any other religious confession. Even during the war years, contrary to general experience, the rate among the Jews continued to rise. The most obvious explanation for this finding is that the financial and industrial

[4] Frederick L. Hoffman, *Suicide Problems,* The Prudential Press, 1928, p. 16.

depression following the war and the disturbed political conditions affected the Jewish people most seriously. The Jews, furthermore, represent largely an urban population, which always has a higher suicide rate than farmers and agricultural workers.

b) From "The Facts of Life from Birth to Death" by Louis I. Dublin, 1951, p. 264. Reprinted by permission of The Macmillan Company, New York.

Is the frequency of suicide related to religious affiliation?

The influence of religion helps to explain some of the differences in the suicide rate among nations. Most of the countries with low suicide rates are those in which the Roman Catholic faith predominates. On the other hand, most Protestant countries record high rates. Needless to say there are several exceptions to these generalizations. France, for example, which is mostly Catholic, has a higher suicide mortality than Protestant Sweden; Northern Ireland, with a predominantly Protestant population, has one of the lowest rates of any country. Suicide is rare where the guidance and authority of religion is accepted.

## 3. Extracts from "Religion and the Class Structure" *

By LISTON POPE. From the *Annals of the American Academy of Political and Social Science*, Vol. 256, March, 1948, pp. 84–91.

* The data contained in these tables were gathered, for the most part, just after the end of the Second World War. It is entirely possible that they would need to be modified to some degree in the light of more recent developments. Fresh data of comparable character are not available, however, and this material is published here as the most recent general summary of its topic.—L. P.

**Table 1—Class Composition of Catholics and Protestants, 1939–40[a]**

| | Per Cent Distribution | | |
| | Upper Class | Middle Class | Lower Class |
| --- | --- | --- | --- |
| *Protestants* | | | |
| In U.S. | 14 | 52 | 34 |
| In South [b] | 8 | 48 | 44 |
| In remainder of U.S. | 17 | 54 | 29 |
| *Catholics* | | | |
| In U.S. | 9 | 50 | 41 |
| In South [c] | 10 | 42 | 48 |
| In remainder of U.S. | 9 | 51 | 40 |

[a] Constructed from data given by Hadley Cantril, "Educational and Economic Composition of Religious Groups," *American Journal of Sociology*, Vol. 47, No. 5 (March, 1943), p. 576, Table 2. Cantril used "social" samples.

[b] The South is overwhelmingly Protestant, and the ratio of church membership to population is higher there than in any other region (*see* Howard W. Odum. *Southern Regions of the United States* [Chapel Hill, 1936], p. 141). The South is also notoriously poor in comparison with other regions, and has proportionately smaller middle and upper classes. Gross inclusion of its figures in national studies therefore results in considerable distortion of the picture for other regions of the country.

[c] Cantril's sample of Southern Catholics is too small—only 165 cases—to support confident generalizations.

**Table 2—Class Composition of Religious Bodies, 1945–46[a]**

| | Per Cent Distribution | | |
| Body | Upper Class | Middle Class | Lower Class |
| --- | --- | --- | --- |
| *Entire Sample* | 13 | 31 | 56 |
| Catholic | 9 | 25 | 66 |
| Jewish | 22 | 32 | 46 |
| Methodist | 13 | 35 | 52 |
| Baptist | 8 | 24 | 68 |
| Presbyterian | 22 | 40 | 38 |
| Lutheran | 11 | 36 | 53 |
| Episcopalian | 24 | 34 | 42 |
| Congregational | 24 | 43 | 33 |

[a] Derived from a breakdown of four polls taken by the American Institute of Public Opinion in 1945–46, covering approximately 12,000 cases. Each poll covered a "voting sample" of approximately 3,000 cases.

**Table 3—Occupational Categories and Trade Union Membership, in Major Religious Bodies, 1945–46[a]**

| | Percentages by Occupational Categories | | | | Percentage belonging to trade unions |
| Body | Business and professional | White collar | Urban manual workers [b] | Farmers | |
| --- | --- | --- | --- | --- | --- |
| *Entire Sample* | 19 | 20 | 44 | 17 | 19 |
| Catholic | 14 | 23 | 55 | 8 | 28 |
| Jewish | 36 | 37 | 27 | 0.6 | 23 |
| Methodist | 19 | 19 | 39 | 23 | 14 |
| Baptist | 12 | 14 | 52 | 22 | 16 |
| Presbyterian | 31 | 21 | 31 | 17 | 13 |
| Lutheran | 13 | 18 | 43 | 26 | 20 |
| Episcopalian | 32 | 25 | 36 | 7 | 13 |
| Congregational | 33 | 19 | 28 | 20 | 12 |

[a] For source of data, see note to Table 2. Figures given above pertain to "the principal breadwinner" in the case of each family interviewed, where the interviewee was not personally employed.

[b] This category includes urban manual workers of all grades of skill, and also incorporates a rather diverse group of "service occupations" that are primarily manual in character (such as domestic servants, policemen, firemen). A great deal of variation is represented within each of the categories in this table, and their relative class status varies from community to community.

### Table 4—Educational Levels in Religious Bodies, 1945–46[a]

Per Cent Distribution

| Body | High school incomplete (or less) | High school graduates (or more) | College graduates |
|---|---|---|---|
| *Entire Sample* | *52* | *48* | *11* |
| Catholic | 57 | 43 | 7 |
| Jewish | 37 | 63 | 16 |
| Methodist | 49 | 51 | 12 |
| Baptist [b] | 65 | 35 | 6 |
| Presbyterian | 37 | 63 | 22 |
| Lutheran | 56 | 44 | 8 |
| Episcopalian | 35 | 65 | 22 |
| Congregational | 29 | 71 | 21 |

[a] For source, see note to Table 2.
[b] As the data for this table were drawn from a *voting* cross-section, virtually no Southern Negro Baptists are represented in these figures.

### Table 5—Political Preferences in Religious Bodies, 1944[a]

| | Per Cent voting for Dewey | Per Cent voting for Roosevelt |
|---|---|---|
| *Entire Sample* | *32* | *42* |
| Catholic | 20 | 54 |
| Jewish | 6 | 75 |
| Methodist | 38 | 37 |
| Baptist | 24 | 42 |
| Presbyterian | 48 | 32 |
| Lutheran | 42 | 35 |
| Episcopalian | 44 | 36 |
| Congregational | 56 | 26 |

[a] For source of data, see note to Table 2.

### Summary

All told, information derived from public opinion polls indicates that Protestant and Jewish adherents come more largely from the middle and upper classes than do Catholics, with significant differences between the major Protestant denominations in this respect. At the same time, Protestants are more largely represented in the lower class than has been commonly supposed; a significant change in this respect may have occurred during World War II. Protestants, and Jews even more largely, come typically from business, professional, white-collar, and service occupations; Catholics are more typically workers; Catholics, Jews, and Episcopalians have comparatively few farmers. Each major religious body has a sizable percentage of trade unionists in its membership. In the over-all picture, Protestants and Jews have had more education than Catholics. Catholics and Jews gave large majorities of their votes to Mr. Roosevelt in 1944; the Protestants divided, with a majority in most denominations voting for Mr. Dewey.

### Negro Stratification

A few statistics will summarize the relation of Negro churchmen to the white religious institutions.[1] Of the more than 14 million Negroes in the United States, about 6.8 million belong to some church. Of these, about 300 thousand are Catholics; two-thirds of the Negro Catholics are in segregated or separate churches. Of the 6.5 million Negro Protestants, about half a million belong to the predominantly white denominations. While Negroes are integrated into denominational affairs to varying degree in higher ecclesiastical bodies (synods, presbyteries, general conferences, and so forth), there is almost no mixing of whites and Negroes at the level of the individual congregation. According to unpublished studies by Frank Loescher, Dwight Culver, and others, less than 1 per cent of the white congregations have any Negro members (and each of these generally has only

[1] For fuller details, see the articles by John LaFarge and by the present writer in *Survey Graphic*, Vol. 36, No. 1 (Jan., 1947), pp. 59 and 61.

two or three), and less than one-half of 1 per cent of the Negro Protestants who belong to "white denominations" worship regularly with white persons.

The remaining 6 million Negro churchmen belong to all-Negro denominations. Nearly all of them are Methodists or Baptists. There are social classes within the Negro community, though the criteria differ from those operative in the white community. Religion tends to be associated with Negro class divisions in a particular context, however, much as it does among whites.[2]

[2] V. E. Daniel, "Ritual and Stratification in Chicago Negro Churches," *American Sociological Review*, Vol. 7, No. 3 (June, 1942), pp. 352–61.

## 4. "The Negro and His Church"

### By WILLIAM W. SWEET

[Extracted from "The Protestant Churches" by William W. Sweet, *The Annals of the American Academy of Political and Social Science*, Vol. 256, March, 1948, pp. 49–50.]

About five-sevenths of the total Negro population in the United States of some 14 million are members of churches, which is a considerably larger proportion than among the country's white population. Of the 9.5 million Negro church members 6.5 million are Baptists and 1.7 million are Methodists; thus about eight-ninths of the church members are identified with these two denominational families. There are thirty-five all-Negro church bodies with a total membership of 8,797,000, while 822,-000 Negroes belong to racially mixed denominations. Of these racially mixed churches the Methodist Church has the largest number of Negro members, with something over 300,000, while according to the most recent Roman Catholic estimates, there are now about the same number of Negroes in that communion. Or to put it another way, there is one Roman Catholic Negro to thirty-two Protestant Negroes.[1] The overwhelming Protestant complexion of the American Negro population is partly due to the fact that the South is the most Protestant section of the nation, and also to the fact that only in Protestantism can the Negro have the opportunity of controlling his own religious expression.

The church has meant more to the Negro than has any other institution, since only in his church has he had an opportunity for self-expression. Strict limits have been placed upon his participation in civic, economic, and political life, but since his emancipation he has managed his own churches, where he has had the chance to develop his own leadership. Although in the organization of his church the Negro has been to a large degree an imitator of his white brethren, in his religion and in the conduct of his worship he has developed distinctive features. His more than two hundred years of slavery have furnished him a central religious theme, which still persists to a greater or less degree. The fact that he continues to feel that he is not yet completely free goes a long way to explain the otherworldli-

[1] These statistics are drawn from *The Negro Handbook*, 1946–1947 (Florence Murray, Ed., New York, 1946), pp. 153–59.

ness which characterizes Negro spirituals and Negro preaching, even in a city environment.

The most distinctive contribution of the Negro, both in the realm of religion and of art, is the spiritual, in which the central theme is most often death and heaven. As Dean W. L. Sperry has well said, "Negro spirituals are perhaps our most moving statement of an inescapable fact and a serene hope." Only in independent Negro churches could these distinctive contributions have been made, and for that reason the Negro will doubtless be reluctant to place himself under the domination of a predominantly white-controlled church where the forms of worship are determined by a different tradition.

# Headquarters of Denominations*

Condensed from the 1955 *Yearbook of American Churches*, BENSON Y. LANDIS, ed., New York: National Council of the Churches of Christ in the U.S.A., 1954, pp. 12–104.

**Adventists, Seventh-day**
6840 Eastern Avenue, N.W.
Takoma Park
Washington 12, D.C.
(formally organized, 1863)

**Assemblies of God**
434 W. Pacific Street
Springfield 1, Missouri
(organized, 1914)

**Baptist Groups:**
American Baptist Convention
152 Madison Avenue
New York 16, N.Y.
(convention formed, 1907)
Southern Baptist Convention
127 9th Avenue, North
Nashville 3, Tenn.
(formed, 1845)
National Baptist Convention, U.S.A., Inc.
3101 S. Parkway [1]
Chicago, Illinois
National Baptist Convention of America
2610 Avenue L [1]
Galveston, Texas
American Baptist Association
214 East Broad Street
Texarkana, Arkansas-Texas
(organized, 1905)
Free Will Baptists
3801 Richland Avenue
Nashville 5, Tenn.
(organized 1727 in South, 1787 in North)

North American Baptist Association
Jacksonville, Texas [1]
(organized, 1950)
United Free Will Baptist Church
Kinston College
1000 University Street
Kinston, North Carolina
(organized, 1870)

**Church of the Brethren**
22 South State Street
Elgin, Illinois

**Church of Christ, Scientist**
107 Falmouth Street
Boston 15, Mass.
(founded, 1879)

**Churches of God:**
Church of God (Cleveland, Tenn.)
Montgomery Avenue
Cleveland, Tenn.
(began, 1886)
Church of God (Anderson, Ind.)
Box 999
Anderson, Indiana
(originated, c. 1880)

**The Church of God in Christ**
958 South 5th Street
Memphis, Tenn.
(organized, 1895)

**Church of the Nazarene**
2923 Troost Avenue
Box 527
Kansas City 41, Missouri
(organized, 1908)

* (with membership of 100,000 or more)

**Churches of Christ** [2]
(reporting separately since 1906)

**Congregational Christian Churches**
287 Fourth Avenue
New York 10, N.Y.
(merger, 1931)

**Disciples of Christ, Int'l Convention**
620 K of P Building
Indianapolis 4, Indiana

**Eastern Churches:**
Armenian Apostolic Orthodox Church
of America
630 Second Avenue
New York 16, N.Y. (East)
or
Armenian Diocese of California
3503 Illinois Avenue
Fresno, California (West)
(established, U.S., 1889)
Greek Archdiocese of North and
South America
10 East 79th Street
New York 21, N.Y.
Russian Orthodox Greek Catholic
Church of North America
59 East 2nd Street
New York 3, N.Y.
Serbian Eastern Orthodox Church
St. Sava Monastery
Libertyville, Illinois
Syrian Antiochian Orthodox Church
239 85th Street
Brooklyn 9, N.Y.

**Evangelical and Reformed Church**
1505 Race Street [1]
Philadelphia 2, Pa.
(formed, 1934)

**Evangelical United Brethren Church**
Knott Building
Dayton 2, Ohio
(merger, 1946)

**Jehovah's Witnesses**
124 Columbia Heights
Brooklyn 1, N.Y.

**Jewish Congregations:**
Union of American Hebrew Congre-
gations
838 Fifth Avenue
New York 21, N.Y.
United Synagogue of America
3080 Broadway
New York 27, N.Y.
Union of Orthodox Jewish Congrega-
tions of America
305 Broadway
New York 7, N.Y.
Central Conference of American
Rabbis
40 West 68 Street
New York, N.Y.
Rabbinical Assembly of America, Inc.
3080 Broadway
New York 27, N.Y.
Rabbinical Council of America, Inc.
331 Madison Avenue
New York 17, N.Y.
Synagogue Council of America
110 West 42nd Street
New York 18, N.Y.
Union of Orthodox Rabbis of the
United States and Canada
132 Nassau Street
New York 38, N.Y.

**Latter-day Saints:**
Church of Jesus Christ of Latter-day
Saints
47 East South Temple Street
Salt Lake City 1, Utah
Reorganized Church of Jesus Christ of
Latter-day Saints
The Auditorium
Independence, Missouri
(organized, c. 1884)

**Lutherans:**
American Lutheran Church [1]
57 East Main Street
Columbus 15, Ohio
(merger, 1930)
Augustana Evangelical Lutheran
Church

Executive Committee
950 Lincoln Avenue
St. Paul, Minnesota
(organized, 1830)
Evangelical Lutheran Church
Church Council
422 South 5th Street
Minneapolis 15, Minnesota
(merger, 1917)
The Lutheran Church—Missouri Synod
The Lutheran Building
210 North Broadway
St. Louis 2, Missouri
(organized, 1847)
Evangelical Lutheran Joint Synod of
Wisconsin & other states
727 Margaret Street [1]
St. Paul 6, Minnesota
(organized, 1850)
United Lutheran Church in America
231 Madison Avenue
New York 16, N.Y.
(merger, 1918)

**Methodist Bodies:**
African Methodist Episcopal Church
1517 North 16th Street
Philadelphia, Pa.
(incorporated, 1816)
African Methodist Episcopal Zion
Church
1421 U Street, N.W.
Washington 9, D.C.
(separated, 1796)
Colored Methodist Episcopal Church
671 Alston
Memphis, Tenn.
(separated, 1870)
The Methodist Church
100 Maryland Avenue, N.E.
Washington 2, D.C.

**United Pentacostal Church, Inc.**
3645 South Grand Blvd.
St. Louis 18, Missouri
(merger, 1945)

**Polish National Catholic Church of
America**
529 East Locust Street
Scranton 5, Pa.
(organized, 1904)

**Presbyterian Bodies:**
Presbyterian Church in the U.S.
341-C Ponce de Leon Avenue [3]
Atlanta 5, Georgia
(established after Civil War)
Presbyterian Church in the United
States of America
510 Witherspoon Building
Philadelphia 7, Pa.
(organized, 1706)
United Presbyterian Church of North
America
209 9th Street
Pittsburgh 22, Pa.

**The Protestant Episcopal Church**
281 Fourth Avenue
New York 10, N.Y.
(name adopted, 1789)

**Reformed Bodies:**
Christian Reformed Church
944 Neland Avenue, S.E.
Grand Rapids 7, Michigan
Reformed Church in America
156 Fifth Avenue
New York 10, N.Y.
(established, 1628)

**Roman Catholic Church**
Apostolic Delegation
3339 Massachusetts Avenue, N.W.
Washington, D.C.

**Int'l General Assembly of Spiritualists**
1915 Omohundro Avenue
Norfolk, Virginia

---

[1] Office of the President.
[2] No general headquarters.
[3] General Council Office.

# Acknowledgments

Many persons, organizations, and church officials provided truly invaluable help with the vast range of materials which have gone into the making of this book.

The series on religion could never have been published without the constant encouragement and unfailing support of Gardner Cowles, editor of *Look*, to whom I am happy to express my particular thanks. The editors, art department, and research staff of *Look* Magazine deserve a tribute for the judgment, taste, and skill with which the articles in the main body of this book were presented to the public—in eighteen issues of *Look* Magazine, from June 17, 1952, through April 5, 1955.

William J. Burke, director of editorial research, was a tireless source of aid and assistance; Barbara J. Kaplan performed the organization of materials for the appendices; Robinette Nixon was of invaluable help and good cheer in analyzing and cross-checking material; David Aldrich, Katherine Hartley, Suzanne Hurley, and Norman Kotker provided special help. Frank Latham, copy chief of *Look*, was unfailingly helpful in many areas. My secretary and assistant, Hazel Harvest, guided the entire project through its many stages with rare judgment and skill.

Our innumerable and often obstinate requests for information met with considerable understanding and generous response from the following, who are listed in alphabetical order: the Rev. C. Rankin Barnes, of the National Council of the Protestant Episcopal Church; the Rev. David W. Barry, of the National Council of the Churches of Christ in the U.S.A.; Dr. Robert Goldenson, of Hunter College; Naomi Grand, of the American Jewish Committee; Rabbi Morris N. Kertzer, of the American Jewish Committee; Helen Knubel, of the National Lutheran Council; Benson Y. Landis, of the *Yearbook of American Churches* (National Council of the Churches of Christ in the U.S.A.); J. Louis Meyer, of *The Official Catholic Directory;* Dr. Cyril Richardson, of Union Theological Seminary; Dr. Paul Scherer, of Union Theological Seminary; Helen F. Smith, of the General Conference of Seventh-day Adventists; Dr. Henry P. Van Dusen, of Union Theological Seminary.

Grateful acknowledgement is made to the following for official permission to reprint valuable material, in part or in whole, from their publications:

Prentice-Hall, Inc., New York, for permission to reprint material from *Building a Successful Marriage* by Landis and Landis;

The Macmillan Company, New York, for permission to reprint excerpts from *The Facts of Life from Birth to Death* by Louis I. Dublin;

The National Council of the Churches of Christ in the U.S.A., New York, for permission to reprint data from the *Yearbook of American Churches*, issues of 1952 and 1955;

Harlan Betts, Lake Forest, Illinois, for permission to reprint excerpts from

*The Beliefs of 700 Ministers* by George Herbert Betts;

Dan Golenpaul Associates, New York, for permission to reprint data from the *1954 Information Please Almanac;*

The Catholic University of America Press, Washington, D.C., for permission to reprint material from *Leakage from a Catholic Parish* by Gerald J. Schnepp;

Louis I. Dublin of the Institute of Life Insurance, New York, for permission to reprint excerpts from his book *To Be or Not to Be;*

Dr. Liston Pope, of Yale University, for permission to reprint extracts from his article, "Religion and the Class Structure";

*The Annals of the American Academy of Political and Social Science,* Philadelphia, for permission to reprint extracts from "The Protestant Churches," by William Sweet, and "Religion and the Class Structure," by Liston Pope;

The American Council on Education, Washington, D.C., for permission to reprint excerpts from *Youth Tell Their Story* by Howard M. Bell;

Houghton Mifflin Company, Boston, for permission to reprint material from *Marriage and the Family* by Meyer Nimkoff;

The National Catholic Welfare Conference, Washington, D.C., for permission to reprint excerpts from "The Christian in Action";

The American Jewish Committee, New York, for permission to reprint material from the *School Calendar,* September, 1954–August, 1955;

The National Jewish Welfare Board, New York, for permission to reprint material from its pamphlets on Jewish holidays and festivals;

St. Anthony's Guild, Paterson, N.J., for permission to reprint material from

*The National Catholic Almanac,* 1955;

The Department of Survey, Statistics, and Information of the Southern Baptist Convention, Nashville, Tenn., for permission to reprint membership statistics;

Dr. Stanley I. Stuber and the *International Journal of Religious Education,* Chicago, Ill., for permission to reprint Dr. Stuber's chart;

Elmo Roper, New York, for permission to reprint several surveys on religion and politics;

The American Institute of Public Opinion, Princeton, N.J., for permission to reprint opinion polls by Dr. George Gallup;

Robert Winston Carden, Schreiner Institute, Kerrville, Texas, for permission to reprint his chart;

P. J. Kenedy & Sons, publishers, New York, for permission to reprint Catholic statistical material from *The Official Catholic Directory,* 1954;

The American Jewish Committee, New York, and The Jewish Publication Society of America, Philadelphia, for permission to reprint statistical material from the *American Jewish Year Book,* 1953 and 1954;

The General Conference of Seventh-day Adventists, New York, for permission to use membership statistics;

Hector Hawton of Watts & Co., Ltd., London, for permission to quote from Gilbert Murray's *Five Stages of Greek Religion;*

The American Association for Jewish Education, New York, for permission to reprint charts on Jewish education.

None of the above is to be held responsible, of course, for my notes, comments, footnotes, interpretations, or errors of judgment.

—Leo Rosten

November 29, 1954
New York, N.Y.

# About the Editor

In addition to fiction and motion-picture scenarios, LEO ROSTEN has written two outstanding studies in the field of social science: a survey of the Hollywood film colony, and another of the Washington correspondents. He is the author of the much-loved book *The Education of H\*Y\*M\*A\*N K\*A\*P\*L\*A\*N*. Mr. Rosten holds a Ph.D. degree from the University of Chicago, where he did his undergraduate study also. He is now special editorial adviser to *Look* magazine.